POWER, NORMS, AND INFLATION

SOCIOLOGY AND ECONOMICS
Controversy and Integration

An Aldine de Gruyter Series of Texts and Monographs

SERIES EDITORS

Paula S. England, *University of Arizona, Tucson*
George Farkas, *University of Texas, Dallas*
Kevin Lang, *Boston University*

Values in the Marketplace
James Burk

Beyond the Marketplace:
Rethinking Economy and Society
Roger Friedland and A. F. Robertson (eds.)

Social Institutions:
Their Emergence, Maintenance and Effects
Michael Hechter, Karl-Dieter Opp and Reinhard Wippler (eds.)

Mothers' Jobs and Children's Lives
Toby L. Parcel and Elizabeth G. Menaghan

Power, Norms, and Inflation: A Skeptical Treatment
Michael R. Smith

POWER, NORMS, AND INFLATION
A Skeptical Treatment

MICHAEL R. SMITH

Routledge
Taylor & Francis Group

LONDON AND NEW YORK

ABOUT THE AUTHOR

Michael R. Smith is Professor and Chair of the Department of Sociology at McGill University. He has published many articles on a variety of subjects on the boundary between sociology and economics including the Canada-U.S. free trade agreement and the postwar inflation.

First published 1992 by Transaction Publishers

Published 2017 by Routledge
2 Park Square, Milton Park, Abingdon, Oxon OX14 4RN
711 Third Avenue, New York, NY 10017, USA

Routledge is an imprint of the Taylor & Francis Group, an informa business

Library of Congress Cataloging-in-Publication Data
Smith, Michael R., 1946–
    Power, norms, and inflation : a skeptical treatment / Michael R. Smith.
      p. cm. — (Sociology and economics)
    Includes bibliographical references and index.
    ISBN 0-202-30429-9 (cloth). — ISBN 0-202-30430-2 (paper)
    1. Inflation (Finance) 2. Power (Social sciences) 3. Pressure groups. 4. Economic policy. I. Title. II. Series.
HG229.S624 1992
332.4'1—dc20
                                          92-3686
                                           CIP

ISBN 13: 978-0-202-30430-4 (pbk)

To Sandra

CONTENTS

ACKNOWLEDGMENTS

My most general intellectual debt is to my colleagues in the department of sociology at McGill. In their work, many of them meander quite happily across conventional academic boundaries. Most of them, it seems to me, are engaged in an attack on one or another disciplinary sacred cow. All of them are lively sources of criticism. Over the years they have provided me with a consistently congenial working environment. I am very grateful to them.

More tangible support to my research has been provided by a number of organizations. Research grants from The Social Sciences and Humanities Research Council of Canada paid for some of my early research on the postwar inflation and for release from teaching for a year, during which the largest part of the first draft of this book was written. For the last eight years, various colleagues and I have received funding for our research on labor markets from the Fonds pour la Formation des Chercheurs et Aide à la Recherche of the Government of Quebec. Having access to a relatively stable source of funds is an enormous advantage to a researcher. I am greatly indebted to the people who designed and administer the FCAR program. Last, but not least, the Faculty of Graduate Studies and Research at McGill has at various times bought me personal computers. Gordon Maclachlan set up the program out of which my computers were funded. As Vice-Principal for Research at McGill he was much more of a friend to research in the social sciences than was sometimes recognized. I know that my own research has been greatly assisted by the program he established.

John Hall, Richard Hamilton, Joe Smucker, and Axel van den Berg read and commented on parts of this book. Comments by them saved me from some errors and helped me to sharpen the argument in it. I owe a more fundamental intellectual debt to Richard Hamilton. Richard was my colleague for a number of years before he was lured away to Ohio State (presumably attracted, among other things, by the prospect of Big Ten football!). I regard him as a model of academic rigor and integrity.

His influence on me has been considerable and all, I think, for the good.

Finally, Daniel and Abigail, who so far have displayed no interest whatsoever in the postwar inflation and its causes, certainly helped to keep in perspective the enterprise that has culminated in this book.

1

INTRODUCTION

Compared to the frenzied last months of the Hungarian pengö when with "fine careless rapture . . . it whizzed across the financial sky in 1946, multiplying itself 300,000 million million million million times" (Cairncross, 1966:414), or to the Weimar inflation of 1922 to 1923 during which workers took their pay home in wheelbarrows (the mark depreciated by 75×10^9), or the Bolshevik destruction of the savings of their class enemies in the Soviet Union in 1922 (a rouble depreciation of 7.3×10^3 produced, apparently, by ineptness rather than design), or even to the more recent currency depreciations in assorted Latin American countries, the postwar inflation in rich capitalist societies is rather small beer.[1] After fairly aggressive stabilizations in Austria and Japan in the late 1940s, inflation in the countries of interest in this study, though persistent, never exceeded 25% per year in even the most inflation-prone cases.

Nonetheless, however so humble (in historical terms), the postwar inflation in rich capitalist economies is of some interest. While there is no consensus on this point a plausible case can be made to the effect that even modest amounts of inflation are harmful, that unexpected inflations produce an arbitrary reallocation of wealth and income and that, because price instability disturbs the environment for rational calculation, inflation deters investment and reduces economic growth. The relative harmfulness of inflation is not my main concern in this book. But the fact that it is *possible* to see it as a practical problem affecting the welfare of large numbers of people provides a good reason for exploring the adequacy of the theories at our disposal for explaining it.

There is, however, a particular interest to these theories. The explanation of inflation has been, and principally remains, the province of economists. But the acceleration of inflation in the 1960s and 1970s and the various economic difficulties that accompanied it were seen by sociologists and political scientists as evidence of the serious inadequacy of conventional economic theory and, by extension, as reason to supplement or even supplant it with an alternative grounded in the different

theoretic premises of sociology and political science. Inflation is only one
of a number of subjects that previously has been, more or less, the
private preserve of economists but has recently been subject to academic
invasion. As we will see in some detail in later chapters of this book,
sociologists and political scientists have applied the same sort of theoretic ideas to other macroeconomic outcomes—in particular to unemployment and growth, with which inflation is usually thought to be
connected. A similar invasion has taken place in other areas—the explanation of earnings differentials (e.g., Colbjørnsen, 1986), the operation
of capital markets (e.g., Stearns, 1990; Mintz and Schwartz, 1990), the
determinants and effects of international trade (e.g., Evans, 1979), and
so on.[2]

All of this has been part of an attempt to create a distinct "economic
sociology" (Swedberg, 1987, 1990; Block, 1990:33–42) made necessary, it
is claimed, by assorted inadequacies of conventional economics. What
then distinguishes sociological from economic analyses of a phenomenon?[3]

First there is a conviction that not only are economic outcomes unfair
but that their unfairness should be at the center of any attempt to explain the outcome. What this means, in practice, is the assertion that
power is a central explanatory factor (Oberschall and Leifer, 1986:245–
246). Thus, international trade is not a neutral process of exchange to the
benefit of both parties; its outcomes are weighted against third world
countries because they are shaped by the interests and institutions of
rich countries, particularly the United States (Chirot, 1977:166; Evans,
1979). The operation of capital markets is distorted by networks of influence involving bankers and the senior executives of major nonfinancial
corporations. Banks, in fact, are "vehicles for the class control of the
economy" (Mintz and Schwartz, 1985:254). Women and blacks earn less
because they are employed in jobs that provide them with negligible
bargaining power (Baron and Newman, 1990). It should be clear that it is
easier to make a global judgment of unfairness on the basis of an explanation in terms of power asymmetries than it is to do so on the basis of
the rather neutral market processes described in standard economics
texts. As compared to standard economics, sociological writing on the
economy is, on the whole I would argue, more morally engaged on the
side of groups thought to be underdogs.[4]

The second distinctive element of sociological approaches to the economy is the assertion that economics is excessively individualistic; that in
most markets people are caught up in, but are also able to exploit, a web
of social obligation (Oberschall and Leifer, 1986:249–250). There are relatives, neighbors, and friends whose sense of obligation can be tapped
for assistance in finding a job (Granovetter, 1974). There are commu-

nities of commodity traders among whom sufficient trust develops to greatly reduce the extent to which transactions have to be finalized with (costly) formal contracts (Coleman, 1988:S98–S99). And I take it that there is at least some truth in Veblen's claim that many choices with respect to what to consume are determined by the esteem attached to the purchase of some good or service rather than more obvious and direct utility (1953: see also Lauman and House, 1973; Hirsch, 1976:20–21). Note, further, that the norms regulating economic behavior are likely to be underpinned and influenced by broadly shared culture, including a morality that enjoins individuals against cheating other people, at least in some contexts (Elster, 1989:248–249).[5]

Sociological analyses of the economy vary in the relative role played by power and norms in producing some outcome. A large proportion of recent sociological analyses of earnings, for example, has largely dispensed with norms as explanatory factors in favor of power (Smith, 1990:837–838). On the other hand, it is a lot easier to find norms than power in Parsons and Smelser's (1956) synoptic treatment of the relations between economy and society. Still, what is most relevant here is the fact that power and norms feature prominently in sociological work of the last decade or so on inflation and other macroeconomic outcomes, and they do so in a very specific way.

Sociological analyses of inflation begin with the power inequalities associated with class position. Ignore, for the purposes of argument, the disputes over precisely how social class should be defined.[6] Assume that there are owners of capital and workers and that they are, in some vaguely Marxist fashion, pitted in a struggle over the functional distribution of income. How much each side gets is determined by the power resources available to it. In the absence of trade unions, capital (again in a vaguely Marxist fashion) normally wins hands down. In doing so it makes enough profits to ensure investment, growth, and the continued viability of the capitalist system. (Set aside for the moment the classic Marxist crisis mechanisms—the falling rate of profit and underconsumptionism.) This, however, is not a stable situation. The untrammeled operation of the market produces altogether too many casualties: society protects itself, in Polanyi's (1957:ch. 11) metaphor. A mass of discontented workers at first produces pressure for political democracy and then, once the apparatus of political democracy is established, including political parties, workers are able to extract both a social safety net and the legal basis for a free trade union movement. The trade union movement, of course, becomes a further source of pressure for measures that will modify the operation of the market in ways likely to produce a more equitable distribution of rewards (Korpi, 1978:ch. 2, 1990; Stephens, 1979:98–112).

So far, then, we have an analysis in which, from the point of view of most sociologists, history unfolds as it should. The distribution of income produced by an unregulated market is judged to be grossly unfair because such a market concentrates too much power in the hands of capitalists.[7] Democracy and trade unions, however, shift power and generate more equitable outcomes.[8] But the story does not end here. We are not quite at the stage of living happily ever after, yet. For trade unions and political parties representing the interests of workers can also impede the proper functioning of capitalism. By shifting the functional distribution of income they reduce capitalist profits. If capitalist profits are insufficient there will be less investment, less job creation, declining tax revenues, and so on. Furthermore, by putting great stress on the protection of workers against changes in technology and the inevitable decline of some industries, they can slow down the process of restructuring required by a dynamic economy. In other words, the growth of trade unions and the political representation of worker interests can throw sand in the gears of the capitalist economy and this can produce a series of perverse macroeconomic outcomes, including relatively poor growth, high unemployment, and high inflation. Note in this respect that the common core of sociological accounts of the postwar inflation is that it is the outcome of a "distributional struggle" between, in particular, capital and labor (Maier, 1978:41; Hirsch, 1978:269; Goldthorpe, 1987a:368–376).

This argument provides a possible explanation for the widespread incidence of inflation in rich capitalist societies and does so in terms congenial to sociological theory; that is, organized power plays a central role. Where does the other theoretic element in sociological writing—norms—come in? These appear in accounts of inflation in two ways. First, it is argued that the distributional struggle has been intensified because, in the amoral environment provided by capitalism, normative restraints on what people demand have been stripped away. Second, norms are relevant in the explanation of the differentials in inflation performance *between* countries. One can reasonably argue that the animus that gives force to the demands of trade unions and political parties is fuelled by a sense of unfairness. Workers develop their own criteria of equitable economic outcomes and these are unlikely to coincide completely with those produced by impersonal market processes.

A principal concern is, of course, the relative returns to capital and labor, and with what capitalists do with their profits. Workers might recognize that, in order to invest, their employers need profits. But it is likely that they will wish to be assured that a significant proportion of the profits *does* actually get reinvested (Schott, 1984a:169–174). They may also wish to be reassured that they really will receive a reasonable share of benefits from the future economic growth produced by the investment (Elster, 1989:221–224). Perhaps even more important are issues of fairness in the relative situations of different groups of workers (see Runciman, 1966). For example, in a general sort of way, at least, many workers may favor reinforcing the pay of the very poor (Elster, 1989:236–238); workers seem frequently to prefer promotion on the basis of seniority to the discretion implied by supervisory judgments of merit (Wood, 1978:182); and there is some reason to think that, once established, interindustry pay differentials become infused with a sense of relative fairness that makes it very hard to change them (Wood, 1978:177–179; Thaler, 1989:179–181).

In securing a properly functioning economy—one that is not catastrophically impeded by the restraints enforced by an organized working class—the problem is, then, to explicitly confront normative issues. *If* bargaining over pay and working conditions transcends simple market criteria and manages to address the fairness concerns of individual workers (to some significant degree) then the working class—or, at least, the organized part of it—can be mobilized in pursuit of growth and rising welfare. This is where norms come in. According to the standard account advanced by sociologists and political scientists (and, it should be noted, some economists), countries that have more successfully integrated fairness concerns into a bargaining process already transformed by a growth in the power of the working class display the best macroeconomic performance including, in some versions, more stable prices.

For a sociologist, this is an immensely appealing account of the postwar inflation because it is a useful vehicle for, to put it bluntly, "sticking it" to economists. There are purely academic reasons why sociologists would want to do this. This is an account that asserts the centrality of power and of norms. Economists build models and construct explanations that, at least in their more abstract versions, are purified of social constraint and tend to produce a distinctly Panglossian vision of the world, purged of power and inequity. If it is necessary to appeal to power and norms to understand prices (of all things), surely no area of economic activity can be properly understood without a significant sociological explanatory component?

Of course, in academic debate as in any other kind of debate, motivations are not confined to issues of lofty academic principle. I think that sociologists are also likely to want to "stick it" to economists out of professional jealousy. Economists earn, on average, more than sociologists. It is clear that the contempt of economists toward sociology to which Leijonhufvud refers in his satire on economics (1973:327) is not just a figment of his imagination. It comes through, in a polite version, in a number of Swedberg's (1990) interviews with economists. And it is likely that most sociologists from time to time bump into expressions of it in day to day university life. Goldthorpe is quoted by Swedberg (1987:11) as describing the characteristic attitude of British sociologists towards economics as follows:

> The basic approach of the subject is disliked, but its practitioners are feared. British sociologists would like to 'take on' the economists directly but hesitate to do so because they know little about economics, are reluctant to learn any and generally lose out to economists when it comes to rigour of analysis and argument.

In my view this sort of attitude is common among North American sociologists too. More importantly, it provides a potent set of incentives to seize with some glee upon any identifiable, or imagined, failing in economists' explanations. This has produced a disciplinary culture in which, in a sociological article or book on an economic subject, it is *de rigueur* to include an exasperated comment on the bewildering naivete of economics.[9] Such comments, it seems to me, engender a rather warm and self-satisfied feeling on the part of sociologists making and reading them but rarely have any other useful purpose.

In saying this I should make it clear at the outset that I share most of the broad premises on which sociological writing on the economy is founded. I do not believe that the actual distribution of economic outcomes in any capitalist society would coincide with the distribution that would be required by any defensible ethical system.[10] I have no doubt that relative power plays an important role in producing various economic outcomes. That there is a normative component to most behavior, including much economic behavior, seems to me to be well established. All this notwithstanding, in this book I argue that the sociological account of the postwar inflation in rich capitalist societies is seriously inadequate and adds only a little to what I take to be the main elements of the standard economic account. In fact, I argue that there are good reasons for believing that the accounts produced not only by sociologists are incorrect, but that the accounts produced by economists who have been influenced by sociological accounts are also incorrect. In this book I lay out in some detail the reasons for this conclusion.

Now, any satisfactory account has to come to grips with the basic facts of the postwar inflation. In Figures 1.1 to 1.3 I have summarized the inflation records of 18 rich capitalist economies that have had democratic political regimes throughout the postwar period (this excludes Greece, Portugal, and Spain).[11] These figures show that the average rate of inflation was relatively low from 1954 to 1972 across countries—between

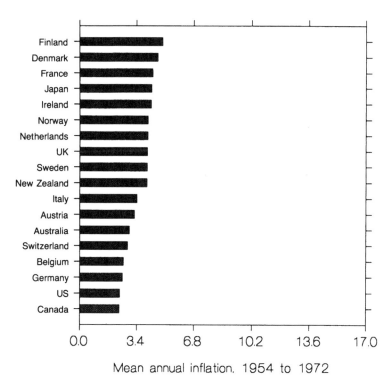

Mean annual inflation, 1954 to 1972

Figure 1.1. Inflation before the oil shocks.

about 2 and 3%. This average for the entire period conceals the fact that rates were higher everywhere from the middle of the 1960s onward. After 1973 (and the first oil shock) inflation accelerated markedly across all 18 countries—but to *very* differing degrees. From 1973 to 1980 Switzerland and Germany had the lowest average rates (about 4 to 5%, and Italy, the United Kingdom, and Ireland the highest (about 14 to 16%). Another distinctive feature of the pattern of inflation not revealed in Figure 1.1 is the fact that a main reason why some countries—including Germany and Switzerland—had a lower average over the entire period was that their rates rose abruptly after 1973 and then fell, whereas in the high inflation countries—Italy, the United Kingdom, and Ireland, inflation rose abruptly, but was very slow to come down again. Figure 1.3 shows that, in the 1980s, the rates remained widely dispersed, but were appreciably lower than in the 1970s. Careful inspection will also reveal marked shifts in the rank of countries across the three periods. I return to these shifts in later chapters.

Any satisfactory social and political account of the postwar inflation also has to come to grips with the fact that inflation has a distinctly

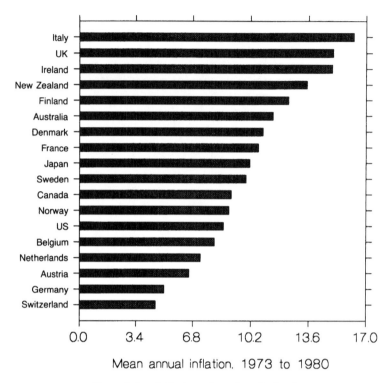

Mean annual inflation, 1973 to 1980

Figure 1.2.   Inflation after the oil shocks.

economic dimension; in other words, it has to link social and political processes to the changes in demand or supply that, I take it we can all assume, have some influence on prices. If demand is at issue, an account of the postwar inflation has to explain why, at some current level of prices, demand increased. For an inflation of any length, it has to explain why the relevant government did not use the policy instruments at its disposal to deflate, or, if it did, why the instruments did not work. If supply is at issue, the explanation has to show why the price at which labor and/or other inputs were supplied increased, at the current level of demand, and why that increase in prices was not offset by a subsequent decline in demand.

To clarify what would be involved in changes of this sort, and because the appraisal of a body of theory involves some consideration of the alternatives against which it is to be compared, in Chapter 2 I present a schematic outline of the major relevant macroeconomic theories and of how they have been applied to the postwar inflation. Then in Chapter 3 I outline and attempt to appraise the political theory that has proved to be most congenial to economists—so-called "public choice" theory.

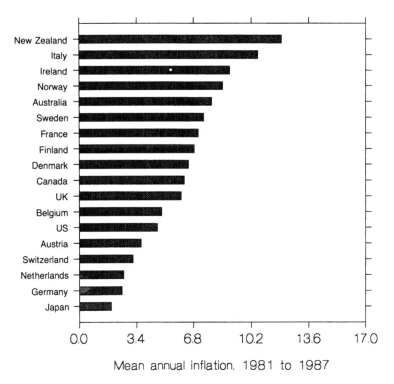

Figure 1.3. Inflation in the 1980s.

This, it should be noted, is typically rather peremptorily dismissed in sociological treatments. I argue that although there is a significant degree of overstatement in "public choice" analyses there are aspects of the postwar inflation that are consistent with a suitably modified version of it.

In Chapter 4 I begin the switch to sociological treatments. Many sociologists and political scientists (who are usually distinctly unenthusiastic about any notion of equilibrium of the sort that features in economic theory) have been attracted to claims that there is some secular process of decline that is conducive to macroeconomic difficulties, including inflation. One such theory makes the claim mentioned above to the effect that capitalism erodes the very moral basis upon which its proper functioning depends; another claims that price instability is one of the outcomes of an inevitable decline in the hegemony of the United States within the international system. In Chapter 4 I present a rather unsympathetic treatment of these accounts. Then I go on to present a theory of secular decline that is rather more consistent with orthodox economic approaches—Mancur Olson's theory of institutional sclerosis—and, while recognizing that the evidence in support of it is not overwhelming, I argue that there is rather more to be said for it as *part* of an explanation of the postwar inflation than can be said for either the moral erosion or declining hegemony accounts.

As I observed above, at the center of sociological accounts of the postwar inflation is rising working class power. The tangible form of this is a tendency for labor costs to rise at rates that cause economic problems. The idea of a *wage-push* is central to sociological accounts, but rarely closely examined in them. In Chapter 5 I review in considerable detail the forms that such an account might take, and what the relevant evidence (suitably appraised) shows. I argue that although there is some evidence of a wage-push, it tends to suggest an altogether weaker economic force than the relevant sociological theory assumes. Then in Chapter 6 I outline and examine the ways in which, it has been claimed, centralized bargaining arrangements—so-called "neocorporatism"—can reduce inflation by introducing normative considerations into the bargains struck between capital and labor. I show that for every presumed advantage of centralized bargaining, there are a number of disadvantages, all of this suggesting that whether or not neocorporatism works to produce superior macroeconomic performance as it is supposed to is an empirical question.

In Chapter 7 I review some relevant evidence. First, there is a set of quantitative studies. In these studies a comparison is made between the macroeconomic performance of countries with different wage bargaining and related institutions. I review the findings of these studies and show that they will not support much of a conclusion for a number of methodological reasons, including the rather fundamental fact that there is significant disagreement over which countries should be allocated to the neocorporatist end of the classification. Then I go on to examine the cases of Germany, Austria, Sweden, and Japan in a bit more detail. Austria and Sweden are almost always, and Germany often, classified as neocorporatist. In a context where there are only 16 to 20 suitable cases to analyze, any quantitative results tending to show that neocorporatism inhibits inflation depend on these countries. I argue that, rather than only comparing crude macroeconomic outcomes (inflation, unemployment, growth), a better strategy involves looking at the processes that (as we will see later) are thought to be involved in and produced by centralized bargaining. This includes, among other things, the extent to which *formal* centralization of bargaining is accompanied by *real* centralization of bargaining, and the extent to which productivity and wage growth are connected. I also argue that in interpreting the macroeconomic performance of these countries it makes sense to take into account factors other than centralized bargaining institutions that might produce superior performance—for example, the role of a distinctively autonomous central bank in the case of Germany and the implications of a heavy dependence on trade with Germany in the case of Austria. Then I look at the case of Japan, which is certainly the most spectacular postwar economic success story and is sometimes classified as neocorporatist. I conclude that, in general, detailed evidence on the economic operation of these countries is not very favorable to the neocorporatist hypothesis.

Now, the neocorporatist account, with its combination of power and norms, is the principal alternative to the standard economic analyses. But, even if hardly anyone else finds it convincing, Marxism continues to exercise some attraction within North American departments of sociology and political science, particularly among those interested in the economy (Swedberg, 1987:78–91). In Chapter 8 I review the various, contradictory, Marxist explanations of the postwar inflation. I argue that, other than the wildly implausible, secular crisis-generating mechanisms on which they rest, each of the Marxist accounts of the postwar inflation is, to all intents and purposes, indistinguishable from one or another of the orthodox economic accounts, except in the rhetoric of moral outrage in which it is couched. I argue that Marxist accounts do not constitute a serious alternative to the orthodox economic account.

It is useful here, I think, to make two general comments about the argument developed in this book. First, it is probably reasonable to recognize that it is likely to be regarded as somewhere between professional disloyalty and apostasy by many of my fellow sociologists, perhaps warranting excommunication.[12] Still, it seems to me that the main objective is to get things right in an explanation rather than to polish the egos of one's colleagues. Second (and perhaps more interestingly), it raises the theoretic question: If it is accepted that power and norms are important in economic behavior and outcomes in general, why is an account of the postwar inflation in which they play a central role incorrect? I return to this issue, albeit briefly, in the concluding chapter.

Notes

1. These figures come from Maier (1978:45–46). For a general treatment of the interwar inflation in Germany see Guttman and Meehan (1975). Maier (1978:49) raises the possibility that the Bolshevik inflation was less deliberate than those producing it claimed.

2. This attempted invasion by sociologists is matched by similar economic imperialism associated, in particular, with Gary Becker (e.g., 1981) and, of particular relevance in this study, Mancur Olson (1965, 1982).

3. For expository convenience in what follows I will describe the approaches of both sociologists and political scientists as "sociological." Maier and Lindberg (1985:571–574) identify sociological accounts with broad processes present in many societies and political science with accounts that stress cross-national institutional differences. But this disciplinary distinction is irrelevant to this study and, on the whole, I am inclined to think that it would be hard to document it.

4. Although it should be noted that the economist Alan Blinder displays a somewhat similar engagement. See in particular his *Hard Heads and Soft Hearts* (1987).

5. The sociological literature on the normative bases of behavior is, of course, immense. For syntheses dealing with economic behavior see Smelser (1976) and Etzioni (1988).

6. For some indication of the disagreements over the definition of class see Wright (1985:ch. 4) and Marshall, Newby, Rose, and Vogler (1988).

7. I take it that this is a reasonable inference about the political judgments of both Korpi and Stephens. Stephens' book is fundamentally an *apologia* for the Swedish version of social democracy. I would argue that the political preferences of most sociologists writing on macroeconomic outcomes are similar to those of Stephens and Korpi and that this is so obvious, if not from political affiliation, then from their choice of language.

8. This is not to say that the shift is thought to have gone far enough. Quite the contrary! Stephens, for example, is quite explicit in viewing this as nothing more than a way station *en route* to a more complete socialism. See also Goldthorpe (1987a:395–396).

9. A fairly extreme example of this is Goldthorpe (1978). Block (1990) is also a fairly fertile source.

10. Although I probably differ from many sociologists in my scepticism with respect to the likelihood that alternative economic systems—including socialism (whatever that might mean)—will produce outcomes that coincide more closely with those required by a defensible ethical system.

11. The data begin in 1954 in order to eliminate from the averages the effects of the Korean war price bulge and its immediate aftermath. Unless otherwise specified the data in the tables and figures in this book come from OECD.

12. Indeed, a recent article in which I made a somewhat similar point about much (but not all) of the recent sociological work on earnings prompted a response that I think can reasonably be described as shrill (see Smith, 1990; Sørensen, 1990).

2

ORTHODOX ECONOMIC
TREATMENTS

Macroeconomists have been divided over the *possibility* and *desirability* of using fiscal and monetary policy to stabilize the economy and, in particular, to reduce unemployment below what it would otherwise be. Broadly speaking, for Keynesians such as James Tobin, Franco Modigliani, Robert Solow, or Alan Blinder, stabilization policies are both possible and desirable; for "Mark I" monetarists such as Milton Friedman or David Laidler, stabilization policies are possible but usually not desirable; and for "Mark II" monetarists such as Lucas, Sargent, Wallace, and the writers in the "new classical" style that have succeeded them, stabilization policies (of the sort that Tobin has in mind) are mostly neither possible nor desirable.[1] In the rest of this chapter I first outline what I take to be the essential elements of each of these approaches and then, second, compare their various aspects.

It should be noted that I begin by presenting a rather antique version of Keynesian theory, that is, I present the version that assumes a long-run, negatively sloped, Phillips curve. As we will see, Keynesians have largely abandoned this idea. But I examine it because the main purpose of this chapter is to review the theory that has been available to inform macroeconomic policy and, possibly, induce policy errors. I do not claim that what follows describes the last word in macroeconomic theory!

Three Macroeconomic Theories

The Keynesian Model

There is a fairly wide diversity of analyses that get subsumed under the label "Keynesian" by those who produce them. What they all share in common is the assumption that capitalist economies are inherently unstable. Both investment expenditures and consumer durable purchases follow erratic paths, the effect of which is to periodically produce unacceptably high levels of unemployment. Poorly judged government policies are another important source of instability. Whether originating in the private or public sectors, the lesson drawn by Keynesians from these instabilities is that the proper task for macroeconomics is to design techniques to smooth out economic fluctuations and, in particular, to prevent *involuntary* unemployment from becoming excessive (Gordon, 1978:345–348; Blinder, 1987:33–36). There are two reasons to be worried about unemployment. First, involuntary unemployment is an unreasonable imposition on those inflicted by it. Second, the underutilized resources that it entails mean that economic growth is less than it would otherwise be, which reduces the welfare of everyone—markedly so when you take into account the year-to-year compounding of sometimes small growth rate differences (Tobin, 1974:13). Keynesians, then, are concerned with the design and implementation of stabilization policies.

After the need for stabilization policies, disagreement begins. In particular, there is a fairly wide disagreement between those who regard themselves as the heirs of Keynes in Britain and North American Keynesians such as Tobin.[2] In the macroeconomic analyses of British Keynesians, wages feature as an important factor explaining inflation. For the purposes of this chapter I will restrict my attention to the North American variant. This is not because I regard it as self-evidently superior, but, rather, because I deal with "wage-push" accounts of inflation in considerable detail in a later chapter.

North American Keynesian analyses of inflation were initially informed by the idea of a long-run Phillips curve that would make stabilization policies fairly straightforward. It gave governments the option of exploiting the fact that higher inflation can, to some extent, be traded-off for lower unemployment, or vice versa (Tobin, 1972, 1974:37–38, 94).

The basis of the long-run Phillips curve is as follows. First, wages are asymmetrically responsive to labor market conditions. Nominal wages rise much more readily in response to tightening than loosening labor market conditions. Wages do not usually decline in loose labor markets (where, that is, unemployment exceeds vacancies) for a number of reasons (Solow, 1979, 1980). Workers are as concerned with relative as with absolute wages (in fact, they are *more* concerned with relative than with absolute wages according to Tobin, 1972:3). Were a group of workers to agree to allow their wages to decline they would have no guarantee that the wages of other workers would also decline. They might end up bearing the costs of a recession themselves and, as a result, slip in the particular earnings hierarchy with which they are concerned (see also Brenner, 1985:136–142). Those running businesses do not force the issue because, to protect their reputation as good employers (and a reputation as a bad employer can be costly when the next upturn takes place), they are willing to concede to their employees some degree of wage stability. Trade unions and public opinion are another source of pressure for wage stability.

Second, the costs of searching for workers, and negotiating new agreements with those they find, provide many employers with an incentive to recognize an "implicit contract," the terms of which provide the worker with some security of employment in the face of variations in the demand for labor (Tobin, 1972:12).

Third, the notion of a single labor market in a given economy is nothing more than a (sometimes) heuristically useful fiction. In fact, national labor markets are made up of many local labor markets, the boundaries of which are determined by the existence of an unwillingness of workers to consider jobs beyond them. Now, the balance of vacancies and unemployment is likely to vary quite widely from local labor market to local labor market. It is this fact, in combination with the other two properties of labor markets described above, that provides a basis for the existence of a long-run, negatively sloped, Phillips curve (Tobin, 1972:10–13: Lipsey, 1960; Archibald, 1969; Holt, 1970; Baumol, 1979).

Suppose you have an economy in which *all* local labor markets have an excess of unemployed over vacancies: the effects of a stimulus to aggregate demand (from a tax cut or reduction in interest rates, or whatever) will have a negligible effect on wages as long as vacancies are exceeded by unemployed. If the stimulus is large enough, vacancies will exceed the numbers unemployed *in some local labor markets*. In those labor markets wages will begin to rise substantially. But the aggregate increase in wage levels will still be quite modest since many local markets still have a surplus of unemployed people. If the stimulus is still larger (or sustained for long enough) most local labor markets will start to have an excess of vacancies over unemployment and the aggregate response of money wages to the stimulus will become substantial. When all labor markets have a surplus of vacancies over unemployed the effects of a demand stimulus can no longer produce a fall in unemployment; in those circumstances, the only effect is on money wages, which, of course, rise, perhaps infinitely so.

What I have described is a curve indicating the relationship between unemployment (on the abscissa) and nominal wages (on the ordinate) that is rather flat at high levels of unemployment, becomes progressively steeper as more local labor markets develop excesses of vacancies, and becomes more or less vertical when all labor markets have excesses of vacancies. I have described, in other words, a regular Phillips curve. The stimulus to aggregate demand will lead not only to rising wages, but also to rising prices, which, affected as they are by employers' responses to the rising wages they have to pay, will follow approximately the same path with respect to unemployment as nominal wage increases (see Tobin, 1980:34).

If, on the other hand, the problem is to reduce a rate of inflation that has become unacceptably high, the government can do that too by reducing aggregate demand (by raising taxes or interest rates), up to a point. As demand slackens the reduced pressure on wages in local labor markets reduces the rate of increase in wages. As consecutive labor markets develop surpluses of unemployed over vacancies the effect of each consecutive reduction in demand on aggregate wage inflation is diminished. Why? The point is that, for the reasons given above, *it is not possible to cause nominal wages to fall*. First, the effects of decreased demand on unemployment are moderated by the tendency of employers to hoard labor (to observe "implicit contracts," that is). Second, because of their concern with relativities, workers resist wage cuts very strongly. So reductions in the demand for labor in individual local labor markets cease having much of a moderating effect on aggregate wages (and inflation) once the point of excess supply is reached. It is true, Tobin acknowledges, that a large and sustained amount of disinflation will eventually lead to a collapse in wages. But, he argued (1972:11), *in practice*, dynamic changes in the economy mean that local labor markets hardly ever reach that state (the 1930s provide an important exception). So, the aggregate floor to wage declines is sustained by the fact that the population of labor markets with floor level wages is in a state of continuous turnover.

It follows that governments can intelligently respond to the waste of resources embodied in a high rate of unemployment by stimulating aggregate demand so that the number of local labor markets with excess supply decreases at the cost of a higher rate of inflation originating in pressure on wages and prices in those local labor markets where vacancies already exceed unemployed. Conversely, inflation can be cut by reducing aggregate demand. But because of the specific shape of the Phillips curve, to do so is likely to be costly. "In the United States, up to 90% of reductions in monetary spending for a year goes into output rather than prices. Two or three point-years of extra unemployment bring down inertial core inflation by only one point" (Tobin, 1981:38).

In fact, for reasons I outline below, Keynesians have tended to abandon the idea of a long-run (negatively sloped) Phillips curve (but the assumption that such a Phillips curve existed informed macroeconomic policy in a number of countries in the early postwar period). The distinctive premise of "new Keynesian" analyses is that, for various reasons, prices fail to adjust to changing market conditions (Mankiw,

1990:1654–1658). In the labor market, unions resist wage cuts and employers of some workers are reluctant to enforce wage cuts because doing so damages the morale and productivity of their workers.[3] In product markets firms are often reluctant to *change* prices (up or down). Doing so sometimes involves significant costs: "the time taken to inform customers, the customer annoyance caused by price changes, and the effort required even to think about a price change" (Mankiw, 1990:1657; see also Cecchetti, 1986). Because prices are slow to adjust to the changing balance of demand and supply, shocks are absorbed by quantity adjustments that produce rising unemployment.

Two further Keynesian views warrant mention. First, if a government wants to reduce inflation it would be well advised to supplement demand restriction policies with some sort of an incomes policy to speed up the process of wage decline. Second, the costs of inflation are not, for the most part, sufficiently high to warrant the higher unemployment that a deflationary policy would produce. Thus, for an *anticipated* inflation, that is a stable rate of inflation, "the ultimate social cost . . . is the wasteful use of resources to economize holdings of currency and other noninterest-bearing means of payment. I suspect that intelligent laymen would be utterly astounded if they realized that *this* is the great evil economists are talking about. They have imagined a much more devastating cataclysm, with Vesuvius vengefully punishing the sinners below. Extra trips between savings banks and commercial banks? What an anticlimax!" (Tobin, 1972:15; see also Solow, 1975).

As I observed earlier, other writers, with credible reasons, are less sanguine about the relative inoffensiveness of inflation. Furthermore, as we will see, Tobin has substantially retreated from this position. But, for the moment, I am concerned with the structure of the Keynesian argument rather than its adequacy.

Mark I Monetarism

Inflation, in this account, originates in government policy. The capitalist economy is not inherently unstable. Left undisturbed, private decisions in competitive markets normally produce the full employment of resources, including labor.

Changes in the price of money are, overwhelmingly, a result of changes in the supply of money. This must be so because the demand for money is, although not rigid, nonetheless a quite stable function of a limited number of variables including interest rates, income, and expected inflation (Friedman, 1968a).[4] Inflation has occurred when governments, for some reason, have increased the supply of money (Friedman, 1968b:21–39). Economic contraction and deflations have occurred when governments have allowed the money supply to contract (Friedman and Schwartz, 1963).

This latter statement, it should be clear, indicates that the effects of government monetary policy are not purely nominal; they can affect the performance of the *real* economy, including output and employment. But the effects are temporary.

> There is always a temporary trade-off between inflation and unemployment; there is no permanent trade-off. The temporary trade-off comes not from inflation per se, but from unanticipated inflation, which generally means from a rising rate of inflation. The widespread belief that there is a permanent trade-off is a sophisticated version of the confusion between 'high' and 'rising' that we all recognize in simpler forms. A rising rate of inflation may reduce unemployment, a high rate will not. (Friedman, 1968a:11)

What lies behind the temporariness of the trade-off?[5] Suppose that a government decides that there is too much unemployment and decides to stimulate aggregate demand, using whatever combination of fiscal and monetary policies it deems appropriate. The effect is that capitalists are confronted with more orders and therefore raise prices and decide to hire more labor to meet the larger volume of orders. Now, the consequence of this is to raise the demand for labor: one might expect that the effect of the increase in demand on production would be offset by the increase in labor costs produced by increasing competition for workers and by the response of those workers to the rising prices of goods they have to purchase. That is not *immediately* so, however.

Workers, it is argued, are much less efficient than capitalists at monitoring market conditions. Capitalists managing enterprises of any size will have full time employees whose responsibility it is to monitor market conditions. Their pricing will respond promptly to increasing demand or costs. Workers, on the other hand, have to monitor the labor market and the cost of the goods they purchase on a part-time basis. Indeed, in many families with an employed husband and a wife working at home the problem of keeping track of the real value of take-home pay will be complicated by the domestic division of labor, with one spouse earning an income and the other spending much of it. Consequently, it is argued, workers are slow to realize that the real value of their wages is falling. Moreover, since their *nominal* wages will rise somewhat in response to increased demand, their difficulty in tracking prices means that they are likely to think that their *real* wages are rising.

In North America the legal framework of industrial relations provides an additional basis for lagging wages. Labor relations in the unionized sector are governed by contracts of up to 3 years. *If* a government chooses to stimulate aggregate demand and *if* there is no provision in the negotiated contract for complete indexation or for reopening the contract in response to a surge in the price index workers are stuck for several months or years with the wages they negotiated before inflation accelerated, whether they realize that their real wages are declining or not.

All of this has important consequences. When aggregate demand goes up employers raise prices but their (labor) costs increase by less than the prices at which they sell their goods. Their profits rise so they invest in more plant and equipment. Because the real cost of labor to them has fallen, they hire more workers. Furthermore, because the increased demand for labor produces an increase in workers' nominal wages that they misconstrue to be a real increase, workers who had been unemployed and looking for a job take jobs that they had previously not considered because they thought the wages the jobs offered were too low. Other workers who have jobs but had considered quitting because they thought their wages were too low become persuaded that their wages are, in fact, acceptable and do not quit. All of this produces an increase in economic activity (as employers increase output and investment) and a decline in unemployment as they take on more (cheaper) workers and as workers themselves become less likely to quit and, if unemployed, more likely to take one of the available jobs. It produces, in other words, a Phillips curve.

Clearly, however, unless one is willing to assume that workers are terminally stupid this cannot go on forever. Eventually they realize that their real wages have lagged (and in North America get the opportunity to do something about it when their contract expires). When this happens they are likely to attempt to negotiate wage increases that both compensate them for any previous decline in purchasing power and include provisions to sufficiently increase wages over the period to which their contract applies to protect them against real wage erosion by inflation. When they do this, employers' incentive to hire the extra workers they took on as a result of the stimulus to aggregate demand evaporates. At the same time, those workers who had taken jobs or continued to hold the jobs they already had on the basis of an overestimate of the real wages they provided, quit. So unemployment rises again, *at least to the level that it was prior to the stimulus to aggregate demand.* But since all contracts (including labor contracts) are now being made on the basis of expectations that inflation will remain at the level it achieved as a result of the government's demand stimulus the economy will tend to settle at a new and permanently higher level of inflation.

Or, at least, it would settle at a new and permanently higher level of inflation if the government chose to do nothing. Suppose, however, that the government regards the new higher rate of inflation as unacceptable and decides to deflate. Orders for products rapidly fall and employers either start to cut prices or, at least, reduce the rate at which they raise them. They begin to lay off workers and, in the new, more difficult economic environment, attempt to restrain the growth of wages. (I am continuing the assumption from the Keynesian account that nominal wages are difficult to cut.) Workers, however, are once again slow to adapt to the changing market conditions. They certainly do not trust their employers who have just effectively—but not necessarily deliberately—cheated them out of some of their wage growth. So they continue to demand wage increases (and to some extent succeed in securing them) that assume the rate of inflation produced by government policy before the government decided to deflate. As a result, the wage bill rises, employers lay off even more workers, and the rate of unemployment rises above what it had been prior to the deliberately induced increase in aggregate demand.

There are two concepts central to this analysis. First, there is the notion of a *short-run Phillips curve*. Second, there is the notion of a *natural rate of unemployment*.[6] Both of these are implicit in the above account. There is a trade-off between inflation and unemployment, but only in the short run. The government does get more production and jobs from a stimulus to aggregate demand but only for as long as workers are either fooled, constrained by their contracts, or both. The process of being fooled is modeled in formalizations of these ideas with the so-called "adaptive expectations augmented Phillips curve." Included among the determinants of inflation is an expectations term that is "adaptive" in the sense that the expectations are assumed to be formed on the basis of past inflation rates.

The term has to be specified in such a way that sooner or later expectations catch up with the real rate of inflation and the economy returns to its *natural rate* of unemployment. And, as a matter of fact, unless the government had been pursuing bad policies prior to its decision to stimulate aggregate demand (such as allowing the collapse of a good part of the credit system, as it is claimed it did during the great depression), it is likely that unemployment, at the time of the stimulus, was at the natural rate.

Where does this leave the government with respect to macroeconomic policy options? It can reduce unemployment but only temporarily. To maintain the lower unemployment at the new, higher, rate of inflation it would have to continue stimulating demand, forcing inflation up to ever higher levels; for only with a consecutive set of unanticipated inflations could the lag of wages behind prices be maintained. But that cannot go on forever because it would ultimately culminate in hyperinflation and the collapse of the currency. Eventually a *reasonable* government has to stop inflating. And, if it turns out that the higher rate of inflation is less economically benign than Tobin has claimed, it is forced to deflate and produce a rate of unemployment above the natural rate, albeit temporarily. If one accepts this analysis there is not much to be said for macroeconomic policies designed to reduce unemployment below the natural rate.

But what if, for some reason, the rate of unemployment is above the natural rate to start with. Even in this case monetarists of this kind are opposed to stabilization policy.

> If it is agreed that in the long run the Phillips curve is essentially vertical—or perhaps even positively sloped . . . . then that certainly does not rule out the possibility of the economy slipping below its natural rate of output in a short run that may be of considerable duration, or the possibility that there exists an appropriate menu of monetary and fiscal policies that might hasten its return to that natural rate without generating any serious costs during the transition. As a first step to exploiting this possibility, though, those in charge of policy would need to know what the natural rates of output and employment actually are. As a second step, they would need accurate information upon where the economy actually is, and where it would move in the absence of a policy change, not to mention at what pace. Armed with this not inconsiderable amount of information, policy makers would know that they were in a position where it might be useful to deploy some policy measure or other. To design the policy would of course require them to know about the size and time path of the economy's response to the measures they might take, factors which even the loosest application of the rational expectations idea tells us are likely to be influenced by the policy measures.
>
> Now I will readily agree that we have the mathematical and statistical tools available for tackling the design of stabilization policy along the foregoing lines, and I also agree that our econometric models contain answers to all the quantitative questions that I have just raised. However the conclusion that I draw from all this is that we are probably rather good at fine-tuning econometric models. One can rest the monetarist case against activist policy on the proposition that markets always clear and that expectations are rational, but one can also rest it on the much more down-to-earth proposition that we are too ignorant of the structure of the economies we live in and of the manner in which that structure is changing to be able safely to implement activist stabilization policy in the present environment, or in the foreseeable future. (Laidler, 1981a:18–19)

This rather lengthy quotation is useful for two reasons. First, it eloquently makes the case against stabilization policy on the grounds that there is not sufficient knowledge of the operation of the economy to allow governments to intelligently intervene at the right time. Even if unemployment is above the natural rate, it is assumed that in the long run the private income-maximizing decisions of capitalists and workers will cause it to return to it on its own. In the meantime, because inevitably ill-informed, government stabilization policy is as likely to make things worse as better. Second, the quotation raises the issue of *rational expectations*, the core of monetarism mark II, which provide additional grounds for eschewing stabilization policy. It is to these that I now turn.

Monetarism Mark II, and the "New Classical" Macroeconomics

If people find their economic welfare seriously damaged as a result of an unanticipated burst of inflation to which they were slow to react, is it likely that they will be as passive about the rate of change of prices in the future? Probably not. It is more likely that they will devote additional time, and sometimes money, to carefully monitoring prices and the factors that influence them. There is an element of unreality about adaptive expectations models of the inflationary process and this is the starting point for *rational expectations* analyses (Maddock and Carter, 1982:40).

Part of the basis of the short-run Phillips curve in North America, for example, is the fact that workers are locked into contracts that bind them to real wages that depreciate as inflation accelerates. But, as Lucas emphasizes, there has to be a reason "why people should choose to bind themselves to contracts which seem to be in no one's self-interest" (1981:564). One answer given by Lucas lies in "informational difficulties." That is to say, workers are ill equipped to monitor price rises in an unexpected inflation. But once bitten is twice shy and workers who have lost from inflation will come to regard as worthwhile the effort involved in forming less inaccurate expectations about inflation.

Those expectations need not be completely accurate. Some workers may overestimate future inflation and others underestimate it. But each time their expectations prove wrong they will correct them for the subsequent period and will also attempt to acquire additional information that will allow a better estimate next time. In fact, the rational expectations model assumes that inaccuracies in people's expectations will be random (Laidler, 1981a:11). This is an important assumption because were they nonrandom it would be possible for the government, if it could figure out in which direction the expectations tended to err, to exploit that knowledge to influence subsequent growth in output and employment. It is, precisely, the systematic tendency for workers to err on the side of underestimating inflation after a period during which prices have tended to increase at a fairly stable rate that allows the stabilization policies inherent in the short-run Phillips curve.

Monetarism mark I, it will be recalled, assumes that there is a short-run Phillips curve that governments might attempt to exploit to stabilize the economy—in effect, to reduce unemployment; but that stabilization policy is impossible because governments do not have at their disposal a sufficiently precise understanding of the economy to allow them to intervene intelligently. Monetarism mark II goes beyond this and argues that there is no short run-Phillips curve to exploit. People acting rationally will react to attempts by the government to exploit their ignorance by acquiring information and changing their behavior. They will, in other words, adjust their behavior to undermine the premises of the policy. Consequently, improved understanding of the economy can never make any difference (as, in theory at least, it might do for mark I monetarists). Countercyclical stabilization policy is, quite simply, impossible.

Rational expectations theory is normally associated with fairly strong assumptions about the capacity of markets to clear. After all, how can they fail to do so when they are made up of individuals working with a model of the economy that allows them to forecast more or less accurately what the economic effects of one or another change in the economic environment (including a change in government) is likely to be? This, however, still leaves to be explained the fairly considerable fluctuations in economic aggregates (output, consumption, employment, etc.) that we observe. The extension of rational expectations theory designed to provide an explanation for fluctuations in economic aggregates is so-called "real business cycle" theory (e.g., Long and Plosser, 1983; Plosser, 1989).

Suppose that productivity levels are unstable and that, for some reason, productivity falls. This implies a lower marginal productivity of labor and, assuming that real wages are connected to marginal productivity, a falling real wage. But if workers are paid less they consume less, so consumption falls; and if the amount workers receive for their work goes down, the attraction of work relative to leisure diminishes and unemployment rises (Mankiw, 1989:83). Increases in productivity will have the inverse effect. If you assume that technology changes in ways that produce highly variable productivity, you have an *equilibrium* explanation for the business cycle. Economic aggregates fluctuate not because of market imperfections that prevent prices from adjusting to clear markets; they fluctuate because, given worker and consumer tastes, changes in the productivity level produce changes in the amount of leisure and consumption that people choose (Prescott, 1986:27–37). Note that changes in government tax and spending policy might have similar (disruptive) effects.

The Theories Compared

In this section I discuss three things. First I contrast the approaches to stabilization policy associated with the macroeconomic theories I have outlined. Second, I venture some judgments about the relative plausibility of each. Third, I look briefly at the kind of factors that these theories suggest might be at the origin of the postwar inflation, starting out with a discussion of the likely effects of alternative exchange rate regimes on the policy options available to governments.

Policy Options

What if there is a relatively high level of unemployment? For Keynesians there is no question: the government should intervene to stimulate aggregate demand. Mark I monetarists would tend to demur. For them, the higher than normal unemployment can only be a transitional phenomenon; it will disappear as people slowly adapt to changed economic circumstances (an abrupt contraction of the money supply or an increase in supply prices, for example) and see the opportunities for profitable investment and employment that had at first been unclear to them. In the meantime (that, as Laidler acknowledges, "may be of considerable duration") the lack of information on and understanding of the fundamental conditions and operation of the economy mean that government intervention is likely to do at least as much harm as good. Thus, Cagan (1979:Part II) has traced the history of postwar macroeconomic policy in the United States in an attempt to show that government policies to "fine tune" the economy—either to reduce unemployment or inflation—were typically implemented or had their effects after the problem that the policies were designed to address had already disappeared; or that the magnitudes of the intervention were wholly inappropriate.[7]

What about mark II monetarists? As Tobin has quite gleefully pointed out (e.g., 1980:41), unemployment is not a problem at all in the models constructed within this tradition. Since people are assumed to quite rapidly correct their understanding of economic conditions to allow them to make mutually profitable contracts, potential employers will quickly perceive the potential opportunities for profitable production available to them and workers will equally quickly develop a realistic understanding of job opportunities and wages. In these circumstances people who want to work will quickly find jobs. The implication of this is that the unemployment level at any time approximates the "natural rate"; that is, given institutional conditions (the existence of unions, of a minimum wage, the investment climate created by the government, etc.) it cannot be any lower. Where unemployment does rise it is a matter, according to the "real business cycle" of the new classical economics, of a change in workers' relative taste for leisure. It is fair to say, I think, that within this tradition, unemployment is simply not a problem.[8]

What if there is a high rate of inflation? Keynesians (of the sort I have considered in this chapter) have responded to inflation in two different ways. In the early 1970s, as we saw earlier, there was a claim that inflation did not matter very much; so there was no pressing need to incur the higher unemployment a deflationary policy would produce (whether in the short or long run). Toward the end of the 1970s there was some retreat from that position and (implicitly, at least) an acknowledgement that some of the effects of inflation were real and damaging. But, consistent with the Keynesian concern with avoiding increases in unemployment under all circumstances, the policy option chosen is a combination of monetary disinflation combined with one or another form of wage and price controls (e.g., Tobin, 1977:467, 1981:39, and, more cautiously, Blinder, 1987:56–59). The assumption behind this is that wage and price controls can reduce the lags in adjustment to changed economic conditions—in this case the switch of government policy to monetary disinflation—and at the same time reduce the amount of unemployment that disinflation will generate.

Part of the monetarist response to high inflation seems to me to have been to say that if intelligent policies had been followed in the first place, inflation would not have happened (see, for example, Laidler, 1981a:22). Monetarists argue that since the government cannot stabilize the economy (whether because of poor models and clumsy policy instruments or because of rational expectations), its best policy is to provide a stable and predictable environment for business decisions: it can do this by having a simple and publicly promulgated rule for growth in the money supply—for instance, tying the growth in the money supply to the rate of growth in productivity (e.g., Friedman, 1968a: Lucas, 1980).

But this does not help very much if, as was the case in the 1970s, a serious inflation is already underway. Monetarists eschew wage and price controls of any kind on the grounds that they will not work. For present purposes we can set aside the reasons why this might be so (Brittan and Lilley, 1977, remain a lucid source), although I will return to the issue when I examine corporatist theories of inflation. The fact is that there is quite a lot of evidence of attempts to use incomes policy to control inflation that have failed in the past and sometimes abysmally so.[9]

If not wage and price controls to reduce inflation then what? Mark I monetarists, acknowledging that there are substantial, unemployment creating, lags in the adjustment of the economy to a contractionary monetary policy, favor a *gradual* process of disinflation to minimize the amount of disruption (Laidler, 1981a:22). Mark II monetarists, who assume that people will rapidly adapt their behavior to circumstances, particularly if they are given accurate information about the government's intentions, favor prompt and widely announced reductions in the money supply (and in inflation-causing government deficits). They would argue, further, that a gradualist approach to the reduction of inflation is likely to be ineffective because less credible than a "once and for all" shift in policy; people simply will not believe that elected governments will be sufficiently resolute to "stay the course" (Sargent, 1986:110–115).

Relative Plausibility

The second general issue I want to address is, are there grounds for confidently plumping for one or another of the alternative theories? There is a huge accumulation of econometric research designed to test each of them. But, it seems to me, Solow (1979:340) was surely correct when, referring to the econometric tests of macroeconomic theories, he argued that "the test of any theory, conformity with the facts, often turns out to be inconclusive and perhaps indecipherable; and it is even possible that the institutional environment of a theory changes so that a theory adequate for one decade may fail in the next." The econometric evidence is, quite simply, not definitive. And, as a matter of fact, when the combatants in macroeconomic disputes seek to take care of their opponents with a knock-out blow they make use of rather broad historical comparisons. Thus, Lucas attempts to put Tobin in his place as follows:

> Keynesian neoclassical orthodoxy or the neoclassical synthesis *is* in deep trouble, the deepest kind of trouble in which an applied body of theory can find itself: It appears to be giving seriously wrong answers to the most basic questions of macroeconomic policy. Proponents of a class of models which promised 3 (and a half) to 4 (and a half) percent unemployment to a society willing to tolerate annual inflation rates of 4 to 5 percent have some explaining to do after a decade such as we have just come through.
>
> Now, Friedman and Phelps had no way of foreseeing the inflation of the 1970s any more than did the rest of us, but the central forecast to which their reasoning led was a conditional one, to the effect that a high-inflation decade should not have less unemployment on average than a low-inflation decade. We got the high inflation decade, and with it as clear-cut

an experimental discrimination as macroeconomics is ever likely to see, and Friedman and Phelps were right. It really is as simple as that. (1981:559–560)

Tobin, on the other hand, seeks to dispose of monetarist objections to stabilization policy by reproducing a chart showing that the variance in growth in output in the United States since the 1960s—the decade when, according to Tobin, stabilization policy began to be seriously attempted—was much lower than it was in previous decades (1980:46–48).

Now, I believe that both Lucas and Tobin are deceiving themselves in regarding each's respective historical comparison as settling the matter. After all, if pressed, Tobin presumably would not claim that the only factor determining the rate of inflation is the rate of unemployment and lots of things other than an increase in the rate of inflation took place in the 1970s. And Lucas might respond to Tobin's chart by pointing out that the presence of *discretionary* stabilization policy was not the only thing that distinguished the period after 1960 from the period before it. In fact, the largest decline in variance came immediately after the second world war. Since there is little evidence of countercyclical policy under Eisenhower's administration of the 1950s, it is necessary to look elsewhere for sources of declining variability. For example, there are the *automatic stabilizers* (insurance of bank deposits, unemployment insurance, and farm support payments) that vary countercyclically (see Friedman, 1968b:72–96).

So the grand historical comparisons do not settle the matter either. Nonetheless, I do think that it is possible to make some judgments on the plausibility of what these alternative models claim about policy options. To start with, it is now largely conceded by Keynesians (and by Tobin in particular: see Tobin, 1980:39) that there is no long-run, significantly nonvertical, Phillips curve. Most people (all but the wholly feckless) clearly do adjust their behavior in the light of experience; the employment-generating effects of a decline in real wages as a result of a government-contrived *unexpected* inflation are likely to dissipate with consecutive uses of the tactic. It is also clear that that process of adaptation will include *some* attempt to anticipate what governments will do in the future. The arrival in power of a Labour government in Britain or a New Democratic Party government in Canada, or, perhaps, a Democratic president in the United States would enter into estimates of future rates of inflation in each country—certainly for a population that has been sensitized to the issue of inflation by a previous episode. Any reasonably competent union would attempt to incorporate the expected rate of inflation in the bargains it struck on behalf of its members. To the extent that it succeeded in doing so it would undermine the premises of employment generation through a short-run Phillips curve.

Rational expectations, then, considerably complicate the problem of formulating stabilization policy. But a number of economists have gone to some lengths to show that stabilization policy remains possible in the context of rational expectations. Both Fischer (1977) and Phelps and Taylor (1977) show that even if expectations are rational, long-term contracts in North America slow the adjustment of wages and prices and that this sometimes produces unemployment. In this context, stabilization policy can usefully be used along familiar Keynesian lines to substitute real for nominal changes in wages and prices.

Furthermore, the rational expectations objection to stabilization policy is only as strong as the assumptions that underlie the model. These go much beyond the notion that people will try to anticipate what governments do. As Laidler (1981a:12) emphasizes, rational expectations writers "model the economy 'as if' markets always clear." They assume, in other words, that if a profitable trade is there to be made, people will make it. In their models workers, for example, will take a pay cut if that is the only way they can protect their jobs. But the existence of rigidities in price responses to changes in market conditions is, surely, beyond dispute.[10] The prices of many goods are set in contracts signed well in advance of delivery dates (Hicks, 1974) and have shown, besides, an increasing inflexibility throughout the twentieth century (Cagan, 1979:ch. 3). The inflexibility of wages also appears to have increased over the twentieth century (Sachs, 1980) and, as we saw earlier, there are all sorts of reasons for expecting wages to be inflexible. All in all, I do not believe that one can argue that rational expectations provide an absolute barrier to stabilization policy. The responses of individuals to government policy will certainly include a rational expectations component and that component will complicate any attempts at countercyclical policy. But the real economy includes systematic lags in adjustment that are excluded from rational expectations models.

Does that mean that sociologists and political scientists should line themselves up behind Tobin (in his short-run Phillips curve incarnation), and construct their theories accordingly? I do not think so, or at least, not entirely. For the problem of the adequacy of the information on which governments formulate policies remains a major one. Stabilization policy requires that governments be able to forecast what would happen to the principal economic aggregates (prices, unemployment, gross national product) in the absence of a change in monetary or fiscal policy and then what would happen after either was changed. The fact is that the forecasting record of the various models of the economy used by Western governments is much more frequently located at the poor to wretched end of the appropriate scale than at the fair to good end.[11] I do not believe that the history of macroeconomic policy errors chronicled by Cagan and by Blinder is purely tendentious. Indeed, Blinder's own sympathies are unambiguously Keynesian.

So if you add inadequacies of information and knowledge to the difficulties posed by the propensity of some people, at least, to react to a period of accelerating inflation by attempting to outguess the government (and in so doing to reduce the government's capacity to secure desired economic outcomes—like declining unemployment—by fooling people), it becomes clear that there are formidable obstacles in the way of successful stabilization policy. Indeed, it is striking that, in a rather forceful attack on the policy inactivism counselled by monetarists, Buiter (1980:47) concludes as follows: "whether 'stabilization policy' has in fact been stabilizing or destabilizing is a separate empirical issue—one that will be extremely difficult to settle with any degree of confidence." It seems to me that there is a long way from this to the certainties of some of Tobin's writings.

A sensible conclusion with respect to the claims about stabilization policy would be something along the following lines. There are enough lags and imperfections in the economy to allow governments to use fiscal and monetary instruments to affect the levels of production and employment and the rate of increase in prices. Sometimes, governments have had some measure of success in manipulating those instruments to secure desired outcomes. Laidler (1981a:19), for example (presumably rather unwillingly), allows that "In the 1950s and 1960s the British government did succeed in fine tuning income and employment variables within the rather narrow bounds laid down by what then appeared to be balance of payments constraints." But this degree of success was achieved within a stable economic environment in which economic aggregates were changing in fairly predictable ways. It does not follow that because stabilization policy worked in the 1950s and 1960s it would have done so in the 1970s, when the quite radical changes in the world economic environment had significant effects on the reliability of the coefficients out of which the various forecasting models were constructed. In a stable environment Western governments probably had some degree of success with stabilization policy. But, of course, in a stable environment there is less need of stabilization policy. In unstable environments forecasting models become increasingly unreliable and the best intentioned government is as likely to have made matters worse as to improve them. The government of the United States seems to have done precisely this during the second half of the 1960s and the first half of the 1970s. It follows that any theory of the postwar inflation

30   Orthodox Economic Treatments

generated by a sociologist or a political scientist that neglects this lim-
itedness of the possibilities of stabilization policy—that assumes, on the
contrary, government macroeconomic omniscience—will be inadequate,
and grossly so.[12]

Explaining the Postwar Inflation

The background to any such discussion is the international transmission of inflation. The revival of monetarism brought with it a shift in
attention to the effects of the world supply of money on national rates of
inflation. After the second world war, rates of exchange for the currencies of the rich capitalist world were negotiated at Bretton Woods. The
governments of the treaty signatories were bound to maintain their
currencies at the negotiated par and were allowed to devalue only under
very specific circumstances. Implementing the terms of Bretton Woods
took several years. At the extreme, Canada became subject to its disposi-
tions only in 1962. Still, until it collapsed in 1971 the fixed exchange rate
regime established at Bretton Woods did effectively restrict the degree of
variation in the exchange rates of its signatories.[13] In doing so it also
substantially tied together the inflation rates of the countries in question—although with different implications for macroeconomic policy
options, depending on the size of the country.

I can illustrate what is involved here by taking the case of Canada and
the United States, the former having an economy about a tenth the size
of the latter, which is its principal trading partner. The mechanisms
involved, however, are quite general.[14] Suppose that, under a fixed
exchange rate regime, the United States government were to provide an
inflationary stimulus to aggregate demand but that the Canadian government responded by restrictive fiscal and monetary policies designed
to avoid a parallel increase in inflation. Other things being equal, the
Canadian dollar would tend to appreciate relative to the U.S. dollar. It
would do this principally because restrictive fiscal and monetary policies
tend to raise interest rates. Higher interest rates would attract U.S.
funds into Canada and, in doing so, bid up the value of the Canadian
currency. If the United States deflated and the Canadian government
tried to maintain a policy of greater stimulus, the reverse would occur.
But if the government is committed to a fixed exchange rate regime it
cannot allow either thing to happen and must adjust its fiscal and monetary policy to keep the Canadian dollar within the agreed on ranges. In
other words, under fixed exchange rates Canada has to inflate when the
United States inflates and deflate when the United States deflates. Canada's inflation rate is tied to that of the United States.

As Fleming (1978:18) puts it, "The situation of a large country is rather different." If the United States chooses to pursue policies that result in a rate of inflation that exceeds that of the rest of the world, is it subject to the same discipline as Canada? The answer is no, and Fleming (1978:18) provides a clear explanation of why.

> If one country does half the world's trade it is natural that other countries should choose to hold about half their foreign exchange reserves in that country's currency as long as it is assumed to be stable. If every country has holdings of this currency it is likely to be used to finance trade with third countries and the demand for it may well rise above 50 per cent of total exchange reserves. In this situation a devaluation of the major currency is unlikely to be a matter of indifference to its major trading partners for three reasons. First it reduces the value of their reserves in terms of the quantities of third-country imports they command; secondly it is likely to accelerate inflation in the large country, thus reducing the purchasing power there of holdings of its currency; and thirdly it represents an increase in the competitiveness of an important rival and thus jeopardizes the other countries' own surplus positions. The minor countries are therefore likely to be ambivalent in their attitude to the major country's exchange rate and this may make them reluctant to press for conversion of their holdings for fear of precipitating a devaluation.

So, fixed exchange rates tie the rates of inflation of countries together but in a different way for small and large countries. The capacity of the governments of small countries to stimulate their economies is limited by the threat to their exchange rate that this poses if they stimulate faster than the large country with which they trade. The government of the large country, on the other hand, can stimulate its economy and drag up the inflation rates of its smaller partners because it is *to some degree* sheltered from pressure on the external value of its currency.

To what degree did the introduction of (more or less) flexible exchange rates in 1971 change all this? It was once argued that with flexible exchange rates countries could effectively insulate themselves from the macroeconomic policy choices of their trading partners (Dunn, 1978:105–106; Dunn, 1971; Wonnacott, 1965). Thus, suppose (to continue with my use for illustrative purposes of Canada and the United States) the government of Canada decided to provide more stimulus to the Canadian economy than was being provided by the U.S. government to its own economy. With flexible exchange rates it would not be prevented from doing so by the resultant depreciation of its currency. The Canadian government could go ahead and exploit the properties of the short-run Phillips curve and maintain lower levels of unemployment than the United States.

Things are not as simple as this, however. A relatively higher economic stimulus in Canada would reduce Canadian interest rates and
provoke a shift of capital out of the country. The flow of funds out of the
country would depreciate the value of the Canadian dollar. People
would have to pay higher prices for imported consumer and investment
goods and wage claims would increase in response to the rising cost of
living (Purvis, 1979). Aggregate demand would also fall since the rising
cost of investment goods and wages would reduce the rate of profits. All
of this is to say that even under flexible exchange rates, the stimulus to
economic activity from an expansionary monetary or fiscal policy would
be rapidly dissipated. Canada would end up with a negligible increase
in economic activity but a higher rate of inflation (see Laidler, 1981b:184).

There is, however, a possible exception to this. A declining exchange
rate will both boost exports and encourage a shift in consumption to
domestically produced goods, including import substitutes. *If* an economy has unused industrial capacity that can be rapidly drawn on to
replace the imports rendered prohibitively expensive by the decline in
the exchange rate, the net effect on economic activity of an economic
stimulus greater than that of trading partners *may* be positive (Bond,
1983). But the least one can say is that the switch from fixed to flexible
exchange rates does not produce nearly the room for autonomous macroeconomic policy that writings prior to the demise of Bretton Woods
advertised. In only one area do flexible exchange rates unambiguously
liberate governments from the constraints of fixed exchange rates.
Laidler (1981b:184) may overstate in writing that "The only degree of
freedom that domestic policy makers get from adopting a flexible exchange rate is the ability to choose the long-run value of the domestic
inflation rate," but not by much.

With this in mind, what explanations of the postwar inflationary process are consistent with the orthodox theories outlined above? It will be
recalled from the previous chapter that, broadly speaking, the postwar
pattern of inflation in rich capitalist societies was as follows: after the
Korean war inflation rates were similar across countries and quite low;
from the mid-1960s rates started to increase but, again within a fairly
narrow band; after 1973 rates went up everywhere as did the level of
unemployment, but to markedly different degrees in different countries;
at the end of the 1970s rates began to come down but much faster in
some countries than others.

The narrowness of the band of rates of inflation to 1971 is easily
explained by the fixed rate regime and the dispersal of rates thereafter
by the shift to rather more flexible rates. The acceleration of rates *across
countries* in the mid-1960s is explained by the fact that the United States
was pursuing a war in Vietnam and at the same time establishing a

broad array of costly social programs without increases in taxes to pay for them.[15] As the largest reserve currency country within a fixed rate currency exchange system it was able to evade the pressure to which any other country would be subject, to devalue or to correct its balance of payments. And, in increasing its expenditures without increasing its taxes it was adding to the world supply of money and causing the rate of inflation to rise in all its trading partners (see, in particular, Darby and Lothian, 1983; also, Bergsten, 1975, ch.7). This part of an explanation of the postwar inflation is, I believe, uncontroversial *amongst orthodox theorists.*

But the following facts remain to be explained. First, why was there persistent inflation throughout the postwar period at all—even at the lower rates of the (post-Korean war) 1950s? Second, why did inflation accelerate everywhere after 1973? Third, why were increases in inflation in the 1970s accompanied by increases in unemployment in almost all countries? Fourth, how are the differences between countries to be explained, including both the narrower differences of the fixed exchange rate period and the broader differences after 1973? Here explanations become much more controversial (and some Keynesians introduce the kind of wage-push accounts that I discuss in Chapter 5).

Differences between the orthodox theories reviewed here in answers to all of these questions are tied to the different approaches to stabilization policy. For Keynesians, some inflation is desirable because it allows a degree of flexibility in *real* prices and, in particular, the price of labor, that is not possible for *nominal* prices (Tobin, 1972:13). Technical change means that some workers become more productive than other workers. Changes in tastes mean that the demand for some goods and services withers away. It is not possible (or, at least, not easy) to reduce the nominal wages of workers the demand for whose labor is declining and whose productivity is stagnant. But a growing economy requires pay differentials that reflect differences in demand and productivity. Suitable differentials can be secured quite quickly without cuts in nominal wages if a steady rate of inflation is allowed to reduce the real wages of workers whose work is in low demand. Presumably, then, part of the generally inflationary tendency in the pre-1971 period arises in the wise policy decisions of some Keynes-inspired governments, who then exported their inflation to the rest of their trading partners because of the fixed exchange rate regime.

Monetarists, on the other hand, are willing to contemplate zero inflation rates with equanimity (e.g., Friedman, 1968b:41, 48), although whether or not the rates are zero or 2% does not seem to be a matter of great moment for them. They typically believe that prices of all kinds are much more flexible than Keynesians assume. In particular, worker concern with relative wages is not typically part of monetarist models and, although it may be conceded that nominal wages are to some degree sticky, they are typically regarded as sufficiently flexible that the problem of reallocating resources (under conditions of steady growth) is not a major one (see Purvis, 1980:98).

Since monetarists do not see inflation as a necessary source of flexibility they would not interpret the gradual inflation of the 1950s as a result of the prudent judgments of some governments. On the contrary, monetarists tend to interpret all inflation as being a result of either poorly informed—by which they mean Keynesian—policy, or the irresponsibility of politicians, or both.[16] This is true of the gradual inflation that preceded the Vietnam war and also of the accelerating inflation that accompanied it and largely originated in the United States.

It is the interpretation of the high inflation and unemployment of the 1970s that seriously divides Keynesians from monetarists. I will illustrate the alternative approaches with analyses of the United States. I examine the record of inflation in some other countries in more detail in a later chapter. For present purposes, it is useful to focus on the United States both because the interpretative issues between Keynesians and monetarists can be illustrated more clearly by avoiding jumping about from country to country and because, given its importance in world trade and capital markets, what happens in the United States is important for all countries.

Feldstein provides a rather typical monetarist analysis. "The historical record shows that the deliberate expansionary policies of successive administrations, particularly the use of monetary expansion in an attempt to limit interest rates, contributed directly to our rising rate of inflation" (1982:65). Specifically, consecutive administrations made the following errors: they interpreted unemployment that in the mid-1960s was largely voluntary (people more disposed to change jobs with the added cushion of more generous unemployment benefits, the increasing proportion of the labor force made up of teenagers whose tastes and behavior mean that they will always have higher unemployment rates) as if it were analogous to the kind of unemployment that was observed in the 1930s; they thought that there was a long-run Phillips curve, offering them a stable menu of long run trade-offs between unemployment and inflation; they forced interest rates down to unnecessarily low levels because they overestimated the effective cost of credit, having neglected to take account of the effects on the real cost of capital of tax deductions; and (misled by Tobin's "shoe leather" rhetoric) they grossly underestimated the real costs of inflation.

In fact, Feldstein argues, inflation has substantial negative effects on the economy and was at the roots of the rising unemployment of the

1970s. When inflation is rising businessmen and consumers are uncertain of the level at which it will finally settle. The resulting uncertainty led to a decision to avoid actions with long-term pay-offs; so there was less saving and investment. There was also less investment because the accounting conventions of the 1960s ("historic cost" and "first-in-first-out" inventory appraisal) led to an overstatement of business profits and, as a result, they were overtaxed. Profits were further reduced, as were the real incomes of consumers, by tax brackets that were not indexed to rising prices. Together, these effects of inflation reduced aggregate demand and investment and, in doing so, reduced growth and employment. So, at the end of the 1970s the United States (and some other capitalist nations) confronted the higher rates of inflation that had become embedded by the policy errors of the 1960s and early 1970s together with the higher unemployment that the inflation itself had produced.

Keynesians explain the stagflation of the 1970s as an outcome of the commodity price shocks—in particular the increases in oil prices in 1973 and 1978, and the policy errors that accompanied them (but, as we will see, different policy errors from those suggested by monetarists).

Blinder (1979) argues that these shocks involved the following process: to start with, the supply of commodities decreased and, because the demand for commodities is fairly inelastic (does not go down by much when prices rise), that produced large price increases. In the short run, the prices of finished goods are largely cost determined ("mark-up pricing"); so the immediate effect of the commodity shocks was to increase the rate of inflation. The shocks also reduced output and employment. People were less willing to buy finished products at their new higher prices, and as demand for higher priced finished goods fell, so did employment. This effect was compounded by the fact that the demand for the goods produced by the industrialized countries was also reduced by the redistribution of income caused by the oil price increases. Income was redistributed to the oil-producing countries and to the shareholders of the oil companies, both of which were disposed to save much more of their income than had been the people from whom the income had been transferred (Blinder, 1979:19–20)[17] Finally, in a number of countries where tax brackets were not indexed, higher inflation also reduced demand by pushing nominal incomes up into higher tax brackets.

According to Blinder, the cost of the oil shock in employment could have been reduced had the U.S. government recognized the depressing effect of the supply shocks on aggregate demand and pursued a more expansionary policy in 1974 and 1975. The higher unemployment component of the stagflation of the 1970s in the United States and to some extent elsewhere (given the importance of the United States in world trade), then, *in part* originated in the inappropriate caution of the U.S. government in 1974 and 1975.

In fact, there is a diversity of broadly "Keynesian" accounts of the macroeconomic events of the 1970s (but they are identifiably "Keynesian" in their explicit preference for policy activism—for, that is, stabilization policy). Bruno and Sachs (1985) add two distinctive elements to the analysis of the stagflation of the 1970s and the policy options open to governments during it. First, they make the point that the capacity for success of a macroeconomic policy depends on the macroeconomic policies being pursued by other countries. If all countries respond to an inflationary supply shock with contractionary policies the total degree of contraction in the world economy will be much larger than what is sought (p. 128). By extension, the policy choices of the governments in each country have to be conditioned by their expectations of what other countries will do. Or they have to be directly coordinated between governments. Second, the stagflationary effects of inflationary shocks are considerably increased where wages are effectively indexed to the cost of living—where, that is, there is real wage rigidity rather than simply nominal wage rigidity. It follows from this that much of the variation in rates of inflation across countries in the 1970s and 1980s was related to differences in wage setting institutions. This aspect of Bruno and Sachs' work is directly related to recent sociological writings on differential macroeconomic performance across nations and I will consider the relevant claims in considerable detail in Chapters 5, 6, and 7 of this book.

To summarize, what are the agreed and disputed elements of what I have called "orthodox" economic accounts of the postwar inflation? That rates of inflation were substantially tied together under Bretton Woods and that in the mid-1960s the United States generated inflation and exported it to the rest of the world are largely uncontroversial (although there are undoubtedly different estimates of magnitudes). Disagreement comes with attempts to explain the general postwar inflationary bias and with the stagflation of the 1970s.

Keynesians have regarded the steady, early, postwar inflation as an outcome of reasonable policy choices by a number of governments and the stagflation of the 1970s as a result of the limits on the ability of markets to clear, given the inflexibility of prices (particularly, but not exclusively, downward) *and* the inadequacy of policy responses. On policy responses, however, there is not even consensus among North American Keynesians. Blinder has argued that the U.S. government erred by not pursuing a sufficiently expansionary policy after 1974. Bruno and Sachs' analysis raises questions about the adequacy of such a response without international macroeconomic policy coordination and institutional arrangements for regulating wage growth.

For monetarists, in contrast, both steady early postwar inflation and stagflation originated in mistaken policies. Feldstein's analysis of the United States attributes its stagflation entirely to errors of analysis and diagnosis. His account leaves open the possibility that the inflation originated in well-intentioned actions of governments. But there is another strand in monetarist writings that attributes the actions of governments to the effects of democratic political pressures (in specific institutional contexts). This is so-called *public choice* analysis.

Notes

1.   The distinction between monetarists Mark I and II comes from Tobin (1981). For a stimulating analysis of the differences between the older form of monetarism embodied in the writings of Friedman and the newer sort embodied in the writings of Lucas see Hoover (1984). Hoover (p. 74) argues that the central difference is divergent approaches to the issue of general equilibrium; Friedman, following Marshall, assumes that "for practical purposes, problems must be partitioned into parts analyzed in detail and parts summarized"; Lucas and the other "new classical" writers, following Walras, "insist that nothing less than a full equilibrium approach, in which the distinction between short run and the long run is abolished, will do."

2.   "I think it's fair to say that such a staunch 'North American Keynesian' as James Tobin would be labelled a monetarist by British Keynesians" (Purvis, 1980:97). It is worth acknowledging that Purvis goes on to say that "expatriate 'British Monetarists' living on this side of the Atlantic are not easily distinguished from the eclectic Keynesians amongst their new colleagues." The former point seems more obviously true to me than the latter.

3.   This involves so-called "efficiency wages." See Yellen (1984) or Stiglitz (1986).

4.   Laidler (1981a:4) acknowledges that there is some evidence that changes in the institutional framework of monetary policy had produced shifts in the demand for money function in the previous decade. Blinder (1987:69–73) makes the point more forcefully.

5.   The principal sources for the account that follows are Phelps (1972b) and Friedman (1975).

6.   The natural rate of unemployment is sometimes more neutrally called the *nonaccelerating inflation rate of unemployment* (or NAIRU). It is worth emphasizing that it is not claimed that governments are unable to reduce the natural rate of unemployment. Anything that cheapens labor (say a cut in the minimum wage or the taxes that employers have to pay on those they hire) or increases its productivity (say government training programs) or makes the operation of labor markets more efficient (by providing information to workers about available jobs and information to employers about available workers) will reduce the

rate of unemployment. What *is* claimed is that deliberate stimuli to demand cannot reduce the natural rate of unemployment in the long run.

7. Blinder (1979:165–167, 198–200), who is unambiguously a Keynesian, provides a similar chronicle of policy errors. The difference is, of course, that whereas monetarists conclude that the litany of policy errors shows that stabilization is, at best, rarely possible, Blinder concludes that stabilization policy is necessary; it should simply be done better.

8. That this implication does not *necessarily* follow from a rational expectations model has been cogently argued by Buiter (1980).

9. For an early survey of the evidence see Parkin, Sumner, and Jones (1972). For a recent survey see Fender (1990:ch. 5). For a detailed study of the inadequacies of incomes policy in Sweden see Jonung (1990). Note, that there is some evidence of modest success in the operation of the Canadian antiinflation program of 1975 to 1978 (Wilton, 1984; McCallum, 1986). It is also true that none of the programs that have been evaluated has been built around the tax incentives that have been urged by those who still favor wage and price controls of one kind or another (e.g., Weintraub, 1978).

10. For the interesting example of prolonged rigidity in the newsstand prices of magazines, see Cecchetti (1986).

11. For a summary of sources on the United Kingdom see Smith (1982:312–13). On Canada see Daub (1984). On the United States see Okun (1983:507–574). The general disillusionment with econometric models for forecasting has, apparently, led to something like the abandonment of their use in academic economics. On this see Mankiw (1990:1645).

12. For a sociological analysis of inflation that seems to assume macroeconomic omniscience on the part of the government see Goldthorpe (1978). For a critique of this aspect of Goldthorpe's analysis see Smith (1982).

13. I will argue later that even though Canada's exchange rate was free to float from 1950 to 1962, *in practice* it was, like all the other industrial countries, tied to the U.S. dollar.

14. What follows is drawn from Smith (1987).

15. For an analysis of the domestic processes producing the Nixon decision to, effectively, scuttle Bretton Woods, see Gowa (1983).

16. For an example of an explanation in terms of error see Johnson (1970). I discuss examples of explanations in terms of political irresponsibility in more detail in the next chapter on public choice theories.

17. Notice that the effect of permanent change in supply prices would be graphed as a shift to the left of the aggregate supply curve and the effect of the redistribution of income as a leftward shift of the aggregate demand curve—both shifting the equilibrium output to the left, that is, reducing it.

3

PURE SELF-INTEREST AND THE
POLITICS OF INFLATION

Keynesians are frequently reproached for their political naivete (e.g., Schott, 1984a:60–61). Their models assume that the economy is made up of self-interested, income (or wealth) maximizing individuals and organizations. This is a necessary assumption since it is the self-interestedness of people that makes their behavior predictable. For example, if businessmen observe that the real wages of their workers are falling during an inflation they can be routinely expected to hire more of them because doing so allows them to make more money. The members of suitably enlightened governments can exploit that fact to raise aggregate levels of output and employment. The question is, what grounds are there for assuming anything resembling enlightenment on the part of the individuals who make up governments?

Politicians and civil servants have their own interests; they have, that is, incomes to maximize too. Why would one suddenly expect people to become noble and generous when they move from the economic to the political arena? Buchanan and Wagner (1977:81) go to some lengths to argue that Keynesian analysis is inadequate precisely because "the presuppositions of Harvey Road"[1] make unreasonable assumptions about the motivations of appointed and elected members of governments. In opposition to the supposed naivete of models—like those of Keynesians—that assume disinterested politicians and civil servants, an alternative class of models has been constructed built on the opposite assumption: "The spirit of such models requires that they leave no concern with the general welfare to affect the political decision making process, except insofar as manifestation of such concern may be instrumental in accumulating political wealth" (Reder, 1982:27). Models of this kind have been applied to a wide range of political and legal phenomena.[2] They have, in particular, been applied to the explanation of inflationary tendencies in modern democracies.

A Democratic Basis for Inflation

Politicians (we will assume for the sake of argument) maximize their incomes by getting reelected. One might think that the way to get reelected is to provide good and honest government, but that is to neglect the opportunities provided by politicians' control over the budgetary process and the limits on the capacity of the electorate to effectively judge politicians' actions. The nub of the issue, according to this line of argument, is that politicians provide cash (in the form of transfer payments), goods, and services to electors to buy votes. There are two possible ways in which this might contribute to the acceleration of inflation: first, if the resulting expansion of the public sector reduces the overall level of efficiency of the economy (by, for example, "crowding out" private investment that would more efficiently generate growth in wealth) and in so doing reduces its capacity to deliver the amounts of goods and services that people have come to expect; second, if the new or expanded programs are paid for using the modern equivalent of printing money. These arguments, then, have two components. The first is an explanation for the growth of government and the second an explanation for the use of an inflationary method to finance that growth.

Now, bear in mind that there are three possible ways in which the expanded provision of government cash grants, goods, and services might be paid for: first, taxes might be increased; second, the government might issue long-term debt; and third the government might "monetize" the deficit. In this latter case it normally orders or induces the central bank to purchase government securities with checks drawn on accounts created by the central bank specifically to allow the checks to clear (see, for example, Gordon, 1978:456–457; Bond and Shearer, 1972:380–391). In other words, the central bank creates by fiat an account out of which the sellers of government securities are paid; in doing so it increases the amount of cash in private hands and, in principle, the effective demand for goods and services.

Even if funded out of taxes there is a mechanism through which governments might buy votes (in the short run, at least).

> The benefits of specific programmes are heavily concentrated among minorities, who do have an incentive to keep informed and to organize. On the other hand, the costs are widely distributed among the bulk of the population for whom the loss is unlikely to be a decisive factor in casting their votes. . . . The minority can be quite a large one, ranging from home buyers to trade union activists; but their incentives to organize and inform themselves are still relatively greater than those of the population at large. (Brittan, 1978:166)

Because of asymmetries in the advantages of acquiring the information necessary to monitor the government there is an incentive to provide vote-buying *targeted* programs, paid for out of taxes.[3]

Furthermore, not only will the size of government expenditures grow because of elected politicians' successful bribing of interest groups, but, in addition, civil servants are themselves a source of pressure for growth. Niskanen (1971) has argued that the salary and perquisites of office of bureaucrats are tied to the size of the bureau they manage. They therefore have an incentive to induce elected politicians to vote ever larger budgets for their bureaus. They have two sources of influence at their disposal. First, they have an information advantage over the politicians with whom they deal. When they confront an appropriations committee the bulk of the information on the performance and benefits of the bureau's services is provided by the bureau itself. Second, civil servants have votes too and the influence of those votes is enhanced by the fact that they are typically concentrated in towns in which government employment is concentrated (Bush and Denzau, 1977).

Growth in government funded through increased taxes—whether as a result of the self-interested efforts of civil servants or the purchase of the votes of interest groups—*may under some circumstances*, have an effect on inflation by reducing overall economic efficiency and in so doing reducing the capacity of the economy to provide the goods and services that people have come to expect. The thrust of public choice writings is, however, to argue that growth in government will be funded through the "monetization" of deficits, with direct inflationary consequences. Why?

Even if individuals tend not to notice small increases in taxes to fund a specific targeted program they sooner or later notice on their tax bills the cumulative consequences of a series of such programs (Brittan, 1978:166–167). Raising taxes is not a good way to win votes. So politicians concerned to buy votes are likely sooner or later to turn either to borrowing money through the issue of securities with maturity dates safely beyond the next election (or beyond the end of their career!) or to the "monetization" of deficits. But, other things being equal, issuing large amounts of government debt will force up interest rates for all borrowers. Causing higher mortgage and consumer loan rates is not likely to curry much support among electors (Buchanan and Wagner, 1977:58–59, 114–121). Ultimately, that leaves the "monetization" of deficits as the preferred method for financing an expanded government for an unscrupulous, vote buying politician (and remember that, within this model, politicians are by definition unscrupulous).

But "monetizing" deficits will tend to produce inflation, which is also unpopular. Why are the popularity gains from the government expenditures not offset by the popularity losses from the resulting inflation? The answer is that the inflation does not happen immediately; it occurs with a lag and has to be "creatively imagined." The benefits of the government programs, on the other hand, are either immediate or, if accruing later, are outlined in lavish detail in election propaganda. So, governments can exploit the limited information available to electors on the long-term effects of the programs they offer to buy votes and, given the negligible difference that any single person's vote can make to the outcome of an election, the incentives to acquire the relevant information are slight.[4] Notice that this is a sort of upside-down Keynesianism. Whereas the lags in the adjustments of people to inflation (and, in particular, of workers) are, in Keynesian models, used to stabilize the economy, in public choice models lags in adjustment are used to gull the electorate.

This inflationary bias in the operation of modern governments is further reinforced by two other factors. First, some people specifically profit from an unexpected inflation. In particular, people or organizations owing debt at a rate of interest fixed during an earlier period of lower inflation are likely to profit. It happens that governments are typically preeminent in this category. A good, unexpected, inflation is one of the best ways available to a government to reduce the real burden of the national debt. Second, the effect of deficit financing of government provided goods and services is to make the real cost of those goods and services appear to be lower than it really is. Because the *relative* cost of government services is reduced, people demand more of the kinds of goods that government provides and less privately provided goods. This reinforces the tendency of governments to provide goods and services and, given the unpopularity of tax increases and the interest rate effects of substantial government borrowing, produces a still stronger impulse toward the monetization of deficits (Buchanan and Wagner, 1977:99).

In sum, lags in the inflationary consequences of the "monetization" of deficits, the limited information at the disposal of electors (and, in particular, their incapacity to foresee the long-term consequences of the policies they are being offered), and the self-interest of politicians produce a tendency toward a larger than preferred size of government and accelerating rates of inflation in democratic polities.

Clearly, on its own this will not do as an account of the postwar inflation. As we saw in Chapter 1 there has been a wide array of national inflation experiences over the postwar period. In fact, the acceleration of inflation rates began only in the mid-1960s though all the 18 governments for which data were presented had been democracies since at least the end of the second world war. For Buchanan and Wagner the origins of the historic shift to higher rates of inflation lie in the first instance in a change in the *ideas* guiding the actions of economic policy makers, specifically, the ideas associated with Keynesianism. Prior to the Keynesian revolution, they claim , the combination of "customary, traditional, and widely accepted precepts" with respect to government finance that they call the "fiscal constitution" prescribed "that public finance and private finance are analogous, and that the norms for prudent conduct are similar." What this meant was that "Barring extraordinary circumstances, public expenditures were supposed to be financed by taxation, just as private spending was supposed to be financed from income" (Buchanan and Wagner, 1977:21). For this simple principle of government finance the Keynesians substituted the notion of "budget balance at high employment" (Buchanan and Wagner, 1977:151–156). Under this principle it is assumed that a deficit under conditions of less than full employment will generate an increase in economic activity that will, itself, restore public finances to a surplus. Hence, the concern shifts from budget balance in any particular year to budget balance over the cycle.

Now, Buchanan and Wagner do not take exception to the economic plausibility of these ideas. The problem, according to them, is that *in practice* there are serious uncertainties involved in applying them. What, for instance, constitutes full employment? This is a matter of controversy in general. And, if one accepts the existence of a long-run Phillips curve with a significant negative slope (and, as we have seen, many economists of the 1960s and early 1970s did so), there is absolutely no unambiguous concept of full employment. If one accepts the existence of a Phillips curve, what constitutes full employment becomes a political issue. Furthermore, the feasibility of a policy of budget balancing at high employment depends on the possibility of accurate econometric forecasting. Determining the appropriate magnitude of the deficit that will, under conditions of relatively high unemployment, produce a subsequent and countervailing surplus under conditions of full employment requires the ability to forecast the effects of any given deficit level. But, as I observed earlier, the accuracy record of econometric forecasting has not been overwhelmingly impressive and it has sometimes been quite wretched.

What is important here is that uncertainty with respect to what constitutes full employment along with the inadequacy and variability of econometric forecasts provides a context within which questions can be resolved on the most politically convenient grounds. Politicians competing for election by offering subsidized or free services can construe full employment in the most generous way possible and can pick and choose among forecasts, selecting the one that requires the largest fiscal stimulus (see Buchanan and Wagner, 1977:155). According to Buchanan and Wagner, a large part of the intercountry variation in postwar rates of inflation can be explained on the basis of the differential diffusion and acceptance of Keynesian ideas.

Some more of the historical record of postwar inflation can be explained in terms of *institutions,* by which they mean the legal and customary restraints on government spending and methods for financing any resultant deficit. Of particular relevance here is the degree of autonomy from political pressures of the central bank. As we saw above, even autonomous central banks, according to Buchanan and Wagner (1977:111–114), are subject to political pressure; they are likely to find it difficult to bear the popular opprobrium that would be caused by the interest rate consequence of an insistence on the financing of deficits through borrowing rather than through the creation of money. Still, writers in the public choice tradition, or influenced by it, do tend to argue that whether or not a country has an autonomous central bank should make a difference. Thus, Parkin (1975:201) has explained the lower rates of inflation in the United States and Germany on the one hand, relative to the United Kingdom and Italy on the other, as a consequence of the more autonomous central banks of the first two countries (see also Brunner, 1975).

The Evidence

I think that it is fair to say that the careful assembly of evidence to test the adequacy of their explanations is not the strong point of most public choice writings. The plausibility of the accounts offered typically rests on a listing of examples of what the writers in question regard as contemporary economic pathologies. Thus: "A regime of permanent budget deficits, inflation, and an increasing public-sector share of national income—these seem to us to be the consequence of the application of Keynesian precepts in American democracy" (Buchanan and Wagner, 1977:72–73). When Buchanan and Wagner published their book in 1977 it was against the background of inflation that had accelerated throughout the industrial world since the mid-1960s and this gave a certain prima facie plausibility to their account. But, as evidence, this obviously will not do, since deficits, inflation, and a growing public sector are, as I will show in some detail in this book, consistent with a number of different interpretations.

In practice, much of the empirical work on macroeconomic outcomes is in the form of writings on the so-called *political business cycle.*[5] This is unfortunate because as I will show shortly, there are important respects in which the political business cycle literature is transparently beside the point as an account of the postwar inflation. Still, some of the issues treated in writings on this subject do require consideration.

The Political Business Cycle

Nordhaus (1975) has provided the most cited analysis within this genre. It goes as follows. Suppose that there is a short-run trade-off between unemployment and inflation (a Phillips curve) that is markedly flatter than the long-run curve (that may in fact be vertical). Suppose also that voters are myopic, that is to say, they fail to foresee the longer run consequences of economic policies. Politicians seeking reelection can then increase their share of the votes by increasing the rate of inflation so that, in the short run, the rate of unemployment and the general level of economic activity will rise. More people will be better off as a result and this will induce them to vote for the incumbent party. In the long run things will be different. There is either no or a negligible trade-off between inflation and unemployment in the long run. The lags that lead unemployment to fall and economic activity to rise will disappear as workers come to terms with the new higher rate of inflation. So in the long run the rate of unemployment returns to at least its former level and, given the disruptive effects of inflation, probably remains at a higher level (it does in the model of Nordhaus 1975:179) and the rate of inflation remains higher too.

Of course, pursuing policies that ultimately produce both higher rates of inflation and unemployment will not, in the long run, endear a particular government to its electorate. To deal with this problem the government, Nordhaus argues, has the following tactic available: it can force up unemployment with a deflationary policy immediately after its election and subsequently stimulate the economy during the rest of its mandate so that unemployment falls "to the purely myopic rate" (p. 184). The electorate in Nordhaus' model neither learns from its past errors nor makes reasonable estimates of the consequences of present policies. People take into account their economic circumstances only at the time of their vote.

Nordhaus tested his model against data on unemployment for nine industrial countries for the period 1947–1972. The results are entirely inconclusive. His theory predicts that unemployment should rise in the 2 years after an election and fall in the 2 years preceding it. Only in three countries—Germany, New Zealand, and the United States—does the data conform to this pattern. In fact, these generally inconclusive results of Nordhaus' test of a political business cycle model largely prefigure the results of subsequent research—although the results are often not presented as if that is so (e.g., Frey and Schneider, 1981).[6]

There are, then, two elements to Nordhaus' analysis: one is an attempt to demonstrate that democratic polities will have rates of inflation higher than the population would prefer, were it not myopic; the second is that there will be a macroeconomic cycle *caused* by deliberate political manipulation. Most of the research has borne on this latter question—as, indeed, does the empirical part of Nordhaus' paper.

Consider the links that this latter argument supposes. First, there ought to be evidence that governments deliberately manipulate the macroeconomic instruments at their disposal—that is to say, taxes, spending, and, if it is under their control, the money supply—to ensure that relative prosperity and elections coincide. Second, if the government is manipulating these instruments with any success there ought to be evidence that macroeconomic performance improves before elections: specifically, that unemployment falls and the rate of growth rises. Third, if this kind of policy works, there ought to be evidence that electors' voting decisions are substantially tied to trends in economic performance. What does the evidence show?

Most studies reveal no (or hardly any) tendency for monetary policy to become distinctly stimulative before elections in the countries in which the relationship has been examined (Beck, 1984, 1987, 1990; Laney and Willett, 1983; Golden and Poterba, 1980; Hibbs, 1987:ch. 8). The studies include the United States (in particular), Germany, and the United Kingdom. An exception is the work of Grier (1987, 1989) that produces some evidence of an association between money supply and time between presidential elections in the United States. Another exception is the work of Frey and Schneider (1978a,b, 1979) that reports some evidence of fluctuations in monetary policy in the United States, the United Kingdom, and Germany associated with the standing of the party in power in public opinion polls. The more substantial effect of standing in the polls that they report for the same three countries and for Switzerland (Schneider, Pommerehne, and Frey, 1981), however, is on the fiscal side, for government expenditures.[7]

Grier's results depend very heavily on an experimentally determined lag structure (1989:379–380) that, one would think, increases the likelihood of establishing a relationship. Frey and Schneider's model has been quite devastatingly criticized by Alt and Chrystal (1983:228–232; and, especially, Alt and Chrystal, 1981). The details of the criticism need not detain us here.[8] It is sufficient to say that they are serious enough to suggest strongly that Frey and Schneider's results be set aside. Furthermore, Dinkel's (1981) analysis of fluctuations in government spending in Germany and the United States reveals no evidence of a political business cycle (see also Payne, 1991). The findings of Chrystal and Alt (1981) for the United Kingdom are broadly similar. Overall, I believe that the most reasonable conclusion is that there is no evidence of a *regular* political business cycle in either monetary policy or in the expenditure side of fiscal policy. I stress the word *regular* because none of this is to say that governments do not sometimes deliberately stimulate the economy for electoral advantage and I will argue shortly that they in fact do so. It is simply to say that there is no evidence that decisions to intervene are a *predictable* response to either the approach of an election or the standing of a party in the public opinion polls. I will return to this issue shortly.

Furthermore since, at best, the evidence that policy *instruments* are coordinated with elections is contradictory, it is not surprising that there is no or negligible evidence that macroeconomic *outcomes* (unemployment, inflation, and growth) that might be partially influenced through the manipulation of policy instruments are coordinated with elections (MacCallum, 1978; Beck, 1982a; Thompson and Zuk, 1983; Paldam, 1979).

What about the last element of the political business cycle argument? To what extent do changing economic conditions influence people's decisions on who to vote for? Only if they do so could politicians hope to influence their electoral support by manipulating the macroeconomic instruments at their disposal, either routinely or occasionally. There are two sorts of studies addressing this issue. One sort examines the association between aggregate support for the incumbent party or president and economic performance, usually operationalized as some measure of unemployment, inflation, or economic growth. The pioneering studies were by Goodhart and Bhansali (1970) for the United Kingdom and Kramer (1971) for the United States. Since those articles there has been a large volume of further research (usefully summarized in Paldam, 1981, and Monroe, 1979; see also, Hibbs and Vasilatos, 1981; Lafay, 1985; Norpoth, 1985). Overall the evidence is quite clear: economic conditions affect aggregate support for incumbents in each country studied for at least some periods.[9] The magnitude of the effect, however, is quite modest.

We can get some further insight into how people respond to changing economic conditions by examining the other sort of research that looks at retrospective survey data on voting decisions and the reasons for them. With data for the United States Kiewit (1983) finds a modest effect of personal economic circumstances (measured in a number of ways: see p. 55) on people's decision whether or not to vote for an incumbent (for comparable data on Norway see Miller and Listhaug, 1985:132). The larger effect, however, comes from respondents' perceptions of national economic conditions. Furthermore, the correlation between personal economic conditions and perceptions of national economic conditions is quite low (p. 89: see also Kinder and Kiewit, 1979). The perceptions of national economic conditions, however, seem to be quite well informed since the correlation between perceptions of national conditions and change in per capita disposable real income was high (p. 134). Kiewit's data suggest that the principal economic determinant of voting decisions is national economic conditions as they are (reasonably accurately) filtered through the perceptions of voters.

We observe, then, that whereas economic conditions do influence the popularity of governments, there is no reliable evidence of a cycle of economic policy or macroeconomic outcomes tied to the schedule of elections or to variations in the popularity of governments. At first sight the absence of short-run cycles of economic policy tied to electoral considerations looks like powerful evidence against a model of political behavior that assumes only unscrupulous politicians concerned with maximizing their prospects of reelection. For, since attitudes toward incumbents *are* affected by economic conditions, what would stop a politician bent on reelection from exploiting the electoral opportunities provided by control over the economic policy apparatus?

One explanation for the absence of evidence of a political business cycle is to argue that politicians are much less narrowly self-interested than public choice models assume. Kelman (1987) has made this argument particularly forcefully. Thus: "My own view is that this account of the operation of the political process is a terrible caricature of reality. It ignores the ability of ideas to defeat interests, and the role that public spirit plays in motivating the behaviour of participants in the political process" (p. 83). In support of his argument he points out that it is very difficult to explain either the huge growth of spending for the poor in the United States in the 1960s and 1970s or the substantial extensions of health and safety legislation as an outcome of the electoral self-interest of politicians since the poor are neither an electoral majority nor very effectively organized;[10] that the process of deregulation of a number of industries during the 1970s directly affronted some powerful interest groups (since the regulation usually protected the interests of both employers and workers in the industries in question); that detailed tracking of politicians in their day-to-day activities turns up an obtrusively responsible, if humdrum, round of activities on committees; and that there is some evidence that the people from whom politicians and civil servants are recruited have a more public spirited attitude than do those from whom businessmen are recruited.

As Kelman himself acknowledges, this is a terribly old fashioned view. It is also theoretically inconvenient. For it is much easier to model people's behavior if one can assume that they act only on the basis of self-interest. (I cite as evidence in support of this claim practically the entire corpus of modern economic theory!) Nonetheless, I believe that the view is fundamentally and profoundly correct. One of the most careful tests of alternative theories of change in economic policy that I know of is John Odell's study of the international monetary policy of the United States. It shows, I believe conclusively, that one of the most powerful sources of change was shifts in ideas about which international monetary arrangements would produce the conditions most conducive to growth in the world economy in general (to which, of course, growth in the U.S. economy is tied). Beliefs and expectations about domestic politics, on the other hand, were not often of any importance (Odell, 1982:366). It does not follow from this that the beliefs politicians hold do actually help people or that they help the people that most need help (although either outcome is possible). The argument is simply that ideas, including ideas about what is morally appropriate, are powerful forces in their own right and weaken the association between politicians' self-interest and their behavior.[11]

The apparent absence of a political business cycle, then, can be partly explained by the fact that politicians are at least occasionally principled. But to conclude from this that we have nothing to learn from public choice analyses of the effects of the electoral concerns of politicians on their choices of economic policy would be, I think, to throw the baby out with the bath water.

As I observed earlier, Tufte's attempt to establish the existence of a political business cycle with quantitative data has been sharply and fairly criticized. But there is another kind of data in Tufte's book. He observes (1978:7) that "News reports, memoirs, and internal political documents abound" demonstrating the concern of incumbent politicians and their advisers with getting right the timing of economic trends and elections. And he provides some examples drawn from these sources. He also provides evidence of attempts to manipulate the payment schedule of various benefits for electoral advantage (pp. 28–44; see also Hibbs, 1987:271–275; Hardiman, 1988:119; Nordhaus, 1989:17). As Alt and Chrystal (1983:120–122) make clear, this does not produce a routine and predictable political business cycle. But that politicians do sometimes attempt to manipulate economic policy for electoral advantage is testified to by an abundance of evidence—disquietingly anecdotal evidence, it is true, but in my view overwhelmingly persuasive, nonetheless. It follows from all this that *if* the assumptions of the political business cycle models were correct *except* for an underestimate of the amount of public spiritedness to be expected from politicians then one might expect to find more evidence of a political business cycle than is the case. The

absence of reliable evidence suggests that there are some other unacceptable assumptions.

The first unacceptable assumption, that is much stressed by Alt and
Chrystal, is that politicians are unconstrained in their efforts to manipulate economic policy for short-term electoral advantage. While the Bretton Woods system governed international currency exchange rates, no
country, except to some extent the United States, could for long pursue
policies that caused its rates of inflation to get much out of line with the
rates of inflation of its trading partners. It is true that a deliberate preelection stimulus of an economy would, given the normal assumptions
of a significantly negatively sloped short-run Phillips curve, produce
inflation only after the election. But remember, Nordhaus assumes that
the cumulative result of this is a generally and consistently higher rate of
inflation than the population would choose (if it were in a position to
make an informed choice) and that a country with less vulnerable institutions (including less enthusiasm for Keynesian policies) would be
likely to arrive at. A government that unreasonably stimulates its economy runs the risk of a foreign exchange crisis at a politically inconvenient
time.[12] Knowledge of that risk may *sometimes* discourage governments
from *substantial* preelection economic stimulation.

They are also likely to be discouraged if the rate of inflation is already
at a high level, either because of the previous "irresponsible" use of
economic policy for electoral advantage or because of causes outside
their control—including the export of inflation from the United States
during the Vietnam war and the effects of the commodity price shocks of
the early 1970s. There are, in fact, two (no doubt related) reasons why
already high levels of inflation are likely to lead a government to be more
cautious. First, a gratuitous economic stimulus on the base of an already
high rate of inflation runs the risk of tipping a country toward hyperinflation (of the Israeli or Brazilian dimensions) and hardly anyone regards that as desirable. Second, the evidence is quite clear that as rates
of inflation rose during the 1970s, so inflation supplanted unemployment as the main concern of the electorate (see, for example, Hibbs,
1982:215–216).

The second unacceptable assumption is that governments can always
freely manipulate the economic instruments at their disposal. Take first
the case of monetary policy. Financing deficits through monetization
requires a cooperative central bank. In some countries the central bank
seems to have enough autonomy to effectively resist political pressures
from the government. This is true of both the United States and Germany and probably of Switzerland, although in the latter case it is not
clear whether the government is ever likely to put pressure on the central bank to monetize a deficit (Banaian, Laney, and Willett, 1983). Even

in countries in which the central bank lacks any formal institutional autonomy, those running it are likely to have considerable influence on the choices made by politicians (see Woolley, 1985:338). For in discussions with governments, they have the advantage of considerable expertise and also of strong ties with the financial community. Suppose a government decides that it wants to stimulate the economy just before an election and is privately opposed by officers of the central bank. Unless the central bank is absolutely leak-proof (and I assume that will not normally be the case) it is likely that financial journalists will get to know about the dispute and will publicize it. In general, that is likely to cause some loss of confidence within the financial community, which may be translated into a politically unpopular currency depreciation. What I am arguing, then, is that the range of policy instruments at the disposal of the government is to some extent limited by the fact that it is usually preferable to maintain the confidence of the financial community; but that will be hard to do if a government chooses to ignore advice on monetary policy originating from the central bank.

What about fiscal policy? Here governments can either cut taxes or increase spending. If the objective is to increase the personal incomes of the electorate by increasing spending or cutting taxes, however, it is not so easy to ensure that the effects will be felt before an election. In the United States the spending and taxing plans of a president have to go through congress, and that can be a time-consuming business (Gordon, 1978:512–513). In a federal country such as Germany many spending plans have to be negotiated with subordinate governments (Knott, 1981). In all countries many spending plans involve a more or less prolonged period during which contracts for the construction or whatever is involved are bid on and the details of whatever is to be done are settled.

Nor are these the only constraints on the effectiveness of monetary and fiscal policy. Much of any attempted preelection stimulus is likely to be lost as funds flow out of the country in question as interest rates fall and money flows to other countries that have not recently stimulated their economy. Under floating exchange rates this effect will be reinforced by the decline in the external value of its currency that results from the autonomous stimulus and that will produce demand-dampening rises in import prices and investment-dampening rises in wages. The extent to which this occurs will vary from country to country, but there are good grounds for thinking that the effect in countries that are closely economically integrated with a larger trading partner—such as Canada to the United States—will be considerable (Smith, 1987).

The third unacceptable assumption is that electors never learn; they remain consistently myopic. This, of course, is entirely inconsistent with

the assumptions of the new classical economics (monetarism mark II).
Now even if the assumed rationality of individuals in the new classical
economics is a bit overdone (to put it mildly), it is pretty widely accepted
that the new classical economists are on to something. That an incumbent produced a recession immediately after coming to office is unlikely
to be forgotten by the entire electorate, especially if the action is repeated more than once. A record of that sort is likely, cumulatively over
consecutive elections, to somewhat handicap a party. Hibbs and Vasilatos (1981:46) provided some evidence to suggest that in the United
States and the United Kingdom the electorate's memory is, in fact, longer than normally assumed. To the extent that this is true and to the
extent that politicians are aware that it is true it provides them with a
reason to take a more long-term perspective on economic policy decisions.

To summarize, preexisting economic conditions and risks may make it
difficult for a government to indulge in preelection economic stimulus; it
may not be able to do what it wants because of the imperfections in its
control of the policy instruments at its disposal; and the members of a
governing party may not want to risk the possible long-term electoral
consequences of becoming identified as the party of fiscal irresponsibility. So, even if disposed to maximize votes, the members of a government may choose not to stimulate an economy before an election.
And even if a government does choose to do so it may be impossible to
discern the consequences of its actions. The consequences of *policy* for
unemployment rates, inflation, and growth, or of the use of *policy instruments* for the usual indicators of their use (interest rate spreads as a
measure of monetary policy, for example: Cameron, 1985:270–273), may
not be discernible because they are swamped by the effects of economic
changes unrelated to policy—such as, for example, the effects of recession in one or more major trading partners, or radical changes in supply
prices.[13]

The lack of evidence for a political business cycle is, therefore, not
terribly surprising. But it should absolutely not be construed as demonstrating that the self-interested behavior of politicians and bureaucrats
does not produce inflationary policies. Trying to increase the rate of
growth of real income or reduce unemployment is one way to win votes
that the documentary evidence suggests is used by politicians from time
to time, although not regularly enough and not sufficiently detached
from other factors to produce a political business cycle. Another way is
to promise to implement programs, or extend the eligibility or improve
the benefits of existing programs, with legislation passed after an election. I have in mind things such as subsidized medical care, pensions,
and unemployment insurance. There is much evidence that there has

been broad support in the electorate for programs such as these (Coughlin, 1980). Consequently, promising to introduce or improve them has been a way in which political parties could improve their chances of winning an election. Clearly, however, since they are part of what is promised in an election their effects show up only after the election. And the distribution of the effects is not limited to the immediate period after the passage of the legislation; it is spread out over many decades as the number of people claiming benefits under the program increases as more and more become familiar with its provisions and sometimes as a result of demographic changes.

The expansion of "entitlement programs" of this sort has been a substantial source of growth in government spending in the postwar period. It can be argued that these programs have expanded because in order to win elections politicians have competed to promise benefits of one kind or another to electorates. Moreover, although it can reasonably be argued that in doing so politicians are simply giving the electorate what it wants (which is what they ought to do in a democracy) it is also true that accumulated budgetary consequences show up only long after the election takes place so that electors' judgments about the benefits and costs of what they are being offered are often likely to be rather ill informed. Furthermore, it is also conceivable that the functionaries administering these programs become advocates for them, in part because their income and perquisites are attached to the size of the program they administer, although there is little or no evidence that this actually happens.

All this is to say that a test of the relationship between the self-interest of politicians (and perhaps of bureaucrats) and inflation requires an examination of the broader international trends in public spending, deficits, and inflation. We want to know whether there is any evidence of the effects of an irregular but cumulatively significant tendency for governments to err in an inflationary direction in their spending and taxing decisions. Do they tend to spend too much, tax too little, and excessively expand the money supply?

Trends in Spending and Deficits

Roubini and Sachs (1989) provide a useful summary of the relevant data. They show that although there is marked variation in the share of public expenditures in total GDP (from a high in 1985 of about 65% in Sweden to a low of about 33% in Japan), the share increased substantially in *all* 15 countries covered in their study. They also show that, from 1973 to 1985, persistent deficits produced rising government debt as a percent of GDP, with the single exception of the United Kingdom (see also Alt and Chrystal, 1983:211; Llewellyn, 1982:15; Tanzi, 1985). In the last 15 years or so there is no question: in all rich capitalist countries governments have not raised enough in revenue to offset their spending. But if governments are willing to tolerate the effects of their borrowing on interest rates the resulting deficits do not have to cause inflation. *Nominal* interest rates tended to rise during the 1970s. Much of that increase, however, was a result of the incorporation into the interest rates of higher inflation. *Real* interest rates have in fact fluctuated markedly, and particularly so in the 1970s. During the early 1970s they fell in most capitalist industrial countries, becoming very low or negative for some periods (Bruno and Sachs, 1985:83). They then rose sharply at the beginning of the 1980s (Dornbusch, 1989:186–187).

What does all this say about public choice theories of the origins of inflation? Bear in mind that it is precisely the secular record of growing government expenditures and deficits in the United States that Buchanan and Wagner cite as evidence for their interpretation. And the abrupt fall in interest rates in the 1970s could be seen as monetization of deficits. Yet, clearly, these data do not in themselves support their account. Interest rates in the 1970s were reduced by a decline in private investment as well as by government monetary policy. Besides, their account requires that the origins of the growth in expenditures and deficits lies in the capacity of self-interested politicians to mislead the electorate, aided and abetted by a set of self-interested bureaucrats. It is conceivable that the growth in government expenditures and deficits accurately reflected some set of popular policy preferences.

To address this issue, consider, first, the sources of the expansion of government expenditure (see Klein, 1985:204; Roubini and Sachs, 1989:106–107; Hicks, Swank, and Ambuhl, 1989). Most of the growth in public expenditures over the post war period has been concentrated in transfer programs rather than in government consumption (that is to say, direct government expenditures on goods and services). Moreover, transfer programs increased the most in some countries that already had high levels of transfer payments and by generally more modest amounts in others. In the Netherlands and Sweden, in particular, there was a substantial proportionate increase in the amount of transfer payments from an already high base.[14] In contrast, the proportionate increase in the share of government consumption was much smaller. It was highest in Denmark, Sweden, and Germany (between 35 and 40%) and it actually fell in the United States. All of this is to say that, for the most part, explaining the growth of government spending during the high inflation years of the 1970s is, above all, a question of explaining the growth in transfer payments.

Now, Wilensky (1975, 1985) has shown that the growth of expenditures on the welfare state (which can include both transfer payments and government consumption) has been associated with the growth in incomes and with population aging. These associations suggest that government expenditures have grown in response to the availability of increased resources (per capita income) and demand for services (an aging population). Neither of these factors would seem to have much to do with the (erratic) actions of unscrupulous politicians and civil servants. There is also considerable evidence that small countries and countries that have had left wing governments tend to have higher public expenditures as a proportion of GDP (Cameron, 1978; 1985:233–240; Castles, 1982, 1986). The small country effect results, according to Cameron, from a government need to protect and stabilize the living standards of its citizens in the face of the considerable vulnerabilities of their small "open" economies to economic disturbances originating with their larger trading partners. These associations also suggest policy choices rather than unscrupulous opportunism. Finally, expenditures tend to grow during wars and recession (Cameron, 1985:231). The growth of transfers in the 1970s clearly had something to do with the recession and rising unemployment that developed at the end of the decade (Hicks, Swank, and Ambuhl, 1989:423). Once again, the growth of government does not appear to be a result of (an irregular) electoral opportunism.

Overall, then, the principal factors explaining growth in government expenditures seem not to be consistent with the process described by Buchanan and Wagner. However, there are some further considerations. First, Wilensky (1975:9–12) notes that the age of a particular program is a predictor of its size; that is to say, it appears that once a program is established those running it become more and more effective in persuading finance ministries to provide funds to expand access to it (Pal, 1988:ch. 5). This could simply be because the experience of running a program brings to light real needs that the program could usefully address; but it is surely just as likely that it is because, along public choice lines, once created a program becomes a base for lobbying. There is certainly evidence that employees in the public sector tend to favor growth in the public sector (Frey and Pommerehne, 1982; Gramlich and Rubinfeld, 1982; Henrekson and Lybek, 1988). Second, whereas public expenditures rise during wars and recessions, they tend not to fall afterward, or at least not to their previous levels (Klein, 1985:217). How can this be explained? In the case of recessions it suggests that if for countercyclical purposes a program is established, or access to it expanded, politicians are unwilling to incur the electoral costs of subsequently taking back the benefits involved and, perhaps, firing the usually unionized public employees administering it. Third, both Alt (1985b) and

Alesina (1989:72–78) report evidence of a distinctive pattern of economic policy making under left wing governments that is relevant here. When parties of the left run for election they typically promise that they will expand benefits to one or another group in the population identified as disadvantaged and reduce unemployment through aggressive government spending. In office, they keep their promise in the first year or so of their mandate.[15] Then they run into the inevitable problems of a depreciating exchange rate and of higher inflation that their policies produce. The rest of their mandate is spent retrenching and, as a result, pushing unemployment back toward the level it was when they first came to power (net of trends in unemployment as a result of international changes in the level of demand). This, of course, is the opposite of the political business cycle described by Nordhaus in which unemployment is forced up in the first year of a mandate and then rapidly reduced as the next election approaches. But it shares with Nordhaus' account the assumption that the electorate gets gulled. Left wing politicians lead the electorate to believe that a number of economic and welfare policy changes can be made costlessly, when that is not in fact the case. Since in this model the politicians themselves may actually believe what they promise there is some difference from the analysis of Buchanan and Wagner, that assumes totally cynical politicians. Nonetheless, averaged over the term of a government, and assuming some difficulty in cutting expenditures once increased, the outcome is higher expenditures originating in the unrealistic promises of politicians.

So, it is clear that much of the growth in the share of government in rich countries is rooted in the growth in income available for expenditures of this kind, in the growth of needs in aging populations, in the policy preferences of governments of the left, and in the concern of the governments of small countries to insulate their populations from external economic shocks. Those factors are not consistent with the public choice account of growing public expenditures. On the other hand, the association of program size with age of program, the difficulties involved in cutting programs once established or expanded, and the fact that parties of the left, in particular, often get into office promising more economic stimulus than they can sustain are *broadly* consistent with the public choice view of economic policy, stressing as it does the opportunism of politicians and civil servants and the tendency of the electorate to get misled about the real costs of policies.

What does all of this have to do with inflation? Buchanan and Wagner argue that if a government increases its spending it will tend not to fund the increases with taxes because taxes are politically unpopular, and that it will not fund the resultant deficit by issuing long-term debt because the effect of that would be to force up interest rates unreasonably and unpopularly. In fact, it is clear that governments with high levels of expenditure do have higher taxes. The countries most frequently controlled by leftist governments that have the highest government expenditures as a percentage of GDP also have the highest taxes (Cameron, 1985:258). So much of the growth in public expenditures has been paid for out of taxes.

However, the rise in the size of deficits across capitalist countries indicates that much of the growth in public expenditures has not been funded out of taxes. So the question becomes, to what extent have deficits been funded in an inflationary fashion? Cameron (1985) has gone to some lengths to show that inflation is neither associated with the policies of left wing governments nor very strongly associated with deficits. He has a set of tables that shows the following: for the period 1963–81 government spending in the United States is positively associated with the rate of inflation (there is effectively no relationship for the period 1948–63); in a sample of 21 countries for the period 1964–1981 there is a slight negative relationship between share of government expenditures in GDP and inflation; for the period 1965–1981, for a sample of 21 countries, having a left or center government is negatively associated with the rate of inflation; for the period 1960–1981 there was a positive relationship between government deficits and inflation in the United States (there was effectively no relationship for the period 1948–1981); for the period 1979–1981 there is a small relationship between government deficits and rates of inflation in 20 countries (there is an even smaller association for the period 1965–1981); for the period 1964–81 for five of a sample of seven rich countries there is a positive association between size of deficits and the growth in the money supply, and for all seven countries there is an association between growth in the money supply and the rate of inflation.

What is to be made of all this? Cameron (1985) concludes that "the argument that leftist parties are more likely to generate inflation than nonleftist parties is simply wrong—or at least time bound and true only for an era when inflation was not a significant macroeconomic problem" (p. 246) and that "Some unidentified processes evidently are at work when leftist parties govern that dampen inflation" (p. 248). He also concludes that "while there is support for strands of the monetarist hypothesis in several nations, it appears highly unlikely that the inflation experienced throughout the advanced capitalist world—and particularly in its three largest economies (the United States, Japan, and West Germany) can be attributed to the budget deficits of government" p. 278).

Now, the issue of leftist governments is relevant here only as it bears on Alt's model of transitory expansionary policies associated with the coming to power of a leftist government. For if leftist governments adopt policies when they take office that lead to an acceleration of inflation (from which they then retreat) how is it that Cameron finds that governments of the left, on average, have lower rates of inflation than governments of the right? I will first deal with this issue and then with Cameron's more general interpretation of the relationship between deficits and inflation.

It was Hibbs (1977) who most forcefully argued for an association between governments of the left and inflation, on the assumption that the natural constituency of left wing governments was more concerned with unemployment than inflation *and* that there is a long-run trade-off between inflation and unemployment. Hibbs' empirical results have been convincingly challenged (Payne, 1979; Beck, 1982c) and he has retreated somewhat from his initial claims (Hibbs, 1979). Indeed, since the notion of a long-run Phillips curve much different from vertical has become largely obsolete, Hibbs' fundamental premise has become untenable. Still, no one else reports data suggesting that left wing parties actually *reduce* inflation (cf., for example, Alt and Chrystal, 1983:114–118).

What makes Cameron's results possible? The distinguishing characteristic of his work in this and other papers is that, almost without exception, his data analysis takes the form of a set of measures of bivariate association with no attention to lag structures. Now, one of the themes much stressed by Alt is that no matter what they *want* to do, what governments *actually* do is greatly constrained by what is allowed to them by economic circumstances. Thus, the Labour government in Britain in the late 1960s was limited in its capacity to stimulate the economy by a series of balance of payments crises. There is also evidence tending to suggest that as rates of inflation increased during the late 1960s and 1970s the concern of the electorate greatly shifted toward inflation instead of unemployment. Presumably in part as a result of that and in part because of a public spirited concern with the dangers of degeneration into hyperinflation, governments of the left in the mid-1970s were likely to have shifted somewhat from their traditional concerns. Again, exactly this occurred in Britain under the Callaghan government (Alt and Chrystal, 1983:116). Finally, it should be borne in mind that the effect of the acceleration of the rate of inflation during the 1970s and the resultant shift in the concerns of the electorate was to help to bring right wing governments to power in a number of countries. But when they came to power those governments had to confront higher rates of inflation that had become embedded under previous governments. The average rate of inflation for governments of the right from 1965 to 1981 is undoubtedly raised by the fact that those governments were brought to power because inflation had become a salient issue and, once a rate of inflation has reached a particular level, it is not easy to bring it down quickly. Therefore, I do not believe that Cameron's crude bivariate analysis of inflation and governing party is very helpful; it certainly does not challenge the general point made by Alt that, other things being equal, parties of the left are likely to stimulate the economy when they first come to office.

What of Cameron's conclusion that deficits are a minor source of inflation? It is based on the very modest associations between deficits and prices reported in his U.S. data and in his comparative data. But as Cameron himself acknowledges (1985:263–265), one of the principal sources of deficits is recessions. Deficits caused by recessions, however, are less likely to be inflationary, since their stimulative effect is offset by the recession itself. When he makes a stab at taking this into account with his U.S. data he finds quite strong evidence of an inflationary, because monetized, set of deficits in the period 1965–1970, that is, in precisely the period during which in orthodox models the United States is thought to have been exporting inflation to the rest of the world. This raises a second issue that Cameron also acknowledges (p. 245). Part of the inflationary process in some countries involves the import of inflation from trading partners. The record of inflation need not be closely associated with the record of deficits in a particular country if international trade and currency movements have been an important source of its inflation. Again, the point is that the crude bivariate analyses with which Cameron attempts to test the deficit explanation of inflation are not suitable; they assume that the cases under study—that is, the years of inflation and deficits in various countries—can be treated as equivalent. That is simply not so. If for a set of years a country has a large deficit and a low rate of inflation, but that is because the country is in a recession, that is not evidence against the public choice theory of inflation. It simply shows that in order to test the theory it is necessary to control for other factors. Cameron's analysis is, quite simply, not a convincing rebuttal of the notion that deficits have played an important part in the postwar inflation.

But then where is the positive evidence of the effects on inflation of the opportunism of politicians and civil servants? The evidence presented in favor of their argument by Buchanan and Wagner is no better than Cameron's. I believe that there is, however, some evidence that the monetization of deficits has contributed significantly to the postwar pattern of inflation. First, remember that Cameron concedes that the United States was running deficits and monetizing them during the Vietnam war period. As we saw earlier, there are good grounds for thinking that under the exchange rate regime of the time the resultant inflation was to a significant extent exported to other countries.

Second, when the oil price shocks hit in the 1970s they produced decreases in real incomes in the rich capitalist countries most affected by them and rises in unemployment. But many of these were countries that had developed elaborate systems of transfer payments, the burden of which rose with the recession caused by the oil shock at the same time that the capacities of the countries to meet the claims made on them diminished. Now, as noted above, real interest rates generally fell after the oil shock, becoming negative in a number of places. In part this was a result of the abrupt increase in the amount of capital available because of the accumulation of savings in a set of OPEC countries whose rulers were not yet terribly skilled at spending the wealth the transfer of which they had engineered (Bruno and Sachs, 1984:25). But after initially uniformly contractionary policies (Bruno and Sachs, 1985:160), some countries seem to have become more "accommodative." This shows up in the fact that real interest rates continued to fall in them while stabilizing or rising in others. The interest rate record, in other words, provides some evidence of monetary accommodation in some countries, with inflationary consequences.

Third, consider the distribution of interest rate changes by country. The largest declines were in the United Kingdom and Italy, Australia, New Zealand, and Finland; all countries that, as we saw earlier, had accelerating rates of inflation. On the other hand, two countries in which the rates remained quite high (relative to their historically customary rates) were Germany and Switzerland. These two countries, of course, have had low inflation rates throughout the postwar period. They are also countries usually identified as having more autonomous central banks than most other countries. That autonomous central banks should produce lower rates of inflation is a central tenet of those sympathetic to the public choice account (such as Parkin or Brunner) and there is, I believe, quite good evidence that they do.

Banaian, Laney, and Willett (1983) have produced a particularly careful examination of the question. They go beyond the crude comparison of postwar inflation rates (though the results of that are pretty striking) and estimate "reaction functions" of the effects of a number of economic trends on monetary policy choices. Their results suggest strongly that among the 12 countries for which they estimate reaction functions Germany and Switzerland have by far the least accommodative monetary policies.

The issue, however, is a little more complicated. Where attempts are made to estimate the relative autonomy of central banks, those of three countries are typically identified as having autonomy—the United States, Switzerland, and Germany (e.g., Fair, 1979:34).[16] Consider these cases in turn.

We have already seen (and Cameron concedes) that in the United

States the Federal Reserve Board appears to have monetized the federal deficits being run up in the second half of the 1960s. Is this because the Federal Reserve is not really autonomous or because the late 1960s were a special time? Woolley (1984) argued at some length that there are very real limits on the autonomy of the Federal Reserve and of all other central banks (Woolley, 1985). He does not, however, argue that the autonomy of all central banks is *equally* limited and has also shown how the Federal Reserve acts autonomously some of the time (Woolley, 1978:170). And the fact is that the late 1960s *were* a special time. The United States was, after all, fighting a war and even Buchanan and Wagner would concede that principles of wartime finance are and should be different from those of peacetime finance. Even if the United States did export inflation to the rest of the world in the late 1960s, in the postwar period as a whole it has had lower rates of inflation than most other countries (see Figures 1.1–1.3) and that is consistent with what one would expect given the institutional descriptions of the operations of the Federal Reserve as compared to either the Bank of England or the central bank of Italy, for example.

Although the Swiss central bank is typically described as being autonomous it is not clear that its autonomy has ever been seriously tested. For the constitutional limits on Swiss government spending are such that it is very difficult for a central government to run up substantial deficits (Aubert, 1979). So it is not at all clear that the Swiss central bank is at all responsible for Switzerland's inflation record; it could just as easily be the Swiss constitution. *But either is fully consistent with a public choice account.*

In the German case the evidence is straightforward. "The Bundesbank has also occasionally refused, in dramatic fashion, to cooperate with announced government policy" (Woolley, 1978:1970). In this case, institutional descriptions, postwar inflation record, and central bank behavior all clearly coincide.

It should be clear, however, that none of this indicates that any central bank is completely autonomous. One suspects that a determined enough elected government can sooner or later bring a recalcitrant central bank to heel. Indeed, precisely that happened in Canada in 1961 when the then governor of the Bank of Canada, James Coyne, attempted to defy the Progressive Conservative government of the time that wanted a lower interest rate policy. Coyne was ultimately forced out and the law governing the central bank was changed (Granatstein, 1986:76–83). Yet this instance also provides some evidence of the difficulty a government faces when it tries to bring a recalcitrant central banker to heel. The Progressive Conservatives had a very great deal of difficulty getting rid of Coyne. He vigorously defended his policy preferences in public and the whole affair is thought to have considerably contributed to the defeat of the government at the next election. Furthermore, the lever the government used to dislodge Coyne was not his resistance to their policies; it was the fact that he had arranged an unusually large pension for himself. That it chose to take him on over that issue rather than his interest rate policy indicates just how dangerous it is for a government to publicly encroach on a central bank that enjoys a substantial amount of autonomy.

I believe that the evidence is quite strong that although central bank autonomy is certainly not absolute in any country, variations in that autonomy are causally associated with variations in rates of inflation. It is simply that the *direct* effect of central bank autonomy is limited to only a very few countries: the United States to some extent, Germany to a greater extent, and Switzerland to an unknown extent.

Public Choice Accounts of Inflation: An Appraisal

Public choice theory makes two central assertions: first that institutions and ideas determine the opportunities available to politicians and functionaries to advance their interests with policies resulting in deficits and inflation (and the two are assumed usually to go together); second, that the resulting amount of inflation is more than the population really wants. So far in this chapter I have been concerned with the first question. Let me first draw the threads together on this issue and then take up the second.

One of the principal specifications of the public choice approach is the so-called "political business cycle." But the evidence on this is overwhelmingly negative, and understandably so. In their account of inflation Buchanan and Wagner identify Keynesian economics as the villain of the piece (along with unscrupulous politicians) because the cumulative result of stabilization policy tended to be, they claimed, the growth of an increasingly hard to finance government. But there is a problem with this view too. As Alt and Chrystal (1983:192; see also Hall, 1989) point out, it is in the United States and Britain that Keynesian economics became most influential (for a while), but neither country has a particularly large government. And, even if Sweden, which does have a very large government, was Keynesian *avant la lettre*, as Goldthorpe (1987a:401) has claimed, it remains the case that it has maintained low deficits because it has financed its expenditures with high taxes. This is not a promising beginning.

However, there are a number of bits and pieces of evidence that are, I think, consistent with a somewhat modified version of a public choice account.

First, the Johnson and Nixon governments in the United States *do* seem to have financed the Vietnam war by monetizing a deficit and those governments *were* at the time influenced by a number of Keynesian economists (see Tobin, 1974). This is important not only because of its effects on the postwar pattern of inflation in the United States but also because the result of it was an acceleration of inflation in the rest of the world. Note, furthermore, that Britain, in which Keynesian policies were most solidly institutionally rooted (Keegan and Pennant-Rea, 1979), and in which senior economic advisors in the 1950s and 1960s reassured cabinet ministers that inflation was generally benign (Shonfield, 1958:188–191; Crossman, 1976:41–42), *did* collapse into one of the highest rates of inflation among rich capitalist countries in the early 1970s. Second, the three countries that have identifiably autonomous central banks (supplemented in the case of Switzerland by a constitution limiting government spending) *do* have generally superior postwar inflation records. Third, Alesina (1989:78–80) has assembled some evidence tending to show that politically unstable countries have higher rates of inflation.[17] Fourth, the deficit problems of governments seem to be substantially rooted in the growth of transfer payments. The effects of the introduction or improvement (including indexation) of these are not typically felt before an election; whatever electoral benefit comes to politicians mostly comes (contrary to political business cycle models) from the promise of benefits in the future rather than from a preelection increase in income. But this delay in the benefits *and costs* of these programs is precisely what makes them politically attractive. People can be persuaded to vote for a government because they are promised a higher pension, or can expect to get higher unemployment payments if they lose their jobs, or because they might receive some cash payment if they have children later on. The ultimate costs of the programs are, however, neither known nor knowable, depending as they do on unforeseeable demographic trends and, in some cases, the extent to which the relevant parts of the population become skilled at taking up the benefits they provide. Fifth, these financial commitments become a particular problem when the growth rate slows, or becomes negative, as it did for a while after 1973. In this case, the relevant point is that politicians competing for election have a very hard time taking away or reducing the cost of or eligibility to programs that may not be working as they were supposed to or that are thought to have become too financially onerous.[18] Sixth, programs *do* tend to grow with age, and that is what one would expect since in creating a program one also creates a lobby for it, including the civil servants employed in administering it.

I therefore believe that there is quite good evidence that suggests that, where institutions allow it—where, that is, there is a central bank that has little or no autonomy (and that is most countries), the democratic process and the interests of civil servants produce a tendency for government to grow or fail to decline and, *irregularly,* to do so in a way that produces inflation, especially where political instability produces a consistent political concern with the short run.

One final issue remains: what evidence do we have that it produces more inflation than people want? Barry (1985) has taken on this question directly. The first part of his argument (and it is an indispensable part of it) is that inflation at the levels found in rich capitalist countries since the war causes no serious problems. Its redistributive effects are modest; it does not undermine democratic civic values; it does not necessarily lead to hyperinflation (which does cause problems); it does not cause the collapse of democratic institutions but rather, where it has accompanied their collapse (as in Weimar Germany), it is a symptom of the causes of the collapse rather than a cause itself. Controlling inflation, on the other hand, causes unemployment (whether transient or not), which involves both real hardship *and* a real threat to democratic institutions.

Barry recognizes that inflation became genuinely unpopular in the 1970s. Does this mean that democratic institutions produced policies that resulted in more inflation than most people want? Well, apparently not, for

> how exactly are the preferences of ordinary citizens for economic outcomes established? When answers to public opinion poll questions are accepted as evidence that inflation is the country's number one problem, what does that actually mean? It ought to mean that people dislike increases in the price level. But do most people have such a clear grasp of economic concepts as this requires? Such studies of popular understandings of economic terms as have been made suggest that, in the absence of inflation, they would have been able to have their latest pay increase and keep its purchasing power through the whole of the subsequent year. Thus, a 10 percent inflation is looked on as equivalent to a 10 percent loss of real income. (Barry, 1985:294).

And, "The deliberate confusion of inflation with a corresponding loss of real income is pervasive."

Now it seems to me that Barry is on very dangerous ground here. Orthodox economic models of inflation do assume, as we saw in the last chapter, that workers' wages tend to lag as a result of an unanticipated inflation. There is at least some evidence that this is true (Smith, 1988). Furthermore, we also saw that economists such as Feldstein (1982) argue at some length that the effects on economic growth of an accelerating inflation are *ultimately* negative—after the short-run Phillips curve has worked itself out. Feldstein regards this as true because of, among other things, the effects of changing inflation rates on the willingness of businessmen to enter into long-run contracts. Barry, on the contrary, regards inflation as essentially benign. The evidence on this matter is rather mixed. Still, there is nothing in Barry's paper to suggest that he has thought the matter through sufficiently carefully to allow him to draw such a categorical conclusion.

But it is important for Barry to be able to claim that the effects of inflation are essentially trivial. For his argument is, quite explicitly, that when people answer pollsters' questions by saying that they regard inflation as a major problem, their judgment is poor. Inflation is really trivial but the benighted public does not realize it, misled as it is by demagogic politicians and irresponsible media.[19] Even if the somewhat arrogant character of this line of argument is ignored, it seems to me that there is some evidence that public concern with inflation rather than unemployment embodies a less superficial judgment than Barry would allow.

Whatever it might or might not have done for (or to) British citizens, the government of Margaret Thatcher has provided quite wonderful near-experimental evidence for social scientists. That government pursued a sustained anti-inflationary policy during almost 8 years of office and at the same time tolerated unprecedented increases in unemployment that have certainly not been concealed by the media or the opposition parties from the public. Nonetheless, it was twice reelected. It is common to attribute the first reelection to the effect of the Falklands war (e.g., Goldthorpe, 1987a:375). The evidence on this is, however, quite mixed; for the 1983 reelection there is, furthermore, some evidence of growing satisfaction with the Thatcher government's economic policies—particularly its tax reductions.[20] Even if one cannot say that Mrs. Thatcher generated great enthusiasm among those who reelected her (but, then, of how many politicians other than Ronald Reagan can that be said?), the fact remains that the British electorate twice had the opportunity to reject her and the unemployment with which she was associated, but did not do so. Barry is quite entitled to think that the part of the electorate that voted for Mrs. Thatcher was wrong in its judgment. But I do not think he is any longer entitled to regard that judgment as uninformed and trivial.

The evidence is overwhelming that in rich capitalist industrial societies most of the public got more inflation than it wanted, at least from the late 1960s onward. They got more inflation than they wanted despite the fact that all the relevant societies are democratic. Public choice accounts of this are overstated. They underestimate the importance of public spiritedness on the part of politicians. In their "political business cycle" versions they are simply wrong. They clearly run into great difficulties in accounting for the wave of elections of conservative governments committed to deflationary policies at the end of the 1970s. Nonetheless, there are bits and pieces of evidence that suggest that, suitably qualified and modified, they have something important to say about the origins of the postwar inflation and its distribution across nations.

Notes

1. The quote is from Harrod's (1951) biography of Keynes. "Harvey road" was where the Keynes family lived.
2. See, for example, Buchanan and Tullock (1962), Posner (1973), and Stigler (1975).
3. One might think that the implication of this is an amount of government spending in excess of what electors would choose if they were fully informed. But the issue is not as simple as that. Whatever tendency there might be to overprovide goods to special interest groups may be to some extent offset by a tendency to underprovide a set of "public goods" (like defense or programs to protect the environment) the benefits from which are hard to monitor but the costs of which are routinely manifest in income tax payments, depending on the form of the tax system. On this see Downs (1965). Notice that it follows from this that government will tend to grow most where it is difficult for individuals to estimate the real cost of that growth. Thus: "complex and indirect payment structures create a fiscal illusion that will systematically produce higher levels of public outlay than those that would be observed under simple-payments structures" (Buchanan and Wagner, 1977:129).
4. For a clear presentation of the argument that voters are typically ill informed on macroeconomic issues, see Suzuki (1991).
5. For a lucid treatment of political business cycles see Alt and Chrystal (1983:ch. 5).
6. One of the most confident assertions of a political business cycle is Tufte (1978). For a cogent criticism, see Alt and Chrystal (1983:120–122). See also Beck (1982). For a more recent attempt that introduces ideological differences between governing parties but still produces mixed results, see Nordhaus (1989).
7. Alt and Chrystal (1983:113) argue that it is not strictly speaking a "political business cycle" model because it ties policy choices to standing in the polls rather than the approach of an election. However, for present purposes I am more interested in the "unscrupulous politicians" assumption that underlies it and all political models inspired by public choice writings.
8. Briefly, Frey and Schneider's model makes an arbitrary assumption about what levels of popularity in the polls are defined by governments as good reason to increase expenditures and, further, excludes GDP (the capacity of a government to tax) when actual popularity is lower than the arbitrarily established level. When GDP is included, the "popularity deficit" effect disappears.
9. But for a criticism of Kramer's study, see Stigler (1973).
10. "Public choice theorists sometimes point to the power of interest groups

representing providers of services to the poor. The hypothesis that an invincible lobby of social workers overwhelmed a defenceless political system is, to put it diplomatically, idiosyncratic" (Kelman, 1987:86).

11.   This has been formally acknowledged within the public choice literature, in particular, in an article by Mueller (1986). A continuing embarrassment for public choice theorists has been the fact that people vote at all, given the fact that the pay-off to an individual of his or her single vote is almost zero. Mueller acknowledges the difficulty and explains the fact of voting (and the fact that public goods do get provided and the existence of relatively civil conduct in queues, etc.) as a result of learned morality. This seems to me to be a long step toward greater realism in public choice writing and, for that matter, toward sociology!

12.   This, of course, is exactly what did happen to a series of British governments during the 1950s and 1960s and paved the way for more fiscally cautious policies on the part of both the Labour and Conservative parties beginning at the end of the 1970s.

13.   This point is particularly clearly made in the context of a discussion of *party effects* on policy in Alt (1985a,b).

14.   The figure approximately doubled in each country, to 32% in the Netherlands and 24% in Sweden. There was also a large increase in Japan from a low base (about 5%) to a level that is still, comparatively speaking, low (about 11%).

15.   An important exception to this is David Lange's Labour government in New Zealand that was brought into office in 1984 and introduced a distinctively unleft wing set of policies. This case provides a useful caution against too easily inferring policy preferences from party label. The general liberalizing character of the economic policies of the New Zealand government are chronicled in successive issues of the Economist Intelligence Unit's *Quarterly Economic Review of New Zealand.*

16.   Alesina (1989:81) adds Japan to the list. As we will see in Chapter 7, the case of Japan tends to reinforce the argument made here.

17.   Having some combination of minority governments, a shift from dictatorship to democracy, the existence of a large communist or extreme right party, or ethnic and regional conflict produce high instability scores on Alesina's index.

18.   A good example of this is the retreat of Canada's Progressive Conservative government from its attempts to reduce eligibility to unemployment insurance and deindex pensions and child benefits. On this see Myles (1988:78–79). Another example is the considerable difficulties in the United States involved in reforming—that is, reducing the benefits of—the social security program. On this see Marmor and Mashaw (1988).

19.   One doubts, frankly, that Barry would have been as sceptical of the well-foundedness of public opinion had majority views continued into the 1970s to regard inflation as a trivial problem.

20.   Sanders, Ward, and Marsh (1987) report a negligible Falklands effect. This finding is disputed by Clarke, Mishler, and Whitely (1990) and defended by Sanders, Marsh, and Ward (1990). Also relevant, and suggesting a substantial Falklands effect, is Norpoth (1987).

4

THEORIES OF SECULAR DECLINE

The political entities that dominated the world in the past, up to and including the British Empire, eventually went into economic decline. Cipolla (1970) outlined some characteristics that have tended to recur in these declines.[1] The state developed an excessive bureaucracy and a penchant for investing unreasonable amounts of money in public monuments. Maintaining an army became an increasingly costly proposition as the pay of rank and file soldiers rose with general living standards. Demands to consume spread from a narrow elite to the wider population and those demands were combined with a declining sense of social obligation. Thus, "as old myths wear out and living conditions improve, more people think in terms of 'rights' rather than in terms of 'duties', in terms of 'enjoyment' rather than in terms of 'work' " (p. 12). A particular problem associated with this was an increasing difficulty in finding people to fill the least attractive jobs. In the case of the Roman Empire, for example, the army was progressively filled with "barbarians" as Roman citizens became ever more adept at evading military service.

How was this rising consumption by both the state and the wider population paid for? Not out of economic growth since another characteristic of the process of decline described by Cipolla was stagnating productivity. People were wedded to customary ways of producing and selling and were slow to either innovate or copy better practices. The political entities described by Cipolla funded their rising obligations by increasing taxes and—what is important for our purposes—by debasing their currencies, that is to say, by *inflation*.

Bloated bureaucracy, rising taxes, unfilled vacancies for unappealing jobs, declining productivity, and inflation all, of course, have a very contemporary ring about them. And contemporary writers have made something of these parallels. Gilpin (1981), for example, has integrated them into a general theory of the rise and decline of political systems (e.g., pp. 164–165, 175–177, 188). But the characteristics of decline listed by Cipolla are largely unexplained.[2] In this chapter I critically examine three theories (including Gilpin's) that attempt to explain why one might expect western capitalist economies to have begun the kind of decline described by Cipolla and each of which has some relevant things to say about the conditions within which the postwar inflation has taken place.

Unbridled Demands

In his influential *Social Limits to Growth* Fred Hirsch (1976) argued that capitalist economies have run into difficulties because they have become less and less able to deliver the economic growth on which their moral credibility rests. As people become richer, he argues, their tastes shift to a class of goods that he calls "positional." The distinguishing characteristic of these goods is that they are finite in either quantity or quality. There are only so many paintings by Rembrandt and it does not matter how many people become billionaires; only a small number can secure them. There is a limited number of lakes suitable for recreational development within a convenient distance of city populations; if the demand for lakeside property is dealt with by denser construction, the quality of the good deteriorates as solitude is lost, the lake becomes polluted, and traveling time rises with road congestion. Similar features attract people to suburban housing. But these too are lost as more people move to the suburbs. The proportion of genuine leadership positions available is also limited and that proportion cannot be expanded to accommodate the increasing numbers who educate themselves to prepare for those positions. These goods, of course, are still available for purchase but their *relative* price increases so that to secure them *it is necessary to be in ever higher percentiles in the income distribution*. Their prices increase by much more than the price of goods in general. This has an important consequence: it is that people have no choice but to concern themselves with their *relative income,* for the acquisition of the positional goods that they increasingly seek requires that they advance in the income distribution (p. 102). The result, then, is a "distributional compulsion," which translates itself into an intensified demand for income.

The problem is compounded by capitalist amorality. Capitalist economic growth is based in the individualistic pursuit of self-interest. But, Hirsch argues, the *pure* pursuit of self-interest is antithetical to capitalism. The point is an extension and specification of the familiar one made by Durkheim (1933:203–219): there are noncontractual bases to contract. Trading is impossible if the parties to it are always trying to cheat each other. Without a minimal amount of trust and confidence, market exchanges are much less likely to take place, or, if they do, will involve a cumbersome, time-consuming, and expensive process of negotiation (see also North 1981:55–58, 201–207).

A properly functioning market, then, requires a moral underpinning. Hirsch is concerned with the importance of two forms of underpinning in particular. First, there is the question of the morality of the governors. Assume, with Keynes, that technical difficulties with the operation of markets (the business cycle, externalities such as pollution, natural monopolies) produce serious enough consequences to require political intervention. If governors are amoral, why should they act in the collective interest rather than their own personal interests? *Unless* it is possible to design institutions that make the interests of civil servants and politicians coincide with the interests of the wider population there is every reason to expect that they will not. That this is a real problem is strongly suggested by the public choice literature that I discussed in the last chapter and by attempts by writers within that genre to specify institutions that will harness the individual interests of those who govern to the collective interest (e.g., Niskanen 1971). Hirsch's point is that as the market has become institutionalized its amoral ethos has progressively spread and that, as a result, people who govern are increasingly affected by it—that is to say, are increasingly amoral and disposed to neglect the collective good where it obstructs their own personal interests.

Just as importantly, the corrosive effects on morality of the market spread to organized interest groups including business (p. 131) and, in particular, labor (p. 145). People organized into groups to advance their interests are more powerful than the unorganized, particularly if they control an array of resources that can be used for leverage. Such is clearly the case for business and labor. The market, which is intrinsically amoral, encourages people to pursue their own interests without concern for others. But what limits are there then on the capacity of those who are organized to divert resources away from the unorganized to themselves? Hirsch's point is that, with the decline of morality caused by the spread of the market ethos, whatever limits exist are clearly inadequate.[3]

What does all of this have to do with inflation? Hirsch himself believed that the process he had uncovered was relevant to understanding the contemporary inflation. Thus: "Economic success on the conventional reckoning contributes in this way to frustration, tension, and inflation" (p. 273). Does it?

Unbridled Demands and Inflation

I argued earlier that any adequate explanation of inflation has to include either, or both, of the following components: (1) it has to explain why demand increased (at the existing level of prices) *and* it has to explain why the government failed to take antiinflationary measures or, if it did, why those measures were ineffective; (2) alternatively, it has to explain why the supply prices of inputs to production increased at the existing level of demand (either a shift in the supply curves of labor, capital, or raw materials to the left or a decline in supply) and why, after the initial resultant rise in retail prices as a result of mark-up pricing, prices did not subsequently fall because of a deficiency of demand at the new, higher, level of prices.

Hirsch's analysis provides a reason for an increase in the supply price of labor. Because of "positional competition" and the resulting "pressure on social scarcity" and also because of the erosion of moral restraints on bargaining tactics and claims, individuals and organized groups are continually attempting to increase their share of the national income and have at least some success in raising their nominal incomes. Prices get marked up on the rising cost of production and the result is inflation. Buy why are wages not subsequently forced down as inadequate demand at the new higher price level forces employers to cut costs? Hirsch briefly addressed this question in a subsequent essay (1978). Inflation, he says, is a mechanism for "easing or accommodating political strife over income distribution" (p. 270). How does it do this? Here he refers back to the "money illusion" that I discussed earlier. Governments can reduce the hard bargaining and strikes that go with the distributional struggle by stimulating aggregate demand, and prices, so that workers are induced to believe that their purchasing power is rising faster than, in reality, it is. Unions concede without the disruptions to production that they would otherwise use to buttress their claims because their members think that they are better off as a result of their wage settlement than they really are. So, the reason that wages are not subsequently forced down is that the government chooses to ratify the higher wages with an inflationary monetary or fiscal policy. Goldthorpe (1978:208) is even more explicit on this point and in the next chapter I deal with his treatment of the issue.

Here, however, we run into the general problem with accounts of inflation based on "money illusion." Only if one assumes that most employees are terminally stupid can this work for long.[4] Sooner or later, as Hirsch acknowledges, people figure out that they have to be more aggressive still since their current conduct is not, in fact, paying off in the rising position in the income distribution that they thought it had been; so whatever social peace was purchased by the government from the initial inflation is lost and, indeed, the government is even worse off than it was before. "As individuals and institutions adapt their behaviour increasingly to anticipation of inflation, the inflationary process becomes self-generating and perhaps accelerating" (1978:270). No reactionary monetarist could have put the matter better! Hirsch's account of inflation requires the addition of an explanation for the choice of the government to deal with the distributional struggle through inflation in the first place. It requires an explanation of the propensity of governments (in those countries where inflation originated) to prize the short over the long run or to fail to realize that whatever benefits are secured through inflation are only temporary.

He addresses this issue by arguing that once the distributional struggle has been heated up by the superimposition onto it of inflationary expectations it "becomes difficult to stop inflation in a distributionally neutral way, so that even groups that do not gain from inflation itself are nonetheless fearful of measures to counter it" (1978:270). Still, unless a government is willing to allow the country it governs to slip into hyperinflation—of Israeli or Brazilian proportions, say—sooner or later it has to intervene. The argument itself assumes that intervening sooner will be less painful than intervening later. Why does the government fail to do so? Clearly, in the first place, the governments with which I am concerned in this book *did* intervene before their countries slipped into hyperinflation, although a number of them made it to what Jackson, Turner, and Wilkinson (1975) called strato-inflation. But their initial decision to prize the short run over the long run requires explanation; or, if they failed to realize that the advantages they gained from allowing inflation to accelerate would only be temporary, that requires explanation too. Hirsch's account requires a supplement. As it stands, it will not do.

The Argument's Assumptions

Can one then consider Hirsch's analysis a useful starting point for a theory of a secular tendency toward inflation in capitalist societies? Certainly, it has frequently been cited approvingly by those sociologists and political scientists who have written on inflation (e.g., Pothier, 1982:198, 216; Lindberg, 1982:21, Maier, 1984:40; Lange, 1984:118; Keohane, 1985; Ruggie, 1982:415; Goldthorpe, 1987a:373). But the argument rests on some exceedingly dubious assumptions for which neither Hirsch nor any of those who have cited him has very much evidence. The problems with Hirsch's analysis are usefully laid out in several essays in a collection edited by Ellis and Kumar (1983).

First, the argument assumes that as people's income rises so does the proportion of it that they would like to spend on positional goods (the income elasticity of demand for positional goods is greater than unity). The evidence for this is cross-sectional data on consumption by income.

But, as Ellis and Heath (1983) point out, it does not follow that because richer people consume more of some good at one point in time, everyone else will want the same goods as their average income rises. I doubt, for example, that the aesthetic preferences of most affluent workers extends to Rembrandts. And, as a matter of fact, the Rembrandts that Hirsch uses to illustrate one kind of positional good early in his book disappear when he later discusses working class demands (cf. p. 20 with p. 173). But even for the goods in which he does think the working class will wish to invest increasing proportions of their rising income the case is not self-evident. Education is often sought as a way of getting ahead and there is considerable evidence to suggest that, other things being equal, the demand for it varies with its rate of return (e.g., Fiorito and Dauffenbach, 1982).[5] Workers whose incomes have risen but who think that a technical training will yield their children a higher income than, say, a B.A. in the social sciences, are likely to encourage their children to follow the former career route rather than the latter. The attractiveness of the peace and quiet of suburban housing (which diminishes as the suburbs are more intensively developed), furthermore, is partly linked to the fact that many people—particularly those with children—cannot afford central city accommodation (Thorns, 1972:45, 68) as well as the undesirability of conditions in inner cities. Where those inner cities have become livable again, quite a lot of people choose to live in them (Gale, 1984:9–15). Not everyone puts a high value on pristine, unsullied surroundings in the choice of their vacations—as the success of quite expensive vacation places such as Disney World or Club Med attests. It simply is not obvious that rising income leads people to desire the particular goods that Hirsch claims it does. Besides, even if there is some tendency for rising income to lead people to seek goods that are intrinsically positional, it does not follow that their preferences are immutably tied to those goods. If more or less pristine recreational lakes were to become unavailable, people can find quite a lot of gratifying, and expensive, things to do on more crowded ones—as visits to many North American lakes on summer weekends will show. In general, one can agree with Gershuny (1983:29) that Hirsch unreasonably assumes that needs are not mutable in the face of varying availabilities of different goods.

Second, Hirsch's argument assumes that the supply of positional goods is inelastic. This assumption is also dubious. There is a long history of successful efforts by forgers to extend the supply of paintings attributable to renowned painters (see, for example, Norman, 1977) and plausible antiques can be manufactured fairly readily (Alexander, 1984). Road networks of rich capitalist countries were upgraded considerably and travel times reduced after the second world war and particularly during the 1960s, that is, during the period when, according to Hirsch capitalism's economic growth was sowing the seeds of the subsequent bitter positional struggle of the 1970s (e.g., Rae, 1971:173–194). The same is true of access to education and one might even argue that the number of the kinds of jobs that would allow people to plausibly regard themselves as upwardly mobile also increased significantly during that period (e.g., Goldthorpe, 1987b:ch. 3). More generally, the notion that people buy things for the prestige attached to them is no doubt true; but it does not follow that, if some goods are not available, people are unable to invent new prestige items. As Gershuny argues at length, there is an unwarranted assumption in Hirsch's work that the current upper middle class sets, and will continue to set, the standards of taste for the rest of the population.

Third, it is not at all clear that the current population is any less morally constrained than previous ones. Interest groups have always acted with varying amounts of scrupulousness. We have a rich history of self-interested lobbying by professional associations (e.g., Friedman, 1962:137–160). Labor history provides us with plentiful evidence of the aggressive pursuit of a higher income, including strikes, violence, and boycotts; such behavior is by no means unique to the prosperous post-war period.[6] *If* organized labor seems to have become more disruptive as living standards have risen over the postwar it does not follow that that is because unionized workers are less *moral*. It may be that it is because they have had more favorable conditions in which to exercise pressure— more supportive legislation, lower unemployment rates, and sympathetic governments. I will consider this in more detail later. The point here is that Hirsch does not provide any evidence of a decline in economic morality; nor is there a prima facie case that such a decline has taken place (see Taylor-Gooby, 1983).

Hirsch's influence on social and political theorists of the postwar inflation does *not* rest on the evidence in support of his claims or the compelling logic of his argument. It is not at all clear that the demand for positional goods *uniformly* increases with income; were it to have done so, there are grounds for thinking that the supply of the goods in question is much more elastic than Hirsch would have us believe; and, in the absence of any evidence to the contrary, the safest bet is that the distribution of morality and amorality has remained pretty much constant. Furthermore, of course, Hirsch's argument does not get us very far in explaining the *details* of the postwar inflation. Why did it accelerate across the capitalist world in the mid-1960s and after 1973? Why do Switzerland, Germany, and, in recent years, Japan have superior inflation records? In fact, the attractiveness of Hirsch's analysis—despite the absence of any evidence in support of it—rests, without question, in the fact that it fits in with the recent theorizing (and attempts to assemble some supportive evidence) about the effects of neocorporatist political institutions on macroeconomic performance.

Institutional Sclerosis

The treatment of inflation in Mancur Olson's *Rise and Decline of Nations* (1982) is rather oblique. Like Hirsch's, his book is fundamentally concerned with economic growth. Where in his final chapter he deals with "stagflation" he has much more to say about unemployment than inflation. Nonetheless, I believe that his analysis has some important things to say about the context within which some governments have had to make macroeconomic decisions in the twentieth century—decisions about whether or not to stimulate inflation or to allow an inflation that originated in an exogenous shock to continue.

The starting point for his analysis is the conclusions of his earlier treatment of collective goods (Olson, 1965). People form associations to advance the interests of their members. Often, they do so by providing "collective goods." These are goods that, once provided to one member of a group, cannot be withheld from any other member (Olson, 1965:14–15). If employers are induced by a union to raise wages they are unlikely to restrict the wage increase to the perhaps limited set of their employees who went on strike. To do so would be to reward militancy and punish tractability. Once a government imposes a tariff the sales of all producers will rise, whether or not the producers in question helped pay for the lobbying effort that securing the tariff required.

If all those in a group receive any collective good once it is secured whether or not they bore any of the costs involved in securing it, members have a strong incentive to allow others in the group to incur the required costs. They have, that is, a strong incentive to be *free riders*. But if most members of a group draw this conclusion the collective good is unlikely ever to be provided—and certainly not in the amounts that would best serve their interests. It is particularly unlikely to be provided where the group in question is large, for the actions of no single member of a large group will make much difference to the likelihood of the good being provided and, besides, it is hard for the members of large groups to police each other's behavior for violations of whatever policy was agreed on (Olson, 1965:33–36, 45).

Nonetheless, we know that workers do sometimes manage to form unions, and producers to lobby effectively. There are various circumstances under which collective goods are likely to get provided: if the group involved is small enough, if the government allows coercion (by not applying laws limiting picketing) or itself provides the coercion (the occupational licensure of professions), if the government or the association itself provides *individual* benefits with membership (insurance, technical information), or where the social relations of membership are valued in their own right so that ostracism or acceptance really matters to would-be free riders. Furthermore, once special interest groups have been formed they rarely fade away; once one objective has been realized they simply shift to another. Two conclusions follow from this: first, because of the difficulties posed by the free rider problem, at any given point in time, people have less collective goods than they would like; second, over time the discrepancy tends to diminish as the available and usable special interest organizations cumulate.

Now, and this is the crux of the argument, most of the objectives secured through lobbying by these organizations hinder economic performance. For they advance their members' interests not by maximizing the amount of goods produced in the economy of which they are a part but rather by *redistributing* the existing income. In doing so, furthermore, they reduce the total amount of goods and services produced. Tariffs raise the supply prices of the protected goods involved and in doing so raise the costs of production of those for whom they are inputs; unions keep the wage for some classes of labor artificially high and prevent the employment and production that would be possible were they lower; and so on. Additional resources are wasted as the pay-offs from it induce more and more resources to be allocated to lobbying (see, in particular, Tullock, 1980:39 ff.).

Distributional coalitions reduce economic welfare. Furthermore, because they tend to accumulate over time, oppose technical and institutional innovation, and succeed in extracting subsidies that obstruct the reallocation of resources to more efficient uses *they slow down economic growth*. Thus, according to Olson, Germany and Japan have had superior postwar growth records because one of the consequences of defeat was the destruction of their special interest organizations—what he calls "distributional coalitions." The apparently inferior records of the United Kingdom and the United States on the other hand are, in part, a result of the fact that immunity from invasion (or revolution) for more than a century has allowed the development of a rich array of effective and encumbering distributional coalitions (pp. 76–78).

There is, however, a very important alternative outcome from the accumulation of distributional coalitions. If, ultimately, the distributional coalitions in a particular society become sufficiently *encompassing*, the interests of their members are changed. If a large proportion of workers belong to the same union (or effectively centralized association of unions), they can no longer so easily increase their welfare at the expense of nonunion workers or workers in other unions, for the pool of workers to be exploited is much diminished. If all employers are similarly organized, their options are limited in the same way. And if they cannot so easily increase their income at the expense of others, they are compelled to consider doing so by maximizing the total income generated by the society. Thus,

> The members of the highly encompassing organization own so much of the society that they have an important incentive to be actively concerned about how productive it is; they are in the same position as a partner in a firm that has only a few partners. (Olson, 1982:48).

As Schwerin (1984:232) notes, however, Olson clearly regards encompassing organizations as inferior substitutes to an economy largely unencumbered by special interest organizations. This is because the political processes within encompassing organizations tend to be time consuming.

> Decision-making under constitutional procedures . . . takes time, especially in larger groups. Decisions may have to wait until everyone is talked out, or until the next board meeting or the next annual meeting, or even until those who favor a change in policy force out those officials who prefer the old policy. (Olson, 1982:55)

Because it takes so long to make a decision, societies with encompassing organizations are ill equipped to make prompt adjustments to changing environmental circumstances. They are much less effective at doing so than are private businesses run by a single manager or by a small group of managers. Jonung's (1990) study of the operation of price controls in Sweden from 1970 to 1987 provides an unusually detailed description of just how cumbersome, time consuming, and costly such bargaining can become.

Institutional Sclerosis and Inflation

Since the 1970s, higher rates of inflation have been accompanied by higher rates of unemployment. More generally, prices of goods and labor have become less downwardly flexible over time in a number of economies and declines in output as a result of falling aggregate demand progressively greater (Olson, 1982:219–224). Why? According to Olson, the answer is that distributional coalitions act to prevent individuals from making mutually profitable transactions. Unions will not allow the wages of their members to fall during a recession; they will also do what they can to prevent nonunion workers who would be willing to work at a lower rate from being hired. Trade associations respond to declining demand by lobbying for protection from foreign competition rather than by cutting prices and are supported in their efforts by their unionized workers. Olson, then, extends his analysis of "distributional coalitions" to explain the observed "stickiness" of factor and product prices in recessions and the unemployment and unused capital that results from them.

But where does inflation come into this? The reason that prices are so sluggish where distributional coalitions are setting them is that it takes the members of these coalitions a long time before they can negotiate a change. This applies, as we have seen, when demand falls. But it also applies when demand rises. This means that the price fixed by the distributional coalition *relative* to prices in the rest of the economy will tend to fall and the inhibition on productive activity imposed by the coalition will be reduced. "In a period of unexpected inflation an economy with a high level of special-interest organization and collusion will be more productive than it normally is" (Olson 1982:206).

Consequently, in institutionally sclerotic societies, governments are likely to find occasional *unexpected* inflations appealing. I emphasize *unexpected* because Olson recognizes that, sooner or later, groups will succeed in tying the prices they charge to the cost of living or will become progressively more sensitive and skilled in suitably adjusting prices to indicators of changes in aggregate demand (1982:206–207, 230).[7] But Olson's analysis provides a reason for expecting governments to find the prospect of an inflation appealing, some of the time.

From there onward, one is pretty much on one's own in applying Olson's model to the postwar inflation. It seems to me that it can reasonably be extended to make the following points. First, those governing institutionally sclerotic societies are likely to have been continually frustrated in whatever efforts they might have chosen to make to secure superior rates of economic growth. Indeed, to the extent that the relative growth performance of nations becomes part of the common currency of domestic politics they are quite likely to get desperate from time to time. That desperation is likely to lead to a floundering around in search of legal and institutional structures to deal with the barriers to growth. I will argue later that, to some extent, the postwar experimentation in Britain with various kinds of incomes policies and legal frameworks for industrial relations can be understood in precisely this way (see, also, Olson, 1982:218).

Second, given the fact that unexpected inflations *initially* produce an acceleration of growth in institutionally sclerotic societies, one would expect politicians who had observed a growth-generating inflation to find deliberately inflationary policies appealing, or to regard a deflationary response to an inflation originating elsewhere definitely unappealing. They would, in other words, tend to think that because inflation "worked" before, it would be likely to work again.

Third, however, because expectations sooner or later catch up with the inflation rate and distributional coalitions appropriately adjust their pricing behavior, each successive time that a government tries to get growth through inflation, it will be less successful. In other words, after the first time, politicians will consistently overestimate the amount of growth that can be secured through an inflation. Furthermore, they would have been encouraged in these mistaken actions by Keynesian economists who failed to recognize the *institutional specificity* of the expansionary policies to deal with slow growth and unemployment that they recommended to politicians. That is to say, because Keynesian analysis does not satisfactorily deal with the *sources* of inflexibility in wages and prices, "some Keynesians in the 1970s recommended ever more expansive policies to cure the unemployment, thereby generating pointless inflation" (Olson, 1982:230–231; see also Olson, 1979:157–158. And, to the extent that they did so, they helped induce governments to adopt incorrect policies. There is in Olson's analysis of inflation, then, an "ignorance and error" component, to use Goldthorpe's (pejorative) term.

The Argument Appraised

One virtue of Olson's theory is that it is specified in a general enough fashion that it can be tested in a variety of contexts. As we have seen, in *The Rise and Decline of Nations,* Olson explains both differentials in economic growth and the increasing durability of unemployment during recessions as products of distributional coalitions. He also applies the analysis to caste endogamy (a way of limiting the supply of labor into a hereditary, occupationally based, distributional coalition), the rise of apartheid in Southern Africa (a device, initially lobbied for by labor unions, for preserving the white/black wage differential), and the tendency for third world countries to develop oversized urban areas (it is much easier to organize distributional coalitions in the cities, which then successfully lobby for protection and subsidies for the industries located in them—producing a much higher urban/rural wage differential than would otherwise obtain). It is true that these applications of his theory can by no means be regarded as rigorous tests. Still, even as rather casual tests their diversity tends to increase one's confidence in the account (see Stinchcombe, 1968:18–20).

More importantly, and in marked contrast to the treatment of Hirsch's ideas, there has been some attempt to more rigorously test Olson's analysis of distributional coalitions and economic growth. Thus, Olson himself (1982:99–114, 1983a:35–44; Kendix and Olson, 1990) presents some quantitative evidence on the states of the United States showing that the longer the time since statehood (and, therefore, the longer the time available to form distributional coalitions), the higher the percentage unionized (as one measure of the presence of distributional coalitions) and that time since statehood and percentage unionized are associated with lower postwar rates of growth and higher unemployment of American states. Furthermore, the confederate states, whose distributional coalitions were devastated by defeat, have had generally higher than average rates of growth.[8] Murrell (1983) shows that old, well-established, heavy industries do less well in the United Kingdom than in Germany and makes the plausible case that that is consistent with Olson's theory since age of industry is associated with the development of special interest organizations and heavy industries, which are capital intensive and pay high wages, are particularly favorable to their development. In these industries, then, the advantage provided to Germany by the wartime destruction of distributional coalitions is most substantial. Choi (1983), Weede (1986a), and Lane and Ersson (1986) test the theory using cross-national data. Choi found that a relatively complicated index of institutional sclerosis predicted economic growth, a finding duplicated by Lane and Ersson for a different sample of countries, with a wider range of controls. Weede has tested for the effects on economic growth and unemployment of distributional coalitions (operationalized as "age of democracy") versus "catch-up" and size of government. Using a variety of specifications, growth turned out to have been lower and unemployment higher in older democracies and in countries with large public sectors. Weede (1986b) has extended the analysis using a pooled regression technique, generating results consistent with Olson's analysis.

There is therefore *some* evidence for Olson's theory. Nonetheless, there are problems. First there is the problem of the indirectness of the indicators of institutional sclerosis. The concept refers to an agglomeration of distributional coalitions, but the measures are all based on the time since some relevant event (the formation of a state, defeat in war, civil disturbance). Scores on the measure are likely to have some association with scores on the concept; but they are also likely to be associated with many other factors that have changed over time (Abramovitz,

1983:83). In effect, the measure of institutional sclerosis is the same as the trend in a time series regression equation, usually included to control for the effects of an array of factors correlated with time rather than as a measure of a specific concept.

Second, some of the applications of his analysis depend on some arguable assumptions about lags. Pryor (1983:91), Kindleberger (1983:6), and Barry (1983:24) have all pointed out that the gap between the devastation of the American Civil War and the period of acceleration of growth in the South in the 1960s is sufficiently long that the notion that the two events might be causally linked strains credulity. Olson (1983b:33–34) has attempted to answer this objection by arguing that it was only after the passage of the Wagner act in 1937 consolidated unions in the Northeast and Middle West that the distributional coalition-free (that is, union free!) South surged ahead. But Olson himself recognizes the "tentative and heuristic" character of his treatment of the South (1982:109–111). Again, there are other factors that might account for the rapid postwar growth in the South (and West) including not only "catch-up" but also the effects of growth in military expenditures during the Vietnam war on a defense industry disproportionately located in those areas. The matter can certainly not be regarded as settled.

Third, particular national economic histories seem not to fit Olson's claims. Asselain and Morrisson (1983) claim that Germany grew rapidly after 1871 and France fairly rapidly after World War II despite well-developed sets of interest groups[9] and De Vries (1983) argues that the same is true of the Dutch Republic in the seventeenth century. He argues further that in the late nineteenth and twentieth centuries Britain ought to have provided one of the less congenial environments for the formation of distributional coalitions since it has been "conspicuous as a land of free trade or low tariffs, as an economy open to the activities of multinational firms, and as a recipient of a flow of Irish and Commonwealth immigrants that was very large relative to the modest increase in demand for labor" (1983:15). On the other hand, for all that the construction of the German empire involved the consolidation of a large national market, that did not herald the elimination of distributional coalitions but rather brought the replacement of guilds with "a comprehensive cartelization of heavy industry, vigorous unionization, protective tariffs, and an extensive bureaucracy" (p. 16).

The fact remains, however, that Olson's theory is more tightly argued than Hirsch's and there is considerably more evidence for it.[10] It does not explain the postwar inflation; nor does Olson attempt to use it to do so. But it does provide reasons why some governments might have been casting around for a way to increase their rate of economic growth and might have considered that inflation was one way of going about getting it, especially where some economists encouraged them (sometimes correctly and sometimes incorrectly) in that belief.

The Decline of Hegemony

Stable international relations, according to Gilpin (1981:29–30), are built around one or a small number of powerful states that "enforce the basic rules and rights" within the system (see also Kindleberger, 1973, 1978). In the modern era the route to international power has passed through leadership in technology and trade and the last two "hegemonic" powers—Britain followed by the United States—in part secured their hegemony by promoting the development of free trade and a world market (Gilpin, 1981:138–139). After the second world war had devastated the industrial infrastructure of its commercial rivals the United States had both the resources and, ultimately, the political will to become the "hegemon" of the capitalist world. It used its power to establish a stable international monetary framework (through Bretton Woods), progressive tariff reductions (through GATT), and stable oil prices (through subversion in the case of Iran and by ensuring the supply of oil under American control to Europe and Japan in times of crisis (Keohane, 1984b:139 ff.). These were all part of the postwar *"regime"* in international relations, a *"regime"* that made possible rapid growth in real incomes in conjunction with prices that remained relatively stable, in part because of the discipline imposed by the fixed exchange rate system established at Bretton Woods. In short, U.S. hegemony made possible superior economic performance throughout the capitalist world.

Hegemony, however, cannot last. U.S. hegemony has been based on the dollar's role as principal reserve currency, the liberal provision of foreign aid, direct investment throughout most of the world by American companies, and technological superiority, all reinforced by military might. But the relative economic power of the United States has declined. It now accounts for a diminished share of world industrial output. Its productivity lead over its trading rivals has narrowed and in some industries has been eliminated altogether. It has been in chronic deficit on its balance of payments throughout most of the postwar period.[11] And it increasingly finds itself with strategic commitments that exceed its military resources (Kennedy, 1988:684).

Gilpin (1981) has provided a number of reasons why hegemony is inevitably transient. What is important for my purposes is that his analysis has provided a convenient source for those, like Keohane (1984a:37), who have sought to explain the economic difficulties of the past 15 or so years in terms of a decline of the United States.[12]

Gilpin's argument goes as follows. Countries achieve the rapid rates of economic growth that make their rise to international power possible by borrowing the technology of the more economically advanced nations. But when they themselves have become economically advanced, their rate of growth slows down as they are forced to take on responsibility for pushing back the technological frontier. Worse yet, other nations grow faster because they are now in a position to appropriate the technology of the leader. This applies to both civilian and military technology. Furthermore, there is a "tendency for the most efficient military techniques to rise in cost" (p. 162) and so the burdens of preserving hegemony become still heavier. This occurs in a context, moreover, in which smaller states tend to "free ride" on the military protection of the hegemonic state (Olson and Zeckhauser, 1966) so that whatever economic advantages might have accrued from hegemony—such as dominance in international trade—are dissipated in military expenditures. As if all this were not enough, there is the corruption from affluence identified by Cipolla: consumption grows faster than production and people become more concerned with rights than responsibilities. And last, and perhaps least, there is the sectoral shift from manufacturing to services, to a sector, that is, in which productivity advances are harder to come by.

For all these reasons, hegemonic nations tend to go into decline and to be replaced as dominant state in the international system, usually after defeat in a war. This is what has been happening to the United States, which is displaying "The classic symptoms of a declining power. . . . in the early 1980s: rampant inflation, chronic balance-of-payments difficulties, and high taxation" (Gilpin, 1981:232).

The Loss of Hegemony and Inflation

Gilpin, then, is quite definite about the association between hegemony in decline and accelerating inflation. Since this is not his principal concern, however, the mechanisms linking decline to inflation are not filled in. But it is quite clear that the model implied is one of inflation in response to an overload on government. First, there is a distributional struggle including at its core the problem of reconciling increasing demands for consumption with the need to continue spending on investment and defense (p. 167). Second, there is the particular problem caused by the fact that defense costs rise faster than costs in general at the same time that the resources available to meet those costs

are dwindling as the technological lead of the hegemonic power evaporates. Governments confronted with these demands in excess of resources deal with the problem by "printing money," that is, by inflation.
These are the mechanisms, associated with the process of hegemonic
decline, that produced accelerating inflation in the United States in the
1960s and, through fixed exchange rates, the rest of the industrialized
world.

Furthermore, U.S. power had created Bretton Woods (Cohen,
1982:465–467; Gardner, 1980) and Bretton Woods had limited the discretion of Western governments to choose inflationary policies. The decline
in U.S. international financial power, most clearly embodied in its
chronic balance of payments deficit, removed the political underpin-
nings of Bretton Woods and produced the (more-or-less) floating exchange rates of the past two decades. Governments could now choose
policies as inflationary as they wanted—and a number chose very inflationary policies indeed.[13]

Now it should be clear that this analysis coincides with a major part of
what I have described as the "orthodox" economic model of the postwar
inflation. In that account, inflation began to accelerate in the 1960s because the United States chose to fund the Vietnam war and the Great
Society programs at the same time, without suitable tax increases. This
produced not only inflation but also the rising government expenditures, balance of payments deficits, and, ultimately, the collapse of Bretton Woods, that are also part of the declining hegemony scenario.

What, then, are the distinctive claims of a "declining hegemony"
account? The first is that declining U.S. influence is a side effect of a
historically repeated, secular, process of decline rather than the outcome
either of some poorly judged policies or of some opportunities available
to the United States provided by the institutional conditions of the time.
In Gilpin's terms it is a question of a "conjunctural" versus a "structural" explanation (1987:341–360).[14] The second is that there is some
relation between hegemonic decline and preference for inflationary
policies.

The Argument Appraised

One should start out by acknowledging that the power of the United
States has certainly declined. But is this a result of the inevitable attrition
of hegemony along the lines sketched out by Gilpin? There are some
fundamental problems with his analysis. First, although it is true that
there are good grounds for expecting a technological lead to narrow as
follower countries appropriate techniques from the hegemonic tech-

nological leader (Choi, 1983; Maddison, 1982) it does not follow that the follower countries ever have to completely catch up. It is easy to imagine a process of catch-up that takes an asymptotic form. And Gilpin provides no reason why the technological catch-up has to culminate in the technological leader being overtaken. Second, the shift from the consumption of manufactured goods to services does not necessarily have the consequence he claims. Not all services are subject to the limitations on productivity increase that seem to apply to much of health and education. And the more general problem with productivity in the service sector is that it is awfully difficult to measure it (Dennison, 1973). There *may* be much more growth in service sector productivity than is typically thought. Third, the evidence does seem to be overwhelming that hegemonic powers pay more than their fair share of the military costs of maintaining order in the international system and Gilpin identifies this as another source of decline. But this will not do either. For this tendency to overpayment is a constant; there is no reason of which I am aware to expect it to increase over time. Indeed, the available estimates of the financial burdens of empire (so to speak) of both Britain and the United States tend to suggest that they fluctuated markedly over time but showed no secular tendency to increase (David and Huttenback, 1982). Finally, there is the "law of the increasing cost of war." There does seem to be something to this argument, although not for the reason given by Gilpin.[15] Kennedy (1988:675) has pointed out that military superiority in the twentieth century has been increasingly tied to the technological *quality* of the equipment involved, a technological quality that tends to come at a very high, and increasing, price.[16]

I would argue, then, that the general processes of hegemonic decline outlined by Gilpin are not persuasive, although the twentieth century does seem to have produced a distinctive problem of defense costs. Hegemonic powers no doubt sooner or later do go into decline, but we have no *general* theory of decline and the fact is that hegemonic powers have managed to maintain their positions over very long periods (Kennedy, 1988:passim). Consider now the alternative, "conjunctural" account of U.S. difficulties over the postwar period.

The extraordinary hegemony of the United States after the second world war was, in an important sense, a fluke (Gilpin, 1987:343). The war was fought on the territories of the United States' principal industrial rivals (in the form of bombing in the case of Britain). The infrastructure of the European countries had been destroyed as well as quite a lot of their young men. But the knowledge and skills required of an industrial nation remained widely available in the remaining population and it was inevitable that they would *to some extent* catch up. It follows from this that inferring hegemonic decline from a comparison of the U.S.

share in world manufacturing value added in 1948 with its share in 1981 (from 57 to 22%), as Bellon and Niosi (1988:29) do, is not entirely reasonable because there is an extraordinarily acute "base point problem" involved.

Still, the *relative* industrial decline of the United States has continued since postwar reconstruction was completed. Why? The Vietnam War was not only lost (in itself seen as a symptom of decline) but also, arguable, considerably damaged the U.S. economy by diverting production to military goods and, in the context of fixed exchange rates, by producing inflation that disrupted investment (see Chapter 2) and priced U.S. goods out of foreign markets. This inflationary tendency was exacerbated by the rising expenditures on the "Great Society" program. Now, although the interpretation is controversial, there is no shortage of writings arguing that the Vietnam war was an error rather than something forced on the United States by its responsibilities as "leader of the free world" (e.g., Janis, 1972; Halberstam, 1972; Tuchman, 1984). For that matter, there is no shortage of writings suggesting (also controversially) that much of the Great Society program was an error too (e.g., Murray, 1984). *If* the policies that produced it were an error, whatever damage was caused by the late 1960s inflation (and the shocks of the early 1970s with which it was connected) was closely related to bad government decisions rather than some ineluctable process of hegemonic decline.

One does not rescue the argument by suggesting that only a hegemonic power can stumble into this sort of error. Even if that is true (and I doubt that it is), if the policy was an error, if not fighting the Vietnam war and not providing food stamps or aid for dependent children would have left the United States at least as externally and internally secure as it was after having spent money on both things, then an explanation in terms of hegemonic decline is simply false.

Moreover, despite the fact that Keohane (1984a:37) has cited Gilpin as authority for the secular decline of hegemony, his own writings provide considerable evidence that the difficulties of the United States in the last 15 or so years can be readily explained in terms of factors other than those identified by Gilpin. The rise of protectionism has its origins, he argues, in the domestic political pressure of European labor unions (1984b:152) rather than U.S. decline. Bretton Woods collapsed because of the error of Vietnam and the inherent instability of a system that required U.S. balance of payments deficits to provide international liquidity but assumed the convertibility of dollars into gold (1984b:149–150). Keohane does claim that the end of stable oil prices was consistent with the effects of hegemonic decline because it followed the depletion of U.S. petroleum reserves. But, as he observes, that (premature) depletion was, in fact, a consequence of domestic lobbying. U.S. oil producers were successful in preventing the Federal government from developing an appropriate reserves policy. Surely domestic lobbying as an explanation is more obviously consistent with public choice theory or, in particular, with Olson's extension of it? Business lobbies, after all, can and do operate in all countries, not only in hegemons (Keohane, 1984b:140–141, 215; 1985:97).

So I think one should start out by recognizing that the case to the effect that the very real (but sometimes, as in Bellon and Niosi's study, exaggerated) relative decline in the United States is connected to a historically recurrent process of loss of hegemony is not all that strong.

But, in any case, whether or not the United States *relative* power has declined is less important than whether or not its power remains strong enough to accomplish its policy goals. In the military field it is clear that the United States has from time to time been overstretched. But as Strange (1982:483) has emphasized (and Keohane has acknowledged) the United States remains, by any measure, a very powerful country indeed—"the undisputed hegemon of the system" (see also Gill, 1990). The theory of hegemonic decline provides absolutely no guidance whatsoever to just how relatively powerful a country has to be in order to be able to maintain its preferred economic regime.

This poses another problem. The premise of the hegemonic decline literature is that hegemons use their power to secure the stability of the world military and financial system as a whole, to the general benefit of the nations incorporated in the system. There is little question that the early postwar policies of the United States, which included the Marshall plan, served the interests of the populations of the other capitalist nations. Those policies, however, also served the strategic military and economic interests of the United States by increasing the attractiveness of remaining in the United States rather than the Soviet sphere of influence and by stimulating a growth in world trade from which U.S. producers considerably profited. In the early postwar period the interests of Europe and of the United States largely coincided.

But one can argue, first, that since the 1960s the economic interests of the United States and Europe have in important respects increasingly diverged and, second, United States governments have been powerful enough to enforce *international financial* outcomes consistent with what those governments perceived to be U.S. interests. Calleo (1982, 1987; see also Bergsten, 1975:ch. 7) has argued that the part of world inflation originating in the United States during the Kennedy and Johnson administrations of the 1960s was a useful device for passing on the costs of its foreign and domestic policies to foreign central banks and citizens. Because exchange rates were fixed and because the reserve role of the dollar and the economic importance of the United States made foreign governments reluctant to force devaluation the Eurodollar market swelled with dollars of a diminishing value. The subsequent period of inflation and flexible exchange rates during the 1970s under Nixon and Ford served to depreciate much of the debt to foreigners that had been accumulated during the 1960s. In the 1980s, monetary stringency and a swelling federal deficit produced high interest rates that attracted investment funds from the rest of the world and contributed to sustained recession in Europe and a consumption-led boom in the United States.[17] For all that these policies no doubt wreaked all sorts of havoc on the American economy (most spectacularly with a rapidly increasing balance of payments deficit under Reagan) they also had a number of advantages. The point I want to make now is that each of these policies, whether ill advised in the long run or not, can be seen as evidence of United States power. The international financial policies in question were (and still are) roundly condemned in Europe but that has not stopped their adoption. The postwar inflation has been profoundly affected by the evolution of international economic arrangements and that evolution seems to have followed U.S. rather than European preferences or interests. Where is the collapsing hegemon here?

Supposing, however, that one emphasizes the aspects of United States relative decline rather than continuing strength: why should one expect the decline of hegemonic power to produce inflation? It may be that constant or growing military obligations in the context of declining relative economic growth puts strains on the budget of a hegemon and those strains lead it to run an inflation-producing deficit. But there are several difficulties with this line of argument.

First, we run into the same problem that applies to Hirsch's analysis. Inflation provides only short-term advantages. Sooner or later, whatever revenue benefits accrue to the government as a result of inflation (see, e.g., Morley, 1979:143) disappear and all that remains is the disruption to markets caused by the uncertainties that accelerating inflation brings to those wishing to make contracts. Why would governments presiding over states struggling to meet the demands of hegemony choose inevitably temporary solutions to their problems? If hegemonic decline is to be linked to inflation it is necessary to come up with an extension of the theory to show why hegemonic states in decline prize the short run over the long run.

Second, the case of Britain poses major problems for a theory linking hegemonic decline to a preference for inflationary policies. It provides the only other case of hegemonic decline that is comparable to the United States.[18] Yet an orthodoxy found in much writing on British economic history is that its governments pursued generally deflationary policies throughout much of the period during which it was in decline. After the first world war British government policies were designed to make possible a return to the gold standard *at the prewar parity.* This required generally deflationary policies both before and after the return to the gold standard (Stewart, 1972:59–63). It has also been argued that British governments in the decade or so after the second world war struggled to maintain an unsustainable rate of exchange with the U.S. dollar, with generally deflationary consequences (Stewart, 1972:247–251; see also Kenen and Lubitz, 1971:80). We have, then, two twentieth-century cases of hegemonic decline: one—Britain—was accompanied by deflationary policies; the other—the United States—was accompanied by inflationary policies. Clearly, the data on the available cases will not support a theory connecting hegemonic decline to inflation.

Third, a fairly strong case can be made that the budget deficits of the United States have been much less produced by excessive spending than by an unwillingness to tax. Calleo observes that "From a French or German perspective, the United States has fiscal deficits not because it spends too much, but because Americans pay too little" (1987:109–113). An unwillingness to tax is not a part of Cipolla's description of the process of decline. It will not do to say that it is the deficit itself, however generated, that is produced by hegemonic decline. To the extent that Gilpin specifies his theory it involves a process of excessive *spending.* By international standards, however, the United States spends rather moderately.

There are therefore grounds for thinking that there is much less to Gilpin's analysis of hegemonic decline than meets the eye. The mechanisms identified by him as being at the origins of decline are in some instances nonexistent and in others unconvincing. There is a quite convincing "conjunctural" account of the changes in the economic order that took place in the 1970s. There is quite a lot of evidence of continuing U.S. power, particularly in international economic matters. And it is not obvious why governments of countries in hegemonic decline should select inflationary policies: in interwar Britain, as a matter of fact, they did not.

This is not, it should be clear, to argue that hegemonic countries do not sooner or later go into relative decline. Of course, they always have. Sooner or later the United States position of world leadership will be lost too. What I am arguing is that Gilpin's analysis of the circumstances that *inevitably* produce this outcome does not much help us in understanding the process that produces the result and, as such, has little to tell us about the origins of the economic difficulties of the last 20 years, including the acceleration of inflation.[19]

Conclusion

In this chapter I have outlined three separate theories of secular decline. Hirsch locates the source of decline in rich countries in the frustrations of growth conjoined with the diffusion of the amorality of the market to wider sections of the population. Olson attributes secular decline to the accumulation of distributional coalitions. And Gilpin explains it with a number of factors but, in particular, the burdens of hegemony. In each case the author himself sees inflation as one of the by-products of this process of decline but the mechanism linking decline to inflation is, in each case, quite different. In Hirsch's account the effect of the distributional struggle is to shift the supply curve of labor to the left as workers demand ever higher wages in an attempt to secure the kinds of income that the acquisition of positional goods requires. The effect of this is to raise supply prices (if we assume an accommodative government policy). In Olson's account inflation occurs because governments see it (sometimes mistakenly) as one of the only ways to secure a politically acceptable level of economic growth in an institutionally sclerotic society. In Gilpin's account inflation is caused when the government of a hegemonic state finds that it cannot pay the costs involved in maintaining its hegemony out of its revenues and is forced to run deficits.

These are quite different explanations of the postwar inflation, but they all appeal for support to the same broad range of economic difficulties that have characterized the capitalist world since the 1970s. The fact is, however, that only Olson's theory has been subject to anything remotely like a rigorous test. Yet it is the work of Hirsch and Gilpin that continues to be approvingly cited in the writings on the postwar inflation of sociologists and political scientists. Olson's *Rise and Decline of Nations* has either been ignored or, where referred to, subject to a generally critical treatment (e.g., Schwerin, 1984).

Notes

1. Cipolla writes about the decline of "empires." But he defines both "empire" and "decline" very broadly indeed. "Empires" are defined by "economic or cultural predominance" and include the Italian city states of the middle ages and the seventeenth-century Netherlands. "Decline" involves "a loss of preeminence" (p. 2) rather than a decrease in per capita income. It is fair to say, I think, that notwithstanding the title of the book, Cipolla is actually concerned with the process of decline of any polity that is powerful within the international system.

2.   The single exception is his discussion of declining productivity in which he argues that there are rational as well as irrational elements to this. The rational element is that productivity advance involves a process of natural selection that can, however, be determined only retrospectively. When a new technique appears (and social techniques such as the corporation are just as important as machines) it is often not obvious *at first* that it involves a real improvement over existing ways of doing things. But in an internationally powerful polity, existing ways of doing things clearly served very well in the past. Making the case for an innovation is all the harder where the innovation has to stand comparison with a record of past success.

3.   Hirsch makes another relevant point that, for the sake of conciseness, I have not dealt with here. He argues that the increase in the size of the array of consumer goods puts pressure on the fixed amount of time available to consume them. Consequently, people are compelled to invest more and more in ways to economize time. For example, they have to buy into an exclusive and expensive tennis club because that is the only way they can be sure that they can fit the matches they want into their overburdened schedule. The membership in the tennis club is purely a means to secure the tennis matches that, with a less charged schedule, could be secured less expensively with a little waiting. But the expenditure on the tennis club membership appears in national accounts data as an increase in gross national product, that is to say, as an increase in economic growth. Since it is only a means to an end (an intermediate good) it, in reality, embodies no increase in welfare. The point of all of this is to say that as larger shares of income go on the intermediate goods that make consumption possible, measured economic growth increasingly overstates the economic growth associated with increasing welfare.

4.   That elaborate social theories that require the assumption that workers are extraordinarily stupid can be and have been constructed is demonstrated in recent writings on the Marxist theory of the state, which I discuss in Chapter 8. On this general point see Parkin (1979:81).

5.   The evidence on the sensitivity of the demand for education to its rate of return is stronger for choices between fields of study at the college level (as in Fiorito and Dauffenbach, 1982) than for the demand for postcompulsory schooling per se. Here it has proven difficult to disentangle shifts in the demand for the good from the effects of government subsidies and rationing policies (see Blaug, 1976:833–836). Nonetheless, the evidence on choices between fields tends to support the general importance of rate of return considerations (which is not to say that they constitute the only considerations).

6.   I take it that this point does not require extensive documentation. That labor history is filled with this sort of thing is a commonplace of recent writing. Brecher (1972) is perhaps the best (albeit overstated) exemplar of this genre. On aggressiveness in pursuit of wage demands in mid-Victorian England see Marshall, Vogler, Rose, and Newby (1987:64). For an argument that there was a surge in industrial conflict after World War I that was stopped only by the great depression see Phelps Brown (1975).

7.   In a later publication Olson (1984:317) goes further and argues that the gains in production from an unexpected inflation will not typically match the losses from an unexpected deflation because the collective resistance to price increases in response to a rise in aggregate demand is likely to be much less than the resistance to a price cut during a deflation.

8.   He also, it should be clear, estimates his equations including a measure of

of relative backwardness as a way of testing for the presence of some "catch-up" process. There are good grounds for thinking that higher rates of economic growth are possible where a political unit has the option of importing technology from wealthier political units. Olson's measure is the deviation of per capita income in each state in each year from the average for all 48 states included in his test.

9. It should be noted, however, that in the same collection Hennart (1983) interprets France's postwar economic performance in a way that is much more sympathetic to Olson.

10. The development in the 1980s of a two tier wage structure in the U.S. airline industry is good evidence of the durability of the influence of a "distributional coalition" (Andriulaitis, 1986:57–59).

11. For data bearing on all this see Block (1977), Bellon and Niosi (1988), and Calleo (1987).

12. Although, as we will see, Keohane himself provides a set of quite different reasons for U.S. decline.

13. See Keohane (1980:150) and, particularly, Calleo (1982:chs. 3–5).

14. Note, however, that along with American hegemonic decline Gilpin incorporates within his "structural" category of explanations secular changes in world supply (exhaustion of cheap labor, a global shortage of capital, a slowing down of technological innovation) and demand (chronically excessive claims on the economy) conditions.

15. He cites Adam Smith (1937:653–659) as his authority for this statement. But Smith's treatment deals with the comparison between citizen and professional armies. The former involve negligible expense; the latter a considerable expense. Clearly, this tells us nothing about what has happened or will be happening during that substantial period of history since professional armies have become normal.

16. Notice that it is not nuclear weapons that increase the costs of defense. Their military attraction is, in fact, their relative cheapness as compared to alternative weapons. The source of the increasing costs is the maintenance of a capacity for waging conventional war parallel with a nuclear capability.

17. For a more rigorous analysis on these lines see Fitoussi and Phelps (1988).

18. There are, of course, other cases of hegemonic decline. Kennedy (1988) analyzes a number in detail. But all but the British and American cases involve undemocratic hegemons in a radically different military and economic context.

19. Note that there is also the possibility that the international authority and influence of a declining hegemon can be replaced by international cooperation (e.g., Keohane, 1984b:243–251). I take it, however, that the transitional difficulties involved in shifting from a hegemonic to a cooperative international regime are sufficiently difficult (if possible at all) that this would be more relevant to the prospects for long-run economic stability than to the explanation of the postwar inflation to this point. Kudrle and Bobrow (1990), however, do claim some modest evidence of effective economic cooperation through the G-7 summits and related negotiations.

5

WAGE-PUSH

In its North American version, economic orthodoxy tends to downplay the role of wages in the generation of inflation. In monetarist accounts (of either sort) nominal wages lag inflation, producing, in the short run, a lag in real wages. Wages do play a part in Keynesian accounts; their relative inflexibility underlies the Phillips curve and the macroeconomic options it has been thought to provide; the downward inflexibility of nominal wages *requires* a certain amount of inflation to allow real wages to adjust suitably to changes in the productivity of different kinds of labor. But in these orthodox economic accounts wage growth has not usually been used to explain the major accelerations of consumer prices across the postwar period. The exception to this is the work of Bruno and Sachs, to which I return later in this chapter.

Wage growth plays a central role in the explanations of inflation of three, rather ill-assorted, groups of writers. First, there are the impeccably conservative antecedents of many of today's monetarists. Writers such as Henry Simons (e.g., 1948:115), Melvin Reder (e.g., 1948:48–51), and Friedrich Hayek (e.g., 1960:272, 280–281) all argued that the growth of trade unionism, combined with the transformation of pricing as a result of market concentration or collusive arrangements between firms, would produce inflation. Unions would force up wages; this would cause a rise in unemployment to which, in the prevailing intellectual climate of the time that they were writing, governments would respond with inflationary, job-creating, deficits. Second, in more recent writings wage-push accounts of inflation have been stressed by generally much less conservative, and sometimes downright radical economists (e.g., Jackson, Turner, and Wilkinson, 1975; Moore, 1979; Rowthorn, 1977)[1] and in Sweden and elsewhere in a so-called "Scandinavian" model (e.g., Balassa, 1964; Aukrust, 1977; Calmfors, 1977). Third, and of particular interest for my purposes, wage-push plays the central role in the accounts of the postwar inflation advanced by most sociologists and political scientists.

In their review of theories of inflation Laidler and Parkin labeled all

wage-push accounts of inflation as "sociological," including those produced by fellow economists (1975:764). Whether post-Keynesians (or the
ghost of Henry Simons!) feel comfortable with that classification, the fact
is that whatever distinctive contribution to the explanation of the postwar inflation has been made by sociologists and political scientists is
tied, almost without exception, to the plausibility of a wage-push account. The "sociological" explanation of inflation stands or falls with
wage-push mechanisms.[2] Consequently, most of the rest of this book is
concerned, directly or indirectly, with theories of wage-push inflation
and the evidence presented in support of them. For convenience, I will
use the term "wage-push" to describe all of these accounts. However,
they can take a form that does not require an increase in wages but,
rather, an increase in unit labor costs produced by a slowdown or decline in productivity growth, in the context of wages growing at the
same rate as before. What I have in mind will become clear in the next
section.

The Mechanics of a Wage-Push

Forms of Wage-Push

The notion that underlies all wage-push processes is that there is an
increase in the relative power of workers in general, or of a large group
of workers, that has macroeconomically significant effects. This can take
a number of forms.

1.   The most straightforward form of wage-push, as an economically
distinctive phenomenon, involves the following: at any particular level
of demand for labor, wages increase by an amount in excess of what
would have occurred in the past.[3] In practice this means that, at some
point, wages were determined by normal competitive market processes
and tended to grow at approximately the same rate as labor productivity; after an increase in worker power they began to grow at a rate that
exceeded the rate of growth of labor productivity.

2.   The rate of growth of wages in response to an increase in the
demand for labor may be unchanged but wages may become less responsive to *decreases* in the demand for labor so that they fail to fall, or at
least to grow at a markedly slower rate, during recessions (e.g., Schott,
1984a:28–30).

3.   The wages of unionized workers may be affected but not the
wages of nonunion workers. Thus, unionized wages may be higher at
any given level of demand, or may become unresponsive during economic downturns, while the wages of nonunion workers remain un-

affected. This would imply, of course, a fall in the share of income going to capital in unionized firms. As we will see shortly, Simons claimed that this decline in the share of income going to capital is particularly likely to happen where production involves a heavy capital investment.

4.   The wages of unionized workers may be increased *at the expense* of nonunion workers. As unionized wages rise relative to nonunion wages, employment in the unionized sector falls and the displaced workers crowd into the nonunion sector where they force down wages (e.g., Johnson and Mieszkowski, 1970; O'Connor, 1973:25–29).

5.   Wages may grow at a rate that exceeds the rate of growth of productivity in industries not subject to international competition. This is the so-called "Scandinavian" model of inflation.[4] Its starting point is that the economy of a small country, heavily dependent on trade, can usefully be divided into "exposed" and "sheltered" sectors. Exposed industries (manufacturing, mining, agriculture) produce for world markets and are compelled to innovate at a rate that allows them to compete with foreign producers. Sheltered industries (construction, utilities, transport and communications, most services) are subject to less pressure to innovate. The result is that the rate of productivity growth in the exposed sector greatly exceeds the rate in the sheltered sector. Wages grow with productivity in the exposed sector. *But the rate of growth in wages produced by the high rate of growth in productivity in the exposed sector spills over into the sheltered sector.* The result is that, in the economy as a whole, average wages grow at a faster rate than productivity.

6.   The level of the total wage bill at any level of demand may be unaffected, but the distribution of wages may be changed. There is some evidence that unions tend to negotiate larger wage increases for lower skilled than for higher skilled workers. The effect of this is to produce an equalization of wages (Phelps Brown, 1977:328; Wood, 1978:182; Dell'Aringa and Lucifora, 1990:392–393).

7.   Wages may be unaffected but unit labor costs (in real terms) may rise either because unions obstruct technological change at the shop floor level or exercise effective political pressure to resist the displacement of labor from low to high productivity growth industries. With respect to the first factor, the literature claiming a "war at the workplace" is relevant (e.g., Rinehart, 1987:143–155; see also Metcalf, 1990:286–290). With respect to the second factor, Olson's (1982) arguments on "institutional sclerosis," discussed in Chapter 4, are relevant.

Note that each of these forms of wage-push may exist independently or in combination with others. With this in mind, how might processes of the kind described above produce an increase in inflation? It is worth dealing with them as three broad types of process.

First, there are those that involve increases in the nominal wages of workers. Wages for all workers (1), for unionized workers (3), or for sheltered sector workers (5) may rise at a rate that exceeds the rate of growth of productivity. There is considerable evidence, drawn from a wide array of countries, that prices are set as a mark-up on costs of production, including wage costs (Brown, 1985:333–335). A rise in wages would, then, produce a corresponding increase in prices. This does not, in itself, provide an explanation of inflation.

Other things being equal, an increase in prices will produce a fall in demand and the higher wages at the lower level of demand will produce falling profits.[5] If that happens, business will reduce investment and employment and *sooner or later* wages will be forced down again (see Jackson, Turner, and Wilkinson, 1975:3–6). Something else is necessary to produce a sustained inflation. There are two possible mechanisms. The government, on the basis of past experience, may recognize the threat to employment of a round of wage increases and offset the effect by using some combination of fiscal and monetary policy to stimulate demand (Rowthorn, 1977: especially pp. 229–235; also Weintraub, 1978:ch. 4). The effect of this will be to *validate* the wage increase. Alternatively, a round of wage increases may force employers to borrow to meet the greater cost of the wage bill. Doing so will put pressure on interest rates and disturb financial markets. If the central monetary authority is concerned "to maintain orderly conditions in the bond markets and stabilize market interest rates" (Moore, 1979:55) it is likely to respond by pursuing a stimulative (real interest rate reducing) monetary policy. Again, the effect would be to *validate* the wage increase and, to the extent repeated, produce a sustained inflation, but in this instance based on a preoccupation with interest rates rather than employment. In either mechanism the money supply becomes endogenous—responds, that is, to wages; the onset of unemployment in response to a wage increase is deferred; and a growth in wages is translated into a sustained growth in prices.

Second, there are processes that increase labor costs by reducing the efficiency of labor or, at least, the growth in the efficiency of labor, relative to the growth in wages. If one assumes that market determined wage differentials produce that particular supply of workers to different jobs that maximizes national output (of goods preferred by consumers), then a union/nonunion wage differential reflecting power rather than market forces (4) or a narrowing of the differential between skilled and unskilled workers (6) will mean lower output. For example, if unions reduce the premium for skills there are likely to be the sorts of bottle-necks in production associated with shortages of skilled workers widely reported in industrial societies in the later postwar period (e.g., Franke and Sobel, 1972; Dodge, 1977; Thomas and Deaton, 1977; Meltz, 1982). If unions force up the union/nonunion premium, then production will be lower than it would otherwise be in the kinds of manufacturing indus-tries where unions tend to be strong, which also tend to be high produc-tivity industries. Output will also be lower if union restrictive practices slow down the growth in productivity within plants or if union lobbying prevents the reallocating of resources from less to more productive in-dustries (7).

How can these processes be translated into inflation? All three have the effect of reducing productivity growth. If wage growth remains the same but productivity growth falls, then we have the same sort of wage-push/inflation links described above, involving government validation of wage-push to protect employment or to hold down interest rates. Even in wage growth falls, the decline in the relative international eco-nomic performance of a country may induce a government to experi-ment with policies designed to accelerate inflation. For example, if wages tend to lag during an unexpected inflation (as orthodox economic theories assume), then a government might be encouraged to use infla-tion to stimulate corporate profits, investment, and therefore growth. Inflation in this version might be produced because a government (or set of governments) in a country with a low growth rate is more likely to experiment with inflationary policies.

Finally, there is the link between downward inflexibility of wages and inflation (2). As we saw in Chapter 2, Keynesians tend to emphasize the downward inflexibility of wages and its implications for macroeconomic policy options. They argue that if unemployment is high governments cannot expect it to fall "naturally" from the pressure of excess labor on nominal wages. Instead, the right thing to do is to inflate so that nomi-nal wages rise but real wages fall. More generally, the need to adjust wages between high and low productivity sectors requires a persistent rate of inflation to allow real wage adjustments without a need to cut nominal wages. The downward inflexibility of wages, then, provides a rationale for generally inflationary policies, and, assuming sensible pol-icy makers (from a Keynesian point of view), an explanation for those policies.

This general link becomes particularly pertinent when an external shock—such as the commodity price shocks of the 1970s—reduces pro-ductivity and output in an economy. Assuming constant shares to labor, capital, and the other functional economic groups, a fall in output requires a reduction in real wages. But since nominal wages cannot be cut (it is assumed) the best way to reduce real wages is by inflating, because real wages tend to lag inflation.

This examination of the processes that might produce a wage-push inflation suggests two interim conclusions. First, in every account, a wage-push cannot produce inflation unless a government (or in the stability-in-money-markets version, a monetary authority) *validates* it. So any credible wage-push theory must include a theory of government and/or monetary authority behavior. Second, there are alternative and *contradictory* wage-push accounts. Some assume that an increase in wages causes governments or monetary authorities to respond to protect employment or interest rates. Others assume that wages lag inflation and that provides an opportunity that governments can exploit to stimulate growth and employment.

Social Bases

Why might a wage-push of one or the other kinds listed above take place? For sociological purposes there are two necessary elements. First, if you assume that behaviour is normatively constrained (and it is hard to imagine a sociological account that does not assume this), there has to be a reason why workers think that they ought to get more than they did in the past. Second, it is not enough for workers to want something; they must also have the power to make employers acquiesce to their demands for higher pay. Sociological accounts address the issues of both aspirations and power.

Several reasons are given for increasing *aspirations* of workers over the postwar period. There is a broad process of accommodation to the acquisitive values of capitalism (Crouch, 1978:227; Goldthorpe, 1978:199). This is an extension of Hirsch's (1976) analysis of the corrosive amorality of capitalist markets (discussed in Chapter 4). At some point in the past, it is argued, people's wants were limited by notions of what was customary and appropriate to a particular status. But the development of capitalism involves the creation of mass markets and the encouragement of people to consume an array of goods, independent of status; or, through advertising, encourages them to imagine themselves in higher statuses and to acquire the appropriate trappings (Galbraith, 1979; McKendrick, Brewer, and Plumb, 1982). Furthermore, according to Goldthorpe, normative limits on aspirations are most effectively embedded in the personal relations between people of different statuses within local communities. Industrialization and the urbanization that went with it have removed most of the population from the small communities where deference was reinforced by day-to-day interactions.

The claim that workers' aspirations have increased is also tied to changes in the composition of the working class (Salvati and Brosio, 1979:48). Over time the proportion marked—and intimidated—by direct experience of the great depression of the 1930s has fallen. Average levels of education have risen. For younger workers, simply having a job is no longer enough. One of the things that they demand, it is claimed, is more interesting work (Westley and Westley, 1971:118; Schrank and Stein, 1971:340; Rinehart, 1987:157–158). But the logic of capitalist production does not allow that so their grander aspirations are channelled into ever more ambitious (in fact, compensatory) wage demands. There is "a more or less anomic (or alienated) pressing of wage demands, wage bargaining as an outlet for aggression" (Lindberg, 1982:12).

What makes it possible for workers to translate their greater aspirations into larger wage increases? This is a question of *power*. There is, to start with, the sustained full employment of the first 25 or so years after the second world war. This shifted the balance of bargaining power to workers (Goldthorpe, 1974:429; Salvati and Brosio, 1979:49). In addition, workers have become increasingly organized (Maier, 1987:11). In most Western capitalist societies the percent unionized increased and in the bulk of them broadly social democratic parties consolidated the position they had established in the interwar period or built on it either to take power or become major components in coalition governments, or to become an opposition strong enough to influence policy (Korpi, 1983:31, 38). All this is part of what Goldthorpe describes as the "emergence of a mature working class" (1978:204). His point is that it is not just the development of organizations expressing working class interests that is at issue. Just as important is the fact that over time the working class has become increasingly self-recruiting. No longer significantly diluted by recruits from rural areas, the working class is now made up of people unrestrained by a carryover of attitudes to status learned in the areas from which migration took place. Most workers now regard unions as normal and appropriate vehicles for advancing their interests.

But the translation into accelerated inflation of grander aspirations and greater power requires that governments commit themselves to preventing the unemployment that the resultant wage-push would, sooner or later, cause. During the inflationary periods of the 1960s and 1970s why did they not simply allow market processes to take their course, produce greater unemployment, and in so doing reduce the rate of growth of nominal wages? A Keynesian economic response would be that sensible economic advisors managed to persuade governments that the loss of output and employment in a recession was too high a price to pay for whatever reduction in inflation could have been achieved. Goldthorpe's (1978:201–210) response was that the power and aspirations of the working class have ruled out deflation.

He argued that the extension of citizenship to the working class in the form of the franchise and the right of association set in motion a dynamic in which the content of the notion of citizenship expanded to include the *right to a job;* thus, "the new thrust of citizenship, in its on-going war with class, is specifically aimed against the idea, coeval with capitalism, of labour as a commodity" (Goldthorpe, 1978:203). So what would happen if a government chose to flout this emerging conception of citizenship? According to Goldthorpe "not only severe electoral punishment, as opportunity for this arises, but more immediately, perhaps, a loss of trade-union cooperation in economic policy making and implementation, and direct industrial and political action in the form of strikes, sit-ins, factory takeovers, mass demonstrations etc." (Goldthorpe, 1978:204).[6] Given the greater power of the working class, in other words, the price of a deflation would be disorder not far short of chaos. Inflationary policies are attractive to governments, then, because they constitute a less politically threatening option: "inflation has the advantage of tending to diffuse the efforts of organized labour: a 'wages free-for-all' encourages sectionalism rather than solidarity" (Goldthorpe, 1978:208).[7]

Economic Bases

There are some accounts by economists of the postwar inflation that treat changing aspirations as an explanatory factor. But they tend to have a distinctly ad hoc and unconvincing character (e.g., Wiles, 1973).[8] It is probably fair to say that by training and inclination economists are not well equipped to deal with normative factors in behaviour.[9] Economic accounts are generally characterized by the assumption that people maximize something or other and usually, in practice, that they maximize income. These accounts therefore typically assume that the aspirations of workers do not change much—that all that changes is the power available to them to realize their omnipresent aspiration to maximize their income. Even within the narrowing confines of this assumption, there are a number of factors that can be said to have produced a wage-push.[10]

There are factors that have increased the bargaining power of workers. Full employment is one. Just as important is the confidence that the government can be expected to intervene to maintain full employment in the future. The commitment to full employment that became an element of the politics of all the rich capitalist industrial societies after the second world war meant that workers did not have to worry that pushing their wages up to uncompetitive levels might cost them their jobs; they could be confident that the government would take whatever measures would be necessary to keep unemployment low.[11] Furthermore, in many countries the legal position of organized labor improved and labor law was more likely than not to move in directions that strengthened the protections against dismissal of workers.[12] Independent of changes in labor law, in most countries, workers could more readily run the risk of a strike or personal dispute with an employer. Higher levels of income mean that they have had the opportunity to accumulate savings to finance themselves during a strike or period of unemployment and the existence of a fairly well-established set of welfare programs provides a minimum protection for their families in either circumstance.

The power of unions has been further increased because of trends in industrial organization that have made particular disputes much more generally disruptive and, because of that, much more liable to induce government intervention. Firm size has increased and when a large firm closes down due to an industrial dispute the ramifications for the surrounding community are correspondingly large. Production is increasingly broken down into consecutive stages with different plants or sections within plants specializing in one or another stage. This produces a pattern of interdependency that means that a work stoppage in one plant, or even section of a plant, can disrupt the flow of work and sometimes stop production in much of an entire industry. The more widely felt the effects within a community or an industry, the more likely it is that governments will be intimidated by the extent of disruption and, depending on the political situation, they may pressure employers to concede.

Employers are more likely to concede both because of increasing vulnerability to labor and, in some instances, because the costs of concession are negligible.

There are several sources of growing vulnerability: in particular, the increasing interdependencies discussed above, an increasing concentration of production in large, costly, production facilities, and a growing dependence on international markets. Where there is a high degree of interdependence of a production process within a single firm, either within a large plant or across a number of plants belonging to the firm, the bargaining power of the workers involved vis-á-vis their employer is increased. Employers are also made vulnerable where they have sunk a great deal of capital into a particular production facility (say, for example, an integrated steel mill). Where a very large investment was neces-

sary to establish a plant its owners have effectively foreclosed the option
of shutting it down in response to rapidly growing labor costs until the
capital costs have been amortized (see Simons, 1948:131). Finally, according to Phelps Brown (1983:154), keeping export markets requires, above
all, meeting delivery dates. So where export markets are involved employers are under strong pressure to concede to wage demands.

In some situations, however, concession is more or less costless. First,
increasing product market concentration (associated to a substantial extent with the trend toward product differentiation) increases the ease
with which producers can pass on cost increases to their clients (see also
Crouch, 1978:224). Second, even where there is a significant number of
producers in an industry the development of industry-wide wage bargaining means that wage increases are common across the industry and
therefore excluded as a source of price differentials between producers.
Third, the importance of the government as employer has increased
and, in the short and perhaps medium run at least, the government has
a bottomless purse out of which to pay for increased wages for its employees (Hanson, 1978:28–29).

So, the argument is that trends that are fairly general across capitalist
societies have strengthened the bargaining position of workers, in some
cases weakened the bargaining position of their employers and in others
rendered them indifferent to increasing wage costs, and have created a
situation in which the government is often likely to interfere in disputes
on the side of workers. One can find in the literature, then, both social
and economic sources of a wage-push. Interestingly, the sociological
analyses of inflation almost entirely ignore the economic sources listed
above (the effects of a growth in concentration are an exception). I will
consider the implications of this later in the chapter. First, however, how
good is the evidence that any of these social and economic processes
thought to produce inflation has actually occurred? Second, how good is
the evidence indicating that wage-push is a source of inflation?

The Evidence

A starting point for any wage-push account is the observation that the
institutional details of wage setting do not coincide with the assumptions of orthodox neoclassical economics (Phelps Brown, 1983:153;
Phelps Brown and Hopkins, 1981:153; Cripps, 1977:108; Flanagan,
Soskice, and Ulman, 1983:29–30; Brown, 1985:275). The labor market is
not made up of a large number of small employers and individual workers with each party on one side carefully appraising the advantages of

entering into a contract implying some wage rate with one or another party on the other side. It is made up of employing organizations that vary greatly in size in which, in some industries in all countries, one or a small number of employers dominates production and sometimes dominates prices and wage rates. It is also made up (to varying degrees in different countries) of workers grouped into unions on various bases. The form and content of contracts are substantially regulated by labor law. We know that the wage-setting practice of large employers frequently involves monitoring wages paid by comparable employers rather than any attempt to directly estimate the overall balance of supply and demand in the particular local labor market where their plants are located.[13] Finally, labor is decidedly nonhomogeneous; the recruitment and training of workers involve considerable costs that make employers reluctant to discharge workers that they have hired and trained, which produces labor hoarding.

This is a perfectly reasonable starting point but it does not show that the postwar inflation originated in a wage-push. After all, many of these characteristics of the wage-setting process are not new; they have been more or less omnipresent throughout the postwar period and many of them to some degree extend back to the interwar period. But sustained inflation across the capitalist world is a postwar phenomenon and its acceleration largely concentrated in the period from the mid-1960s. To properly appraise claims that a wage-push explains the postwar inflation it is necessary to examine the evidence bearing specifically on the mechanisms thought to have produced that wage-push and on the evidence on the specific form of any link between wages and prices. Consider, first, the evidence bearing on the economic mechanisms thought to produce a wage-push.

Economic Bases: (1) The General Context

During the postwar period unemployment did remain low, until the very end of the 1970s. As compared to the interwar period there is no question; the lower level of unemployment would have increased the bargaining power of labor, both individually and in the organized form involved in trade union membership. It is likely that workers' attitudes were affected by their experience of full employment. Whether as individuals or when voting on whether or not to ratify a contract negotiated by their unions, most workers in (say) 1969 would surely not have been greatly concerned that they might price themselves out of employment.[14]

Furthermore, although the pattern varied, in most rich capitalist countries programs providing fairly generous unemployment benefits had been established by the middle of the postwar period.[15] Even if some workers did price themselves out of a job or, by their aggressiveness, induced their employer to find some way of firing them, they would have had a reasonable level of unemployment insurance benefits to fall back on in a number of industrial countries.

It is also true that the legal position of labor strengthened in several capitalist countries. This can be shown very clearly in the case of Britain (e.g., Lewis, 1983; Hepple, 1983; Meade, 1982:ch. 5)—until the onset of Mrs. Thatcher! In France and Italy the upheavals of the late 1960s brought substantial legislative gains for labor (Bruno and Sachs, 1985:168; Brandini, 1975; Templeman, 1981:14). In Canada, the federal government and some of the provincial governments legislated during the 1960s to facilitate public sector unionization (Carter, 1982:36–37) and most jurisdictions improved union security (Muir, 1975:103). In broad terms, other countries made legal advances from the interwar to the postwar period, in an extreme form with the reconstruction of the framework of labor relations in Germany Italy, Japan, and Austria, and in less extreme forms in other countries. Only in the United States is their evidence of a deterioration of the relative legal position of labor from the interwar to the postwar period. The Taft-Hartley act (1947) stands out in this respect. Along with a number of related statutes it prohibited the closed shop and introduced other restrictions on union activities, including strikes and boycotts (Burtt, 1979:276–287). With the exception of the United States, it is fairly clear that legal trends have tended to increase the probability of some sort of wage-push.

Full employment and the law, then, have tended to reinforce the position of labor in general and organized labor in particular. The other factors mentioned in wage-push interpretations advanced by economists are much more dubious. Take, first of all, the case of personal savings, unemployment insurance, and social welfare payments, as incentives to strike. It is true, of course, that since the second world war most of the unionized population earns an income well above the starvation level. Consequently workers could, *in principle*, accumulate a solid financial reserve to be drawn on in a struggle with an employer. However, there is some evidence that, *in practice*, rising incomes are associated with rising debt (e.g., Eastwood, 1985:257)—particularly, the debt involved in purchasing a home (and in some countries a country cottage). Quite a lot of workers spend much of their lives in debt. Their debts combined with the standard of living to which they have become accustomed, which requires a steady flow of income, provide a considerable disincentive to engage in a prolonged strike.

The effect on striking of welfare payments has been a major preoccupation in Britain. The families of strikers in Britain are entitled to receive "supplementary benefit" from the government and it has been claimed that this allows workers to strike more often and for longer than they would otherwise. It is certainly true that many British strikers have claimed supplementary benefits. But detailed research on how particular strikers financed themselves showed that supplementary benefit constituted a minor part of the income of strikers. This is because the amounts involved are quite small and because entitlement usually began 2 weeks into a strike (Gennard, 1977; Gennard and Lasko, 1975). Furthermore, Clegg (1979:283) has pointed out that public provision of funds to strikers is not a uniquely postwar phenomenon and that the generosity of the amounts involved had not much increased since 1956. The evidence for supplementary benefit-induced strikes is not strong in the British case and I am not aware of any stronger evidence that has been presented for other countries.

Economic Bases: (2) Firm and Industry-Specific Effects

The growth in the size of government is an indisputable trend in the postwar period. This has meant a growth in the proportion of the labor force employed by the government. Is the government a particularly soft touch for unionized workers? It is very hard to know. Answering the question depends on comparing the remuneration of jobs in the private and public sectors. There have been many attempts to do so but the process is fraught with difficulties. Many jobs are not comparable; it is difficult to quantify the importance of pace of work; it is clear that public employment usually brings greater job security, but how much that is worth is less clear (Christensen, 1980:10–11).

The published research on public/private sector pay differentials, then, does not inspire overwhelming confidence. In fact, conclusions vary from study to study. Hammermesh (1975) compared the private and public sector earnings of three sets of unionized workers in the United States and found no difference for two of the groups and a 12% premium for public sector workers in the third. Christensen reports that during the early 1960s public sector pay in Canada probably lagged the private sector, but subsequently overtook it (Christensen, 1980:12–22). Davies (1983:444–445) reports that differentials in Britain tended to fluctuate widely. During the incomes policies that punctuated the pre-Thatcher period in Britain public sector wages were most severely affected but tended to rise dramatically after the incomes policies were taken off. Evidence from other countries is similarly mixed. But, overall, it does not suggest that there has been a general tendency for public sector salaries to rise relative to private sector salaries during the period of accelerating inflation.

The claim that increasing product market concentration (partly based on greater product differentiation) provides a basis for less stringent policies on the part of employers is similarly dubious. Take the case of the United States, for instance. It has been widely observed that concentration ratios tended to rise through the postwar period (Allen, 1976; Shepherd, 1979). But these concentration ratios ignore imports. They also ignore deregulation. When imports and deregulation are taken into account the evidence points overwhelmingly to an *increase* in competition (Shepherd, 1982). Data for other countries tend to be less complete. But what exists suggests that something similar has gone on. The growth of large firms has produced greater concentration of output *within* countries. But national concentration ratios have become increasingly meaningless. The reduction of tariffs associated with the European Economic Community, the European Free Trade Area, and consecutive rounds of the General Agreement on Tariffs and Trade have greatly increased competition. On balance, the case is overwhelming, I think, that the amount of competition confronted by firms in capitalist industrial countries has greatly increased.

What about the importance of delivery dates in exports? Do they compel employers to concede? Perhaps, but there is another offsetting factor. For the increase in trade seems to have been accompanied by an increase in the mobility of capital. As stable political conditions spread throughout all of the rich world and significant parts of the third world it is ever more common for large corporations to have plants to which they can shift production in response to a work stoppage in a particular country. And if there is a prolonged period of labor unrest it is relatively easy *in some industries* to close down production altogether in the country involved and move it elsewhere (Bluestone and Harrison, 1982; Perrucci et al., 1988:20–43). This is clearly not the case where a plant construction (or mine development) required a substantial investment. But it is possible in many other industrial contexts and it is a threat that seems to have become more acute since the second world war. Even if the tyranny of export order delivery dates forces concessions, the option of capital mobility in many industries is likely to stiffen the spines of the relevant employers.

Perhaps, then, it is the growth of industry-wide bargaining, removing wage differentials as a cost factor discriminating between employers, that makes the difference? But, once again, the growth of international competition means that industry-wide bargaining within a single nation (and that is the only way it is organized at present) is increasingly irrelevant. If the same set of wage increases were to be negotiated throughout the steel industry in Germany that would not much reduce the competitive pressures on German steel producers since they increasingly originate in Italy, or Japan, or Korea, or elsewhere. Besides, a country with one of the worst inflation records during the postwar period, namely Britain, experienced a collapse of industry-wide bargaining and that collapse is often associated with Britain's apparent wage control difficulties (Clegg, 1979:12–19).

Finally, what about the effects on the power of workers of scale and technological interdependence? There may be something to this. A small group of workers in a part of a sequentially arranged production process within a single plant can close the entire plant down. In the early 1970s some Italian trade unions effectively exploited this possibility with *"scioperi articolati"* in which groups of workers in a single plant consecutively stopped work (Aaron, 1972:93). Air traffic controllers, maintenance workers in power stations, and port workers can paralyze a modern industrial nation. They do have immense power. Yet what is striking is the extent to which the power of small groups within a single plant or key groups in an entire economy is institutionally remediable. The Italian *"scioperi articolati"* were made possible by a labor law that, in most instances, prohibited lock-outs. Employers did not have the option of freely responding to half-hearted work or consecutive stoppages by work groups by closing down a plant. In North America they can and the result is that such disruption is relatively uncommon. Similarly, while air traffic controllers can paralyze a nation's communications, it is also possible for a determined government to disband their union and send its leaders to prison, as the Reagan administration did in 1981 (Shostak and Skocik, 1986). The point is not, of course, that it is possible for every government to act in such a way (although few commentators thought that Margaret Thatcher could do what she did, before she did it!). The point is that it is not the technology itself that makes the difference but rather the legal framework within which the technology exists. And legal frameworks are by no means immutable. The same general point applies to the effects of growth in scale. Governments may feel impelled to put an end to an industrial dispute involving a large number of workers in order to protect some wider community interest. But there is no reason why they *have* to intervene on behalf of the workers involved. Indeed, during the 1980s, there is some evidence that governments intervened increasingly on behalf of employers (e.g., Panitch and Swartz, 1988). It is not the technology that determines the form of the intervention; it is the political preferences and the political will of the government.

Social Bases: (1) Aspirations

There is, as I observed in Chapter 4, not much evidence of a decline in normative restraint. There have always been interest groups. Strikes, boycotts, and violence are not in the least unique to postwar labor history. It is true that the amount of disruption in labor relations increased during the late 1960s and 1970s; but it is not clear that they increased to historically unprecedented levels. Phelps Brown (1975), for example, has argued that what was involved in the 1960s was a return to the levels of conflict of the period immediately after the first world war. In fact, for almost all capitalist industrial societies, rates of industrial conflict during the 1960s were generally *below* those reached in the early interwar period (see Paldum and Pederson, 1984). It could be argued that this fact is quite consistent with the collapse in normative restraint that is at the heart of Goldthorpe's account, because capitalism had already by the beginning of the first world war undermined the norms of deference that underpinned restraint. It would follow from this that, had it not been for the great depression, capitalism would have become *generally*, and intolerably, inflationary much earlier, as it did indeed in Germany, France, and several other countries in the 1920s.[16]

This is possible, but the evidence on status hierarchies provided to support the argument is actually rather mixed. It comes from a paper by Goldthorpe and Bevan (1977) on Britain. They cite some ethnographies reporting a status order that "as a structure of morally-grounded inequality, . . . serves to legitimate the, often extreme, forms of economic and political inequality and domination which co-ordinate with it" (Goldthorpe and Bevan, 1977:303). But they also cite some studies that report generally conflictual relationships within local communities (pp. 303–304). They provide no evidence that the integrated form is the more typical. And later in their paper they express some skepticism about the sorts of studies they use as evidence of integration, or the lack of it, in rural communities. Thus, "the parallel attempt to draw on the 'fieldwork' methods of social anthropology in the investigation of class and status relations has been generally less successful, since the methods in question are restricted in their applicability to relatively small-scale social situations and have in any event always lacked an adequate statement of either their basic *rationale* or their specific procedures" (Goldthorpe and Bevan, 1977:317). The point is that the rather cautious treatment of the available evidence in the 1977 paper becomes transformed into something like an empirical certainty in Goldthorpe's 1978 paper on inflation. And the fragility of the underpinning evidence is obscured even further in the (widespread) uses of Goldthorpe's paper in subsequent writings on the subject. In a recent attempt to find evidence of the decay of status orders Roche (1990:202–203) cites the numerous studies documenting difficult labor relations and pay bargaining in Britain. But this, of course, involves a transparently circular line of reasoning.

It is not so much that there is evidence directly contradicting the "normative restraint" component of recent analyses of inflation; it is rather that there is precious little evidence in support of it.[17] Goldthorpe cites only British evidence. The evidence he cites does not really support his claim. And in other European countries there is fairly good evidence of fairly persistently antagonistic rural relations, going back quite a long way (e.g., Hamilton, 1967:128–130). The normatively integrated rural community (extended into small towns) does not seem to have been a particularly common phenomenon.[18]

The claim that young workers, better educated and unmarked by the great depression, have greater aspirations, is, on the whole, contradicted by the best available evidence. The *systematic* evidence typically cited in support of this claim shows that younger workers report higher levels of job dissatisfaction than older workers (e.g., Quinn et al., 1974). But this higher level of young worker dissatisfaction is consistent with *either* a generational effect or with a "life cycle" effect. That is to say, it is possible either that young workers are more likely to be discontented because they tend to expect more than their elders or it is possible that they are discontented because, being at the start of their careers, they have objectively worse jobs. Using U.S. data Wright and Hamilton have provided the most careful examination of this question. They found, first, that education and job satisfaction were unrelated among blue-collar workers, which raises some doubts about a hypothesis to the effect that education increases work dissatisfaction (1979:66; see also Martin and Shehan, 1989); second, that over time younger workers have been persistently relatively dissatisfied with their work, which poses serious problems for a "generational effect" (Wright and Hamilton, 1978:1148–1152); third, that the distribution of aspirations with respect to work over the life cycle is consistent with a model in which, in their youth, workers are most concerned with the prospects attached to a particular job and therefore often put themselves in jobs that in terms of income or conditions are "bad" but that contain the promise of future movement to something better (Wright and Hamilton, 1978:1148–1152; see also Taveggia and Ross, 1978; Glenn, Taylor, and Weaver, 1977). These results do not suggest a younger generation that is distinctly aggressive. They suggest a younger generation with about the same preoccupations as earlier generations; most of them seek jobs that, although often bad, promise to lead to something better.[19]

The claim that aggression generated by increasingly alienating work gets displaced into, and takes the form of, ever more ferocious wage demands will not do either. Since Braverman's (1974) classic treatment there have been a large number of studies purporting to show that the logic of capitalism produces increasingly fragmented, dull, and oppressive work (e.g., Clawson, 1980; Crompton and Reid, 1982). More careful subsequent research tends to show no clear trend in skill levels, with as many instances of upgrading as downgrading (Littler, 1982; Penn, 1982; Adler, 1985; Spenner, 1979, 1983).

Neither is there any clear evidence that the degree of "alienation" among workers has increased. There is controversy over the matter; but responses to questions on work satisfaction are sometimes seen as indicators of the presence or absence of alienation. Hamilton and Wright (1986:219–272) have reviewed the relevant data for the United States and report rather confused results. Some studies do show declines in work satisfaction from the 1960s to the 1970s but most do not. Even if one rejects work satisfaction data, as some writers do (e.g., Rinehart, 1978), the relevant behavioral data do not clearly support an inference of rising alienation. The amount of industrial conflict did, of course, rise during the 1960s and 1970s in all western capitalist societies. There is also some evidence of rising quit rates and absenteeism (see Hamilton and Wright, 1986:274–279). But the incidence of all three phenomena tends to increase as the rate of unemployment falls, and unemployment was generally low during the 1960s and first few years of the early 1970s.[20]

That the rate of industrial conflict tended to continue to rise or remain high as the rate of unemployment rose during the mid 1970s is not surprising. First, high rates of inflation also tend to produce higher rates of industrial conflict and inflation, as we saw, accelerated rapidly during the mid-1970s. Second, both monetarist and Keynesian analyses assume that the labor market responses of workers tend to lag actual conditions. If workers' price expectations are (adaptively) based on past prices one would expect them to continue striking at a higher than usual level beyond the point at which the unemployment rate stopped falling, or started to rise. Third, during the 1970s, for various reasons, taxes tended to rise so that the take-home pay of employees did not rise as rapidly as their wage rate. There are good grounds for thinking that this was a source of increases in industrial conflict in a significant number of Western industrial countries (Flanagan, Soskice, and Ulman, 1983:657–660).[21]

Finally, what about the claim that workers' conception of citizenship has expanded to include the right to a job so that, when combined with greater worker power, deflationary macroeconomic policies have been precluded? Here Goldthorpe (1978:201–204) did not even make a stab at providing systematic evidence in support of his argument. He simply asserts that this is so. Now, there is little question but that during the first 25 years or thereabouts after the second world war workers became accustomed to full employment. They probably came to *expect* it. That this might have been so is a common enough argument that is also made, as a matter of fact, by a number of economists. But Goldthorpe is at pains to distinguish his version. Thus:

> In other words, it is not sufficient, in seeking to explain the force of resistance to such measures, simply to invoke changes in expectations created by two decades or more of virtually full employment following the Second World War. Workers' expectations that they will not be exposed to unemployment, or at least not of a widespread and long-term kind, have to be seen as ones which by now have *normative* and not merely *empirical* grounding—as ones relating to rights and not just to probabilities. (1978:203)

It is surely quite reasonable to argue that workers believe that they ought not to be unemployed—that there is, in short, a normative component to their attitude to the phenomenon. What is less clear is that workers ever thought differently. Indeed, I suspect (speculating right along with Goldthorpe) that this judgment had something to do with the rise of socialist parties in Western Europe. But it does not follow that because they believe unemployment unjust they do not resign themselves to it when it becomes endemic. In other words, where no practicable alternative course of action is available, even normatively colored judgments tend not to lead to protest. Barrington Moore (1978) showed this brilliantly in his *Injustice.* So I doubt that it is the presence of a distinctive normative judgment about unemployment that distinguishes the postwar from the prewar (and Goldthorpe, let it be clear, provides not a shred of evidence to contradict this view). The real issue is, was there a power shift after World War II that allowed workers to make governments take their normative judgment into account?

Social Bases: (2) Power

After the second world war unions and social democratic parties were stronger in most Western countries than they had been before it. Because they grew the unions had more resources at their disposal when they tried to influence government policy. When social democratic parties held office the unions dealt with governments that were generally receptive to their policy preferences. Thus, in Sweden there has been considerable overlap in policy formation between the unions and the SDP (Gourevitch, et al., 1984:193–194). In Britain, the unions scuttled an attempt to legislate restrictions on their behavior during the first Wilson government (Smith 1982:316) and extracted substantial legislative concessions under a later one and under the Callaghan government that succeeded it (Lewis, 1983:373–375; Hepple, 1983:408–410). Something

similar happened when the German SDP achieved office within a Christian Democratic led coalition government in 1966 and, subsequently,
became the dominant coalition partner in 1969 (Gourevitch et al.,
1984:133–141). Even where social democratic parties did not hold office
their presence as a viable electoral alternative (as well as, in the earlier
period in particular, a communist presence) put pressure on conservative governments to treat labor with some caution. This, then, was a
clear source of increasing working class power.

   In general one can assume that, given their principal constituencies,
both unions and social democratic parties are a source of pressure for
full employment policies. Hibbs (1977:1472) provided some evidence
that this was so during the 1960s. Countries such as Sweden, Finland,
Norway, Denmark, and the Netherlands, with mainly or entirely socialist governments in the period, had markedly lower unemployment
than did the United States and Canada, neither of which has ever been
governed by a party of the left. The generally low unemployment rates
of these countries persisted into the later postwar period. To the extent
that emphasizing full employment introduces an inflationary bias to
policies, the increase in the strength of unions and the left from the
interwar to the postwar period is a source of increased inflation, a source
that can be reasonably described as originating in greater working class
power. Indeed, as Hibbs showed, the five low unemployment countries
listed above did have relatively high rates of inflation (although not
conspicuously so in the case of Norway).

   But Goldthorpe's (influential) sociological account of the postwar inflation goes beyond this. For him it is not simply a question of the
political coloration of the party in government. For Goldthorpe, the crux
of the matter is that the "maturity" of the working class—its habituation
to unions and to the notion of a collective interest to be advanced[22]—
precludes deflationary policies of any magnitude because such policies
would threaten disorder, of a fairly (but not revolutionary) kind. There
are, however, some serious difficulties with this argument.

   First, there is the question of the attitudes of workers toward unions.
The "maturation thesis" argues that workers come to regard unions as
right and proper instruments in the advancement of their interests. Yet
as Batstone (1984:319) pointed out, much of the labor force is not unionized in Britain (and elsewhere) and the part that is unionized has social
ties likely to weaken their commitment to unions (parents who were not
members of unions, upwardly mobile children). Not surprisingly, the
survey data on workers' attitudes toward unions reveal a widespread
ambivalence toward them, particularly when they forcefully exercise
their power. In Canada there is clear evidence of widespread antipathy
toward unions and union leaders *among members of union households* and

the incidence of antipathy increased during the time of increased industrial disputes at the end of the 1960s. In fact, by 1976, 60% of respondents in union households thought that too many union leaders were
trouble-makers and in 1972 almost three-quarters of blue-collar workers
favored additional restrictions on the right to strike (Smith, 1978:466–
469). Nor is this simply a question of a perverse result originating in a
country with a weak tradition of trade unionism. There is evidence of
widespread antipathy toward unions in Britain (which contains Goldthorpe's paradigmatic mature working class!), an antipathy that is quite
widely shared by union members themselves (e.g., Clemens, 1983:62–
63) and that increases whenever unions exercise their power by striking
(Edwards and Bain, 1988). Furthermore, along with the rest of the working class, union members have increasingly voted for parties other than
the Labour party and in 1979 and 1983 about a third of them voted for
Margaret Thatcher (Minkin, 1986:202; Webb, 1987).[23] The irreducible fact
is that many union members in Britain, Canada, and elsewhere are
considerably more ambivalent about the institutions to which they pay
dues than one would expect if Goldthorpe's "working class maturity"
thesis were correct.

Second, the premise of Goldthorpe's argument is that governments
eschewed deflationary policies because unemployment constitutes a
more serious threat to order than accelerating inflation. He argues that
inflation tends to exacerbate the sectionalist tendencies within the working class as groups of workers get caught in a spiral of competitive wage
claims. Unemployment, however, which is disproportionately concentrated among blue-collar workers, further exposes the illegitimate moral
bases of capitalism and their particular class form. This premise is, I
would argue, wildly implausible.[24]

Consider the two broad policy options at the disposal of governments
in relatively democratic societies for determining the general experience
and capacity for action of workers. One of the options is to pursue a
tight money, deflationary, policy that would generate some bankruptcies
and a more or less prolonged spell of above normal unemployment. The
other option would be to pursue a full employment policy as far as
possible, using expansionary credit policies to maintain tight labor markets. The resulting inflation would require the occasional use of incomes
policies since inflation tends to be politically unpopular.[25]

Which of these options would be likely to generate the most serious
threat to social peace? Take the effects of full employment policy first of
all. Full employment itself tends to increase workers' propensity to strike
because it increases their bargaining power (e.g., Ashenfelter and Johnson, 1969; Pencavel, 1970; Smith, 1979b, 1981).[26] If the policy of full
employment produces accelerating inflation it is likely to produce great-

er discontent in a number of ways. Inflation, for example, requires the constant renegotiation of wage levels. Consequently, a structure of wage differentials that was formerly to a greater or lesser extent sanctioned by custom is continuously put into question by the need under inflationary conditions to frequently negotiate *substantial* wage changes. The result is that "issues which had seemed closed have to be reopened" (Hicks, 1974:79; see also Hyman and Brough, 1975:47–61). The general level of discontent is also likely to be heightened by the fact that under rapid inflationary conditions, at any given time, most people's incomes will be perceptibly falling. Even if, say, annual pay awards mean that the long-term trend of their incomes keeps up with or goes ahead of inflation, at any given time, most people will experience their income as in decline. Thus, "almost everybody can sincerely feel *his* real income is falling when *average* real incomes are rising" (Jackson, Turner, and Wilkinson, 1975:39).

So, even if the resulting discontents are diffuse, focusing on one or another salient pay comparison rather than on the question of the relative shares of capital and labor, the net result is likely to be a generally higher level of discontent than would be obtained under stable prices. At the least that means that the government would find it hard to get reelected. It might also mean the pursuit of wage gains with considerable aggressiveness and accompanying disorder.

The whole problem is compounded when an attempt is made to deal with inflation through an incomes policy. To start with, incomes policies tend to fail outright (e.g., Lipsey and Parkin, 1970; Brittan and Lilley, 1977; Flanagan, Soskice, and Ulman, 1983:688) or produce rather modest results (e.g., Wilton, 1984).[27] Typically, they produce a temporary restraint of wage and price increases followed by a subsequent surge that incorporates the trend rate of increase in addition to the increases foregone during the time the incomes policy was enforced. More importantly, however, the single most obvious effect of an incomes policy is to politicize class relations; it replaces the apparent neutrality of the market process of wage determination with a process in which political organization is critical and the relative shares of capital and labor inevitably come to the fore. That is, as a matter of fact, one of the grounds on which incomes policies have been criticized (Lipsey, 1976).

Now compare all this with the other method for dealing with the broad problem of class relations, through the use of monetary restraint and unemployment. Let us assume, also, that the problem is compounded by the fact that the government decides to deflate after an inflationary episode.[28] Monetary restraint following an inflationary period is likely to generate some bankruptcies as marginal firms surviving on credit no longer find that credit available. Other firms will cut back production as aggregate demand falls. This will throw some workers out of their jobs and make them decidedly unhappy. But *most* workers will not become unemployed and those that do are likely to be concentrated within particular areas and within particular categories (in particular among those with least seniority). *Here* is a basis for segmentation within the working class. In addition, throwing people out of work severs them from that organizational base that is indispensable if people are to protest effectively, for the most important organizational basis for most union movements is the workplace and the social relations it involves.[29] All this is to say that a high unemployment policy is neither likely to unite working class opposition, since the incidence of unemployment tends to be concentrated within rather delimited parts of the labor force, nor to provide a very general or effective basis for political protest, because its effect is to undercut workers' organizational base (Bradley and Gelb, 1980).

The answer to the question I raised above as to "which of these options would be likely to generate the most serious threat to social peace?" should by now be quite clear. Full employment increases the strength and aggressiveness of the working class. An incomes policy provides a common focus of concern across the working class. It provides a basis for class unity in opposition and raises the whole question of the relative shares of capital and labor. At the same time, the organizational basis of working class resistance, the trade union movement, remains largely intact. If, then, a government above all wishes to secure social peace and to diffuse class solidarity, I submit that it would be considerably wiser to deflate the economy and put some people out of work than maintain full employment and use an incomes policy to restrain prices.

Third, and finally, there is the question of events since Goldthorpe wrote his (widely cited) analysis. During the early 1980s unemployment rose dramatically throughout the capitalist world including, and spectacularly, in Britain. What happened to the power of the working class? Why did it not force governments to bring back full employment? Did it suddenly lose its "maturity?" Moreover, the increase did not produce anything remotely like the range of disorders that Goldthorpe predicted. Indeed, for the most part, industrial relations cooled down throughout Western capitalist societies with the incidence of strikes falling as unemployment rose, exactly as the bargaining power model would predict (Brown, 1990:219–221).

Where then does this leave us with respect to the social bases of an increase in the bargaining power of workers? Full employment did increase worker bargaining power in capitalist countries into the middle of the 1970s. This full employment was in some countries *in part* based on the greater political influence of social democratic parties and unions, as compared to the interwar period. But social democratic parties have to get elected or reelected.[30] That has meant they have had to come to grips with very high, and very unpopular, rates of inflation. As a result, during the 1970s they were almost as likely as governments of the right to pursue deflationary policies.[31]

I would argue that the greater predisposition of social democratic governments to pursue full employment, somewhat inflationary, policies rested on rather wide popular consensus about the importance of minimizing unemployment. In the case of Britain, for example, support for greater attention to unemployment *rallied a majority of all classes* in the 1960s (Smith, 1982:304–307), and the fact that the majority was larger among blue-collar workers does not change this fact.[32] So social democratic governments could pursue full employment policies because inflation was not as salient a concern for most of the electorate—not just for the working class. But the rise in inflation during the 1970s reversed this. The consensus on the primary importance of keeping unemployment low evaporated and social democratic parties changed their policies accordingly.

This puts a wage-push account based on the rise in political influence of social democratic parties and unions in a somewhat different light. The power of unions to produce wage increases that governments then ratified with inflationary policies ultimately rested on a broad political consensus that full employment was a primary concern. When that consensus evaporated, so did the power. For it was absolutely not a concern with political order that produced inflationary policies.

Direct Evidence of a Wage-Push

So far in this chapter I have assumed that it can be clearly shown that a wage-push (in one of the senses defined above) took place. This, of course, contradicts those accounts that I have described as "orthodox" since they assert that wages tend to lag prices. Consider now the evidence directly bearing on this. I will deal with this evidence in three parts: first, the evidence on wage inflexibility; second, the evidence directly bearing on the existence of a wage-push; and third, the evidence bearing on productivity changes and their likely effects on inflation.

Wage Inflexibility

The issue here is, are nominal wages sufficiently inflexible to encourage real output growth in response to a demand stimulus but to produce rather durable unemployment in response to a recession? The evidence, in a variety of forms, is quite overwhelming that nominal wages are significantly unresponsive to changes in demand. First, in numerous equations, covering a number of different countries and time periods, unemployment—the measure of demand most relevant to wages— turns out to be weakly or insignificantly related to wage growth (Laidler and Parkin, 1975:706; Wood, 1978:206; Blanchard, 1987:72; Brown, 1985:256). The interpretation of this result is not straightforward. For example, there are a number of difficulties in the measurement and meaning of the unemployment rate. In the periods for which equations have been estimated there have been improvements in unemployment benefits in some countries and increases in all countries in the propor- tion of young people and women in the labor force, each of which category has a somewhat higher than average likelihood of being unem- ployed (see Wood, 1978:207–208 for a critical discussion of these claims). These changes in the character of unemployment are likely to have attenuated any relationship between a single measure of unemployment and wage growth. Still, there are now enough findings of a weak rela- tionship between labor market conditions and wage growth over differ- ent time periods and in different institutional contexts, to warrant about as confident a conclusion as the social sciences allow: the effects of unemployment on wage growth often operate with an important lag.

Second, in the same or other equations, wage growth is substantially predicted by wage growth in an earlier period (Brown, 1985:276). This mechanism has been formalized in equations testing the so-called "tar- get real wage hypothesis" (Henry, Sawyer, and Smith, 1976; Henry and Ormerod, 1978). The assumption behind analyses based on this hypoth- esis is that, on the basis of their past experience, employees form some idea of what level of real *after tax* earnings growth is acceptable and succeed in forcing employers to concede nominal wage increases that are to some degree responsive to this conception. In operational terms this means the replacement of a measure of unemployment in an equa- tion predicting nominal wages with a measure of past growth in real (after tax) earnings. In wage equations testing this hypothesis the mea- sure of past earnings growth turns out to be positively and significantly signed. The work of Henry et al. remains quite controversial (e.g., War- burton, 1980). But the general pattern this kind of equation assumes, in which wage growth is to an important extent a function of past wage growth, is quite widely established and provides additional evidence of inertial growth in wages.

Third, those directly involved in bargaining are likely to report (in England, at least) that the rate of unemployment and profitability of the firm have little effect on the outcome of wage negotiations but that target wage rates, price increases, and relativities have substantial effects (Sheriff, 1980:213; Daniel, 1976).

The evidence of a significant degree of nominal wage inflexibility is, I believe, overwhelming. What does this mean for the explanation of the postwar inflation? Can variations in wage responsiveness be used to account for international differences in inflation? I will consecutively consider this in terms of the international and temporal patterns of postwar inflation.

It is sometimes argued that countries vary in the amount of nominal wage rigidity generated by their labor markets. If this were so it would mean that different governments confronted different macroeconomic options and that would be likely to produce different inflation records. Where nominal wages are somewhat rigid there is the possibility of using inflation to produce growth. Where nominal wages are not slow to adapt to either changes in demand or to *prices*—where, that is, *real* wages are rigid—government cannot engineer an inflation as a method for securing an increase in output and employment; all it can produce with a stimulative policy (insofar as its effects on the labor market are concerned) is more inflation.

Bruno and Sachs (1985:232–240) have argued that, in broad terms, the United States and Canada can be distinguished along these lines from most European countries and Japan. In North America wages lag prices but in Europe they closely track them. Thus, in North America there is *nominal* wage rigidity and in Europe there is *real* wage rigidity. Bruno and Sachs (1985:240) discuss two implications for macroeconomic performance of this difference. First, nominal wage stickiness in the United States and Canada meant that only some of the increase in prices as a result of the supply shocks of the 1970s was translated into wage increases, so that the negative effects on employment of the supply shock were moderated. Real wage stickiness in Europe, on the other hand, meant that the supply shocks produced corresponding increases in wages at the same time that profits were falling, also as a result of the supply shock: the net effect of increasing wages and falling profits was a substantial increase in unemployment. Second, nominal wage stickiness meant that is was *possible* for the United States to inflate its way out of a recession, and it did so in 1974.

All this might take us some way toward explaining international differences in inflation (but only in combination with some consideration of government policy preferences). However, the evidence on differences in nominal wage stickiness between the United States and Europe, in the words of Helliwell (1988:13), "was never very strong." Estimates of nominal wage rigidity depend very heavily on the specification of the estimating equation. Thus, estimates of nominal wage stickiness depend on whether or not some attempt is made to explicitly model the "war-ranted" rate of wage change by incorporating a measure or measures tapping productivity growth and changes in the prices of imported in-puts.[33] Bruno and Sachs method of modeling this "warranted" rate is not very satisfactory.

In fact Helliwell's review shows that the relevant studies all tend to produce estimates of nominal wage rigidity that are higher for the United States than for European countries but raise the possibility that what makes the major difference to U.S. real wage responsiveness is greater flexibility in prices. Real wages may fall in the United States not so much because nominal wages are rigid as because prices tend to rise more rapidly in response to an increase in demand (Helliwell, 1988:17). To the extent that this is true it has major implications for the specific form of any wage-push account of output and employment trends. It suggests, to be exact, that the higher unemployment in a number of European countries in recent years that frames the policy choices of governments in the relevant countries may originate in sluggish pricing practices rather than, or as much as, in labor market institutions. Three-year contracts and, in the United States, more flexible pricing do seem to distinguish North America from Europe. Differential wage rigidity may contribute to the explanation of international differences in mac-roeconomic performance. But to what extent is unclear.[34]

Does the spread of nominal wage rigidity explain the temporal pattern of inflation? In North America the establishment of 3-year contracts is both a source of wage stickiness and, largely, a postwar phenomenon (Gordon, 1982:41; see also Sachs, 1980). Persistent inflation has also been a postwar phenomenon. In many European countries, that have also experienced inflation, the limits on the timing of wage-setting that are found in North America simply do not exist. This has, of course, spec-tacularly been the case in Britain where wage setting has remained largely unregulated until recently (except when incomes policies have been in effect). So, insofar as it has provided a distinctive context for policy makers, the fairly widespread use of 3-year contracts in North America may have produced some macroeconomic consequences, *per-haps* starting with a greater nominal wage rigidity, but it cannot explain the persistence of postwar inflation across countries or its surge begin-ning in the mid-1960s.

What then distinguishes the postwar period across Western capitalist countries? In explaining greater postwar price rigidity Cagan (1979:91–94) has argued that "a reduction has occurred in the magnitude of price response to excess capacity because of a growing general belief that inflationary movements will not be reversed" and this because of "the postwar history of government failures to curb inflation." Wages are one

kind of price and it is to be expected that they would be similarly affected. Now, remember that there are two directions of rigidity involved. The persistence of postwar inflation clearly would not have
made wages more sticky in response to *increases* in demand. Quite the
contrary. Persistent inflation during the 1970s probably reduced nominal
wage rigidity in North America by encouraging the widespread adoption of cost of living adjustment clauses. But the other form of stickiness,
the failure of wages to fall during a recession would be exacerbated by
persistent inflation. With a background of persistent and accelerating
inflation it is likely that the effects of labor market conditions on the
bargaining behavior of workers and their unions would be largely offset
by the effect of price expectations. Furthermore, the background to the
persistence of inflation is the "greater public sensitivity to unemployment since the Great Depression" (Cagan, 1979:29). Up until the latter
part of the 1970s the preservation of something like full employment
was, arguably, a preoccupation of the governments of all Western industrial nations. This meant that through the mid-1970s, no matter what
wage rate they negotiated, workers and their union leaders could reasonably expect to keep their jobs or, at worst, to find another. In this
context the incentives for restraint were rather modest and the likelihood of wage stickiness in the downward direction substantial.

So where does all of this leave us with respect to a possible connection
between nominal wage stickiness and the postwar inflation? First, in
North America wages do seem to be nominally sticky in both directions,
to some degree; in Europe they seem to be nominally sticky in the
downward direction. Second, nominal wage rigidity provides an incentive for governments to adopt inflationary macroeconomic policies along
the standard Keynesian lines. Third, this is not, however, the case
where nominal wage rigidity on the downside is accompanied by real
wage rigidity on the upside. Fourth, real wage rigidity on the upside
provides a limit on the effectiveness of Keynesian policies that appears
to some extent to apply to Europe, but not to North America, although
the evidence on this is not entirely clear. Fifth, and finally, it should be
clear that, as part of an explanation of the postwar inflation, wage
rigidity has to be combined with government policy choices—specifically, the choice to preserve full employment (through the mid-1970s) and
the decision (either sensible or ill advised) to exploit the opportunities
provided by wage rigidity to use inflation to stimulate output and employment.

The Autonomous Growth of Wages

There is evidence that in a number of Western industrial nations the
rate of increase of hourly wages began to accelerate between about 1969

and 1970 (Phelps Brown, 1983:155–157). This increase was quite general, although Sachs (1979) does present some data suggesting that the increase was particularly large within the manufacturing sector, which is heavily unionized. The counterpart of this surge is that standard wage equations (incorporating measures of labor market conditions) estimated for a number of European countries for the postwar period up to the end of the 1960s significantly underpredict the observed rate of wage inflation in the early 1970s. Some proportion of the labor force in the countries in question was able to protect its *real* wages in the face of the escalating prices that resulted from the commodity price shocks of the time, including the 1973 rise in oil prices, by more than labor market conditions would have led one to expect (Flanagan, Soskice, and Ulman, 1983: 654). A shift in the relationship between labor market conditions and wage growth constitutes one sort of evidence in favor of a wage-push.

A second sort of evidence links the growth of wages to "militancy." Militancy has usually been measured either by unionization (Hines, 1964, 1971; Ashenfelter and Pencavel, 1972) or by the incidence of industrial conflict (Godfrey, 1971; Johnston, 1972; Sylos-Labini, 1974:90–92). These measures prove to be significant predictors of wage growth in the relevant equations, using time series data.

The third sort of evidence links wage growth to price inflation, indirectly or directly. Moore (1979), with U.S. data, estimates a "central bank reaction function" that includes measures of earnings among its predictors. It turns out that earnings are a significant predictor of the monetary base, which he interprets to mean that money supply increases likely to produce inflation are sometimes a form of central bank "accommodation" to pressure on interest rates caused by employer borrowings to finance an increased wage bill. Brown (1985:306) and Shannon and Wallace (1985) attempt to establish the causal priority of wages with respect to prices. In their data wage growth tends to be a stronger predictor of price inflation than price inflation of wage growth. Bruno and Sachs (1985:204–208) estimated price equations for eight countries including a "wage-gap" variable. This latter measures the percentage deviation of the real wage from what it ought to be under full employment, in the economy in question. The variable significantly contributes to the explanation of variations in the rate of inflation in most of the countries. A number of studies lend credence to the Scandinavian model of inflation in which wage increases grow with productivity in the (price-taking) traded goods sector and set the standard for wage increases in the sheltered sector, producing a wage-push inflation in that sector. Thus, Calmfors (1977:509) found that, for the period he analyzed, prices in the traded goods sector tended to follow world prices but followed unit labor costs in the sheltered sector.

Finally, as broad evidence of the increased power of labor Sachs (1979:276; see also Bruno and Sachs, 1985:162) has shown that the share of value-added accruing to labor rose somewhat in a number of European countries over the decade of the 1970s. Furthermore, that growth was mostly concentrated within the heavily unionized manufacturing sector.[35] And the rising share of labor is mirrored by, and presumably causally related to, "a remarkable decline in the pretax rate of return to capital in manufacturing" (Bruno and Sachs, 1985:164).

There is, then, a variety of evidence tending to indicate the existence of a wage-push. Is this evidence definitive? The answer is, quite simply, no. It is quite a bit less than conclusive for a number of reasons. There are two sorts of data involved. There are, first, the time series regressions covering year-to-year changes in prices and wages over a good part of the postwar period. There are, second, a number of studies focusing particularly on distinctive characteristics of the 1970s. Consider, first of all, the studies of year-to-year changes over much of the postwar period.

These have been used to show that the money supply responds to earnings growth, that wage increases cause price increases (sometimes involving the specific mechanisms of the Scandinavian model), and that growth in wages is in part a response to militancy. Results like these, however, tend to be quite fragile. There is the general problem of establishing a causal sequence using time series data (Cagan, 1979:62). It is in general difficult to disentangle which variable causes which, or to what degree one causes the other, and the problem is compounded by the fact that the length and form of lagged effects of exogenous variables in time series regressions are, typically, determined by trial and error. It takes scholarly principle of heroic proportions to prefer the lag structure that produces results inconsistent with one's preferred hypothesis. I am not suggesting that the coefficients estimated using time series regressions should be discounted, simply that they should be treated with some caution.

This can be illustrated with the estimates of the effects of "union militancy." We know that both strikes and union growth tend to *respond* to real wage changes (on the former see, for example, Ashenfelter and Johnson, 1969; on the latter see Bain and Elsheikh, 1976). Even where tests of causal direction are used (e.g., the so-called test for "Granger causality") the discretion in model construction allowed through lag specification means that the results should be treated with some caution unless they prove to be extremely robust—that is, to be reproduced with differently specified models, covering different periods. The "militancy" analyses did not produce robust results (see Johnston and Timbrell, 1973; Ward and Zis, 1974). And the unreliability of the results is compounded by the dubiousness of the measure of "militancy." Growth in union membership, for example, has often taken place as a result of a deliberate government policy of encouragement (e.g., Bain, 1970:142–182; Bain and Elsheikh, 1976:87; Chaison, 1982:148–150) rather than as a result of any distinctive surge in the aggressiveness of union leaders or members. In addition, as Purdy and Zis (1973) pointed out, there is a confounding factor at work here. Union membership may grow not only as a result of additional recruitment within a particular sector but also as a result of a reallocation of labor from sectors with low union density to those with high union densities. If high union density sectors also have higher wages (and it is clear that they tend to do so), that would produce the association between growth in union membership and increasing wages that has been used in support of wage-push interpretations. Purdy and Zis have provided some evidence that this has in fact happened.

In general, the time series studies indicating a postwar wage-push are not replicated or themselves report some results casting doubt on their reliability. Shannon and Wallace, for example, managed to generate an equation in which prices have absolutely no effect on unit labor costs. This is surprising (workers wage claims are unaffected by the rise in the cost of living!) and, the authors acknowledge, a little "troublesome" (1985:188). It is not something that inspires confidence in their other results. Evidence for the Scandinavian model, involving wage leadership from the tradable goods sector, is somewhat stronger. There are Calmfors' results for Sweden (1977) and estimates for a number of countries made by Maynard and van Ryckeghem (1976:Ch. 8). But the relevant process does not apply to all countries. In a number, prices of traded goods rose much more rapidly than world prices (and productivity), causing devaluations (the United Kingdom, Ireland, and France). Even in Sweden, the effect of world prices on domestic prices seems to be much more substantial for centrally negotiated agreements than for overall wage costs, which include a substantial "wage drift" component (Flanagan, Soskice, and Ulman, 1983:311). So there is some evidence for the Scandinavian model of wage-push. But it does not seem to apply to all countries and, where centrally negotiated agreements are involved, seems to be partially offset by wage drift, which is less affected by trends in world prices and productivity growth than by normal conditions of demand and supply.

The best than can be said of the direct evidence of a wage-push of this kind is that it is mixed. Little credence can be put in the results of econometric attempts to measure militancy or to show that wages lead prices rather than vice versa. The Scandinavian model, however, does seem to apply in some countries, although it applies better to negotiated wage rates than to earnings and unit labor costs, which incorporate wage drift.

What about the data tending to show that the 1970s displayed some distinctive economic characteristics, consistent with a wage-push? Here the evidence is stronger. Wage and price equations estimated for the earlier period underpredict for the later period. The share of labor in value added increased fairly clearly from the 1960s to the 1970s in France (in Bruno and Sachs, 1985, but less clearly so in Sachs, 1979), Belgium, Denmark, Germany, Japan, Italy, and the United Kingdom. And Bruno and Sachs report that a real wage-gap measure contributes significantly in explaining the higher inflation of the 1970s in Belgium, Denmark, Germany, Japan, the United Kingdom, and the United States.

These data, however, also raise some problems. First, Bruno and Sachs' wage-gap measure involves, as I noted above, a number of conceptual problems (Helliwell, 1988:18–21). For example, calculating a full employment wage, against which the real wage is to be compared, requires taking into account technical progress. For if labor productivity increases so will the wage compatible with full employment. Bruno and Sachs do not satisfactorily resolve this problem and it is Helliwell's view that their particular solution contributes, along with a number of other problems, to producing an overstated wage gap. Second, that wage growth is underpredicted in the 1970s by equations estimated for the 1960s is by no means catastrophic for orthodox, particularly Keynesian, economic accounts. Such accounts assume lags in adjustment and the 1970s supply shocks did produce a downturn in economic growth to which workers, one would expect, would have been slow to adapt, producing higher than warranted wage growth and higher unemployment during the period of adaptation. Third, Sachs (1979:277) explains the rise in the share of labor in the 1970s in part as a result of a response to the pressure on wages, particularly in the form of incomes policies, during the 1960s.

This is a rather odd sort of wage-push. It really involves an effort to restore the status quo ante and, as such, is hardly evidence of greater worker power. Sachs also claims that the resulting increase in the share of labor in the 1970s was reinforced by legislative concessions to labor in a number of countries and by government policy that ratified the wage-push. But, once again, this means that in order to explain this inflationary episode we have to explain government choices. Organized worker power (as opposed to the power of workers at the ballot box, as citizens) is one explanation of government conduct, but there may be others.

The Problem of Productivity

Inflation can occur because wage growth continues at some customary rate but productivity growth declines (assuming that the government "validates" the wage-push). A "war at the workplace," likely to produce a decline in productivity growth, features in some sociological accounts of postwar labor relations (Rinehart, 1987:143–152). But accounts of the postwar inflation produced by either sociologists or political scientists have not discussed this possible source in any detail. Both Maier (1985:13) and Lindberg (1985:33–34; see also Lindberg, 1982:8–9) acknowledge that declining productivity after 1973 was likely causally linked to accelerating inflation but do not elaborate. Zysman (1985) has emphasized the role of "adjustment difficulties"—that is, difficulties in the reallocation of labor from less to more productive employments—in the generation of inflation. But that is about all there is.

For the purposes of this chapter, there are two separate issues: first, is there any evidence linking declines in the rate of productivity increase to the postwar inflation? Second, if there is a link, does it have anything to do with working class power used (1) to produce an equalization of pay likely to undermine work incentives, (2) to resist technological innovation at the shop floor level, or (3) to prevent the run-down of industries in decline?

The best general source on trends in pay inequalities is Saunders and Marsden's (1981) study. They find the following. First, there are quite wide variations in the amount of pay inequality between countries. But the differences are not closely related to countries' inflation experience. For example, both the United Kingdom and the Netherlands had fairly high inflation rates during the 1960s but were at opposite ends in Saunders and Marsden's ranking of country by degree of pay inequality— with, across different measures, Britain having a consistently high amount of inequality and the Netherlands a consistently low amount (pp. 18–20). Second, if one focuses on manual skill differentials (that are most likely to have been affected by egalitarian trade union policies) the most marked decline in Britain and France took place well before the postwar period. In the United States, however, the decline continued to the mid-1960s, when skill differentials began to turn up (pp. 156–157) again. Third, more detailed analysis of the 1960s and 1970s shows stability in differentials in France and Germany (pp. 176, 187) and some catch-up by unskilled workers in Britain (p. 169) and in Italy (p. 196). Note, furthermore, that the narrowing of differentials in Italy certainly had something to do with worker power since there was a fairly abrupt narrowing after the "hot autumn" of 1969 and, in the later period, a union-encouraged shift to a flat-rate system of indexation, tending to favor lower paid workers (Dell'Aringa and Lucifora, 1990:392–394).

Does this, then, suggest that a narrowing of skill differentials has contributed to inflation by disturbing incentives and reducing productivity? Probably not. It is true that the two high inflation countries—

Britain and Italy—had the largest narrowing. But the narrowing in Italy, at least, took place *after* inflation had already accelerated in the early 1960s. Besides, there is no evidence that the pay distribution in either Britain or Italy is pathologically egalitarian. On the contrary, despite the somewhat egalitarian trend in the 1960s both have fairly high levels of pay inequality. That worker power produced a narrowing of pay differentials is clear in the case of Italy and the same sort of thing probably occurred in Britain, as a result of the flat-rate form of pay increases allowed during some incomes policies. But the evidence tends not to suggest that the result was a productivity damaging pay structure. On the whole, I think that the shifts in the pay structure in Italy and Britain were more a product of inflation than vice versa.

What about resistance to technological innovation within the plant or to industrial restructuring? Neither seems relevant for the pre-1973 period. Across the rich capitalist world productivity grew rapidly until the very end of the 1960s. Now, the generalized acceleration in inflation of the early 1960s was *not* accompanied by a decline in the rate of growth of productivity. In fact, a close examination of the pattern of wage growth, inflation, and productivity growth in Quebec showed that when inflation hit its earlier peak, in 1968 and 1969, labor productivity was growing at rates well above trend and, in each case, at a rate in excess of earnings (Smith, 1988:592–593). This pattern seems to apply more generally (Bruno and Sachs, 1985:249). There is no reason to attribute this earlier acceleration in the rate of inflation to an inertial increase in wages in the context of productivity decline. The brute fact that productivity was growing at a rapid rate throughout the capitalist world at exactly the same time that inflation was accelerating suggests that, for this period, whatever "war at the workplace" might have been underway did not have as an effect a rise in unit labor costs likely to produce, in one way or another, inflation.

The later period is more promising. The rate of growth in productivity turned down at the very end of the 1960s. The exact point of the turndown seems to have varied from country to country. The series presented by Bruno and Sachs suggests that productivity growth in manufacturing started to decelerate as early as 1966 in Italy and as late as 1976 in Ireland and 1977 in Canada, with an overall tendency for the turn-down to cluster around 1973 (1985:250). It is also clear that inflation accelerated throughout the capitalist world after 1973. Did a decline in the growth of productivity produce an acceleration in inflation and, if so, did the decline in the growth of productivity have its origins in an increasing resistance on the part of workers to managerial authority on the shop floor or to a more successful resistance to attempts to shift labor from less to more productive employments?

Bruno and Sachs (1985:206–207) attempted to estimate the contribution of productivity decline to 1970s inflation. The premise of their analysis is that, for a given rate of increase in wages, a decline in the rate of increase in productivity worsens the menu of combinations of unemployment and inflation available to policy makers (the short-run Phillips curve). Assuming that there are limits on the amount of unemployment policy makers are willing to tolerate, this means that a decline in productivity growth is likely to produce a rise in inflation. They have estimated the magnitude of this effect for eight countries.[36] Their estimates suggest that in Belgium, Denmark, and the United States it substantially increased the inflation rate for at least one subperiod during the 1970s. It had smaller effects in France, Germany, Japan, and the United Kingdom. There is, then, some evidence that declining productivity growth in the 1970s produced higher inflation, in some countries for some periods. But this was only one cause of higher inflation in the 1970s among several. For most countries, the direct effect of rising import prices was much larger.

Accepting, then, that declining productivity played some role in increasing inflation in the 1970s, what caused the decline in productivity? In part it was caused by rising raw material prices and, in particular, the rise in oil prices. Production equipment and processes designed to exploit cheap oil became unprofitable and therefore underutilized when the price of oil relative to other inputs rose. Furthermore, the transfer of wealth from oil-consuming to oil-producing countries reduced demand in the consuming countries and that produced higher unemployment, which, among other things, reduced economies of scale and slowed investment (Bruno and Sachs, 1985:249–251). Clearly, this part of the productivity decline was not *initiated* by labor militancy.

However, Bruno and Sachs' estimates suggest that the decline in manufacturing began in some countries before 1973.[37] In these cases the oil shock does not provide an explanation. Was this earlier decline in productivity growth produced by militancy? Here is a list, taken from Bruno and Sachs (1985:250), of the countries in which manufacturing productivity growth turned down before 1973 and of the year when the turn-down occurred.

United States	1972
Germany	1969
Italy	1966
Sweden	1970
Austria	1969
Norway	1970
Switzerland	1970

What is striking about it is the overrepresentation of countries with typically low levels of industrial conflict. Five of the seven countries— Germany, Austria, Norway, Sweden, and Switzerland—are low industrial conflict countries and, besides, countries usually or often asserted to have "neocorporatist" institutions that harness labor in a collective endeavor to secure long-run benefits from productivity growth. I critically examine the hypothesized connection between neocorporatist institutions and economic performance in the next chapter. For now I simply want to observe that the fact that the turn-down was more likely to have occurred before 1973 in countries with very modest amounts of industrial conflict raises some doubts about an idea that it was militancy that produced these earlier downturns, rather than any one of a number of other factors (e.g., unusually low rates of unemployment that meant that plant and equipment was operating at levels of capacity utilization beyond the point of optimal efficiency).

So there is some evidence that a decline in the rate of productivity increase contributed to the acceleration of inflation in the 1970s but no evidence that the decline in productivity growth was principally caused by labor militancy. Yet that does not mean that worker power was irrelevant. It is quite clear that powerful union movements were able, to some extent, to protect their members by slowing down the transfer of resources out of industries in decline. One conspicuous example (and in the light of the content of subsequent chapters there is considerable irony in this) is Sweden, where a series of industries in decline (shipbuilding, steel, remotely located forest products) were heavily subsidized during the 1970s (Lawrence and Bosworth, 1987:70; Gramlich, 1987:280). The oil shock made a shift of production away from energy-intensive industries of this kind all the more imperative. But strong trade unions, with considerable political weight, were able to defer the appropriate structural adjustments in a number of countries.

On the whole, then, there is evidence that productivity decline contributed to the acceleration of inflation in the 1970s but no evidence that that decline originated in a heating up of the "war at the workplace." However, it is clear that in some countries the productivity-enhancing adjustments in industrial structure that were already underway before the oil shock, were deferred as powerful trade unions succeeded in extracting subsidies to declining industries. Where this occurred its effect would have been to further worsen the menu of (short-run) choices between unemployment and inflation available to governments and to increase the probability that, in order to maintain an acceptable level of unemployment, they had to tolerate even higher levels of inflation.

Conclusion

There are two sorts of evidence that might be mobilized to demonstrate the presence and the importance of a wage-push as a source of inflation. First, it is possible to list a set of institutional changes likely, at a given level of demand for labor, to induce workers to seek higher wages than they have sought in the past, and others that make it possible for workers to force employers to concede. *If* there is evidence that such institutional changes have occurred the plausibility of a wage-push account is correspondingly increased—but not by very much. To test the theory properly it is necessary to go beyond institutional description and show that changes in labor costs of one kind or another have been associated with increases in prices. This second method for testing a wage-push account means demonstrating covariation over time or across countries and, best of all, in a form that allows establishing that the increase in worker aspirations or power preceded the acceleration of inflation.

The work on inflation by sociologists and political scientists has been restricted to the first of these two methods. This is rather unsatisfactory. It is true that the second poses fairly considerable methodological difficulties. But simply listing institutional changes that might be associated with greater worker power and aspirations does not show that the power and aspirations have in fact been transformed into wage increases that can be used to account for inflation. Besides, there are two other fundamental problems with wage-push accounts that have been proposed or assumed by sociologists and political scientists. One is that many of the changes in institutions that have been asserted turn out, on close inspection, not to have taken place or, if they have taken place, not to have had the effects claimed for them. The other is that it is not possible to test a theory unless the mechanisms it involves have been specified. In the case of wage-push accounts of inflation this means specifying whether the wage-push takes the form of an increase in the downward rigidity of wages, or a shift in the supply curve of labor caused by either an increase in the real wages demanded, or a shift in the supply curve of labor caused by a decrease in the productivity of labor at any given real wage.

Consider, first of all, the list of institutional changes that are supposed to have taken place. For a number there is no evidence (the decline of normative restraint, the greater commitment to trade unionism as a result of the maturing of the working class, the financial reserve that makes striking easier, the decline in competition). Others are not obviously likely to produce a wage-push (industry-wide bargaining, government employment, export dependence). Still other institutional changes, however, have both taken place and are likely to have produced a wage-push. This is the case in a number of countries where there has been a growth in the percentage unionized and/or improvements in the legal rights of unions and their members, and in all countries there was a commitment to full employment after the second world war and, probably, increased technical interdependence in the production process. So, although most of the institutional changes purported to have produced a wage-push are sheer fiction, there is a solid basis for several others.

But how good is the evidence that these increases in worker bargaining power have been translated into inflation? On the whole, rather weak. Only in the case of Scandinavian countries is there any good evidence of a causal path going from wages to prices (the spillover of wages from the exposed to the sheltered sector). But even in that case the relationship is strong for negotiated wages but rather weak for earnings; and it is earnings that count for wage costs. After 1973 national rates of productivity growth do seem to be associated with inflation rates. But there is little evidence that rates of productivity growth varied with worker militancy or cooperativeness. And although it is clear that nominal wages are relatively rigid in response to changes in the demand for labor the evidence that variations in the rigidity of wages between countries and over time account for variations in inflation is not strong.

So I would argue that the evidence for a wage-push account of the postwar inflation is much weaker than its proponents typically allow. That wage setting institutions have something to do with the process of inflation seems certain. But in what form and to what degree are much less certain. Furthermore, consider once again the institutional changes that clearly have increased worker power—a higher percentage unionized compared to the interwar period, legal reinforcement, sustained full employment (ending in the late 1970s in some countries), and increasingly technically interdependent production. All of these factors are subject to the discretion of governments. Governments can allow unemployment to rise and can legislate to weaken the bargaining power of labor as well as to weaken the union security that sustains higher levels of union membership. A number of governments have done precisely this. Even the effect on labor relations of increased technical interdependence is to some extent conditioned by government policy. After all, *scioperi articolati* in Italy would not have been nearly as effective had employers not had the right to lock-out taken away from them. All this is to say that any credible wage-push account must incorporate an explanation for the relevant policy choices of governments. Why did governments commit themselves to full employment and, in some cases, ex-right.

panded legal rights for trade unions after the second world war? Without an answer to that question there is no complete wage-push account.

Notes

1. Economists in Britain and the United States who stress the role of wage-push in the explanation of the postwar inflation often identify themselves as "post-Keynesians."
2. Rare sociological exceptions can be found in the work of Blumberg (1980:177–178) and Cuneo (1979:11–14), each of whom stresses monopoly pricing and asserts that wages tend to lag inflation, and, in a more general form, in Smith (1982, 1987, 1988).
3. In other words, the supply curve for labor shifts to the left as illustrated, for example, in Trevithick and Mulvey (1975:88).
4. A good discussion can be found in Maynard and van Ryckeghem (1976:Ch. 8).
5. It will not do to say that the increase in wages in itself allows demand to rise to meet the price increase. First, the income of a substantial proportion of the population of every capitalist country is derived either from savings or transfer payments or from profits. These will not normally have increased to match the wage increase (although this may be so in countries with very high levels of inflation and widespread indexation, as in the case of Israel). Second, if overall wages or unionized wages are involved much of the demand is overseas and the price increase will either produce lost markets, or a depreciating exchange rate (which causes a number of problems, as we saw in Chapter 2), or both.
6. It is interesting that, in a more recent version of his argument, Goldthorpe somewhat reduces the weight of this sort of disorder and stresses the electoral consequences of a deflation (1987a:372).
7. Related sociological analyses can be found in Gilbert (1981, 1986) and Skidelsky (1979).
8. Goldthorpe's (1978) seminal sociological analysis of the postwar inflation provides a suitably scathing examination of economists' use of aspirations as an explanatory factor. See, in particular, his discussion of "residual categories" on pp. 187–194.
9. One should not confuse the issue of normative components of behavior, about which economics has very little to say, with normative economics, which deals with the relative desirability of alternative economic arrangements, assuming maximizing—that is, nonnormative behavior. For a discussion of the difference between positive and normative economics see Buchanan (1987:Ch. 1). The work of Herbert Simon with its assertion of the importance of "satisficing" (e.g., 1979) inevitably leads to the introduction of normative elements into behavior. But Simon's ideas continue to be largely neglected by mainstream economics and, where to some accepted (e.g., in the work of Oliver Williamson, 1985), are not applied to macroeconomic issues.
10. As noted above, British economists feature prominently in the production of analyses of this sort. I have used Meade (1982:26–28) and Phelps Brown

(1983:154–155) as my principal sources. Other sources are cited in the text. Although the source is British economists it should be noted that the mechanisms they are describing *ought* to have a more general relevance.

11. This factor was particularly stressed by Reder (1948:52–53), Simons (1948:291), and Hayek (1960:280–281).

12. One might reasonably regard legal changes as sociological rather than economic. But specific legislative changes have not been incorporated in explanations constructed by sociologists. Here I am classifying the factor as sociological or economic according to the discipline of those adducing it rather than in terms of the inherent properties of the factor.

13. Note that although monitoring the wages paid by comparable employers does, of course, involve a degree of sensitivity to local labor market conditions it also introduces rigidity. Suppose that a downturn in the demand for labor means that it becomes a lot easier to find workers; if wage rates are set on the basis of a survey of comparable employers rather than the number of qualified candidates those rates will tend not to fall, although their rate of increase is likely to slow. The resultant wage rates are not impervious to changes in market conditions; they are simply slow to respond and their response does not take the form of a wage cut.

14. Alt (1979:53–57) reports that, in Britain, expectations of unemployment in any given year (t_1) are more closely correlated with unemployment in the following year (t_2) than the preceding year (t_0), suggesting that past experience is less important in forming expectations than the forecasts of economists, diffused through the media. This may be so. But in practice the economic models of economists are likely to include some effects from past economic conditions that are themselves likely to be associated with past unemployment. One way or another it seems to me certain that the record of unemployment in the past affects expectations of unemployment in the future.

15. For examples of the sorts of benefits that were provided see Minford (1983:135–137, 244–250) on Britain, Germany, Italy, and France. On Canada see Pal (1988:33–51).

16. See Maier (1978, and, in more depth, 1975).

17. It is worth noting that a "traditional" situation, for which precious little evidence was advanced, played a central part in Goldthorpe's earlier work on the affluent worker (Goldthorpe et al., 1968, 1969). As Benson puts the matter: "The central criticism being advanced is that the 'traditional' worker displays far too much of a tendency to appear in the guise of a *deus ex machina* whose function it is to validate a prepared theoretical position" (Benson, 1978:156). I am arguing that the same criticism applies to Goldthorpe's analysis of inflation.

18. Goldthorpe (1990:438) has recently noted that he would like to undertake a large scale study "of the decay of status structures." I take it that this indicates some acknowledgement on his part of the paucity of the evidence documenting the process that nonetheless plays a central part in his account of the postwar inflation.

19. The literature on young worker discontent includes a large amount of more qualitative research. For a devastating critique of the bulk of that research see Hamilton and Wright (1986:19–38, and Chapter 6).

20. Note furthermore that there were important changes in the composition of the labor force in the 1960s likely to increase absenteeism and quit rates. The labor force grew rapidly during that period producing a higher proportion of younger workers. Young workers tend to have higher absenteeism and quit

rates. So do women, whose labor force participation increased considerably. See Hamilton and Wright (1986:276, 279).

21. The claim that alienation was producing all sorts of behavioral symptoms of discontent during the 1960s and 1970s has been—and continues to be—made quite stridently in Canada (e.g., Crispo and Arthurs, 1968; Rinehart, 1987). For a review of the evidence tending to contradict these claims see Smith (1979a).

22. Goldthorpe (1978:207) describes a "mature working class" as "one which remains only very imperfectly accommodated by the capitalist system *per se*, in that its members lack any value commitment to the basic principle of this system—namely that the life-chances and welfare of individuals are most appropriately determined by the 'free' working out of market forces" and goes on (p. 208) to describe it as having "the potential for action of a more concerted kind." I take it that with this Goldthorpe is indicating that workers have some (politically significant) sense of a collective interest.

23. On declining working class support for the Labour Party see Kavanagh (1990).

24. The next several paragraphs are adapted from Smith (1982:317 ff).

25. Goldthorpe (1978:208–209; 1987a:382–385) acknowledges this.

26. For some well thought out reservations with respect to the bargaining power model of strikes see Lacroix (1987). Nonetheless, in my judgment the balance of the evidence seems to show that the amount of industrial conflict is negatively related to the unemployment rate.

27. Perhaps the most positive appraisals of an incomes policy can be found in McCallum (1986, 1990).

28. I assume that this would be more socially disruptive than a sustained policy of monetary restraint that avoided inflation in the first place. The argument I am making, then, would be strengthened if one assumed that government had, through monetary restraint, consistently *avoided* inflation.

29. France, where the organization of workers at the shop floor level was relatively weak, may have constituted a partial exception to this generalization during the earlier part of the postwar period, at least if Shorter and Tilly (1974:189) are to be believed.

30. Unions are typically better insulated from democratic pressures as the notion of "representational monopoly," that is central to neocorporatist analyses, shows. I discuss this in some detail in the next chapter.

31. Although it probably took a conservative government to produce as vigorously pursued a deflation as occurred in Britain from 1979 to 1981 (Alt and Chrystal, 1983:118).

32. For evidence suggesting that in Sweden in the early 1970s it was middle-income respondents who responded most negatively to rising unemployment see Jonung and Wadensjö (1987:206).

33. If there are two countries with similar rates of price increase and similar levels of unemployment it makes sense that the country with the higher productivity growth will have a higher rate of wage increase. Besides, it is quite conceivable that the higher productivity increase will change the *form* of the relationship between price increases and wage increases, that Bruno and Sachs use as their measure of nominal wage stickiness.

34. See also Fitoussi and Phelps (1988:4–5).

35. Careful comparison of the relevant table in Sachs (1979) with the table in Bruno and Sachs reveals fairly divergent numbers. One of the divergencies is explained in Bruno and Sachs. For France, they use French data rather than the

U.S. Bureau of Labor Statistics data employed for the rest of the·countries covered in their table. They note that "the French national source" shows "a considerably higher share of value added and a more sharply rising profile than the BLS series" (Bruno and Sachs, 1985:162).

36.   Belgium, Canada, Denmark, France, Germany, Japan and United Kingdom, and the United States.

37.   These declines in the rate of increase in manufacturing productivity that took place before 1973 are, oddly, ignored by Bruno and Sachs.

6

CORPORATISM
AND THE LONG RUN

Inflation rates have varied between capitalist countries over the postwar period, particularly since 1973. Sociological analyses have explained the postwar inflation as an outcome of the class conflict that is endemic to capitalist society. If class conflict is common to capitalist societies but inflation rates vary between them it makes sense to seek an explanation in the presence or absence of institutions that can contain the disruptive effects of class conflict by regulating its operation. Broadly speaking, in the twentieth century two intellectual traditions concerned with outlining the institutional arrangements that can put an end to the social and economic disruptiveness of class conflict have been produced. One, of course, is *communism*, which purports to deal with the problem by eliminating classes. The other is *corporatism* and it is a *variant* of this that has appealed to a number of social scientists both as explanation for the differential inflation performance of capitalist nations and/or as a desirable set of institutions to be copied (e.g., Crouch, 1985; Lange, 1984; Goldthorpe, 1984; Bruno and Sachs, 1985).[1]

Now corporatism has a rather bad name as a result of its association with some extremely unpleasant political regimes—fascist before the second world war and authoritarian after it (see, e.g., P. Williamson, 1985:chs. 6–8). It should be clear at the outset that the current proponents of corporatist institutions are advocating polities that look like neither those of Italy under Mussolini nor Portugal under Salazar. They distinguish the institutions they are describing from the more oppressive versions by referring to "neocorporatism" (Crouch, 1985), "liberal corporatism" (Lehmbruch, 1979:54), "societal corporatism" (Schmitter, 1979:65), "contract corporatism" (P. Williamson, 1985:ch. 10), or "bargained corporatism" (Crouch, 1979:189) and all of these terms are designed to indicate that the political form in question is not rooted in force in the same way that its unpleasant antecedents were. But the use of the term "corporatism" (whether "neo," "liberal," or whatever) also indicates that there are some continuities between the two forms. It is useful to start with those continuities because, I think, they are at the root of some of the theoretic difficulties posed by the recent attempts to explain variations in macroeconomic performance in terms of the presence or absence of corporatist institutions.[2]

The common features of neocorporatist and early twentieth-century corporatist polities are as follows. First, as a noncommunist response to class conflict, they are founded on an economy in which most property is privately owned. Second, they assume that parliamentary institutions of the usual kind (with representatives elected by district or at large) are unable adequately to come to grips with class conflict and its results. Parliamentary institutions are thought not to provide a suitable forum within which workers and employers can negotiate lasting settlements of their differences and, in so doing, prevent disorder and disruption. Consequently, and third, parliamentary institutions have to be supplemented with some form of representation of "functional" interests— that is, with some sort of organization within which both capital and labor are incorporated so that these otherwise contending classes are forced to examine in what respects their interests are shared. Fourth, the "state" has a responsibility to do more than simply "hold the ring" for a market economy. It is obliged to intervene more or less aggressively to induce citizens and organizations to act in ways that are compatible with some more general social and economic goals.

This latter is a very important point and it provides a suitable starting place for an analysis of the distinctive characteristics of neocorporatist polities. In early twentieth-century corporatist theories the objective to be sought was some sort of social justice that the untrammeled operation of the market was thought not to produce. In recent neocorporatist writings the transcendent goal has been *stable* economic growth, that is, economic growth with a minimum of unemployment and that avoids extremes of inflation. It is often asserted that corporatist polities tend to spend a lot on social welfare and to have lower levels of inequality (e.g., Goldthorpe, 1984:337; Barber and McCallum, 1982:6–13; Klein, 1985: 221–222). But although certainly regarded as desirable attributes, in the analyses that concern us here these are treated as a means to the general end of stable, full employment maintaining economic growth rather than as corporatist objectives in themselves.

Neocorporatism and Economic Performance

The underlying premise of neocorporatist writings is that the most substantial threat to economic performance is posed by the growing power and assertiveness of organized labor, of which the wage-push discussed in the previous chapter is one outcome.[3] Countries that develop suitable institutional arrangements to come to grips with this threat

achieve superior growth with lower unemployment. The suitable institutional arrangement identified by neocorporatists is bargaining over
wage increases and related economic matters between a (more or less)
centrally organized union movement that includes much of the labor
force as members and a (more or less) centrally organized group of
major employers, under the aegis of a government that both encourages
and reinforces the centralized bargaining because it sees the institutions
as a way of reducing the extent to which class conflict poses an obstacle
to stable economic growth. Note that this arrangement is corporatist in
that the centralized bargaining between employers and unions is organized around the "function" of production, in that it to some significant
extent shifts real decision-making power outside of parliament, and in
that the state plays an important role in both supporting the process of
bargaining and in encouraging the parties involved to direct their attention to broader economic performance.[4]

Why might this institutional arrangement be expected to produce
higher growth, lower unemployment, and more stable prices than are
found where centralized bargaining is absent (Crouch calls such polities
"liberal systems")? Different analysts of neocorporatism have offered
different reasons, of which the most frequently given are as follows.

1. Suppose that workers in an economy with something like full
employment are powerful enough to negotiate a series of wage increases
that exceed the rate of increase in productivity. This is likely to be the
case where unions have organized all the firms in an industry or group
of industries. Where an entire industry is organized "excessive" wage
increases in one firm cannot be offset by a decline in demand for the
products of that firm and an expansion of production in other firms in
the industry. Where the entire industry is organized the real wage increase sticks; employment may decline but most workers keep their jobs
and are quite willing to tolerate the unemployment of former work-
mates, or the continued unemployment of the currently unemployed, or
of new entrants to the labor force. In any case, if the government responds to the wage increase by stimulating demand, there need be no
short-run increase in unemployment. Instead, inflation will accelerate. If
economists such as Cagan or Feldstein are correct (discussed in Chapter
2) unemployment and slower growth will be a longer run effect of the
inflation—but, in any case, will be produced beyond the time horizon of
the union leaders who negotiated the "excessive" wage increase.

Note, furthermore, that even if all workers and their leaders recognized the existence of this trade-off between wage growth in excess of
productivity on the one hand and some combination of inflation, unemployment, and slow growth on the other (and that is unlikely), it would

still not be in the interests of any particular set of workers to restrain their wage demand to something equivalent to the rate of increase in productivity because there is the real possibility that all other workers would continue to demand higher wages. Any resultant inflation would leave them worse off rather than simply no better off than they would have been without the wage increase.

Now suppose that in a particular economy there is only one union that includes all workers within it and one employers' association that includes all employers within it. Suppose further that the leaders of the two groups are able to guarantee that their members accept the wage that is centrally negotiated for them. *If* union leaders can be persuaded that, beyond a certain point, wage increases will come only at the expense of employment (and growth), or inflation, or both, then they will be willing to bargain a rate of wage increase that corresponds (more or less) to the rate of productivity increase and to make it stick with their members. The same applies to the employers' association, which will be able to compel members inclined to respond to labor shortages with "excessive" wage increases to toe the line. In this situation, unions and employers bargain over the *real* rather than the *nominal* wage, and concern themselves with employment and output too (Flanagan, Soskice, and Ulman, 1983:27–29).

The best formal model of centralized bargaining can be found in Calmfors and Driffill (1988). It produces a real wage increase for fully centralized bargaining (one union, one employers' association) that is identical to the real wage increase that would be produced in a perfectly competitive labor market. The assumptions of such models are endlessly debatable. Still, it is the best model we have. One of the things that makes it interesting is that it implies that the major source of economic superiority of centralized bargaining (in terms of real wage restraint) comes from the fact that the alternative to it is *partially centralized bargaining*. Complete centralization may be preferable, then, because there is no prospect of a fully competitive labor market in a rich capitalist economy. Unions are here to stay (with the possible exception of the United States) and often organize an entire industry. Centralization produces the same real wage increase as does a fully competitive labor market and is a lot more feasible.

Neocorporatist institutions that *approximately* resemble the total centralization described above, then, may produce superior economic performance by forcing the parties to wage bargaining to "take a somewhat less parochial view" (Olson, 1982:50). Each side is forced to confront the consequences for employment and inflation of the bargain it seeks to strike, modifies its demands accordingly, and ensures that its members respect the bargain that is struck. In view of the previous chapter it is worth noting, however, that this is necessary only where unions have sufficient power to force through wage increases that are in excess of the rate of increase of productivity to a disruptive (in terms of price and employment) degree. As Calmfors and Driffill make clear, this advantage of corporatism assumes that, in the absence of the institutions, there is a significant wage-push.

2. There is a corollary to all of this that embodies a separate real wage restraining effect. The presence of an effectively centralized union movement means that, *by definition*, interunion rivalry is no longer possible. Unions clearly do base their wage claims, in part, on what other unions have negotiated (Dunlop, 1957; Ross, 1948; Bourdon, 1979). Such "orbits of coercive comparison" exist even in times of price stability. But inflation exacerbates the rivalries involved. For when inflation accelerates, wages tend to increase in abrupt and newsworthy leaps. A newsworthy leap becomes a model for, and part of the justification of, the wage claims of other union leaders. And so on, ad infinitum (Hicks, 1974:78–79).[5] The growth of wages, then, becomes self-feeding and, assuming some sort of mark-up pricing, inflationary.

Whether in times of price stability or during inflation, however, effectively centralized bargaining makes all of this impossible. The separate bargaining units within the overall federation are forced to come to terms with each other and to resolve their mutual resentments over wage differentials within the centrally negotiated framework (Bruno and Sachs, 1985:231–232).

3. Neocorporatist models (in their pure form) assume that the government plays an active role in the process of centralized bargaining. One of the courses of action open to it is to induce the unions to make what it deems to be realistic real wage demands by offering, as an alternative, what is sometimes called a "social wage." In exchange for wage restraint it can offer welfare programs, more generous unemployment insurance, more heavily subsidized higher education, enlarged access to free medical services, better pensions, and so on. Or, alternatively, the government can cut taxes so that the take-home pay of workers rises despite the fact that real wages are kept under control (Bruno and Sachs, 1985:231; see also Hibbs, 1978:165).

Either way, it is the fact that government has centralized counterparts with whom to negotiate and that can reasonably be expected to deliver something like compliance that makes the difference. Real wage growth can be controlled, so the argument goes, not only because the government has something to offer in exchange for it, but also because the corporatist institutions make possible the relevant trade-offs between wages, taxes, and benefits.

4. Once a neocorporatist bargaining relationship gets established it allows *sequential trade-offs over time* (Lange, 1984:101–106; Crouch,

1985:74). This means that each individual negotiation need no longer be viewed as an all-or-nothing matter. Crouch (1985:112) puts the point as follows.

> This routine participation prevents excessive expectations being invested in individual "big deals". The sheer multiplicity of transactions reduces the risk involved in any one of them and makes it possible for concessions made on one issue to be offset against gains on another. As Lehmbruch has put it: "Corporatism will tend to be stable . . . to the degree that concessions in one field . . . appear to yield a long-run pay-off in the other domains."[6]

Note that there are two major sources of real wage restraint in what Lange calls an "iterated game" of corporatist bargaining. One is that repeating negotiations over time reduces the risk attached to any single negotiation. The second is that it becomes possible to formally and realistically consider *long-run* outcomes. If you assume that the advantage to workers of a wage-push are likely to be transient this is an important matter.

Now, although it is in principle conceivable that workers might *individually* be persuaded that an iterated game involving occasional wage restraint is a good thing, in practice, this is not likely given the problems posed by free riding. Individual workers, who have to confront the day-to-day problems of making a living, are unlikely to put a great deal of stress on the long run. The best possible outcome for any particular worker is if he or she maximizes income while everybody else practices wage restraint. The same thing applies for a small group of workers. In either case a large wage increase will have a negligible effect on employment in the firm but a large impact on the take-home pay of the worker or small group of workers in question.

However, according to Lange, centralizing the bargaining structure facilitates trade-offs over time in two ways. First, to some extent it allows the centralized unions to coerce their members (Lange, 1984:107).[7] Even if individual union members are not disposed to trade off short-run advantage for long-term benefits or are sceptical that the long-run benefits will ever be delivered, their union leaders, who have better information, can act on their behalf, in their true interests. (The continuity with old style corporatism should be clear here.) The same is, in principle, true of the relationship between the heads of employer associations and their members.

Second, according to Lange, centralization encourages workers to develop a normative identification with a larger workers' movement and in doing so to be more willing to run the short-term risk associated with wage restraint. His rationale for this claim is to the effect that, in perceiving the tie between their own fate and the fate of their class, workers necessarily enlarge their time horizons. He seems to be arguing that if workers understand that other workers are in the same situation and have the same interests as themselves they are more likely to think that those other workers might also decide to act *responsibly* and defer wage claims in some long-run, collective, interest. I am inclined to think that this is a *non sequitur,* but let that pass for the moment.[8]

Lange also argues that the establishment and maintenance of a relationship between workers and employers that allows trade-offs over time is facilitated by the presence of a social democratic government. This is partly on account of the possibility of a trade-off between a 'social wage' and real wage increases, as outlined above. It is also because a government of the left "can play a role as a 'guarantor'"; if workers agree to forego a wage increase so that a higher proportion of national income can be devoted to investment the presence of a social democratic government, willing to increase taxes on the rich and expand the role of public enterprise in the economy, is likely to reassure them that the funds freed up by the wage restraint will actually go into investment rather than into riotous capitalist consumption.[9]

5. Much of the interest in the relative performance of corporatist economies originated during the economic difficulties that began after the oil shocks of the 1970s. It has been argued that corporatist institutions are particularly suitable for handling the adjustments necessary when economic growth declines substantially. In these analyses, however, the definition of corporatism is typically extended beyond centralized bargaining between capital and labor under the aegis of the government to include, *in practice,* a high level of government spending on welfare (Bruno and Sachs, 1985:224) combined with a fundamental commitment to full employment (Barber and McCallum, 1982:6–12; Blais and McCallum, 1986:164–166).[10]

The argument goes as follows. When economic growth is knocked off track by, for example, a substantial rise in oil prices, the problem is to speed up as much as possible the process of adjustment to the shock. People running businesses have to come to terms with the change in their costs and, in particular, unions and workers have to come to terms with the absolute decline, or substantial decline in the rate of increase, of their real wages. The centralized negotiating institutions are particularly efficient at disseminating information on the real state of the economy. But, in addition, the institutions as well as the welfare expenditures and low unemployment that accompany them build a social consensus that leads to an acceptance of the need for a scaling down of wage claims. They do so in two different ways. First, the centralized negotiation of wage increases necessarily involves a consideration of the distributional implications of whatever increases are agreed on. Instead of allowing a market to blindly and impersonally determine who gets what central negotiators have to confront the issue of who *ought* to get what. This often involves an attempt to equalize wages but, in any case, it infuses normative considerations into the income determination process. In corporatist societies, it is argued, wage levels and the shares of labor and capital have a moral content. Consequently, workers are more likely to accept the adjustment decisions that are made necessary by the shock. They will scale down their demands because their experience of its outcomes convinces them of the fairness of the wage determination process in their society. The low level of unemployment and the high level of expenditure on social programs further increase the probability of acceptance in that workers and their families have less to fear during an adjustment process.[11]

Second, to the extent that the process of adjustment requires changes at the level of the firm, including both wage restraint and reorganizations of the production process, workers in neocorporatist systems are more likely to accept those required changes than workers in alternative (liberal) systems. Thus, Barber and McCallum (1982:2; see also McCallum, 1983:785) seem to argue that the infusion of moral legitimacy that goes with centralized wage negotiations and large expenditures on social programs extends to relations between employers and workers *within firms*. As a result, in a neocorporatist society, when an employer tells a group of workers that they have to forego a wage increase or shift to new jobs within the plant or change the way they do their current job, the workers are more likely to believe that the changes are necessary.

The result of all this is that economies with neocorporatist institutions adapt much less painfully, in terms of industrial disputes, inflation, and unemployment, than do their liberal counterparts. And, in fact, the argument implies that the consensus or trust that is supposed to characterize them is likely to enhance the process of technological change in normal times as well as when it is necessary to adjust to shocks (Muszynski and Wolfe, 1989:252).

Some Reservations

The background to the analyses of the corporatism described above is the apparently superior economic performance during the 1970s of a number of countries that have been identified as having neocorporatist institutions. The combined inflation and unemployment record of Sweden, Norway, and Austria was quite good, and these countries do have neocorporatist institutions. The Anglo-American democracies (the United Kingdom, the United States, Canada, Australia, and New Zealand) had higher rates of unemployment and inflation and are thought not to have neocorporatist institutions.

Now, the obvious way of testing whether or not the claims about corporatist routes to superior economic performance are true is to compare the inflation, unemployment, and growth records of corporatist with liberal polities. But, as I will show in the next chapter when I do look at the relevant data, that is no easy matter. For it turns out that there is a lot of elasticity in the process of classifying countries as corporatist or liberal. And some of the issues raised in the classification decisions require that one carefully consider the premises of the theory of economic performance and corporatist institutions. That is what I do in the remainder of this chapter.

The Negotiation of Real Wages

Centralization is supposed to redirect the attention of labor and capital from nominal to real wages and, in fact, has probably done so, at least some of the time. The direction of attention to real wages is on the credit side of corporatism's ledger (so to speak). But there are a number of things that *might* appropriately be allocated to the debit side.

First, centralized negotiations are likely to produce (either deliberately or unintentionally) a schedule of wages not only different from what would be produced through the multitude of bargains struck within a decentralized system but also, *arguably* one which, because less of a response to local conditions, fails to produce the income differentials appropriate for securing the movement between more and less productive jobs that economic growth requires. Centralized negotiations may produce an inefficient allocation of labor.

Second, the delegation of responsibility for bargaining to representatives of business and labour, and to government the obligation to channel those negotiations in some socially desirable direction, runs into the public choice objection that the bargainers have their own personal interests that are likely to contaminate their actions. The central establishment of a wage schedule for even a modest sized economy will usually require a fair-sized bureaucracy whose members, if Niskanen (1971) is correct, have an interest in maximizing their incomes by maximizing the size of the bureau they direct, and in so doing producing wasteful spending and wasteful regulations.

Third, even if the centralized negotiations generate a wage schedule likely to produce an efficient allocation of labor, in which civil servants and union and employer association bureaucrats do not reallocate excessive amounts of resources to themselves, there is still the problem raised by Mancur Olson. The existence of encompassing groups may serve to force labor and capital to think in terms of real rather than nominal wages; but the fact that they are forced to secure agreement over a wide range of issues *may* mean that it takes a long time for them to make decisions and, therefore, reduce their adaptability to changing circumstances. This is what Olson (1982:55) calls the problem of "crowded agendas."

Inter-Union Rivalry

If there is only one union you cannot have interunion rivalry. But, among western capitalist nations, there is no instance in which there is only one union. Of the relevant countries Sweden has one of the most centralized union movements. But it has three separate federations; LO for blue-collar workers, TCO for white-collar workers, and SACO for professionals. In the earlier postwar period, the blue-collar federation clearly dominated the union movement. In 1960 LO had a 75% share of union membership to TCO's 20% and SACO's less than 4%. But this dominant position has been eroded: in 1980 LO's share had declined to 62%, and TCO and SACO had risen to 31 and 7%, respectively.[12] The relationships between these federations have not always been harmonious.

The issue here is not whether or not centralization allows the negotiation of real wages. I have already conceded that it does so (although, possibly, at a significant cost). The issue is whether or not a more, *but not completely*, centralized union movement implies an interunion rivalry that is less likely to intensify the concern with relativities and therefore real wage growth than a more decentralized union movement. In fact, a little thought should show that it is not self-evident that reducing the number of parts of a union movement will reduce the extent of disruptive struggles over relativities.

The issue is often treated empirically. Cameron (1984:169), for example, has shown that "organizational unity" of the labor movement—which is a subjective scale of centralization created by Cameron—is associated with a lower rate of working days lost per thousand in the labor force. Does this settle the issue? I do not think so. Clearly, a group can have power even if it does not actually exercise it. What may make the difference is the *threat* of the use of the instruments of power (Bachrach and Baratz, 1970:ch. 3). In fact, Ingham (1974:57) explains the low level of industrial conflict in Sweden *in part* as a result of the "fear of escalation" produced by highly centralized labor relations. To put the matter another way, having a small number of extremely powerful unions may be accompanied by an intense preoccupation with rela- tivities but a relatively small amount of working days lost from strikes because employers, either of their own volition or at the behest of gov- ernment, usually give in. And then the government adjusts its mac- roeconomic policy accordingly to protect employment, for as long as it is able to do so.

Now I do recognize that with this sort of argument one treads on rather dangerous ground. Postulating an unobserved and perhaps un- observable power is the easy course taken by the shoddiest of conspir- acy theorists. I will come back to the matter of evidence in the next chapter. For the moment, however, I simply want to show that one can derive conclusions about the consequences for economic performance of corporatist institutional arrangements that are different from those drawn by Crouch, Bruno, and Sachs, McCallum, and their ilk. The fact is that no Western capitalist society has a completely centralized union movement and there is no a priori reason why the struggle over rela- tivities within a small group of very powerful union organizations should produce a smaller gap between real wage and productivity growth than the struggle among a larger number of less powerful small- er union organizations. And the data on centralization and industrial conflict do not contradict this!

Note, furthermore, that the effects of centralization on both real wage *and* productivity growth are at issue here. A group of powerful, cen- tralized, unions may not only be able to force "excessive" wage in- creases; they may also be able to resist the kinds of adjustment involving movement of labor and capital from less to more productive industry that are critical to economic growth (see Zysman, 1985). It may be that with more centralized union movements there is less difficulty with the kinds of jurisdictional disputes that seem to have hindered economic growth in Britain (e.g., Maitland, 1983:ch. 4). But if a set of old industries in decline has a predominant political position within the centralized union movement (say, for instance, steel or shipbuilding—and given the role of workers in such industries in the development of union move- ments that is surely likely to be the case) its power may be used to coerce governments to subsidize or protect the industries and in doing so to prevent the shifting of resources to more productive areas.

Trading Off "Real Wages" for a "Social Wage"

Can a government reduce the growth of real wages by offering in exchange to a centralized union movement either a reduction in taxes, or an increase in government expenditures on social programs, or both? Perhaps, but there are limits to this process. Consider, to start with, the question of social programs.

First, there are good grounds for thinking that people are not infinitely enthusiastic at the replacement of increments in disposable income with better social benefits. Some of the benefits are likely to be perceived as largely irrelevant by a substantial part of the population. This is clearly the case for unemployment insurance, particularly where the unemployment rate is very low, as it is in some of the polities that have been classified as neocorporatist. It is also to some extent the case for subsidized access to higher education, from which the children of a good part of the working class will never profit. It is conceivable that quite a lot of younger adults would prefer disposable income with which they can purchase housing rather than better medical benefits.

The more general point is that social benefits are clearly not infinitely substitutable for disposable income. Unless the government in a neocorporatist polity starts providing automobiles, *and* other consumer durables, *and* restaurant meals, *and* recreation accommodation, *and* becomes the principal provider of new housing, among other things (and in doing so manages to respond as adequately to popular tastes as private producers do), much of the unionized population is unlikely to respond to expanded social benefits with overwhelming enthusiasm. Beyond a certain point they are unlikely to endorse trade-offs between real wage growth and increases in social benefits, *if they are given the choice*. There is, in fact, evidence that political support for the welfare state declined in Scandinavia during the late 1960s and 1970s (Cerny, 1977), suggesting that whatever trade-off between social benefit increases and real wage growth took place during that time was not enthusiastically endorsed by much of the population on whose behalf the trade-off was made.

Second, the expanded social benefits have to be paid for somehow. If they are paid for by printing money they will produce inflation. If the government pays for them by issuing long-term debt, interest rates are likely to rise, deter private investment, and produce slower growth ("crowding out") and will, besides, decrease the margin of flexibility of the government in the future as interest payments occupy a larger and larger part of the national budget (and this has certainly occurred across both corporatist and liberal Western countries: see Courant, 1987:427). If the government pays for them by raising marginal taxes on income it is *conceivable* that work effort will be deterred (e.g., Browning and Johnson, 1984) but almost certain that increasing amounts of economic activity will be channelled into the "black economy" where taxes and work regulations can be avoided.[13]

The general point is that the substitution of social benefits for real wage increases is not costless. And to write as if it is (as Bruno and Sachs, for example, do) is grossly misleading.

What about the substitution of tax cuts for real wage growth? Whether or not this is feasible depends on the budgetary situation of the government (assuming it wishes to avoid inflationary financing or long-term borrowing). Furthermore, the possibility of this exchange depends on the capacity of the centralized negotiators to make their wage increase decisions stick. That is to say, if some groups of workers in a part of the labor market where demand is particularly tight can both have their taxes cut and induce their employers to raise their wages they are unlikely to sacrifice the opportunity. I will have more to say about this shortly. The general point I wish to make is that there is a strong tendency to identify neocorporatism with the extensive provision of social benefits. If the path to stable growth is via tax cuts and ultimately therefore reduced benefits, neocorporatist theorists will sooner or later have to determine whether their conception of institutional arrangements involves finite limits on tax cuts or, alternatively, does not necessarily require extensive social benefits.

Sequential Trade-Offs and the Long Run

Lange has argued that the existence of centralized negotiations, especially where an SDP provides the normal governing policy, allows sequential trade-offs and this reduces the stake of any particular negotiated outcome. Reducing the stakes in any particular negotiation, he claims, makes possible settlements that embody a concern with the long run.

One of the reasons that this is so, according to Lange, is that workers who are drawn into an organization that encompasses much of the working class are more likely to think that their own restraint will be matched by restraint on the part of other workers. However, this argument is quite dubious. It might rest on two related grounds. One is that self-interested workers run less risk in exercising restraint where the existence of a centralized union movement allows some possibility of restraint elsewhere. But this does not change the fact that income maximizing workers are still better off not exercising restraint while the rest of the union movement does so (see also Hardiman, 1988:15). To the extent that compliance is voluntary, a centralized union movement does not overcome the free rider problem.

The other, related, ground is to the effect that the existence of a centralized union movement encourages the development of solidaristic norms. Individual workers exercise restraint because they identify with the interests of a larger working class and because (and this relates to the pure self-interest ground) they believe that the same normative restraint is probable on the part of other workers, who share their sentiments. But there is precious little evidence of the widespread existence of the kind of sentimental attachment to a larger working class that this argument presumes. Lange (1984:108) suggests that the fact that Norwegian workers often vote to ratify centrally negotiated collective agreements is evidence of normative consensus. But that is nonsense. Failing to ratify a contract involves potential costs in the form of a strike and the presentation of an often complicated contract is normally associated with an endorsement of what has been agreed on by the union leadership. It takes fairly determined and intellectually independent workers to vote down a contract—and that is one reason why most contracts get ratified in North America too, despite its liberal system.

I would go further than this and argue that the negotiation of contracts at the plant level provides some grounds for greater normative consensus than is likely to be present within a centralized system. If the management of a plant negotiates with its employees in more or less good faith over a prolonged period of time there is no reason why the kind of confidence that goes with sequential trade-offs (and that serves to reduce the stake in any particular negotiation) cannot be built up. Indeed, the workers observing the negotiating process surely have a better basis for accumulated confidence; they actually know the personnel involved in the negotiations and can supplement knowledge about their past performance with estimates of the personal reliability of those involved. They are much less able to do this where the negotiations are conducted by the inevitably remote negotiating teams of an immense union federation and its immense employer association counterpart. We need to look elsewhere for any advantage of neocorporatist bargaining in the production of decisions likely to address long-run outcomes.

Assume (as, I think reasonably, the neocorporatists do) that the distribution of information about the long-run effects of a particular path of real wage growth means that the leaders of a centralized union are more likely than their members to recognize the economically damaging effects of a real wage increase. How might those leaders of a centralized union movement induce their members to accept settlements that favor better long-run outcomes? I have not discovered any very systematic treatments of this in the neocorporatist writings. But if one is to properly appraise the neocorporatist claims it is necessary to sort this issue out.

First, they might provide their members with a great deal of information that makes them see what is in their real, long-run, interests. Second, they might provide the members with misinformation that makes them think that they are making smaller sacrifices for the long run than they really are or that is designed to show exaggerated benefits of previous settlements negotiated with the long run in mind. Third, they might simply negotiate a settlement and give members no option but to accept it. This could be enforced in a pure neocorporatist system since such a system involves, by definition, a "representational monopoly" (Lehmbruch, 1984:612), that is, some means of preventing the emergence of alternative organizations to represent workers.

The first method—rational persuasion—is associated with the "social consensus" version of neocorporatism. I objected to Lange's version of it above and will critically examine some other versions in the next section. The second—disinformation—seems of rather limited utility in countries with a free press and minimally adequate parliamentary opposition. I doubt that, in a free society, you can fool most of the people all of the time (to paraphrase Abraham Lincoln).[14] The crude facts of economic performance—the growth in the cost of living, the amounts by which wage increase over a decade or so—will sooner or later impinge on the consciousness of ordinary workers (although probably not as rapidly as rational expectations theorists would have us believe!). That leaves coercion.

As we saw earlier, Lange (1984:107) acknowledges the role of coercion (although only in a form that can be put in quotation marks) and Barber and McCallum (1982:13, 99–103) make it quite clear that where there is not much prospect of building social consensus (Canada is the case they have in mind) they favor resort to the direct coercion implied in a statutory incomes policy. The question then becomes, is the coercive character of neocorporatist institutions likely to produce economic decisions, particularly on wage growth, that produce better outcomes in the long run?

The first difficulty with this is that it assumes that centralized negotiators are *able* to perceive what is in the best interests of the people whose long-run interests they are advancing. This must be fairly tricky. Consider the way Lange (1984:105) describes the issue from the point of view of the ordinary worker:

> the likelihood that any worker will cooperate with wage regulation will be a function of his risk of loss in the present contract period and the rate at which he discounts his future advantages from extensive co-operation if it were sustained. . . . . the higher his rate of discount, the less likely he is to cooperate conditionally with wage regulation.

Now, to be quite honest, I am not at all certain at what rate I would choose to discount my personal future income stream to a present value. I suspect that this is also the case for most workers. Nor do I think it likely that most individual workers have a very good estimate of the probability that the long-term benefits forecasted to come from a wage increase foregone will actually be delivered. More particularly, I submit that there are good grounds for thinking that union, business, and government negotiators do not have good estimates of the discount rates of the people on behalf of whom they are negotiating.[15] Indeed, how can they if the workers themselves do not have adequate estimates? Coercion does not solve the problem. There is still no obvious method available that would allow central negotiators to determine the balance of long- versus short-run income that would most gratify those on behalf of whom they are negotiating.

There are, in fact, two separate issues here. The first is the problem of estimating the preferences of individuals as between present and future income, that I have already discussed. The second is the problem of forecasting the outcomes from alternative macroeconomic policies (and in a centralized bargaining system the wage rates negotiated are very clearly a part of macroeconomic policy). In Chapter 2 I outlined some of the arguments against the possibility of an effective macroeconomic stabilization policy based in the limits on the information and the understanding required to formulate and implement the policy, and the capacity of capitalists and workers to undermine the intentions of a policy by anticipating some of its characteristics. Both of these general difficulties are relevant here. One can, then, raise questions about the *capacity* of centralized negotiators to serve the interests of those on behalf of whom they negotiate.

Even if negotiators could decide on what is in the long-term interests of those on behalf of whom they are negotiating, it is not clear to what extent they can make their decisions stick, if those decisions go against the broad trend of market forces. An employer who is short of one or another kind of labor and has a full order book, at prices out of which a profit can be made, is likely to find some way to raise pay to attract workers of the type sought (and in so doing to undermine the centrally negotiated macroeconomic policies). Even if the vigilance of local union officials prevents the employer from raising the wage rate for a particular job (but it is hard to imagine local union officials enthusiastically preventing their members from getting higher wages—at least, if they want to remain local union officials!) there is always the possibility of regrading the job so that it formally warrants a higher rate.

Something like this clearly does go on in neocorporatist systems. Flanagan, Soskice, and Ulman (1983:675) report that

It is clear . . . that wage drift continued to limit the achievements of European incomes policies during the 1970s as it had in earlier decades. In virtually every country in which a statistical analysis was possible, our wage-change estimating equations indicated that wage drift was sensitive to labor-market pressure. At the same time, in our statistical analyses we uncovered very little evidence of a significant negative relation between changes in wage drift and changes in negotiated rates, and we found no evidence at all of a compensatory equal proportionate relation, which would have implied that changes in negotiated rates have been exactly offset by opposite changes in drift and hence could not affect total money earnings and real wages.

Therefore, much of whatever restraint in official wage rates gets accomplished through neocorporatist bargaining is lost in wage drift.

Moreover, it is not just a problem of devious attempts by employers to deal with their own short-run production problems at the expense of the long-run interest of the population at large. There were forceful rejections of centrally negotiated agreements involving wildcat strikes by substantial groups of workers in many of the European countries that have been typically classified as neocorporatist (e.g., Crouch and Pizzorno, 1978; Barkin, 1975). A model that assumes that centrally negotiated wage rates determine what people actually get paid is a wildly inaccurate portrayal of what happens anywhere, including Sweden.

Social Consensus

Neocorporatist arguments typically assert that one of the sources of macroeconomic superiority of the relevant countries is the moral legitimacy that neocorporatist practices bestow on the distribution of income. Because neocorporatist bargaining explicitly takes into account the moral appropriateness of wage settlements people are more likely to accept the results of the bargaining and, moreover, to trust the government and employers when the onset of hard times requires real wage cuts or, at least, a significant slowing in the rate of increase of wages.

I have not come across a shred of direct evidence of greater moral approval of the inequality in societies whose polities are typically classified as neocorporatist. There is some evidence to the contrary. Scase (1977:23), for example, reported more resentment over income inequality in Sweden than in Britain.[16] (I review other relevant evidence in the next chapter.) In principle, there are certainly some problems with the argument. Once again, I would suggest that the remoteness of the highly centralized negotiators tends to undermine the moral authority of the settlements they negotiate. And besides, is it likely that the particular aspects of inequality that get addressed in negotiations coincide with those that are morally salient to those on behalf of whom the negotiations are being negotiated? I think not.

There is, of course, the difficulty of establishing the moral preferences of the relevant community. But even if that can be done, there is no guarantee that the settlement most suitable for economic growth coincides with the settlement that addresses the moral concerns of that constituency. For example, if Goldthorpe (1978:203; 1984:320) is correct, the notion of citizenship in industrial societies has been extended to include some degree of proprietorship over one's job. That is an issue of what is fair; it is a moral matter. But superior long-run economic performance requires phasing out less productive jobs (that are likely to be clustered in particular industries) and replacing them with more productive jobs, with a high potential for growth in productivity. The popular moral judgment is, then, that people should keep their jobs; the requirement of growth is that some people—quite a lot—should lose them. A suitable job placement scheme of the sort thought to exist under Sweden's active labor market policy *might* address this issue. But it is not obvious that someone losing his or her job in an industry in decline is going to be much enthused by the need to retrain, move jobs, and, perhaps, relocate from one part of the country to another, even with an active labor market policy. Such a person is likely to use all the moral suasion at his or her disposal to mobilize political sentiment—that is, to generate moral outrage at the phasing out of an industry that happens to be unproductive. The general point is, simply, that economic policies that generate moral approval are, much of the time, likely not to coincide with the economic policies that are consistent with economic growth.

Besides, we do know that moral judgments about inequality are not shared across the working class. Much of the resentment of workers is directed at the pay of other workers and there are some grounds for thinking that this is not simply a question of outrage at the distribution of income produced by the blind and impersonal workings of the market. Quite apart from anything else, there is no current capitalist society in which the pattern of inequality can reasonably be attributed to blind impersonal market mechanisms. Even the United States has some unions and welfare programs. But beyond this, the behavior of skilled workers tends to suggest that they regard substantial skill differentials as appropriate and, historically, they have created and maintained trade unions to protect those differences (Littler, 1982:77, 167) or caused problems within unions where the leadership pursued policies deemed to be inappropriately egalitarian (Hinton, 1973:166 ff.; Flanagan, Soskice, and Ulman, 1983:372). There is no shortage of resentments of white-collar workers towards blue-collar worker wages, and vice versa—and this in both liberal and neocorporatist societies (on the former see Bain, 1970:49; on the latter, Martin, 1984:212–213; Lash and Urry, 1987:246–248). I believe that the potential for moral legitimacy of a centrally negotiated set of wages is greatly limited by the lack of consensus on what an appropriate wage distribution would look like between blue- and white-collar workers, skilled and unskilled workers, male and female workers, graduate and nongraduate workers, ad infinitum.[17]

Supposing, furthermore, that as part of the trade-off of a real wage increase for a better "social wage" it is decided to increase taxes to fund improved social benefits. Most of the cost of those benefits will have to be paid for by the unionized constituency of the central union federation. It is fairly well established that there are limits to the revenue generating capacities of aggressively redistributive tax schemes (Atkinson, 1983:ch. 15). So after the provision of social benefits funded by taxes as *an alternative to a real wage increase*, workers are likely to find themselves paid less than they would have been had they pushed their market power aggressively, with their disposable incomes reduced by higher taxes, and provided with a set of benefits about which they are likely to have mixed feelings (because they coincide less precisely with the range of the things workers would have chosen to purchase, had they had the choice). This, it seems to me, would not do wonders for social consensus.

Finally, there is the question of the protection of the interests of those excluded from the central bargaining process (Schmitter, 1985:44). Neocorporatism, by definition, involves political decision making in which parliamentary institutions are partially replaced by direct negotiations between business and labor. If large employers and unionized labor have a disproportionate weight in determining economic outcomes there are some grounds for expecting the interests of the groups that are not represented within those centralized organizations to be neglected. Small business comes to mind immediately. So does nonunion labor.[18] If significant groups get excluded as a result of centralized bargaining between organized labor and business the members of those groups are not likely to enthusiastically share in the consensus that is advertised as one of the benefits of corporatism. Indeed, the notion of "consensus" loses much of its meaning.

A More Fundamental Issue

In appraising the economic performance of alternative institutional arrangements it is hard to avoid making some judgment about the performance of markets. The underlying premise of neocorporatist theorizing is that markets produce unsatisfactory outcomes because the workers who formerly had no option but to accept the costs of the fluctuations and inequalities generated by markets are now, with well-established unions, strong enough to secure some protection against economic fluctuations and to attack some of the features of the inequality that markets produce (see, especially, Goldthorpe, 1984:321–322). But, the argument goes, they have a largely negative power until their organizations are, through the construction of neocorporatist institutions, enlisted in the national pursuit of a very general social welfare. That is to say, until its constructive political participation is secured the union movement's efforts to protect the interests of its members simply foul the gears of economic growth by obstructing technological innovation and pushing up wages.

The problem with the arguments of those advancing this interpretation is that, to the extent that they go beyond classifying countries as neocorporatist and neoliberal and comparing their macroeconomic performance, they tend to simply produce examples of benefits that might flow from the centralization of wage negotiation and, in some versions, the development of a welfare state, without ever considering the economic and social problems that might be expected to be produced by any substantial supplanting of market processes.[19]

Consider one final problem that illustrates the difficulties with this approach rather well. The argument typically assumes that centralized wage negotiations involving a powerful union movement produce an agreement to more or less tie wage increases to the growth of productivity. But why should a powerful union movement settle for this? If it is really powerful would it not be tempted to go further and secure a change in the shares of gross national product going to capital and labor, that is, in the functional distribution of income? Assuming, for the sake of argument, that union leaders in neocorporatist polities continue to seek to advance the interests of their members—that there has been no substantial Michelsian corruption of their intentions (Michels, 1962)—what data could be used to persuade them that they should halt their demands at the point where private capital maintains its share of income? One possible response is that it does not matter if they do so, that there is nothing sacrosanct about any particular functional distribution of income, and that if unions manage to extract a larger share of national income for their workers, so much the better for them. This seems to be the view, not always clearly articulated, of some neocorporatist theorists.[20]

But such a response simply will not do. Neocorporatist theory, like its early twentieth-century antecedent, assumes that the economy will continue to be organized on the basis of private property. Such an economy leaves a significant share of the decision to invest in the hands of private

capital. A substantial shift away from capital in the functional distribution of income implies a decline in the rate of return on capital and a
reduction in the incentive to invest. A collapse in investment is in the
interests of no one. Now, the crux of the neocorporatist argument is,
precisely, that centralized bargaining allows the union movement to be
enlisted in the common pursuit of growth, which implies, of course, a
recognition of the need for investment. Thus, Schott has constructed
a model in which "workers will sometimes agree, quite rationally,
not to press for all the resources they could potentially command"
(1984b:92). Yet this is only a *model* designed to show how it is possible for
a rational set of workers to agree to allow their leaders to negotiate
agreements embodying sufficient restraint to allow investment to continue at a satisfactory level. There are two critical issues that it does not
address. First, how is it possible for the leaders of a labor movement to
determine the appropriate functional distribution of income? Second,
how is it possible for the leaders of that movement to induce its members to accept that the functional distribution they have decided on is
appropriate?

The answer to the first problem could be given by the solution to an
econometric model of the economy. That is to say, a model could be used
that predicts future investment and growth under alternative assumptions about wage growth and trends in the distribution of employment
between industries. But that is no real answer since, as we saw in Chapter 2, there is a multiplicity of such models the forecasting record of
which is at best mixed and at worst atrocious. Because the results of
econometric models are substantially determined by their assumptions,
the choice of one for policy purposes is itself a political act, likely to be
determined by political power rather than technical considerations.
There is no obvious solution to the first problem.

The solution to the second problem depends on the aspect of neocorporatism emphasized. If its coercive aspect is emphasized union leaders
can simply tell the members they represent what is good for them (for
the sake of argument I am assuming now that the first problem has been
resolved). Whether they like it or not, they are stuck with the decision
because of the union's representational monopoly. But if one allows
some limits to coercion or stresses the "social consensus" component of
neocorporatism the problem becomes, I think, insoluble.

First, as Schott makes clear (1984b:94–96), the incentive for workers to
forego consumption decreases where the anticipated rate of economic
growth is low. The process he has in mind is as follows: economic
growth tends to accelerate in response to a wave of technological inno-
vations that generate a high rate of return on capital.[21] Where the rate of
return on capital is high workers have an incentive to forego present

consumption by accepting modest wage increases because capitalists are likely to invest rather than consume most of the income that accrues to them and the product of those investments is more goods and services to be consumed by workers and their children in the future. But as the possibilities of the innovation are exhausted the rate of return on investment falls and capitalists are likely to respond to this by consuming a larger share of their income—that is to say, of their profits. In this *stagnationary* situation the incentive for workers to forego wage increases diminishes greatly. For there is no guarantee that the income they forego will actually be invested. It might simply be frittered away by capitalists in an orgy of conspicuous consumption. All of this is to say, then, that it is not always rational for workers to choose to respect the existing functional division of labor. This is a problem because the only way to escape from stagnation is through additional investment.

Second, even during those times when it is rational for workers to forego consumption it does not follow that they will be persuaded that that is so. The investment forecasts from one or another econometric model under different wage assumptions are unlikely to cut much ice. Workers look at what is in their pay packet and at the security of their jobs. It is not obvious how *individual* workers can be persuaded (1) that it is necessary to forego their particular wage increase (the impact of which on their own and their children's welfare is considerably more evident than whatever is promised from some percentage increase in the rate of investment); (2) that in the interests of growth their particular jobs should be cut to allow the shifting of resources to high productivity growth sectors; and (3) that capitalists can be counted on to do anything useful to offset their own personal wage or employment sacrifices. None of the rather romantic appeals to "social consensus" provides a solution to these problems.

I would argue, then, that neocorporatist theory does not provide any *satisfactory* answer to the question of why a union movement would ever agree to restrain its power and leave the functional distribution of income intact or, more precisely, leave the share of capital sufficiently high to allow appropriate levels of investment to continue.

There is, however, a way out of this problem. It is to suggest that an economy organized around private property is only one way of securing investment, and not necessarily the best one. Stephens (1979:188–194), in what is to a substantial extent a socialist tract, emphasized the role of Swedish employee investment funds (so-called "wage funds") in both building socialism and in ensuring adequate investment.

It is will known that the Swedish social democrats, in association with the blue-collar union federation, developed a "solidaristic wages policy" that involved negotiating wage increases that tend to be equal, irrespective of the past productivity growth or future productivity potential of an enterprise. The effect of this (to the extent that it is not offset by wage drift) has been to force down profits in low productivity sectors and allow unusually high profits in high productivity sectors. This tended to concentrate wealth in the hands of the owners of high productivity growth industry.

In principle, of course, this concentration of wealth is not *necessarily* against the interests of workers—if the profits are intelligently reinvested and produce growing levels of welfare. But a group within the LO and the Swedish Social Democratic Party either regarded the investments by capitalists in high productivity sectors as inadequate or the concentration of wealth as an issue in its own right.[22] In any case, they responded to it by recommending a policy that would require the transfer to the unions of a portion of the profits of companies with more than 100 employees in the form of newly issued equity. The effect of this, in the long run, would have been to transfer the ownership of companies to the union movement. As Stephens (1979:189) puts it, "In fifty or sixty years, the Swedish economy would be essentially socialist because the huge majority of equity capital would be collectively owned." In the wake of the political controversy caused by this plan (see Martin, 1985:448–452) it was adopted in a highly watered down form, in which shares had to be purchased on the open market from a fund largely provided for out of a payroll tax, supplemented by a 20% tax on "surplus profits." It does seem, however, that a number of writers advocating broadly neocorporatist interpretations are sympathetic with the more radical version of the plan (e.g., Goldthorpe, 1984:339) and, as such, they clearly regard the existing functional distribution of income as unessential to investment and growth.

Now, this would be a perfectly defensible position were there any serious analysis on the part of those who advocate it of the likely economic performance of a nonmarket economy of the sort they are advocating.[23] But, as is commonly the case in the political economy tradition in which they are writing, much more attention is devoted to the performance inadequacies of capitalism than to the sources of performance improvements to be gained from a noncapitalist economy. Their writings on the advantages of neocorporatist institutions do not address this question. The hallmark of corporatist writings, ancient and modern, is that they assume a private market economy, onto which some distinctive political arrangements get grafted. But the process of drastically modifying the functional distribution of income is actually a process of eliminating a private market economy, as Stephens (gleefully) noted and the theorists of neocorporatism have no serious analysis of what would replace it. My argument is, then, that a fundamental difficulty of neocorporatist analyses (but only one of a number of difficulties) is that they have no theory with which to determine the ultimate functional distribution of income that will be accepted by a powerful and centralized labor movement.

Notes

1.   Note that I have not listed *socialism* as an alternative. This might seem like a serious omission. But bear in mind that the precise relation of socialism to capitalist institutions has always been a difficult issue and besides, as we will see shortly, there is a strong association between neocorporatism and the form that socialism has taken in some noncommunist countries since the second world war. Thus, according to Grant (1985:6), "Neo-corporatism has generally been seen as a doctrinal companion of social democracy, and there is no doubt that social democrats have given a considerable impetus to the spread of corporatist arrangements, both in theory and practice."

2.   In what follows I depend heavily on P. Williamson (1985). Unless otherwise specified, in the rest of this chapter I use the terms "neocorporatism" and "corporatism" interchangeably to describe the modern form.

3.   This is particularly explicitly argued by Goldthorpe (1978, 1984), but is an essential premise, more or less explicitly stated in all the work within this genre. For a programmatic statement along these lines see Maier (1987:11).

4.   For examples of definitions along these lines see Lehmbruch (1984:61), Calmfors and Driffill (1988), and, in particular P. Williamson (1985:ch. 10).

5.   For some detailed data on just how discontinuous wage increases can be in an inflationary period see Smith (1988).

6.   The citation is to Lehmbruch (1983).

7.   Lange, writing specifically about unions, puts *coerce* in quotation marks. Frankly, I think that this is a fairly clear symptom of the intellectual evasiveness of a number of the analysts of neocorporatist economies who have also become protagonists of the institutional arrangement. One assumes that the quotation marks are there to indicate that what is involved is something other than real coercion. But this is nonsense. Either the union members are forced to be more passive than they would otherwise be in the face of a centrally negotiated agreement or they are not. It is, of course, precisely the coercive aspect of corporatism that Panitch has continually emphasized (Panitch, 1976, 1977a,b, 1980).

8.   It is perhaps worth quoting Lange (1984:106) at length here so that readers can make up their own minds. He argues that "for co-operation to become likely under conditions of uncertainty some normative factors creating the inclination to cooperate rather than defect must be present. Such a norm would override the risk of cooperation in the first game and would promote co-operation rather than defection when the player was uncertain whether his individual failure to co-operate might provoke the collapse of all co-operation. While the possible sources of such a norm are many, in the case of workers one of the most likely would seem to be a minimal degree of *extensive group commitment:* an identification with workers beyond one's bargaining unit which prompted a willingness to take small, short term risks by co-operating when this might be consistent

consistent with longer-term self-interest and which was tied to a belief that other workers had a similar identification."

9. But one of the advantages claimed for neocorporatism is that it allows governments to influence economic policy indirectly, through influence on the centralized bargainers, and thus allows it to protect "its ability to exercise legitimate power," presumably by sparing it from direct responsibility for economic failures (Grant, 1985:8; Streek, 1984:145). If government ensures that centrally negotiated wage restraint produces more investment, either through tax policy or through public investment, it abandons that particular political advantage of corporatism.

10. I noted above that one of the sources of restraint on real wages is the possibility of trading-off wage growth for social expenditures, including expenditures to reduce unemployment. This tends to suggest that high government expenditures on social programs are a natural outcome of corporatism. However, two observations are in order here. First, some writers within the corporatist tradition have classified Switzerland as corporatist, and Switzerland has a decidedly low level of government expenditures. Second, the mechanisms that have been argued to link government expenditures to economic performance in a corporatist context are tied to the response to an economic shock rather than to economic performance under normal circumstances.

11. It will surely not have escaped the reader's notice that the coercive character of neocorporatist wage determination in the previous section becomes normative acceptance in this version of the argument.

12. The source for these figures is Martin (1984:345).

13. For a useful systematic list of the costs and benefits of high government expenditures see Blais and McCallum (1986:164–166).

14. Although such deception was possible during wartime in Britain. During the second world war the British consumer price index was to some extent falsified (see Clegg, 1971:1).

15. The proper techniques for determining an appropriate rate of discounting, and for discounting an income stream to a present value remain controversial. See, for example, Mishan, 1982:237–260.

16. For an unconvincing attempt to argue around this conclusion see Gilbert (1986:162–165).

17. This problem is recognized by Goldthorpe (1987a:389 396), but he seems to think that it can be overcome if union leaders encourage sentiments of class solidarity among their members. This, it seems to me, is the analytic equivalent of waving a magic wand.

18. Remember, Sweden is almost unique in having practically its whole labor force unionized. Most other countries identified as more or less corporatist— including Austria—have substantial nonunion sectors. For a general analysis of this difficulty in corporatist institutions see Bendix (1964:89–126).

19. For the honorable exception to this see Blais and McCallum (1985).

20. Thus, for example, Goldthorpe's clearly positive evaluation of neocorporatist institutions is tied to its redistributive effects (1984:336–337). See also Grant, 1985:24–25.

21. For a discussion of models of economic growth emphasizing the effects of waves of technological innovation see Coombs, Saviotti, and Walsh (1987:ch. 7) and Berry (1991:35–60).

22. In fact Stephens (1979:193) points out that both the LO and the TCO—the

white-collar federation—justified the employee investment fund plan in terms of the need to stimulate investment, but the TCO put more emphasis on the need for investment than did the LO. See also Korpi (1978:329).

23.   For an exceptional attempt to address issues of this sort see Przeworski and Wallerstein (1988).

7
THE EFFECTS OF INSTITUTIONS ON MACROECONOMIC PERFORMANCE

In Chapter 5 I showed that there was little evidence for the detailed mechanisms that, it is often supposed, link class conflict to inflation. Many of the institutional changes thought to produce a wage-push inflation seem to exist in a more tangible form in the hands of those asserting them than in identifiable historical processes (e.g., Goldthorpe's ideas about the effects of a collapsing status order, maturing working class, and extended notions of citizenship). Other changes do clearly exist but no robust evidence exists that they have actually produced a wage-push (e.g., an increase in government employment, the rise in the percentage unionized from the pre- to the postwar period).

It is true that there were, during the postwar period, some institutional changes likely to produce a wage-push effect of some sort. This was particularly the case for the liberalized labor laws adopted in a number of countries after the second world war, subsequently extended in some of them. Even here, however, it is not at all clear that labor law liberalization was *forced* on governments by a newly powerful and determined working class. The period of successful labor law retrenchment after the mid-1970s suggests that governments probably always had more latitude to legislate to weaken the labor movement than some politicians thought.

So on what does the evidence rest for the existence of a wage-push inflation of the sort outlined in recent analyses by sociologists and political scientists? Largely, it turns out, it rests on studies on the relative macroeconomic performance of different countries. Note that although the particular outcome that is at issue in this study is the postwar inflation, theoretic considerations direct attention to a wider range of explanandums.

First, there is unemployment. Some of the writing on the postwar inflation produced by sociologists and political scientists has assumed the existence of a long-run Phillips curve (e.g., Hibbs, 1977; Barry,

1985:300). Even where that is not assumed, it might still be argued that governments in a country with a persistently high rate of unemployment are likely to be tempted from time to time to seek to escape the political opprobrium it causes by pursuing inflationary macroeconomic policies that exploit the temporary unemployment-reducing effects of the short-run Phillips curve (e.g., Olson, 1982:218). High unemployment, in other words, might produce inflationary policies. Indeed, that is precisely what seems to have happened in a number of countries after the 1973 oil shock (Bruno and Sachs, 1985:160). Second, and related to the above, governments might be less likely to stumble into inflationary policies if they preside over economies with satisfactory records of economic growth. Britain had a record of low economic growth and its political rhetoric in the 1960s was filled with rather vague ideas about "going for growth" that, in practice, meant stimulative economic policies (e.g., Stewart, 1967:252–258). Third, there are other macroeconomic outcomes thought to be associated with the operation of neocorporatist institutions. For example, it is usually argued that a large government presence in the economy and some substantial amount of income redistribution are principal parts of the mechanism through which neocorporatism produces superior economic outcomes (e.g., Barber and McCallum, 1982:2; Bruno and Sachs, 1985:224).

Consequently, in what follows, I consider not only evidence bearing directly on differences in the rates of inflation between countries but also evidence on the other macroeconomic outcomes that are relevant to theories of the inflationary process. I begin with an appraisal of the quantitative and cross-national studies of aggregate economic performance—studies mainly inspired by the analyses of neocorporatism outlined and criticized in the previous chapter. How good are the results from those studies? To be blunt, I will argue that they are not very good at all.

Quantitative Studies: Some Methodological Problems

There is a set of countries with varying records of inflation, unemployment, and economic growth. Making use of this set, an obvious technique available for testing theories about the implications of neocorporatism is as follows: countries can be classified into those with institutions thought to be associated with neocorporatism and those without them and the records of economic performance of the two groups over some period examined either through the comparison of means (e.g., Crouch, 1985:121–122, 124) or by categorizing the countries and displaying the array of scores on each performance measure (e.g., Wilensky and Turner, 1987:19).[1] Or, if the presence of neocorporatist institutions can somehow be scaled (and this is a very popular technique), the relationship between neocorporatism and economic performance can be plotted on a graph (e.g., Barber and McCallum, 1982:5; Crouch, 1985:120–124; Schmidt, 1989:118; Masters and Robertson, 1988:1190). Finally, once neocorporatism is scaled its relative effect on macroeconomic outcomes, net of other likely influences, can be estimated using multiple regression techniques (e.g., McCallum, 1983; Bruno and Sachs, 1985:228–232; Friedland and Sanders, 1985; Lange and Garrett, 1985; Garrett and Lange, 1986; Hicks, 1988; Alvarez, Garrett, and Lange, 1991).

At first sight all this seems rather straightforward. In fact, however, there are a number of problems.

Which Countries Are Neocorporatist?

Whether comparing means, drawing a graph, or estimating regression coefficients, the results are only as valid as the scores measuring the presence or absence, or degree of neocorporatism. The first problem is the validity and reliability of measures of neocorporatism. The extent to which this is a problem can be seen in Chart 7.1.[2] It shows the range of ways in which countries have been classified between neocorporatist and nonneocorporatist categories.[3] There is, it is true, some consensus. Austria, Norway, and Sweden *almost always* fall into the most corporatist category (in Schmidt's most recent effort Sweden drops to the medium category). Where included, the United States, Canada, Ireland, and Italy are always in the least corporatist category, and France is almost always in there too (the exception is, again, Schmidt, 1989). After that, things get more complicated. The Netherlands is sometimes allocated to the most neocorporatist category and sometimes to the medium one. Australia shifts between the medium and the least neocorporatist categories. However, no spectacular inconsistency is involved for those cases. The United Kingdom, Belgium, Japan, Finland, Denmark, Switzerland, and Germany are quite another matter. Across studies their placement varies from the highest to the lowest category.

This, I submit, is a major problem. After all, measurement of the effects of neocorporatism is impossible without agreement on what it is. And if the location of 7 of the 18 or so cases that typically show up in relevant studies can shift so widely between categories (and most of the rest shift across a narrower band) it is fairly clear that there is some

Chart 7.1. Which Countries have Corporatist (or Related) Systems?

Source	High	Medium	Low	Description
Schmidt, 1982 (1974–78)	Austria Japan Norway Sweden Switzerland	Australia Belgium Denmark Finland Iceland Germany Israel Luxembourg New Zealand Netherlands	Canada France Ireland Italy UK US	Corporatism
Lehmbruch, 1982	Austria Sweden Netherlands	Denmark Germany UK	France	Liberal corporatism
Schmitter, 1981	Austria Norway Denmark Finland Sweden	Netherlands Belgium Germany Switzerland	Canada Ireland US France UK Italy	Societal corporatism
Crouch, 1985	Austria Denmark Finland Netherlands Norway Sweden Switzerland Germany	Australia Belgium Canada France Ireland Italy Japan New Zealand UK US		Neocorporatism
Barber and McCallum, 1982	Austria Belgium Denmark Japan Germany Netherlands Norway Switzerland Sweden	New Zealand UK Australia Ireland US Canada France Finland Italy		Social consensus
Bruno and Sachs, 1985;	Austria Germany	Denmark Japan	Australia Canada	Labor Market Corporatism

(continued)

Chart 7.1. (Continued)

Source	High	Medium	Low	Description
Blais and McCallum, 1986	Netherlands Norway Sweden	Finland Switzerland	France Ireland UK US Belgium Italy New Zealand	
Wilensky, 1987	Austria Sweden Netherlands Germany	Japan France	UK US	Corporatism
Maier, 1984	Sweden Norway Germany Austria Switzerland Netherlands		France Italy UK US	Consensual wage determination
Lange and Garrett, 1985 (1)	Sweden Norway Austria Belgium Denmark Finland	Netherlands Australia UK Germany	Italy Canada US France Japan	Labour organization index
Lange and Garrett, 1985 (2)	Austria Norway UK Denmark Germany	Sweden Netherlands Finland Australia Belgium	Canada Japan US France Italy	Left Cabinet Participation (1974–1980)
Lange and Garrett, 1985 (3)	Norway Austria Denmark Sweden UK	Germany Finland Netherlands Belgium Australia	Italy France Japan Canada US	Cross product of Lange and Garrett (1) and (2)
Marks, 1986 (1)	Sweden Norway Belgium Austria	UK Germany Netherlands Finland	Denmark Italy France US Canada Ireland	Neocorporatist incomes policy

(continued)

Chart 7.1.   (Continued)

Source	High	Medium	Low	Description
Marks, 1986 (2)	Sweden Norway Austria Denmark	UK Finland Belgium Germany Netherlands Switzerland	Italy France US Canada Ireland	Socialist government participation (1946–76)
Tarantelli, 1986	Austria Germany Japan Sweden Denmark Norway	Netherlands Australia Finland US Belgium Canada	New Zealand France UK Italy	Neocorporatism
Schmidt, 1989	Norway Japan Germany Austria Switzerland	Ireland Denmark France Belgium Finland Netherlands Sweden	Portugal Spain Greece U.K. Canada Australia New Zealand USA	Concertation/ Consensus
Cameron, 1984	Austria Sweden Norway Denmark Finland Belgium	UK Germany Australia Switzerland Netherlands Ireland	France Italy Spain Japan US Canada	Organizational power of labour
Hicks, Swank, and Ambuhl, 1989	Austria Belgium Finland Netherlands Norway Sweden		Australia Canada France Germany Ireland Italy Japan Switzerland UK US	Union strength/ 'Corporatism'

disagreement over what the concept means. It is also clear that the differences of means and regression coefficients from a set of studies with this characteristic cannot easily be compared.

There is a more forceful point to be made here. With a maximum of 18 to 20 cases, the economic performance effects uncovered depend very heavily on how countries are classified. In particular, it is the placement of the countries with very good or very poor records that determines whether or not neocorporatism is associated with superior macroeconomic performance. Switzerland has a postwar history of low inflation and practically nonexistent unemployment. Until recently, Germany did almost as well in both inflation and unemployment and maintained a good record of economic growth too. Italy, on the other hand, has had the worst record of inflation and unemployment among industrial countries (although at first sight quite good economic growth). Over the last two decades, the United Kingdom and Ireland appear to have done badly at practically everything. To a substantial extent what you find when you use some method to test for a relationship between neocorporatism and macroeconomic outcomes depends on where you put these countries.

Japan matters even more. It has the highest average annual rate of growth among industrial countries, a consistently low rate of official unemployment, and, since the mid-1970s, a low rate of inflation. There are two interesting features of the way Japan has been classified in the literature. There are, first, the criteria used to classify Japan with neocorporatist countries. In Barber and McCallum (1982) the usual corporatist countries (Sweden, Austria, Norway) plus some others are put into one group. Then Japan, on its own, is put into a second group.[4] These two groups contain the countries that have the institutional bases for "social consensus." Why does Japan go into its own group? Because, according to Barber and McCallum (1982:11), although it does not have centralized bargaining, "Japanese firms offer 'lifetime' employment and these, together with very low unemployment rates, provide a high degree of job security to the worker." There is also some evidence that it has only a moderately unequal distribution of income. Schmidt (1989) argues somewhat similarly: he groups Japan with Norway, Austria, Germany, and Switzerland because "while labour found itself excluded at the national level" it was "included at the enterprise level" (p. 110) and this appears to have produced "a high degree of concerted policy formation and high levels of stable consensus between capital and labour" (p. 116).

In effect, this introduces "functional alternatives" into the analysis (Merton, 1949:35–38). A country does not actually have to develop centralized bargaining and a social democratic government to secure "social consensus" or "concerted policy formation." Other arrangements can produce the same consequence.[5] Now in principle this is all very well, and it may even be true; but it does make the falsification of hypotheses about the effects of neocorporatism a bit difficult. In particular, it makes it rather easy to deal with cases that do not have the defining characteristics of neocorporatism by discovering other traits that can stand in their stead. That there is a general problem of falsifiability with arguments couched in terms of "functional alternatives" was made abundantly clear in the splendid article published some time ago by Carl Hempel (1959).

A second feature is that Japan is only unambiguously assigned to the least corporatist category in studies using Lange and Garrett's (1985) measures (Garrett and Lange, 1986; Hicks, 1988). These, however, are studies in which the classification decision is based on an arithmetic operation rather than a subjective judgment.[6] In other words, only where the classification rules prevent the classification decision from being fudged does Japan end up in the least corporatist category.

Time Period Analyzed

The extent to which the institutions of some countries warrant their assignment to a neocorporatist category varies over time (this explains some—but not all—of the classificatory inconsistencies described in the previous section). The collapse of centrally negotiated incomes policies in the Netherlands between 1962 and 1963 is, of course, well known (e.g., Shonfield, 1965:212–217). To a substantial extent, the history of economic policy in the United Kingdom from the 1950s to the end of the 1970s is dominated by the attempt to construct some sort of centralized bargaining relations, with accompanying wage restraint.[7] All this, of course, came to an end when Margaret Thatcher came to power in 1979. In Germany, on the other hand, it is easier to allocate the country to the neocorporatist category during the early part of the Social Democratic interregnum (as part of coalitions) from 1966 to 1974 than for the period before or after (Allen, 1989:262).[8]

Furthermore, social democratic parties tend to be in and out of government. And even when they are in government, as we saw in Chapter 3, their policies often become progressively more conservative. To the extent that, according to some theory, social democratic parties are supposed to be part of the neocorporatist institutional system, and that their effects are mediated through specific interventionist policies, attempts to estimate the effects of neocorporatism need to take into account whether a social democratic party is present or absent in government *and* whether there is anything distinctively social democratic about its policies.

Economic conditions also change. The most obvious change occurred with the oil shock of 1973, after which average levels of growth fell throughout the West. This established a wholly different environment for economic policy making. In the 1960s macroeconomic performance was relatively good throughout the capitalist world (even, in retrospect, in the United Kingdom); living standards were carried upward by the overall growth of world trade; unemployment was low and inflation, while rising, was still at moderate levels. In this period, one might reasonably argue that there was room for governments to tinker with all sorts of institutional arrangements and, as long as they remained open to trade, to maintain a politically acceptable growth performance. It was the arrival of difficult times in 1973 that made policy differences really matter. It follows from this that studies of time periods that average across the pre- and post-1973 period are likely to eliminate much of the interesting variance in economic performance (see also Castles, 1987:385–386).

Thus, it can be seen from Figures 1.1 to 1.3, 7.1, and 7.2 that the critical issue in differentiating the postwar economic performance of Western nations is *the extent to which their performance deteriorated after 1973*. Relative to other countries, the inflation performance of Canada and the United States (going from low to medium) and Italy, New Zealand, Australia, and the United Kingdom (going from medium to high)

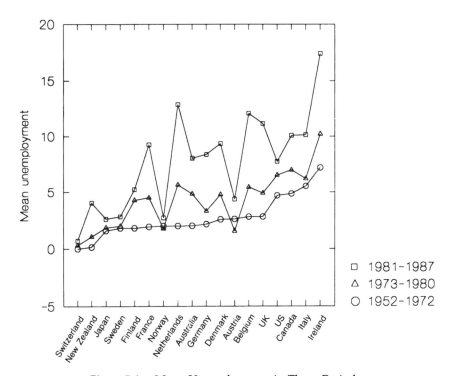

Figure 7.1. Mean Unemployment in Three Periods.

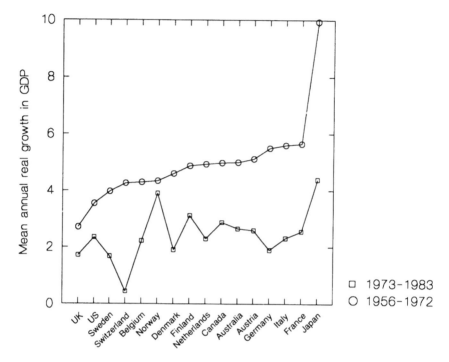

Figure 7.2. Growth Before and After the Oil Shock.

deteriorated after the oil shock, whereas Japan's performance improved considerably. Average growth fell everywhere after 1973, but least in Norway, the United Kingdom, and the United States (these latter two already had a rather low rate of growth) and most in Sweden, Switzerland, Denmark, Canada, Australia, Austria, Italy, France, and, in particular, Germany. It also fell substantially in Japan, but from a very high level to a still distinctively high level. Unemployment rose everywhere after the oil shock, but by very little in Norway, Austria, Switzerland, Japan, and Sweden and by a distinctively large amount in France, the Netherlands, Australia, Germany, Denmark, Belgium, the United Kingdom, Canada, Italy and Ireland. It rose only moderately in the United States.

To illustrate the problem with the relative indifference to time period in the relevant studies in Chart 7.2 I summarize the treatment of Germany, the Netherlands, and the United Kingdom in some of the main quantitative studies of macroeconomic performance. This chart shows several things. It shows that Germany and the Netherlands get classified as corporatist in studies that extend across the entire period from 1950 to

Chart 7.2. Time Periods and Classification Decisions

	Selected Dependent Variables	Time Period of Dependent Variables	Corporatism Classification, Germany, Netherlands, UK	Left Vote
Crouch, 1985	growth in inflation	Peak inflation in the mid 1970s minus mean inflation, 1964 to 1967	Germany=high Neth.=high UK=low	not analyzed
Master and Robertson, 1985	growth in public employment	1965–1983	Germany=medium Neth.=medium UK=low	not analyzed
Lange and Garrett, 1985	change in average economic growth	mean growth 1974 to 1980 minus mean growth 1960 to 1973	Germany=high Neth.=medium UK=high	mean percent cabinet portfolios held 1974 to 1980; mean percent left vote 1960 to 1980
McCallum, 1983	mean annual inflation	1973 to 1979	Germany=high Neth.=high UK=low	not analyzed
Blais and McCallum, 1986	annual average percent change in GDP	1960 to 1981	Germany=high Neth.=high UK=low (note: Japan excluded)	not analyzed
Bruno and Sachs, 1985	rise in misery index	mean score 1973 to 1979 minus mean score 1965 to 1973	Germany=high Neth.=high UK=low	not analyzed

(continued)

Chart 7.2. (Continued)

	Selected Dependent Variables	Time Period of Dependent Variables	Corporatism Classification, Germany, Netherlands, UK	Left Vote
Cameron, 1984	average annual percent unemployed	1965 to 1982	Germany=medium Neth.=medium UK=low	mean percent cabinet portfolio held; mean percent seats held as percent of number needed for a majority (1965 to 1982)
Wilensky and Turner, 1987	(1) average annual unemployment, (2) average annual economic growth, (3) average annual inflation	1950 to 1974, 1975 to 1979, 1980 to 1984	Germany=high Neth.=medium+ UK=low	not analyzed
Schmidt, 1989	average annual misery index, 1974 to 1984	1974 to 1984	Germany=high Neth.=medium UK=low	not analyzed
Friedland and Sanders, 1985	economic growth over one, two, or three years	1965 to 1980 (pooled sample)	not analyzed	not analyzed

1984 whereas, with the exception of Lange and Garrett's (1985) study, over the same time period, the United Kingdom is uniformly classified as noncorporatist. It also shows that many studies aggregate data from before and after the oil shock (Crouch, 1985; Masters and Robertson, 1988; Blais and McCallum, 1986; Cameron, 1984; Friedland and Sanders, 1985). Finally, it shows that although, in general, the social democratic element in neocorporatist theory is ignored in quantitative studies, where it is included (Lange and Garrett, 1985; Cameron, 1984), it involves averaging some form of left political presence over a substantial time period.

All of these features suggest serious problems with much of this quantitative literature. The least that can be said about the cases of Germany, the Netherlands, and the United Kingdom is that, from the point of view of neocorporatist theory, they are complicated. This complexity is ignored in the quantitative literature. In averaging economic performance data from before and after the oil shock, most studies gloss over the extent to which the real difference in economic performance between nations is a matter of how they dealt with the post-oil shock difficulties. And, in averaging left political presence over substantial time periods, the studies detach the social democratic presence in government from the actual record of policy making. For example, by averaging cabinet presence and left vote over almost 20 years from 1965 to 1982 and treating the result as a unitary independent variable, Cameron submerges the distinct shift in politics and policy in Britain in 1979—a shift that showed up rather promptly in a dramatic rise in unemployment and fall in economic growth. And, for that matter, this method makes it impossible to take into account the fact that governments of the left typically stop behaving in very distinctive ways after they have been in office for several years.

The Independence of Cases

In Chapter 2 I pointed out that flexible exchange rates or not, small countries tend to be constrained to follow the policy lead of larger trading partners. I illustrated this with the case of Canada, but the same principle applies more widely. We know that Ireland has had difficulty in stabilizing the exchange rate of the Irish pound with the other currencies of the European Monetary System precisely because Ireland trades so heavily with the United Kingdom that it is compelled to align its currency with sterling and, by extension, its rate of inflation with that in the United Kingdom (Crouigneau, 1986; Hardiman, 1988:42–43, 243–244). In an article some years ago (Smith, 1987) I showed that the currencies of the small countries contiguous with Germany (Austria, Belgium, Denmark, the Netherlands, Switzerland) have tended not to vary greatly in relation to the mark and that their rates of inflation have been correlated with Germany's. Further, the greater the extent to which each country's trade is concentrated with Germany (and, therefore its economy is integrated with the larger country), the lower the exchange rate variability with respect to the mark and the closer the correlation between rates of inflation.

This raises an interesting methodological problem. If macroeconomic policy in a number of small countries is to an important extent constrained by the need to align their currency with a larger trading neighbor, can one really call those countries *independent cases* in a quantitative analysis? In practice, a major element of Canada's macroeconomic policy has involved limiting the variation of the value of the Canadian with respect to the U.S. dollar. This produces a rate of inflation in Canada that is usually similar to the rate in the United States. Where, then, cross-national data including both the United States and Canada is employed to explain differences in inflation rates once might reasonably argue that the United States is being counted twice: and, to the extent that the same phenomenon applies to the smaller countries contiguous to Germany, that Germany is being counted up to six times.

It is also true, of course, that where a small country trades heavily with a larger country, its economic growth and unemployment records are largely determined by the rate of economic growth of the larger trading partner. This is another reason why many of the cases used in samples in studies of neocorporatism are not even remotely independent.

The Measurement of Economic Growth

Higher rates of economic growth are sometimes seen as a benefit of neocorporatism; in addition, by taking the edge off the distributive struggle it is claimed that they also reduce the rate of inflation (e.g., Gilbert, 1981:199, 1986:43–44). Now, rates of economic growth between countries certainly vary and, assuming away the methodological difficulties discussed above, in principle it ought to be possible to establish whether or not countries with neocorporatist institutions have higher or lower rates of economic growth.

However, in estimating the extent to which neocorporatist institutions enhance economic growth it is necessary to bear in mind that, in the long run, economic growth depends largely on productivity improvements, and it is a lot easier to improve productivity if improved techniques do not have to be created but, rather, can be adopted from a technological leader.[9] At the end of the second world war the world technological leader was the United States, followed by Canada (Maddison, 1982:98). In aggregate, the United States still has the highest productivity levels in the world, but the gap has narrowed and it has done so *principally* because in order to upgrade its productivity the United States has had to push back the technological frontier whereas other countries have been able to tinker with (and in some cases, it is true, improve on) technologies mainly developed and applied in the United States.

It is not only the relative position of the United States that is at issue here. The farther a country was from United States technological best practice in 1950, the larger the feasible *inexpensive* productivity gains available to it. Thus, Canada, Australia, the United Kingdom, Sweden, Belgium, the Netherlands, and Switzerland were closer to U.S. productivity levels than most other countries and so would have had rather more difficulty in generating impressive rates of productivity growth than Japan, Italy, Germany, and Austria, all of which in 1950 had very low levels of labor productivity compared to the United States. Furthermore, Germany and Austria should be differentiated from Japan and Italy; the low productivity levels of Germany and Austria in 1950 represented a dip from their prewar relative level, presumably because of destruction during World War II. In other words, those two countries had a particular advantage in that they not only started from a lower postwar productivity base but, in addition, they had a labor force accustomed to more modern equipment and thus better equipped to use that equipment efficiently.

Just how important this factor is can be seen from Figure 7.3, that I have adapted from Helliwell (1988:122; see also Dowrick and Nguyen, 1989). It shows that growth in labor productivity from 1960 to 1985 is strongly negatively related to the initial level of productivity in 1960 (r^2 = 0.74).[10] Another way to look at what is at issue here is with Figure 7.4, which is also adapted from Helliwell (1988). It shows to what extent each country's productivity growth differs from what would be predicted by its initial productivity level. What is interesting is that the superior performers (in that they have had rates of productivity growth in excess of what would be predicted from their initial level) include the resolutely noncorporatist United States and Canada and the underperformers include Sweden and Denmark—the former the corporatist paragon and the latter a country that is also often classified as corporatist (e.g., Crouch, 1985).

This raises the question, to what extent has initial productivity level been controlled for in quantitative, cross-national, studies of economic

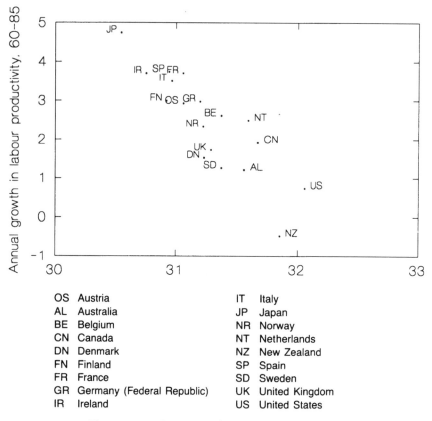

OS Austria   IT Italy
AL Australia   JP Japan
BE Belgium   NR Norway
CN Canada   NT Netherlands
DN Denmark   NZ New Zealand
FN Finland   SP Spain
FR France   SD Sweden
GR Germany (Federal Republic)   UK United Kingdom
IR Ireland   US United States

Figure 7.3   Labor Productivity: Growth by Level

growth? The answer is that in many studies it has not been controlled (e.g., Friedland and Sanders, 1985; Wilensky and Turner, 1987; Schmidt, 1989:114–115; Lange and Garrett, 1985; Garrett and Lange, 1986; Alvarez, Garrett, and Lange, 1991).[11] Therefore the economic growth measures that are used in these studies to discriminate between corporatist and liberal performance are difficult to interpret.

Controlling for Third, Fourth, etc., Factors

The importance of international interdependence, and of labor productivity at the beginning point of any analysis of economic growth are particular examples of a more general methodological problem: this is the exclusive or principal use of bivariate evidence to test the hypothesis

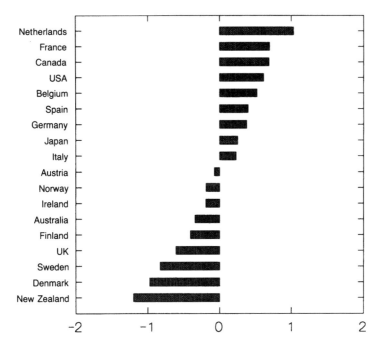

Average annual growth 1960-1985: observed minus predicted

Figure 7.4   Labor Productivity Growth Performance.

that neocorporatist institutions produce superior economic performance. There *are* attempts to estimate the effects of neocorporatism
using multivariate methods (e.g., McCallum, 1983; Bruno and Sachs,
1985; Friedland and Sanders, 1985; Lange and Garrett, 1985; Garret and
Lange, 1986; Hicks, 1988; Alvarez, Garrett, and Lange, 1991). But there
is a large number of studies, some of them frequently cited, that put
great emphasis on one or several breakdowns of macroeconomic performance by neocorporatism score (e.g., Cameron, 1984:160, 1985:246;
Crouch, 1985:119–127; Tarantelli, 1986; Wilensky and Turner, 1987:19;
Schmidt, 1989:105–116; Zeigler, 1988:89–116; Korpi, 1990).[12] It should be
clear that the quantitative data in these studies are always combined
with a more qualitative discussion of two or more cases—such as the
discussion that occupies the second part of this chapter. But the bivariate
analyses are presented as if they constitute evidence of some substance.
Now, I think it is reasonable to recognize that *some* data are always better
than *no* data and that, since definitive tests in the social sciences are hard
to come by, it makes sense to make the most of the available evidence,
even if it is flawed. Still, it is important to actually identify flaws and

"bivariateness" (so to speak) in what is so obviously a multivariate world is a *major* flaw.

We know that macroeconomic outcomes are affected by a number of factors other than, or in addition to, centralized bargaining. One is the relative prices of imports and exports. For the New Zealand economy, for example, a (perhaps *the*) critical determinant of trends in growth and employment has been the fate of export prices of butter and mutton (Blyth, 1977). All Western industrialized countries were hurt by the oil shocks, but the effect of the first oil shock was moderated for significant producers like Canada, the United States, and Norway. Another such factor is variation in national financial institutions. For example, there is variation in the autonomy of central banks. This is an important "third factor" because, as we saw in Chapter 3, it is stressed in the public choice accounts of international differences in rates of inflation and, to the extent that inflation has real consequences, unemployment and growth. Countries also vary in the importance of international financial transactions in the national economy and, therefore, the weight of the preferences of private financial institutions in government policy decision. Alt (1988:155–161), for instance, has emphasized the extent to which economic policy in the United Kingdom is constrained by the economic importance of the financial sector in its balance of payments, given the high degree of international mobility of financial capital.[13]

The two factors outlined above do not, of course, exhaust the list of things that one would wish to control in an attempt to estimate the effects of neocorporatist institutions on macroeconomic performance. But they are all potentially important, at least for some cases. And, where the sample rarely exceeds 18, single cases (that significantly diverge from the mean of the variables of interest) matter.

Summary

It would be possible to begin an article reporting, quite truthfully, something like the following: "There is a large accumulation of quantitative evidence suggesting positive effects of neocorporatist institutions on macroeconomic performance." Then one could cite in support a dozen or so studies. But what I have tried to show in the first section of this chapter is that there is much less to this accumulation of evidence than meets the eye. Some studies display all the flaws listed above: dubious assignment of cases to corporatist or noncorporatist categories, lack of attention to the implications of international interdependence for small country policy autonomy, inappropriate averaging over discrepant time periods, failure to control for initial productivity levels in analyses of economic growth, and failure to control for other factors. The evidence from such studies (Cameron, 1984, 1985; Crouch, 1985; Wilensky and Turner, 1987; Schmidt, 1989) has little or no value. This reduces the absolute amount of supportive quantitative evidence by more than a third.

Furthermore, *none* of the remaining studies is sheltered from all of these criticisms. It is true that the studies by the economists McCallum (1983) and Bruno and Sachs (1985) include controls and a recognition of the need to distinguish the pre- from the post-oil shock period. But their studies are flawed by the classification between corporatist and noncorporatist countries that they adopted. In each case they cite Crouch's 1985 paper as the source of the scale scores of corporatism that they incorporate into their analyses. Crouch's paper, however, was part of a collection based on a conference that took place quite some time before the conference papers were published. So both McCallum, and Bruno and Sachs used the original, unpublished, version of Crouch's paper. In the published version, however, *the scale scores were dropped* in favor of a simple categorical distinction between neocorporatist and liberal economies. In other words, McCallum, and Bruno and Sachs, estimated equations with a set of corporatism scores that the developer of those scores did not himself feel sufficiently confident to publish![14]

All this is to say, then, that the quantitative evidence on corporatism and macroeconomic performance at our disposal settles nothing. Perhaps, at some future point in time, someone will develop a better quantitative test (although problems of data quality and model specification make me skeptical that this will happen). In the meantime, we can get a firmer grasp of the relationship between institutions and economic performance by examining selected country cases in a little more detail. Regression estimates are disproportionately determined by cases at the extremes of a regression line. In the research on neocorporatism, that means Austria, Sweden, and, sometimes, Germany at the corporatist end of the regression line. In addition, given its extraordinary postwar economic performance and the fact that it has sometimes been classified as corporatist (or equivalent), the case of Japan is of particular interest.

Institutions and Performance: Claims and Alternatives

In the previous chapter I outlined the main claims about the effects of neocorporatist institutions on economic performance. These claims can be grouped into two sets. First, there are claims about the institutions of neocorporatism and how they operate:

1. Bargaining takes place between a more or less centralized organization of labor unions and a more or less centralized organization of employers.
2. The policy options of the government are enlarged because a substantial part of GDP passes through government coffers.
3. These policy options include trading-off tax relief or government services for wage restraint.
4. There is a well-developed welfare state that serves to remove some of the anxiety and tension from relations between employers and workers.
5. These institutions produce a somewhat higher degree of normative consensus than would be found in their absence, so that workers are less mistrustful of their employers and less sceptical about the appropriateness of existing levels of inequality.
6. In the absence of centralized bargaining or some of the other institutions outlined above, there are "functional alternatives" that produce outcomes similar to those found in classic neocorporatist economies, such as Sweden (e.g., lifetime employment in Japan, or statutory incomes policies elsewhere).

Second, there are claims about the effects of these institutional arrangements. Neocorporatist institutions produce

1. a narrower dispersion of wages;
2. less difficulty in moving resources out of industries in decline;
3. less "leapfrogging" in the wage-determination process;
4. less industrial conflict;
5. a superior growth record;
6. both as a result of a superior growth record and of the attempt by governments within neocorporatist systems to protect workers against the vicissitudes of the unregulated operation of markets, lower unemployment;
7. and, finally, related to all of the above, *either* lower rates of wage and price inflation in general *or* lower rates in response to supply-side shocks.

Now, as a test of neocorporatist theory it would be unreasonably stringent to require that *all* of the institutional arrangements and outcomes be present in any economy thought to fit into the neocorporatist category. Clearly, however, some significant proportion of them should be present. At the same time, in appraising the economic performance of selected cases, it makes sense to examine the extent to which factors other than those incorporated into the standard analyses might produce the outcomes that are thought to be desirable. In previous discussions I have raised a number of such possibilities some of which are listed below.

1. The amount of industrial conflict is likely to be affected by the legislative framework of labor relations and, in particular, the harshness or laxity with which striking is treated.
2. For writers within the public choice tradition central bank independence is a critical factor that can explain lower rates of inflation and, to the extent that unstable prices disrupt the process of making contracts, superior economic growth and lower unemployment.
3. Welfare systems should be judged not only by the size and nature of the benefits they provide. Also important is the extent to which they provide more or less coercive measures for ensuring that people move promptly from unemployment into jobs.
4. How well a country does depends on its international context and, for small countries in particular, what is happening to the economies of their larger trading partners. Note, in this connection, that a country can attempt to deal with some of its economic difficulties by devaluing its currency.
5. Ideas make a difference to policy choices. Some diagnoses of policy options are better than others. According to monetarists, policies inspired by Keynesian theory are generally pernicious and have produced excessive inflation and poor records of growth and employment.

In what follows I review the postwar economic performance of the country cases listed above with these considerations in mind.

Germany

From economic devastation at the end of the second world war the Federal Republic of Germany has grown into the preeminent economic power in Europe. At first sight its economic growth performance is nothing short of stunning. However, it makes sense to bear in mind that, by the interwar period, Germany had already become an economic power within Europe, at the leading edge of technology across a variety of industries (Landes, 1972:411–412, 435, 468). At the end of World War II, although devastated, the country had lost its economically backward Eastern part and had a labor force that, with U.S. assistance, enabled it to quickly regain its earlier levels of labor productivity. It is certainly true that Germany has a better record of economic growth than the United Kingdom; but, then, so do most rich industrial countries.

Figure 7.4 shows that, in fact, Germany did *a bit better* than one might have expected, given its low early postwar level of productivity. Figures 1.1 to 1.3, 7.1, and 7.2 show that its relative performance worsened appreciably after the first oil shock, but that it has improved again relative to other countries in the late 1980s. More clearly superior has been its postwar unemployment record. Until recently, Germany has maintained a generally lower than average unemployment rate. Most clearly superior is Germany's inflation record. It retained one of the lowest rates of inflation across industrial countries before, between, and after, the oil shocks. By any measure, then, Germany has been a superior macroeconomic performer in the postwar period. Is this because it has neocorporatist institutions?

Institutions and Policies

The organizing principle of Germany's economic policy, the "social market economy," has tended to preclude extensive government intervention in the economy; for example, German governments have made very modest use of Keynesian stabilization policy (Katzenstein, 1987:92–96; Allen, 1989) and those efforts to stabilize that have been made appear to have been as unsuccessful as everywhere else (Kloten, Ketterer, and Vollmer, 1985:380; Westphal, 1986). Why, then, has it been allocated to the neocorporatist category in some studies? In several (McCallum, 1983; Bruno and Sachs, 1985; Blais and McCallum, 1986), Crouch (1985) is cited as the authority for the classificatory decision. So we can focus our attention on Crouch's rationale.

First, Crouch claims that the German labor movement behaves responsibly because it is incorporated into the polity (1985:111–112). It is true that the SDP has been excluded from the federal government for much of the postwar period; but it has sufficient influence at the *Länder* level to ensure that labor's interests are taken into account. Furthermore, "the unique system of codetermination through worker representation on supervisory boards and, more important, on powerful statutory works councils makes it difficult for German employers to pursue a strategy of eliminating worker representation" (p. 112). Second, there is a history of employer cartellization. Consequently, although there is no employer equivalent of the Swedish SAF, "employers' associations play an important part in bargaining, help employers maintain a common front against unions, and even maintain strike protection funds" (1985:129). Third, among industrial unions, the very large *IG Metall* is wage leader and "performs something like the function of confederal bargaining coordination" (p. 130). Finally, the system of codetermination weakens the power of workers on the shop floor; it provides a channel for dealing with worker grievances and, in so doing, undercuts would-be shop floor militants (p. 130).

In addition, much is sometimes made of the "concerted action" policy established by the (coalition) SDP government in 1966, under which trade union leaders "bargained within the range of targets that officials announced would not endanger growth and stability" (Maier, 1984:48; Marks, 1986:260–261). Here, it is claimed, is an unambiguous example of centrally negotiated restraint.[15]

Consider, first of all, the extent to which labor is effectively represented in the polity. At the federal level, the SDP was excluded from government—and from power—until 1966 (Esping-Andersen and Korpi, 1984:195). In 1966 it entered into a grand coalition with the Christian Democrats and then in 1969 with the Free Democrats. In 1982 it lost office to a Christian Democratic government. In the early years of Social Democratic coalition government the party initiated a number of measures it regarded as reforms.[16] Under the practical pressures of government, however, the party moved to the right and adopted macroeconomic policies that are not readily distinguishable from those that would have been preferred by a Christian Democrat (Kloten, Ketterer, and Vollmer, 1985:386; Markovits and Allen, 1984:142). So distinctive labor influence *at the federal level* is more or less restricted to the period 1966 to, about, 1973. It is true, of course, that many *Länder* have been governed by the Social Democrats and the *Länder* have substantial constitutional power in the Federal Republic (Kloten, Ketterer, and Vollmer, 1985:367). But there is no evidence that they have any significant influence over monetary policy and their influence over fiscal policy seems to be largely negative in character. Their independence, in fact, makes it difficult for the federal government to pursue a coherent stabilization policy (Knott, 1981; Kloten, Ketterer, and Vollmer, 1985:381–382).

In sum, organized labor was excluded from the federal polity until 1966, had a 6- or 7-year period of influence during the early SDP coalition governments, and thereafter was excluded by either increasingly conservative SDP coalitions or the resolutely conservative Kohl governments. At the local level organized labor's *macroeconomic* influence was of a largely negative kind; it would have been confined to obstructing federal initiatives. I submit that this is a history of *very* modest labor influence on government policy. What about the centralization of collective bargaining?

The bulk of the unionized labor force is organized into 16 industrial unions. Employers tend to cooperate with each other, and the unions have large strike funds. *IG Metall* serves as pace setter. The result, according to Scharpf (1989:90), at least by the 1980s, was about as much centralization of labor relations as exists in Sweden.

However, note first that the extent to which employers cooperate is controversial. Renshaw (1986:50–51) argues that there is less concentration in German than in British industry and that it is not clear that this is offset by the greater presence of banks in industrial administration. Furthermore, only about 40% of the German labor force is unionized. This is not only much less than the unambiguously neocorporatist case of Sweden, it is also significantly less than the level in the United Kingdom, prior to the accession of Margaret Thatcher (Adams, 1982:474). A good part of the labor force escapes whatever institutional centralization of bargaining might be provided by the union movement. The major union confederation, the DGB, has very little power; Schmidt (1972:38; see also Bergmann and Muller-Jentsch, 1975:245) equates its amount of power with that of the TUC in Britain. There is a significant number of independent unions, largely involving white-collar workers (Schmidt, 1972:38). *IG Metall* has from time to time resisted centrally negotiated wage restraint (Bergmann and Muller-Jentsch, 1975:245). In sum, there is a distinct lack of detailed, institutional, evidence showing centralized wage bargaining.

Besides, it is hard to see how such a system could display a high degree of centralization. Calmfors and Driffil's (1988) model produces outcomes equal to those of a competitive market where there is a single employer and a single union. That is, of course, only a model. But one might reasonably expect that in making a classificatory decision that is so central to his analysis, Crouch ought to show how it has been possible for 16 industrial unions within a decentralized confederation, and assorted independent white-collar unions, to agree on what the warranted increase of wages actually is, and how different categories of workers should fare under conditions of wage restraint. And one might hope for some evidence that this has actually taken place.

But what we have, at best, is the fact of "concerted action" after 1966 when there was some wage restraint negotiated between the unions and the government of which the SDP was a part.[17] This, however, rapidly collapsed. By 1969, the period of restraint was followed by an outburst of militancy that has been extensively documented and by a collapse of the putative incomes policy (e.g., Markovits and Allen, 1984:134–139). By the early 1970s policy had returned to traditional and rather conservative macroeconomic management. Three years is a thin reed on which to base a decision to classify Germany as a neocorporatist industrial relations system!

There is a final institutional characteristic of neocorporatist systems.

They are, it will be recalled, thought to be *fairer* than liberal systems and this encourages workers to be less reticent in the face of needed structural change. Does Germany have a set of institutions likely to produce distinctively *fair* outcomes?

Germany does, as Barber and McCallum (1982:10) observe, have a fairly large government. It also spends a significant proportion of GDP on income maintenance (Klein, 1985:213). However, its welfare system is distinct in the extent to which it is *insurance based.* By this I mean that pension, sickness, and unemployment benefits are largely tied to contributions (rather than some general entitlement) and amounts received are, therefore, related to income received when employed (see Mitton, Wilmott, and Wilmott, 1983:89–91). Furthermore, Minford (1983:98–99, 105) claims that income assistance is often associated with a rather stringent obligation for unemployed workers to seek employment. Esping-Andersen (1990:52) concludes that Germany has an approximately intermediate degree of "decommodification" in its welfare system (which means the extent to which welfare is based on an insurance principle as opposed to general entitlement). To put this in context, the inequality of benefits in Germany is much greater than Sweden, rather greater than the United Kingdom, and almost as great as Canada. That Germany has a welfare state is not in question. But it is also clear that its system for providing welfare differs substantially from Sweden's where access to benefits is a matter of general entitlement rather than contribution based.

Policies and Outcomes

By international standards, the German industrial relations systems produces *very* low levels of industrial conflict.[18] This outcome is sometimes treated as evidence of social consensus in Germany (e.g., Barber and McCallum, 1982). But is this really evidence of social consensus and, if so, of what kind? Markovits and Allen (1984:119–120) claim that, for most of the postwar period the unions have accepted the basic principles of the social market economy in which, of course, inequalities are determined by market forces rather than by the centrally coordinated moral judgments that are supposed to characterize neocorporatist industrial relations systems.

Not surprisingly, there is evidence of struggles over relative wages in Germany. In the early part of the postwar period (through the 1950s), and perhaps beyond, there was considerable resentment toward *IG Metall* and its wage-leadership pretensions (Markovits and Allen, 1984:113–114). More generally, while DGB industrial (and some independent) unions set basic wages, plant-specific works councils (the importance of which has increased over time) negotiate over bonuses and fringe benefits and these play a significant role in the total remuneration package (Markovits and Allen, 1984:121; Brandt, 1984:17). This has contributed to the wage drift that appears to characterize all industrial relations systems where wages are negotiated at the industry or economy-wide level. Clearly, there are no grounds for concluding that Germany has had an industrial relations system that has succeeded any better than anywhere else in suppressing the struggle over wage relativities.

Despite what looks like a relatively decentralized wage bargaining system (or, perhaps, because of it!) the cost of German labor has, for the most part, grown at or below the rate of increase in labor productivity (Flanagan, Soskice, and Ulman, 1983:224). There is splendid irony in the fact that the important exception to this pattern is the much heralded, but relatively brief, period of "concerted action" after 1966. Almost the only period when labor costs grew at a rate greatly in excess of productivity was from 1968 to about 1972, that is, in the period when unions and the government were supposed to be concerting their actions![19] Moreover, while German industrial agreements were modified by wage drift (sometimes substantially), in the period 1965 to 1975, the drift was *almost* as likely to be downward as upward (Flanagan, Soskice, and Ulman, 1983:247). But the one period when wage drift was most consistently positive was 1968 to 1973! Concerted action was not, of course, the only change in the bargaining environment in this period. Nonetheless, the data clearly do not support the view that concerted action made a substantial contribution to the problem of aligning wage and productivity growth.

As indicated in Chapter 6, neocorporatism is supposed to have three other outcomes. First, its institutions reduce income inequality. This reduction in inequality, along with the infusion of morality into the bargaining process and labor market protections provided to workers, is supposed to increase worker trust and (this is the second outcome) worker willingness to cooperate in the process of technological change at the workplace. Third, the incorporation of unions in a centralized bargaining process is supposed to facilitate industrial restructuring because unions are less likely to demand subsidies for declining industries. How does Germany fare in these respects?

First, by any measure, Germany comes out as having one of the higher degrees of income inequality among industrial societies (Sawyer, 1976:19; Ringen, 1987:260), certainly, a higher degree than the United Kingdom, Canada, or the United States.

Second, although we have little detailed information about the relative cooperativeness of German workers in the face of technical change,[20] the fact that labor productivity has tended to grow at a better than average rate and has not fallen behind wages does *suggest* some degree of cooperativeness *in practice*. However, this does not seem to be accompanied by any greater degree of "moral solidarity." Thus, comparative survey data (Hondrich, 1989; Yuchtman-Yaar, 1989) show that, as compared to citizens of the United States (the paradigmatic market society), Germans were much more likely to consider "unconventional" political action (such as demonstrations) as legitimate (9.5 versus 3.6% in 1974); much more likely to feel unable to change an "unjust or harmful local regulation or national law" (about a fifteen percentage point difference at both local and national levels in 1974); were more sceptical about economic growth (64% in the United States thought its effects on employment were good versus 54% in Germany, with an even larger difference for blue-collar workers); were considerably less committed to their work (68% reported high work commitment in the United States versus 42% in Germany); and in attitudes to technological change produced frequencies that were sometimes more positive (e.g., relative to Americans, Germans were more likely to report that technological change had made their jobs clean and reduced the physical strain involved) and sometimes less positive (Germans thought their jobs were made more difficult and were less likely to think technology had made them more interesting).

Third, although there is no question that German governments have subsidized industry, they do not appear to do it to a greater degree than other governments. In fact, they probably do it less. Esping-Andersen and Korpi (1984:198) note that the "first steps to regional investment policy" were taken in 1969, which was, I would have thought, later than elsewhere. It is true that the German government responded to the crisis of the 1970s by providing financial assistance to companies that were in difficulty; but, at least in the case described by Streeck (1984:298–303), the assistance came with fairly stringent strings attached (reduced employment, reduced redundancy payments, reduced pension benefits, frozen wages) that were enforced over the objections of the union—*IG Metall*.

In summary, for most of the postwar period Germany appears not to have had centralized bargaining institutions; when it did, under concerted action, its productivity performance deteriorated; it is a highly unequal society with a population exhibiting higher levels of mistrust than are found in the United States; and it appears not to be overly generous in easing the problems of workers who find themselves employed in industries in decline. Is this a case that can reasonably be classified as neocorporatist and treated as evidence of the benefits of neocorporatism?

Performance in a Wider Context

Germany remains a postwar economic success with a growth record
that is a bit better than would be warranted by its level of productivity
after the war, low levels of unemployment until recently, and consistently low inflation. How can these outcomes be explained, if not by
corporatism? Consider now some other factors that distinguish the German political economy.

First, there is an unusually autonomous central bank. As we saw in
Chapter 3, when central bank independence is analyzed, the German
Bundesbank is always put in the most independent category (e.g., Banaian, Laney, and Willett, 1983: Alesina, 1989:81). This is not, it should
be clear, merely a question of a nominal, legal, independence. The
SDP/FDP government attempted to reflate after 1973 and, as part of that
policy, to induce the Bundesbank to pursue a more expansionary monetary policy. But the Bundesbank successfully resisted its attempt (Wool-
ey, 1978:170; Esping-Andersen, 1990:184–185).

Second, Germany has a set of labor laws that is relatively repressive.
As in North America, collective agreements are legally enforceable. Unlike North America, it is illegal to strike over a grievance, a worker who
goes on an illegal strike is liable to lose social benefits (including medical
coverage), and sympathy strikes are illegal (Giugni, 1972:133; Tylecote,
1981:93).[21] Unlike the United Kingdom and Canada, closed shops are
illegal (Flanagan, Soskice, and Ulman, 1983:231). Unlike most Western
countries, political strikes are illegal, and unions that engage in them are
liable for damages. Unlike Italy, the courts have established an employer
right to lock out workers, although with some limitations (see Mueckenberger, 1986:241–249). I would submit, therefore, that Germany has one
of the most conservative bodies of labor law among Western capitalist
countries.

Add to an autonomous central bank and a repressive body of labor law
the following facts: as in a number of other countries immigration provided a supply of cheap labor but, unlike most other countries, rising
unemployment in the 1970s could be partially dealt with by failing to
renew the work permits of part of the immigrant labor force. Between
1973 and 1979 about three quarters of a million people were removed
from the labor force in this way (Webber and Nass, 1984:177); the German welfare system (pension, unemployment insurance, welfare) provides a strong incentive for workers to maximize their incomes because
benefits are income related; according to Minford the administration of
the unemployment insurance system involves an element of coercion so
that it is particularly difficult for a worker to refuse a job when it becomes available; German macroeconomic policy has rarely been inspired

by Keynesian principles; Germany seems to have succeeded in maintaining an internationally superior system of vocational education (Renshaw, 1986:89–90, 94–96). All of these characteristics of German institutions and policy provide the basis for an explanation of superior macroeconomic performance entirely different from corporatism (for which the institutional evidence is, in any case, skimpy, at best).

An autonomous central bank harboring traditional central bank concerns with price stability, accounts for most of Germany's superior inflation performance.[22] Price stability provides a favorable context for making contracts and, therefore, for investment, growth, and employment. So (according to monetarists) does the absence of Keynesian policies that have usually not worked where they have been tried and have, on the contrary (despite short-run benefits), introduced uncertainties into the economy likely to deter investment. Lower unemployment rates and good economic growth have been facilitated by the fact that the German labor market has been less rigid than its rivals because its trade unions are weakened by repressive legislation, because there has been access to immigrant labor (and in the early postwar period, to refugees from Eastern Europe who brought considerable skills with them), because the insurance-based welfare system maintains strong incentives for people to work, and because the vocational training system reduces the incidence of bottlenecks of skilled labor. The opportunity to expel excess labor in the 1970s also helped to keep lower unemployment levels.

Now, I can hardly claim that I have shown that this latter interpretation of Germany's macroeconomic performance is correct. But I do think I can claim that it is quite a bit more consistent with the available evidence than is Crouch's interpretation in terms of the effects of corporatism.

Austria

Austria's postwar macroeconomic performance has been widely celebrated. Katzenstein (1984:34) has described it as "spectacular" (see also Katzenstein, 1985; Frisch, 1986; Scharpf, 1984:259, 263; Scharpf, 1989:87). As we can see from Figures 1.1 to 1.3, 7.1, and 7.2, Austria had a strong relative growth performance both before and after the oil shock, and has maintained low unemployment rates and a low rate of inflation, moving to a still lower *relative* rate after the first oil shock.

Once again, however, assessing relative growth performance requires that one adjust for Austria's (very low) early postwar level of labor productivity. Maddison (1982:98) estimates that in 1950 Austria's productivity was about 29% of that of the United States, a bit more than half of the U.K. level, and not even as high as that of Italy. After World War II Austria was clearly positioned to experience a great deal of catch-up in living standards. It was greatly helped in doing so by "massive" amounts of aid from the United States (Haberler, 1982:66). Adjusting for its initial productivity level (but not for American aid) we can see in Figure 7.4 that Austria has done *a bit* better than its initial level of productivity would have led one to predict. So, in the Austrian case what we need to explain is *adequate* but not, as Katzenstein states, *spectacular* growth, combined with a much more impressive history of price stability and full employment.

Institutions and Policies

It requires a great deal of imagination, or a relatively brutal treatment of the evidence (pick your own description, according to taste), to force West Germany into the corporatist category. This is not so for Austria. Austria certainly has corporatist institutions. First, along classic corporatist lines, in addition to a parliament, there is functional representation of interest groups in "economic chambers," membership in which is compulsory (Gill, 1989:104–105). These are described by Katzenstein (1984:60) as follows:

> Public law defines their membership and organizational mission, and even though the government cannot influence the internal process of decision making in the chambers, it enjoys the right of legal supervision. The Federal Economic Chamber . . . represents the crafts, commerce, and industry, and business interests more generally; the Federal Chamber of Labor . . . speaks for wage and salary earners, as well as for consumer interests. There are also chambers of agriculture . . . at the provincial level. Austria's most important private interest groups, the Federation of Austrian Industrialists . . . and the Austrian Trade Union Federation (the ÖGB), cooperate closely with their respective chambers.[23]

These chambers provide a forum within which the interests of both labor and capital are effectively expressed across a range of issues, an institutional context within which labor and capital are compelled to negotiate some sort of cooperative policy.

Second, most of the unionized population belongs to one of 16 unions, "organized generally along industrial lines" (Flanagan, Soskice, and Ulman, 1983:51); these unions are, in turn, subject to considerable control of their finances by the ÖGB, which also employs the general secretary of each union.[24] Thus, the ÖGB controls about four-fifths of the membership dues generated by the constituent unions and administers their strike funds. Business and industry, however, is quite a bit less centralized although the existence of the Federal Economic Chamber does provide a fairly convenient venue for the "aggregation of interests" (Katzenstein, 1984:61). Note, furthermore, that these institutional arrangements provide a strong basis for the "representational monopoly" on which corporatism rests. Thus,

> the state provides rather detailed legislation which helps the interest group leaders to assert themselves in their relationship with the respective rank and file. These include obligatory membership in the chamber organizations, a closely knit web of regulations of industrial relations at the plant level and the possibility of sanctions *vis à vis* price breakers. If necessary, this can even result in enforcing membership acceptance of jointly negotiated compromises. (Gerlich, Grande, and Müller, 1988:216–217)

The third relevant element of Austrian institutions is the permanent regulation of *some* prices and wages (see Flanagan, Soskice, and Ulman, 1983:58–62). There is a Parity Commission for Wages and Prices with a separate subcommittee devoted to each. The subcommittee on prices is chaired by a member of the Federal Economic Chamber. In general, it links allowable price increases to unavoidable cost increases. Note, however, that the committee has regulatory authority over only about 20% of prices and compliance is voluntary; employers are not compelled to submit prices for review. If the committee's regulation of prices were really stringent, employers would be unlikely to submit to it their price increases. Furthermore, the committee has no authority to reduce prices if costs *decrease*. The subcommittee on wages is alternately chaired by a member of the Federal Economic Chamber and a representative of the ÖGB. It also depends on voluntary compliance by trade unions (although the ÖGB would be breathing heavily down their necks) and it influences wage rates by approving when negotiations for a new contract should be started.

Fourth, a large (but diminishing) part of Austrian industry is owned by the government. For much of the postwar period, public utilities, banks, a fifth of Austrian manufacturing (including the iron and steel industry), and a number of larger theatres have been publicly owned (Seidel, 1982:10).

What policies are generated by these institutions? The unions, as responsible partners in the formulation of economic policy, allow their wage negotiating to be influenced by considerations of "productivity, solidarity, and cyclical stabilization" (Flanagan, Soskice, and Ulman, 1983:53; see also Duda and Tödtling, 1986:243–244). In practice this means that they accept that wage growth should be tied to long-run

growth in productivity; they seek to avoid increasing wage gaps between workers in strong and weak sectors or unions (although, apparently, not to *narrow* existing gaps); and, in the short run, they want
wages to rise faster during recessions than during upturns in economic
activity.

What is distinctive about the government's policies? First, it makes the
maintenance of full employment a first priority. In particular, during
economic downturns it uses the large public sector to mop up excess
labor (Katzenstein, 1984:40; Duda and Tödtling, 1986:229–230). Second,
it is sometimes claimed that the Austrian government has pursued
countercyclical Keynesian stabilization policies (e.g., Katzenstein,
1984:243; Jessop, Jacobi, and Kastendiek, 1986:3; Scharpf, 1984:264;
1989:87). This, however, is controversial (see Tichy, 1984:367–369;
Haberler, 1982:68; Seidel, 1982:15).

Finally, it is worth noting that little attention has been paid to the
extent to which the centralized bargaining institutions in Austria produce distinctive policy preferences on the part of employers. It is true
that much of the economy has been owned by the Austrian government
so that, presumably, the policy preferences of its managers coincide with
those of the government (officially at least). But much of the growth of
private industry in Austria since World War II has come from foreign
investment (Katzenstein, 1984:56–57) and it is not clear how those inves-
tors have reacted to, or lobbied about, the institutions of "social partnership."

Policies and Outcomes

By the normal macroeconomic criteria, Austria has a superior record,
particularly in price stability and low unemployment. It also has centralized bargaining institutions and some degree of regulation of prices
and wages. It is often claimed that these institutions are supplemented
by a relatively aggressive Keynesian policy of economic stabilization.
The first question to be addressed is, are the more detailed aspects of
postwar wage growth and economic performance consistent with the
operation of a neocorporatist system?

Note first, that, unlike many other European countries, including
Germany, there was no wage explosion in Austria at the end of the 1960s.
Austria appears to have escaped the wage explosion because, unlike
Germany and other countries, it did not adopt wage restraint policies in
the mid-1960s. At first sight this looks like—and may indeed have been—
a product of the wage growth smoothing effects of neocorporatist bargaining. But, also relevant, and a bit less consistent with the neocor-

poratist model, was the fact that the Austrian economy had been operating further below capacity than most other European countries (Flanagan, Soskice, and Ulman, 1983:43). Note also that, consistent with the view that Austrian prices are to an important degree centrally regulated, Flanagan, Soskice, and Ulman (1983:67) found that price increases are better predicted by unit labor cost changes than by a measure of demand.[25] Here are two pieces of evidence that, to some degree, suggest that Austrian neocorporatist institutions work as they are supposed to.

Now here is some evidence that suggests that they do not. First, the countercyclical wage policy seems not to work very well. Whatever the intentions of the parity committee on wages, negotiated rates rise most as unemployment falls and least as it rises (Flanagan, Soskice, and Ulman, 1983:53). Second, no doubt in part because works councils negotiate agreements supplemental to whatever their unions have negotiated, wage drift in Austria has been quite substantial and, in particular, offset the attempts to deal with the supply shocks of 1973 (Flanagan, Soskice, and Ulman, 1983:55, 74). Third, despite the commitment to some sort of solidaristic wages policy (protecting weaker unions and industries), wage differentials fluctuate with the business cycle, as they do elsewhere, and wages have tended to fall behind in weak industries, such as textiles and apparel (Duda and Tödtling, 1986:244–245). Fourth, whatever the unions' commitment to relating wages to productivity might have been, when economic difficulties set in at the beginning of the 1970s unit labor costs rose relative to Austria's competitors (Artus, 1982). Fifth, although the Austrian government attempted in 1974 to deal with rising unit labor costs by trading-off tax reductions for wage restraint, the attempt failed and wages rose by unusually large amounts (Flanagan, Soskice, and Ulman, 1983:63). Sixth, the Parity Commission has had very mixed success in exercising its control over the 20% of prices subject to its jurisdiction: although regulated prices rose more slowly than unregulated prices from 1969 to 1971, in 4 of the next 5 years (while unit labor costs were rising), regulated prices grew by more than unregulated prices and, sometimes substantially so (Flanagan, Soskice, and Ulman, 1983:69). In other words, effective price regulation appears to be a short-term phenomenon, liable to be offset in the longer run. Finally, *pace Scharpf* (e.g., 1984:264) and others, Austrian policy cannot be characterized in normal Keynesian terms. Government budgets do not display a consistently countercyclical pattern (Frisch, 1982:51) and, even when countercyclical, usually fluctuate with automatic changes in government revenues and expenditures (tax revenues decline in a recession and unemployment insurance expenditures go up) rather than as a result of deliberate intervention (Tichy, 1984:367). Indeed, Austrian economists appear to be as inept as their counterparts elsewhere at providing the predictions that would allow effective policy intervention and their models failed completely in the face of the economic difficulties of 1974–1975 (Katzenstein, 1984:39).

In general, then, Austria's macroeconomic performance has been very good; many of the details of policy implementation and wage outcomes seem, however, to diverge from what one would expect if neocorporatist institutions were principally responsible for those outcomes.

Performance in a Wider Context

The premise of Keynesian stabilization policy is that, since wages tend to lag prices, employment and growth can be increased by stimulating demand so that inflation redistributes income from workers to capitalists. Governments should adopt policies producing this outcome, it is claimed, if they are concerned to minimize unemployment. Now, it is clear that Austria's governments have been concerned to minimize unemployment but, for the most part, they have not done so with the technique described above. The distinctive Austrian approach to economic policy is sometimes described as "Austro-Keynesianism." What does it involve?

One critical element is the protection of the value of its currency. After the second world war, prices in Austria rose rapidly. The American government used the suspension of aid to force on Austria an aggressive currency stabilization involving restrictions on bank credit, sharply reduced government expenditures, and devaluation (Haberler, 1982:68–69). Inflation came down rapidly. From then until the 1970s, Bretton Woods provided the framework for Austrian exchange rate policy, as it did for much of the rest of the industrial world. In 1971, Bretton Woods fell apart. But Austria's trade is heavily concentrated with Germany, which takes about 40% of its exports, and sends 30% of its imports (Smith, 1987:379). A widely fluctuating schilling/mark exchange rate would disrupt this trade (and probably be politically unpopular too!). In 1971, therefore, the Austrian government formalized the "hard currency option" that involved tying the schilling to the mark (Flanagan, Soskice, and Ulman, 1983:45–46; Tichy, 1984:369).[26] Consequently, Austria has tied its rate of inflation to Germany's. In other words, given this policy choice, at least since 1971 Austria's low rate of inflation is explained by Germany's.

A second element of Austro-Keynesianism (and the only part that is remotely Keynesian!) is a concern with unemployment. How has unemployment been minimized? As mentioned above, the public sector was used to absorb excess labor in the 1970s (Seidel, 1982:11). This policy was supplemented by statutory reductions in work hours and a substantial

reduction in the foreign labor force (Butschek, 1982:107–108). In addition, youth unemployment is particularly low in Austria, apparently
because of low minimum wages, as least as compared to the United
States (Kosters, 1982:125). Add to this the facts that Austrian unemployment insurance replaces a modest portion of earnings and that the obligation to take an available job is rather stringently enforced (Butschek,
1982:110–111).

To what extent are the hard currency option and the unemployment-
reducing measures consistent with the normal models of neocorporatism? It is conceivable that, as Flanagan, Soskice, and Ulman
(1983:47) argue, the hard currency option is possible only because of the
existence of the institutions of social partnership. This may be so, but
there is some evidence that suggests that the direction of causation runs
the other way. I have shown elsewhere (Smith, 1987) that, of the five
small countries contiguous with Germany, the three with superior inflation performance are the ones that depend most heavily on trade with
Germany. I also showed that Canada's inflation record has, like its trade,
been tied to that of the United States. As I explained in Chapter 2, small
countries have a strong incentive to stabilize their exchange rate with a
larger partner on which much of their trade depends; that, in turn,
determines their rate of inflation. Since small countries seem, in general,
to tie their currencies to the currencies of larger trading partners one
does not need Austria's social partnership institutions to explain its hard
currency option.

How do we interpret the low rate of unemployment? Clearly, the
government seeks to avoid unemployment, no doubt in part because of
the political weight of the left in Austria's coalition governments and the
influence of the trade unions in the institutions of social partnership
(Katzenstein, 1984:36 ff.). But job creation through public employment
does not involve the sort of reallocation of labor from less to more
productive jobs at which neocorporatist systems are supposed to excel.
Indeed, by the end of the 1970s, Austria was paying a high economic
price for its policies in the form of rapidly increasing government debt
(Frisch, 1982:51). Furthermore, note that there is a distinct, market-rein-
forcing character to a number of the unemployment-reducing policies
that does not usually feature in models of corporatism. Strong incentives not to remain unemployed are embedded in the low replacement
rate of unemployment insurance and in the compulsion to find jobs
originating in the rules and practices of the employment service. Young
workers are more likely to be hired because minimum wage laws do not
prevent paying them very low wages. And so on. Indeed, the result
seems to be a society of considerable and increasing inequality (Esping-
Anderson and Korpi, 1984:194).

What about Austria's good economic growth performance? If the monetarists are right, good economic performance is secured by stable prices and the absence of an activist stabilization policy. Austria, of course, qualifies on both counts. Moreover, the method for securing stable prices—the hard currency option—is not obviously an attribute of corporatism; and some analyses of corporatism assume the presence of the kind of Keynesian demand management that is largely absent from Austria's postwar economic policy. Furthermore, given its trade dependence, it should be no surprise that Austrian economic growth is closely tied to demand originating in Germany—to German economic growth (Cooper, 1987:589; Flanagan, Soskice, and Ulman, 1983:43).[27] Austria, then, has grown because Germany has grown, and because the hard currency option protects and nurtures the trade tie with Germany. Finally, consistent with its apparently high degree of income inequality, Austria has tax laws that, by allowing rapid depreciation, treat investment favorably. It will be recollected from Chapter 2 that Feldstein (1982) has argued that the negative effects on profits of U.S. tax laws (in the inflationary context of the 1960s and 1970s) were a serious obstacle to U.S. growth.

Sweden

Sweden has become something of a social democratic lodestar for the North American left, providing a distant Northern glimmer of a successful attempt to reconcile growth with equity. This has produced a literature that, on occasion, has a distinctly reverential cast (e.g., Stephens, 1979:176–194; Milner, 1989). In terms of the three macroeconomic indicators that concern us here, however, it is only in unemployment levels that Sweden excels. Figure 7.1 shows that Swedish unemployment levels stayed remarkably low through all three time periods covered. But its inflation record is not impressive: before and after the first oil shock its rate of inflation was approximately at the midpoint among the 18 industrial countries for which data are provided; then in the 1980s its relative position deteriorated somewhat, falling into the highest inflation third of the list (Figure 1.3). Its growth performance was quite good until about 1960, but since then has been unimpressive to poor (Dowrick and Nguyen, 1989). Figure 7.2 shows that, over the entire period before the oil shock, annual average growth rates in Sweden were among the lowest among the 18 industrial countries; and after the oil shock the growth rate fell substantially—a much larger drop than occurred in the United States. Productivity growth is, of course, particularly important.

Figure 7.4 reports annual average productivity growth rates from 1960 to 1985, controlling for productivity level at the beginning of the period. Sweden's performance proves to be particularly poor: it fell farther short of productivity growth that would have been predicted from its 1960 level than, even, the United Kingdom!

Institutions and Policies

Sweden is clearly corporatist.[28] More than 80% of the labor force is unionized. In the private sector, there is highly centralized bargaining between a confederation of Swedish employers (SAF) and large labor federations. In the private sector, in principle, bargaining takes place independent of the government; in the public sector there is bargaining between a consortium of public sector employer associations (OASEN) and the public sector unions that belong to LO, TCO, or SACO. For much of the postwar period the largest union federation, the LO, pursued a so-called "solidaristic wages policy" the purpose of which was to weaken the link between wages and worker productivity. Wages of low paid (and presumably less productive) workers were forced up faster than those of higher paid workers both for reasons of equity and as part of a mechanism to speed up the shift of production from low to high productivity sectors and firms (see Hibbs, 1991).

The Social Democratic Party has governed for most of the postwar period—although usually in a minority position or as part of a coalition.[29] Swedish governments, including the "bourgeois" government of 1976 to 1982, have been consistently committed to maintaining low rates of unemployment. They have also constructed an elaborate welfare state that, according to Esping-Andersen (1990:52), displays a high degree of "decommodification" of labor. And they have constructed a set of labor market policies designed to facilitate the mobility of labor involving, principally, an elaborate system of labor exchanges (that also administer mobility allowances) and widely available training programs. All of this has produced less posttax income inequality than most other countries for which data are available (Sawyer, 1976:17; Ringen, 1987:260).

Now, on what policies does the Swedish success in maintaining low rates of unemployment rest? One possibility is that Swedish unemployment is low because labor costs in Sweden grow at the same rate as productivity, so that excessive wages never force employers to lay off workers. This is the way neocorporatism is supposed to work. Another possibility is that unemployment is low because active labor market policies—training programs and government employment—remove large numbers of workers from the unemployment rolls. This, of course, is less clearly an attribute of neocorporatism, although it could be argued that this is one of the ways that the confidence and cooperation of workers in the pursuit of growth-enhancing technical change and economic restructuring are secured (e.g., Muszynski and Wolfe, 1989:252). The final possibility is that full employment is maintained through an aggressive stabilization policy of a Keynesian kind.[30] I will return to the first two possible sources of full employment in the next section. To finish this section, consider the question of Swedish stabilization policy.

Pekkarinen (1989:318) presents a rather sanguine summary of countercyclical policy in Sweden (noting the important addition to it of supply side industrial and labor market policies). This view is rather unusual. Lindbeck (1974:238–239) reports a mixture of success and failure in stabilization policy for the period up to the early 1970s—not so very different from what Laidler (1981a:19) reports for Britain. Lundberg (1985:26–27) presents a still more negative view for the period since the mid-1970s.

In fact, one can raise questions about the extent to which Sweden provides the adequate institutional conditions for a Keynesian policy for reducing unemployment. Remember, from Chapter 2, that the standard Keynesian technique for reducing unemployment involves, to be blunt, fooling workers. Governments stimulate economic activity, which increases prices. But because wages tend to lag prices, profits and investment increase, and so does employment.[31] The extent to which this works beyond the short term within liberal industrial relations systems is controversial. But it is hard to see how policies of this sort could work within a genuine corporatist system. After all, centralized bargaining institutions, according to Lange (1984) and others, both depend on and create trust on the part of those bargaining. But for how long would worker trust persist in the face of the repeated experience of being fooled?[32] Besides, neocorporatist bargaining is supposed to involve negotiation over *real* rather than *nominal* wages whereas the worker-fooling techniques of Keynesian policy presuppose a divergence between real and nominal wages. Finally, the Swedish commitment to egalitarian objectives has precluded the use of a number of Keynesian policy instruments (e.g., cuts in taxes), on the grounds that they would favor the rich (Lindbeck, 1974:239).

Now, there does seem to have been *some* success in Sweden with countercyclical public investments and investment subsidies. There have also been substantial failures rooted in inadequate forecasting and delays in policy implementation (Lindbeck, 1974:238–239). So Swedish stabilization policy has, in practice, disproportionately involved rather direct, job-creating, public expenditures.

Policies and Outcomes

One of the fundamental differences between the economics of the
Stockholm school and the economics of Keynes is that Keynes constructed a closed economy model whereas the Stockholm school was,
from the outset, preoccupied with Sweden's position as a small country
dependent on international trade. In the postwar period this concern
became formalized in the Scandinavian (or Aukrust) two sector model,
discussed in Chapter 5. It will be recalled that the crux of this model is
that firms competing on international markets are price-takers, and allow their wages to rise with productivity. These wage increases are
transferred to firms sheltered from international competition and to the
public sector. In the sheltered sector, then, wages are to some extent
disconnected from productivity and inflation represents the difference
between productivity growth in the sheltered sector and the wage
growth transferred from the competitive to the sheltered sector.

  This model has provided the frame of reference for economists in the
government and in the union and employer federations (e.g., Martin,
1984:225–226; 242–246). A first criterion for judging the performance of
Swedish institutions is, then, the extent to which wage growth fits the
Aukrust model, with wages growing with productivity in the exposed
sector, which serves as wage-setter for the sheltered sector. By this
standard there is rather more evidence of failure than success in the
Swedish model.

  First, there is the widely observed fact that a very large part of earnings growth takes the form of "wage drift." Flanagan, Soskice, and
Ulman (1983:313) note that "From the mid 1950s to the end of the 1960s
wage drift exceeded the total of negotiated wage increases and
amounted to nearly half the increase in wage costs, including fringes
and benefit payments by employers." It remained a very large proportion of wage growth through the 1970s and 1980s (Bosworth, 1987:40),
sufficiently so that provision was made in the central agreement to compensate workers disadvantaged by it (Hibbs, 1991:96–99). The one fairly
clear attribute of wage drift is that it largely originates at the plant level
and is predicted by measures of the demand for labor. Consequently,
the magnitude of wage drift is hard to reconcile with a centralized model
of wage determination.[33]

  Second, wages in the exposed sector have tended to grow at rates
appreciably in excess of the rate of productivity increase. This has created a chronic problem of inadequate profitability in this sector
(Flanagan, Soskice, and Ulman, 1983:309–311; Lawrence and Bosworth,
1987:62). Nor has nominal wage growth as a whole been responsive to

changes in Sweden's international competitive position, measured by previous year's current account balance as a percent of GDP (Bosworth, 1987:51). Not only, then, does the Aukrust model not accurately describe wage determination in Sweden (other than the fact of a spillover of wage growth from the exposed to the sheltered sector in some periods), in addition, Swedish corporatism has *not* succeeded in tying earnings to productivity growth where and when it really mattered.

Third, whereas in the early postwar period it is fairly clear that the private sector negotiations involving the SAF and the LO set the pattern of wage growth for the rest of the economy, by the 1970s this had begun to break down. In Sweden (as elsewhere), the weight of the public sector in employment grew throughout the postwar period. It is clear that as their weight in the union movement and the economy grew, the public sector unions became increasingly unwilling to accept wage leadership from the private, let alone the exposed, sector (Martin, 1984:239, 265–266, 315; Lash and Urry, 1987:238–239; Ahlen, 1988a,b, 1989; Albåge, 1986). So, by the late 1970s, one of the institutional bases for the Swedish model—wage leadership by the exposed sector—had largely broken down.

Fourth, bargaining is no longer as solidly centralized as it once was. The relations between the three union centrals have been increasingly fractious (although, patched up from time to time) and in 1984, the large Metal Workers Union withdrew from LO bargaining because it judged that the solidaristic wage policy was being pushed too far (Lash and Urry, 1987:244–245).

All of this indicates that wage growth outcomes seem for the most part not to coincide with what neocorporatist institutions should produce and, more recently, the extent to which Sweden actually has neocorporatist institutions has become somewhat problematic. What about Sweden's success in maintaining full employment?

Stabilization policy has had only modest success and what success it had was concentrated in the first two decades after the second world war. As in most other countries, the attainment of successful stabilization policies became very difficult in the more turbulent post-oil shock economic environment. Nor is there much evidence that full employment has originated in a distinctive Swedish capacity to tie wage and productivity growth together. The major method for maintaining internationally competitive labor costs in Sweden has been, in fact, devaluation of the Kronor—five times since the second world war (Wijkman, 1987:93). So where does full employment originate? Labor market programs absorb a *very* large part of the labor force likely to be counted as unemployed in other countries. Heclo and Madsen (1987:74–75) present figures that suggest that if workers in job creation programs, in labor market training programs, and in jobs for which wage subsidies have been provided by the government were added to the formally unemployed, the rate since the mid-1970s would more than double (see also van den Berg and Smucker, 1992). There is, no doubt, a substantial component of error in this estimate. Still, it is hard to avoid the conclusion that a lot of unemployment in Sweden is effectively concealed. In addition, as in Austria, Swedish governments (in particular the bourgeois government of the late 1970s) have quite deliberately expanded the public sector to absorb excess labor and, during the difficult years of the 1970s, subsidized industries in decline—such as steel and shipbuilding (Lundberg, 1985:26; Lawrence and Bosworth, 1987:73–75).

Now, whether or not these are good policies is not at issue here. One might argue that it is better to put people in training programs than to leave them to collect unemployment insurance or welfare, even if the probability of getting jobs from those programs is rather low.[34] It is not my intention to take issue with such an argument here. The point I want to make is, rather, that there is precious little evidence that the low unemployment rate in Sweden originates in the distinctive wage setting practices of neocorporatist centralized bargaining. If neocorporatist institutions reduce unemployment in Sweden it is because they provide a forum within which organized labor can bring pressure to bear on the government *to do whatever it takes to keep the unemployment rate low,* even if that involves (contrary, I would suggest, to neocorporatist theory) make-work programs and subsidies to declining industries.

Performance in a Wider Context

It is still the case that if any country can be described as neocorporatist, it is Sweden. Corporatist institutions have no doubt induced groups of workers to act in a restrained way from time to time. Heclo and Madsen (1987:325–326), for example, show that downsizing the textile industry was a lot easier when the social democratic party was in office than during the "bourgeois" interregnum. And the connections between the LO and the social democratic party are so strong that they have no doubt produced some LO bargaining restraint. But, in practice, the Swedish system diverges from the neocorporatist models in two important ways. First, after wage drift is taken into account, not much of the central bargain on *aggregate* wage growth is left.[35] Second, there is a degree of centralized coercion (not in quotation marks) in Swedish neocorporatism that is not prominent in most of the models. The election of the leadership of the unions and of the LO is indirect; the period between congresses has tended to lengthen; by the 1970s many union officers were appointed rather than elected; and most union decisions on contract ratification are not subject to membership referendums (Korpi, 1978:216–224; Martin, 1985:410–411; van Otter, 1975:203–204). Korpi's (1978:225) study of the attitude of rank and file members of the metal workers union reveals what can only be called widespread political alienation of the rank and file from the union leadership.[36] There is no evidence that I know of that the gulf between union leaders and members in Sweden is any greater than elsewhere. But the fact remains that a gulf exists that poses some serious problems for models of neocorporatism that postulate some process of moral incorporation.

Japan

By the conventional standards of macroeconomic performance, Japan's postwar record is extraordinary. As Figures 1.1 to 1.3, 7.1, and 7.2 show, Japan has a spectacular record of economic growth and a consistently low rate of unemployment. Its record on inflation is a bit more mixed. Up to the first oil shock it was a high inflation country; after that shock its performance improved relative to other countries so that, after the second shock, it had one of the lowest rates among capitalist industrial countries.

Because its record is so good, in studies of the effects of neocorporatist institutions on performance, how Japan is classified makes a great deal of difference. As we saw in Chart 7.1 the placement of Japan varies from the most to least corporatist category (and in several studies it is dropped altogether). How *should* Japanese institutions be classified? And what effect do those institutions have on economic performance?

Institutions and Policies

The first stylized fact about Japan is the coherence of its business elite. With the assistance of a government concerned to foster a constructive collaboration among businesses designed to facilitate the conquest of foreign markets, the Japanese business elite acts, it is claimed, with a distinctive unity (Vogel, 1979; Rosenbluth, 1989:11). The second stylized fact is that its "lifetime employment system" builds social consensus (e.g., Barber and McCallum, 1982:69–70). A third stylized fact is that Japan's industrial relations system is built around "enterprise unions." By directly tying the fate of a single union to the fate of a single employer, these also help to build consensus. Furthermore, by conventional measures, Japan has a fairly low level of income inequality

(Sawyer, 1976:16; McKean, 1989:202). It is these factors, it is claimed, that warrant the allocation of Japan to the corporatist category.

It will be no surprise, I suppose, that I have used the term "stylized fact" because I want to argue that the evidence on each of these issues is by no means straightforward.

Take, first of all, the issue of complicity among business, in association with government, in pursuit of long-run economic performance. Actually, on many issues, Japanese businesses seem to be as mutually suspicious as businesses elsewhere. In an account sympathetic to the "Japan Inc." view, Ouchi (1984:106–123) presents ample evidence of corporate reticence in the face of government attempts to induce collaboration in computer development and little evidence of government success.[37] On the other hand, there is some evidence of rather effective collaboration in dealing with labor. The first oil crisis was followed by a substantial acceleration in the rate of inflation in Japan—to over 20% in 1974 (Suzuki, 1986:134) and by considerable concern on the part of Japanese business leaders about international competitiveness. Their reaction was *not* to consult with labour leaders. Rather,

> between the 1974 and 1975 wage rounds there was a closing of ranks among employers and high government officials and close coordination between them, culminating in the adoption of specific targets. Apart from displays of 'formal' and 'symbolic' tripartism, the government did not consult the major labour organizations until after its wage targets were determined, and offered the unions only vague promises of "preparing favourable environments" in return for wage moderation. (Shalev, 1990:82–83)

In response to the 1973 oil shock, then, there was employer collaboration, but *against* rather than *with* labor.

Indeed, it would be difficult for employers to collaborate with organized labor, even if they wanted to. For the Japanese labor movement is highly decentralized. The 30% or so of the Japanese labor force that is unionized is spread among a "vast number of unions—over 72,000 in 1980" (Shonfield, 1984:111).[38] Nor is it true that Japanese unions are exclusively enterprise based. Almost 300,000 workers belong to *craft* trade unions (especially in the building trades), and most enterprise unions are affiliated with industrial union federations (Koike, 1987:314). It is true that it is at the enterprise or establishment level that bargaining usually takes place (Shinkai, 1982:182)—as it does in Britain and, to an important extent, everywhere else. But the overall structure of the labor movement, while no doubt less untidy than Britain's nonetheless, is neither centralized, nor *uniformly* based on enterprises (see also Shalev, 1990:69). So the evidence tends to suggest that business can combine but that the structure of the union movement would make it difficult for organized labor to do so.

Still, there is lifetime employment. Does this produce moral solidarity? Shonfield (1984:107) estimates the proportion of lifetime employment workers in the Japanese labor force at about a third, but concedes that this is a near guess. Chalmers (1989:33) estimates the proportion to be about a quarter. By any estimate, the bulk of the labor force is not covered by lifetime employment. We know that a substantial proportion of workers without lifetime employment are in a precarious position; they are also disproportionately women (Shonfield, 1984:111–112; Chalmers, 1989). The basis for moral solidarity between these workers and their employers is not evident. Are the permanent employees, at least, likely to be morally solidary? Koike (1987:308–13; see also Shigeyoshi, 1984) describes permanent employment as a "myth" and claims that redundancy in large firms is "not rare"; in fact, in a survey in 1978, more than 20% of firms with 1000 or more employees had declared workers redundant in the previous 3 years. Furthermore, the typical criteria for redundancies are both different from the practice of most other rich capitalist societies and unlikely to engender trust. Whereas in North America, worker redundancies tend to be skewed by the last-in-first-out principle, in large Japanese firms it is workers over 45 (who, with a steeply age-graded pay hierarchy, are more expensive) and those judged to be poorer performers that get fired.

Moreover, what is at issue here is not just whether or not Japanese management practices are likely to generate moral solidarity; there is also the question of the extent to which those practices, and the institutions in which they are embedded, are likely to generate cooperation through *intimidation*. Remember that in Japan, most workers in the private sector do not belong to trade unions; many workers outside of large firms experience considerable precariousness of employment; even workers in large firms risk being fired in the sort of difficult economic circumstances that developed in the mid 1970s—*and seniority does not protect them from dismissal*. All of this might make workers likely to think twice before risking offending an employer. Their minds also might be concentrated on cooperation by the fact that, notwithstanding a relatively equal distribution of income, for most of the postwar period Japan has had a distinctively niggardly welfare system—one in which housing, pensions, and retirement benefits were provided by the employer rather than by the government (Shonfield, 1984:112–113; Shalev, 1990:76, Bronfenbrenner and Yasuba, 1987:135; Noguchi, 1987:188).[39] It has been, besides, a fairly "commodified" welfare system, tying benefits to income (Esping-Andersen, 1990:52).

Note, finally, that the relative weakness of organized labor in Japan has a definite historic origin: the American occupation administration reacted to a postwar crisis of inflation in Japan and to what it saw as an increasing threat of communism in the Far East by enforcing a series of extremely conservative policies. The Japanese government was obliged to balance its budget, and to retire a set of loans at the same time; antimonopoly policies were markedly diluted; subsidies were reduced; government employees were deprived of the right to strike; identifiable union militants in the private sector were dismissed, along with large numbers of other workers (Nakamura, 1981:35–40; Uchino, 1983:44–54; Hadley, 1989:296–299). The result of all this was a serious recession and the cowing of a labour movement that had been both growing and becoming increasingly aggressive.

Policies and Outcomes

I started this section observing that, relative to other capitalist industrial economies, Japan had a postwar record of high growth, low unemployment, and high inflation until the oil shock but declining inflation thereafter, to a very low rate by the 1980s. Now consider this performance in a bit more detail, starting with Japan's growth performance.

After the second world war Japan had lower labor productivity than any other capitalist industrial nation—less than half of Italy's, which was less than a third of the level in the United States (Maddison, 1982:98). Here was a place with plenty of room for catch-up. If you look at Figure 7.4 the implication of this shows up very clearly: Japan had only slightly better growth in labor productivity from 1960 to 1985 than would have been predicted from its 1960 labor productivity level. However, if the same analysis is run using GNP per capita, Japan considerably *overperforms*, that is, its annual growth rate in GNP per capita is about one and a half percentage points higher than would be predicted from its 1960 level.[40] Why? The reason is that Japan has an unusually high rate of investment (Helliwell, 1990:124–125). In interpreting Japan's high economic growth rate, then, what is at issue is the institutional conditions that have made possible a high rate of investment.

Corporatism is supposed to accomplish this. But Japan does not have even remotely corporatist institutions, so it cannot be that. It is sometimes thought that by reducing the amplitude of investment-discouraging recessions Keynesian policy accomplishes this. But the policies enforced by the U.S. Government in response to the postwar crisis established a background of fiscal orthodoxy that persisted until, at least, 1965 (Hadley, 1989:304). Since then the Japanese government has tended to accumulate budget deficits. This, however, has had nothing to do with Keynesian stabilization policies; it is rather that, as in the United States, expenditures on transfer payments have risen with eligibility but tax revenues have remained static (Noguchi, 1987:193, 213). Indeed, the evidence tends to suggest that there is no long-run Phillips curve in Japan that significantly deviates from the vertical (Suzuki, 1986:150). That particular structural condition for a countercyclical stabilization policy has simply not been present.

If neither corporatism nor stabilization policy accounts for the high rate of investment in Japan, what does? Certainly, the government has attempted to foster investment. For much of the postwar period the Japanese government has actively pursued a low interest rate policy. Suzuki (1986:4–9, 17) argues that, in general, the policy had negligible effects, but there was an important exception in direct loans by the Japanese government and preferential treatment for exporters. Investment in export industries has been encouraged by a government interest rate policy that favors exporters. It has also been encouraged by a political system that seems to have been capable of limiting the extent to which the fruits of growth were distributed to the wider population in improvements in housing (a major consumer of capital in other countries) and other living conditions (Galenson and Odaka, 1976:668; Sato, 1987:142–143; Calder, 1988:ch. 9). So, the feature of Japanese growth performance that is identifiably superior has substantially rested on the capacity of governments to withhold commonly accepted Western living standards from the bulk of its population and, in so doing, to support a high rate of investment in productive capital. Note, however, that there is no evidence that this rests on negotiation involving organized labor, capital, and the government. Quite the contrary! Japanese labor seems to have been largely excluded from politics.

What about Japan's persistently low rate of unemployment? Here, there is widespread agreement that the reported figures considerably underestimate real unemployment. The dual structure of the labor market—with particular precariousness of employment concentrated among women—is accompanied by a pronounced tendency to withdraw from the labor market on the part of workers discouraged by a failure to find a job. Japanese statistical agencies use a rather stringent definition of job search activity so that workers who would be classified as unemployed in the United States are considered out of the labor force in Japan. And, in comparison to European countries in particular, there is a large part of the labor force that is officially self-employed, but earns such a low and erratic income that it is rather close to being unemployed (Bruno and Sachs, 1985:220–221; Lebaube, 1986:9–10). This does not necessarily mean that, using the same criteria, the Japanese unemployment rate would approximate levels in Canada or the United States. But, as in the case of Sweden, it does mean that the Japanese performance on this particular statistical aggregate is less impressive than it seems when aggregated by Schmidt (1989:118), for example, into a "misery index" (the sum of the inflation and unemployment rates). In fact, the real unemployment rate in Japan is probably more than double the reported rate (Shalev, 1990:76). It is also worth noting that a significant proportion of the total compensation of Japanese workers in the lifetime employment sector is made up of bonuses, so that when demand goes down labor costs can be reduced by what are, in effect, pay cuts rather than layoffs (Abegglen and Stalk, 1985:197).

Finally, there is Japan's success in transforming itself from a high inflation country before the 1973 oil shock to a low inflation country thereafter. How did it accomplish this? Not, as we have seen, through any centralized negotiations involving labor. Instead, Japan seems to have accomplished price stability through a shift on the part of the Bank of Japan to policies of impeccable monetarist rectitude.

The 1973 oil shock caused inflation in Japan to surge to well over 20% in 1974. The direct effect of the rise in oil prices was amplified by hoarding behavior by consumers and businesses. The Bank of Japan responded with a "period of monetary restraint that far surpassed any that had been seen previously" (Nakamura, 1981:229). The commitment to restrained monetary supply growth remained a basic part of Bank of Japan policy thereafter, and was the principal source of the relative price stability maintained in Japan through the 1978 oil shock.[41]

Performance in a Wider Context

Japan has been classified as "corporatism without labour" (Pempel and Tsunekawa, 1979) and has from time to time been included within the corporatist category in comparisons of macroeconomic performance. However, even if collaboration between government and business in Japan warrants categorization as corporatist it remains the case that *without labor* none of the hypothesized sources of superior performance outlined in the previous chapter can operate. Japan does, however, have a superior growth performance; where does it comes from?

As we saw above, it comes from a distinctively high rate of investment. And that high rate of investment is made possible not only by government policies that procure low interest rates for exporters but also by the fact that Japanese workers have been unable to extract the living standards increases that would be commonplace elsewhere in Western capitalist societies. It is possible to explain this failure of living standards to grow as follows: the union movement is weak and fragmented; the

workers in the so-called life time employment sector have little opportunity to quit and move to jobs elsewhere that would be as attractive—
but they might be fired, irrespective of seniority, if they get defined as
poor performers; and the alternative to a job in the life time employment
sector seems to involve a rather high probability of precarious and marginal employment. Since the early 1970s, moreover, the Japanese economy has continued to grow within the context of a generally nonaccom-
modative stance on the part of the Bank of Japan.

I suggest that this is a case in which the explanation for what is
superior about economic growth in Japan is the rather ferociously liberal
character of its economy. That is to say, in Japan, the labor market is
much less trammeled than elsewhere by restraints imposed by the moral
concerns that in other countries would be forced on employers by a
powerful union movement or political party.

Conclusion

Among sociologists and political scientists the predominant account
of the postwar inflation attributes high rates of inflation to class conflict
and the lower rates of inflation in some countries to the presence of
institutions that, by explicitly introducing a more substantial element of
equity into distributional outcomes, produces superior economic performance and introduces a degree of collaboration across classes. There is a
significant number of quantitative studies purporting to document this.
However, on closer scrutiny, it becomes clear that there is much less to
these studies than meets the eye. Their results are produced by an
erratic and dubious classification of countries into corporatist and noncorporatist categories; they vary in time period and countries covered in
ways likely to influence results (for example, several studies simply
drop two countries—Japan and Switzerland—that have superior economic records but do not fit easily into the corporatist category); most
that measure economic growth do so without controlling for initial productivity levels; and many of them draw conclusions without controlling
for other potentially relevant factors. Overall, I would argue, the accumulated research on the economic effects of corporatism is not very
good.

Now, consider this accumulation of research in a more general way.
On the one hand, there is a body of theory that specifies the *mechanisms*
through which neocorporatist institutions produce superior economic
outcomes, including price stability (bargaining takes place over real
wages, wage leap-frogging is eliminated, governments trade-off social

benefits and tax reductions for wage restraint, sequential trade-offs over time are possible, and the maintenance of economic security increases the cooperativeness of workers). On the other hand, this theory is usually tested using nothing but aggregate data on macroeconomic performance. Without denying that some data are always better than no data, I would nonetheless argue that the more direct way to test the theory is to look at whether or not countries that are supposed to be corporatist actually produce centrally negotiated, reasonably binding, agreements that effectively tie real wages to productivity growth; whether attempts to trade off government-provided social benefits or tax cuts for real wage restraint have actually worked; and whether there is any evidence of greater moral solidarity (for example, greater trust) on the part of workers. In other words, what is lacking in research on neocorporatism is attention to the intervening variables that tie institutions to the most aggregate macroeconomic outcomes.

In this respect the brief country case studies presented above are revealing. No matter what the centralizing institutions might be, there is in each case a substantial tendency for final earnings increases to respond to local market conditions in ways that subvert national agreements. Where wage bargaining appears to be centralized—in Sweden and Austria, and in Germany under "concerted action"—there is no evidence that wage growth is closely or distinctively connected to productivity increases; indeed, wages in Germany seem to have been *most* disconnected from productivity growth during "concerted action." And in supposedly corporatist Germany and unambiguously corporatist Austria, workers display less evidence of moral solidarity than they do in the aggressive market economy of the United States. Bear in mind, furthermore, that Scase (1977:23) reported more resentment over income inequality in Sweden than in Britain! I submit that, because more directly related to theoretic claims, this evidence is considerably more germane in testing neocorporatist theory than are the (in any case inadequate) products of the quantitative studies of macroeconomic performance.

But even if one stuck to those studies and the kind of evidence they marshall, the brief case studies above pose, at the very least, some serious problems for neocorporatist claims. The classification of Germany (with its 16 industrial unions and significant plant level bargaining component) as neocorporatist is a bit odd. The classification of Japan as corporatist (with no effective labor central and lifetime employment that is both circumscribed in coverage and considerably less than absolute) is quite simply bizarre. Austria and Sweden do have neocorporatist institutions. But (bearing in mind that maintaining stable prices is likely to be assisted by a superior growth record) neither has a record of growth that is much different from what might be expected, given its early postwar level of productivity. And although there is no evidence that their low rates of unemployment are produced by their ability to tie wage growth to productivity, it *is* clear that they substantially reduce unemployment through government programs of various sorts (including expanded public sector employment).

Before considering the more general implications of all this, and, in particular, of the factors that *do* seem to have played a role in these countries' macroeconomic outcomes, in the next chapter I examine the other kind of class conflict related explanation of the postwar inflation that has appealed to some sociologists and political scientists—Marxist accounts.

Notes

1.   Note that many of the studies I cite and discuss below do not use the term "neocorporatism"; the institutional variable measured might involve percentage of the labor force unionized, or centralization of collective bargaining, or strength of left parties, or some combination of these variables. But it is quite clear that their working hypotheses are derived from, or broadly related to, the set of ideas claiming that centralized bargaining over income shares, reinforced by a strong left (sympathetic to labor union demands), produces better macroeconomic performance.

2.   Where the source uses a scale score rather than categories I have assigned cases to broad categories, corresponding to the rank of their score.

3.   Pryor (1988) reports generally consistent classificatory decisions, except for Japan and France. However, he reviews only six studies.

4.   Korpi (1990) also allocates Japan to a category on its own.

5.   Barber and McCallum classify Switzerland in the first group but claim that, in addition to low unemployment, its firms offer lifetime employment (although they offer no documentation for the latter claim) so that it might have been put in group 2 with Japan.

6.   Lange and Garrett constructed their index as follows: first, they summed countries' standardized scores on percentage unionized and centralization of the labor movement (the latter an index drawn from Cameron, 1982); second, they measured labor's political power as *either* mean participation of left parties in government cabinets (1974–80) *or* as mean vote for left parties (1960–1980); third, they multiplied the labor centralization/unionization scores by each of the left political power scores.

7.   Panitch (1988:816) describes this period as follows: "In fact, British unions practised corporatist wage restraint of a draconian kind for longer periods than any other labour movement did through the 1960s and 1970s." In this short review article he does not provide any evidence in support of this claim and, in my view, it is probably exaggerated. Still, there is no question but that there was a continuous effort during this period to create and improve institutions designed to secure wage restraint (e.g., Smith, 1982:315).

8.   The Social Democratic Party remained in power until 1982 but, under

Helmut Schmidt, reverted to quite conventionally conservative macroeconomic policies. See Kloten, Ketterer, and Vollmer (1985:386–398). I would note in passing that in the second half of this chapter I will dispute the claim that it makes much sense to describe Germany as neocorporatist, even during the 1966–1973 period.

9.   Clearly, this assumes that a country has a sufficiently educated labor force that it can import more modern techniques and a sufficiently stable political and legal environment that capitalists are willing to invest. This, of course, rules out a good proportion of the third world. But in this book I am concerned only with rich capitalist societies.

10.   Note that the stricture about breaking down postwar economic performance into pre- and post-1973 periods does not apply here since I am interested only in how much of the variance of productivity growth can be exhausted by initial productivity level. In a multivariate equation it would probably be necessary to somehow take into account the shift in performance after 1973. Note also that using 1960 as the base year reduces or eliminates the effect on the performance of Germany and Austria of recovery from war time destruction.

11.   Hicks (1988:688), however, does include an explicit control.

12.   Korpi's (1990) analysis of international differences in level of unemployment is rather odd. In the first part he provides a multivariate analysis of the effects of economic factors. But when he introduces political factors in the second part his analysis becomes effectively bivariate.

13.   Alt goes on (1988:191–192) to argue that centralized bargaining institutions would have provided British governments with a different, and superior, set of policy options. For further attempts to attribute a part of Britain's economic difficulties to the City of London see Ingham (1984) and Newton and Porter (1988).

14.   As quite striking evidence of the casualness with which economists tend to approach institutional issues, Helliwell (1988:18) again cites the Crouch index that did not get published, as if it had been published.

15.   Wilensky and Turner (1987:43) go further and claim that "West Germany has had continuous incomes policies, formal or informal, since the early 1950s." They cite two authorities for this, one of which is Flanagan, Soskice, and Ulman (1983). As we will see shortly, this is to considerably overstate what Flanagan, Soskice, and Ulman actually argue.

16.   These included expanded programs for worker retraining and legal recognition of unions on the shop floor (Markovits and Allen, 1984:138–139).

17.   But consider the following description of "concerted action": it "did not arrive at binding decisions and was primarily an occasion for the government to present 'orientation' data to the unions and employers so that they would be better informed about the consequences of their prospective policies. In fact wage agreements kept within government figures only during recession periods like 1967–8 and 1975–6. The trade unions resented the narrow scope of its subject matter, and the withdrawal in 1977 was eventually the cause of its collapse" (Dyson, 1982:38). See also Katzenstein (1987:98–99).

18.   Relevant data are readily available. To give some idea of the magnitudes involved, for the period 1969 to 1978, the working days lost total in Germany was about a twenty-fifth of Italy's, a twentieth of Canada's, a tenth of the United State's, and almost the same as Sweden's (Adams, 1982:470).

19.   The other period was at the very beginning of the 1960s.

20.   But the case study evidence in Maitland (1983) does suggest that they have been quite a bit more cooperative than British workers.

21.   This is an important enough point that it is worth quoting Tylecote. He writes: "In Germany a worker who goes on strike without official union support, and strike pay, is more or less from that moment uninsured (so that a serious illness in the family could ruin him). Neither he nor his family can expect any support from the State. Sympathy strikes by one group in support of another—which can be very effective—are illegal."

22.   It is plausibly claimed that this general central bank preference for price stability is reinforced in the Germany case as a result of the hyperinflation of the 1920s.

23.   Flanagan, Soskice, and Ulman (1983:49) translate the Federal Economic Chamber as the Chamber of Commerce.

24.   Katzenstein (1984:61) and Marin (1985:97) give the total as 15 unions. This does not make any difference to the argument that follows.

25.   Aggregate demand was measured by the deviation of GDP from trend.

26.   It should be noted that Austria had already, for many years, been tying the schilling to the mark. To an important extent, the hard currency option formalized what had already developed.

27.   This dependence on the German market is also evident from a reading of consecutive issues of the Economist Intelligence Unit's *Quarterly Economic Report* on Austria.

28.   For useful sources for what I summarize below, see Martin (1984) and Heclo and Madsen (1987).

29.   The interludes were from 1958 to 1960 and 1968 to 1970, when there were social democratic majorities, and from 1976 to 1982, when there was a "bourgeois" government.

30.   The Swedish version of "Keynesianism" is associated with the so-called "Stockholm school." There are a number of important differences between the economics of the Stockholm school and what has become defined as Keynesian economics. It is clear, however, that each assumes that capitalist economies are not self-equilibrating within an acceptable time span. For a brief discussion of the Stockholm school, see Lundberg (1985:7–12).

31.   For a splendidly described, apparently successful, exercise in worker fooling see Giavazzi and Spaventa's (1989) analysis of post-oil shock economic policy in Italy.

32.   Unless it is only union *leaders'* trust that matters. But that gets us back to the issue of coercion (in quotation marks in Lange's version).

33.   Calmfors (1987:179) raises the possibility that wage drift may be anticipated by central negotiators and negotiated rates adjusted to offset it. But my guess is that an accurate forecast of aggregate wage drift is usually beyond the capacities of central negotiators and, more importantly, that it would be impossible for them to anticipate the multitude of differentials introduced by plant level agreements.

34.   Note, in this respect, that despite the huge apparatus of Swedish labor market programs, just like other capitalist countries, Sweden has serious shortages of skilled workers (Lundberg, 1985:26). Whether the magnitudes of the shortages are less in Sweden than in, say, Canada or Britain is not clear.

35.   Although as Hibbs (1991) makes clear, bargains did, as intended, produce a cumulative decrease in wage dispersal.

36.   Thus, *of those who expressed an opinion*, 71% said that "common" members

of the union did not have enough influence, 60% said that union leaders did not know enough about what it was like to be a worker, and 58% described union leader contact with the members as "bad."

37.   In Ouchi's account, MITI encouraged computer manufacturers to pool research and development and to focus on different market segments: but the companies concealed important research findings from each other; they lobbied for subsidies without cooperation; and Ouchi felt obliged to conclude with respect to one of the major collaborative efforts, "Whether the project yielded truly significant joint scientific achievements is not clear" (p. 117).

38.   Note, furthermore, that about a third of the union membership is in the public sector—so that private sector union density in Japan is, by international standards, modest (Shalev, 1990:69).

39.   Noguchi (1987:191) argues that the modest coverage and level of expenditure on social security is simply a result of lags in the development of the Japanese social security system and that when all those eligible qualify the Japanese program will be comparable to the programs in other Western countries. Still, the fact remains that there has been a substantial gap between social security protection in Japan and in other Western countries for most of the postwar period. Interestingly, McKean (1989:215–216) suggests that increases in welfare provision in Japan have had the effect of increasing inequality!

40.   Its nearest rival, Norway, is about three quarters of a percent beyond what would be predicted from its 1960 level. Norway's GNP growth, of course, substantially reflects the effects on exports of oil discoveries. Notwithstanding its neocorporatist institutions, until its oil was commercialized, Norway had a poor growth record (Dowrick and Nguyen, 1989:1026).

41.   The other part was the experience gained by consumers and businesses. Hoarding in 1973–1974 caused consumers and businesses to encumber themselves with excessive stocks of overpriced commodities. Each appears to have learnt from the experience during the later oil shock (Suzuki, 1986:130–131).

8

MARXIST THEORIES

It would be churlish to begrude Marxists their obvious pleasure at the marked deterioration in the economic performance of the capitalist nations in the 1970s and early 1980s. After all, their academic and political opponents had made the most of the surge in economic growth throughout the capitalist world in the earlier postwar period, interpreting it as clear cut evidence of the inadequacy of Marxist analysis. Certainly, the onset of slower growth, markedly increased unemployment, and accelerating inflation tended to enhance the credibility of a body of theory at the center of which is the inherent instability of capitalism; it allowed Marxists to more confidently announce the bankruptcy of bourgeois economics (de Brunhoff and Cartelier, 1974:47; Mattick, 1978:27–55; Franklin, 1977:216–228; Mandel, 1978:9).[1]

Furthermore, *in principle*, Marxist theory starts out with a distinct advantage in the explanation of macroeconomic outcomes. We know that they are affected by government policy choices and it is clear that there is a tradition within Marxist theorizing stressing the inevitable integratedness of the political and the economic (e.g., Gough, 1979: 10)—something that has not been true of orthodox economic analyses until the quite recent efflorescence of public choice writings. *In practice*, the Marxist literature has not been especially superior in this respect. Major Marxist economic treatments have incorporated no explicit political analysis (e.g., Baran and Sweezy, 1966; Mattick, 1969; Mandel, 1975; Glyn and Sutcliffe, 1972; Glyn and Harrison, 1980; Harvey, 1982) and major political analyses (e.g., Miliband, 1969; Poulantzas, 1975; and the essays in Holloway and Picciotto, 1978) have tended to content themselves with accounting for the growth in government intervention in capitalist economies without specifying the particular economic problems with which government decisions have been concerned. Thus, Holloway and Picciotto (1978:2–3) have observed that

> Some analyses pay little or no attention to the specificity of the political and argue (or more often assume) that the actions of the state flow more or less directly from the requirements of capital: such analyses are sometimes

accused of 'reductionism' or 'economic determinism'. Other analyses, in over-reaction to this approach, have insisted on the 'relative autonomy' of the political, denying (or more often overlooking) the need for theorists of the political to pay close attention to the conditions of capital accumulation: this tendency may perhaps be termed 'politicist'. What both poles of this dichotomy—which does not, of course, always present itself as more than an underlying tendency—have in common is an inadequate theorization of the relation between the economic and the political as discrete forms of capitalist social relations.

It is fair to say that in recent years a number of Marxist writers, especially, James O'Connor, Ian Gough, and Manuel Castells, have made serious attempts to transcend this gulf. But it remains the case (and this seems not to have been noticed or remarked on) that notwithstanding the roots of Marxism in *political economy*, Marxist theorizing has been no quicker than orthodox economics to construct theory that synthesizes political and economic processes. Indeed, Stigler's pioneering work on public choice antedates the recent Marxist attempts at synthesis.

In this chapter I will argue that, with or without a synthesis of the political and economic, Marxist theorizing contributes nothing of use to the explanation of postwar macroeconomic performance and, in particular, the acceleration of inflation. Specifically, I will try to show two things: first, that when Marxists attempt to explain the postwar inflation the accounts that they produce are in most important respects indistinguishable from one or the other of the non-Marxist theories I have reviewed earlier; second, that what *is* distinguishable about their accounts, namely the assertion and identification of an *underlying* crisis causing mechanism, is, for the most part, rather unconvincing. It should be recognized, of course, that there is no such thing as *a* Marxist theory of the postwar inflation. There are as many varieties of explanation of the postwar inflation claiming to be Marxist as there are non-Marxist varieties and, as I will show, each variety tends to produce an account that coincides quite closely with a non-Marxist account, distinguished only by the rhetoric of outrage in terms of which the account is couched and the particular secular crisis tendency stressed.

I will begin by outlining Marxist crisis theories and examining their logical difficulties. There is no shortage of summary treatments of Marxist theories of crisis (e.g., O'Connor, 1987) so I will present them in a quite concise fashion. Two points need noting at the outset. First, it should be understood that none of the theories is formulated in such a way that it implies that any source of crisis is likely to produce a collapse of capitalism in the foreseeable future. They all allow for "countertendencies" and, indeed, "always imply the *temporary resolutions of the contradictions . . .* and thus repeatedly create the conditions for a new period of capitalist accumulation" (Altvater, 1973:76). All they suggest is that capitalist economies are chronically unstable and, in some versions, that they are likely to function most of the time at considerably less than their full capacity. Second, two or more of the sources of crisis outlined below are likely to be combined in any particular analysis of postwar economic difficulties, in one or another of their versions.[2] I have separated them out to facilitate analysis.

Theories of Crisis

The Falling Rate of Profit

Start out by assuming either a competitive economy or that oligopolistic industrial structures do not significantly free price and output decisions from the constraints of competition. Competition means that businessmen who want to maximize their profits are compelled to innovate. It is *assumed* that over the long haul innovation means substituting capital for labor. But, for the capitalist class as a whole, profit depends on the surplus value extracted from labor. Assume further that there is only so much surplus value that can be extracted per laborer (defined either by subsistence or a rather woolly notion of a customary standard of living—see, e.g., Harvey, 1982:50). If the profit of capitalists depends on the surplus value produced by workers, any substitution of capital equipment for labor will reduce the base from which that surplus can be extracted. The substitution of capital for labor (the rising "organic composition of capital") causes a fall in the rate of profit, which in turn produces unemployment and economic crisis.

It is worth stressing that this has remained the *fundamental tendency* of capitalism for a whole series of major Marxist writers. Mattick (1969:61) describes it as an *"immanent* law of capital accumulation" and, for Mandel (1975:210; see also Yaffe, 1973; Fine and Harris, 1976; Gamble and Walton, 1976:125–135; Lipietz, 1985:31, 110),

> with increasing automation, increasing organic composition of capital and the onset of a fall in the total man-hours worked by productive laborers, it is impossible in the long run seriously to continue to increase real wages and at the same time maintain a constant mass of surplus-value. One of the two quantities will diminish. Since under normal conditions, i.e., without fascism or war, a significant decline in real wages can be excluded, there emerges *an historical crisis of the valorization of capital* and an inevitable decline, first in the mass of surplus value and then also in the rate of

surplus value, and hence there follows an abrupt fall in the average rate of profit.

Underconsumption

Modern underconsumption theory emerged as a Marxist response to the interest in monopoly pricing of the 1930s (e.g., Robinson, 1933; Chamberlain, 1933).[3] The best known postwar version of this analysis goes as follows. Assume that the existence of stock options guarantees that managers in corporations that they do not own nonetheless maximize profits. Now, however, profit-maximizing decisions are taken within an oligopolistic context, which means that competition no longer forces the managers to reduce prices as they improve productivity (e.g., Steindl, 1976:3). But since they profit maximize the managers do continue to innovate and reduce the costs of production. The result is stable or rising prices and falling costs (each in real terms) and a tendency for the absolute "surplus" accumulated by capitalists to rise. Because perfect competition has been replaced with oligopolistic competition, profit does not fall (Sweezy, 1942:102 ff.).

But the resulting surplus must be disposed of, for this rising surplus means that national income is being shifted from labor to capital and there is a problem of aggregate demand (it is assumed that capitalists cannot consume all of the rising surplus accruing to them). Stagnant or declining demand means falling investment and a secular tendency to stagnation. Clearly, the mass of profits must fall as declining demand forces some firms out of business and other firms to produce at less than capacity. At first, at least, the *profit margin* is not reduced for "in an industry which approximates to the oligopolistic type, where the driving out of competitors is difficult, the profit margin at given utilization is inelastic" (Steindl, 1976:122). Ultimately, of course, as crisis deepens, even the profit margins would become insecure.

James O'Connor (1973) has produced a somewhat more elaborate version of this argument, which combines the core ideas of underconsumption with the "dual economy" ideas of Averitt (1968).[4] The private economy is divided into a monopoly and a competitive sector. In the monopoly sector prices are relatively insensitive to demand and, in particular, do not decline when demand falls or when productivity rises (and it is assumed that the monopoly sector is characterized by steady productivity increases). So "many or most gains from productivity increases . . . are not distributed evenly throughout the population but rather are 'bottled up' in the monopoly sector" (p. 21). At the same time, "the absence of effective unions in the competitive sector and the bifurcation of the wage- and price-determination process in the competitive and monopoly sectors keep consumer demand (in terms of average wage increases) from advancing as rapidly as productive capacity in monopoly industries" (p. 25).[5] O'Connor's analysis, then, arrives at underconsumption from a sectoral model of the capitalist economy. Monopolies administer prices that render those prices inflexible in the face of declining demand. Workers outside of the monopoly industry, devoid of unions (or, at least, effective ones) and facing employers rendered intransigent by the competitive conditions they face, have wages that are too low to pick up the slack. All of this produces a chronic tendency to excess capacity in the monopoly sector and inadequate growth of employment.

Because of a number of difficulties with this line of argument (that I discuss later in this chapter) an alternative "underconsumption" interpretation has been asserted. It assumes competitive rather than monopoly pricing. In this version capitalists are driven by competition "to produce to the limit set by the productive forces . . . without any consideration of the market or needs backed by ability to pay" (Harvey, 1982:93). In particular, this means that capitalists are continually squeezing labor costs so that they are also undercutting the markets for their products (Lebowitz, 1982:17; Weeks, 1981:ch. 6), a problem they compound by saving the income that is transferred to them from workers rather than by spending it (Bleaney, 1976:211).[6] But, at the same time, they are compelled to continue investing; first, there is an incentive to introduce new plant and equipment to replace labor that is always less tractable than the equipment that replaces it; second, to provide the growth that the "middle layers" of managers and white-collar workers require to keep them motivated and loyal; and third, to forestall loss of markets to rivals (Devine, 1983:6–7).

As Devine points out, neither of these arguments makes a lot of sense if workers are in a sufficiently strong bargaining position to effectively resist the redistribution of income to capital that the underconsumption argument assumes. Thus, "underconsumption forces are more important in undermining an economic boom in a labor-abundant economy, where agricultural or foreign labor-power reserves and the weakness of working-class organization prevent wages from rising with productivity during an economic expansion" (Devine, 1983:4). So either the monopoly or the competitive version of underconsumption theory assumes a generally weak working class.

Class Struggle

Class struggle is, of course, an element of all Marxist crisis theories. The economic damage wrought by the falling rate of profit or by the rising surplus produces political outcomes by intensifying class conflict. But there is a set of writers who regard themselves as Marxist but who have abandoned or, at least, downplayed the underlying economic mechanisms that have been at the core of more orthodox Marxist treatments. They have been labeled (pejoratively) neo-Ricardians by more orthodox Marxists. Their "error" is that they accord an unacceptable degree of independent causal influence to "the sphere of exchange" for "All analyses of economic practice must centre on the complete concept of capital in which production is primary" (Fine and Harris, 1976:101). To put it more simply, the neo-Ricardians assign a central role to the confrontation between capital and labor over wages in the labor market and in the political arena over the broad reinforcement to the position of workers provided by the welfare state and downplay the importance of the process of pricing and selling goods, that is central to the two crisis theories I have so far reviewed.

The assertion that all of these analyses share is that full employment is a threat to profits because of its effects on the bargaining position of labor. In Gough's (1975, 1979) version, in the capitalist world in the postwar period there have been two major developments: first, full employment, and, second, the creation and expansion of the welfare state. As a precondition for support during the war and because a repeat of the 1930s was deemed to be politically too dangerous, Western governments responded to the needs of capital by introducing a broadly Keynesian policy of full employment and by creating or expanding the welfare state (see also Glyn and Sutcliffe, 1972:34–36). But full employment itself further strengthened the labor movement (Gough, 1975:69–70) and the welfare state created a set of strong public sector unions that themselves ratcheted the level of class conflict up another notch (Gough, 1979:86).

Other versions of this argument stress other factors. The postwar boom exhausted the supplies of reserve labor in agricultural regions of Europe and North America (Glyn and Harrison, 1980:7–11; Gonick, 1983:31; O'Connor, 1984:70–79). The development of the welfare state safety net undermined work discipline (Gonick, 1983:34–35). All of these factors, or some combination of them, tilted relative bargaining power in favor of labor and against capital and produced a strong wage-push that *tended* to cut into profits and produce a general crisis for capital since "the demand for higher real wages and working class income resulted in the diffusion of economic struggle into all spheres of circulation, including the credit sphere" (O'Connor, 1984:94).

Credit Institutions

The approach to credit institutions is not so much that they cause crises as that they compound and amplify crises originating in one or another of the processes described above. Thus, "The credit system is a product of capital's own endeavours to deal with the internal contradictions of capitalism. What Marx will show us is how capital's solution ends up heightening rather than diminishing contradictions" (Harvey, 1982:239; see also Lipietz, 1985:81–106).

Investment requires large outlays of capital and they in turn require financial institutions and instruments to mobilize capital and transfer it through the economy. This process is a source of instability in the following ways (Harvey, 1982:284–295). First, it speeds up the process of investment and, therefore, of innovation. But if you accept the falling rate of profit argument (as Harvey to some extent does) that produces an acceleration of the rate at which the organic composition of capital rises and of the rate at which profits are likely to fall. Second, in this system, bankers become powerful and act in their own self-interest in ways likely to disrupt the process of accumulation. Third, since the whole process involves competition to loan money for profit with competition among borrowers for capital there is a strong incentive to make loans secured by more or less valueless collateral. At their core financial markets have a speculative character likely to magnify the damage caused by a crisis originating in the productive core of the economy (as, arguably, the stock market crash of 1929 did).

Marxist Accounts of the Postwar Inflation

In the previous section I identified four sources of crisis in capitalist economies described and outlined in Marxist writings—the falling rate of profit, underconsumption, class conflict, and as a complement to and amplifier of the three previous sources of crisis, instability in the credit system. How are these sources of crisis linked to the acceleration of inflation in the postwar period? The link is not obvious in the case of the first two sources of crisis, which produce reductions in economic activity and unemployment rather than inflation. However, in the 1970s, at least, high rates of inflation *were* associated with increasing unemployment so that Marxist accounts, at the core of which is a tendency toward stagnation, start out with a certain surface plausibility when applied to the *stagflation* that began in the 1970s.

For both falling rate of profit and underconsumption writers the explanation of inflation is quite straightforward. It is a device used by governments (who are predisposed from the start to choose policies that protect capitalism and, in the long run, capitalists) for restoring economic activity. The problem is to make it worthwhile for capitalists to invest.

For Mattick (1969:183–184; 1978:16–17, 36), Mandel (1975:42, 448 ff.), and Harvey (1982:312–313) inflation serves to shift income away from workers and helps to buttress the profit rate (see also Gamble and Walton, 1976:160 ff.). It does this, moreover, in a way that is supposed to be partially obscured from the worker by the fact that money wages are rising even if real wages are falling. Underconsumptionists stress the same income shift (Baran, 1957:123–125; Morris, 1973:6; The Editors, 1981:5; Sherman, 1976) as part of the efforts of governments to use budgetary deficits to generate economic activity.[7] In O'Connor's dual economy version of underconsumption theory the government has to spend even more. It has to provide the infrastructure and education that are required to maintain the profitability of the technologically advanced and large scale monopoly sector; and it has to spend to offset the chronic tendency to inadequate demand caused by the bottling up of profits within the monopoly sector.

This does not, of course, explain why inflation was absent in the 1930s but accelerated, in particular, in the 1960s. How have Marxist's explained the periodicity of twentieth-century inflation? First, there is the argument by both falling rate of profit and underconsumptionist writers that postwar inflation has its roots in the adoption of Keynesian policies to counteract the tendency of capitalist economies to stagnate (Mandel, 1975:415 ff.; 1978:60–68); Mattick, 1978:14; Morris, 1973:12; The Editors, 1974; Altvater, 1973:80). In the 1970s this inflationary bias was compounded by the breakdown of the Bretton Woods system and the international financial discipline that it involved, including the accumulated effects of the U.S. balance of payments deficits that had started to build up in the mid-1960s (de Brunhoff and Cartelier, 1974:57–58; Gough, 1975:80).

So for both falling rate of profit and underconsumption theorists the postwar inflation originated in the chronic stagnationary tendencies of capitalism in the context of a Keynesian intellectual tradition that legitimated government deficits, and was exacerbated by the collapse of the Bretton Woods system through which the United States had been able to impose financial discipline on the rest of the capitalist world. Before critically examining these notions, let us consider the class conflict account of the postwar inflation.

Here inflation is quite readily explained. After the second world war the working class in capitalist nations became much more powerful. Workers were, therefore, able to extract increases in wages in excess of the rate of increase in productivity (Gough, 1975:86) and capitalists attempted to defend themselves by increasing prices: hence inflation (see also Glyn and Sutcliffe, 1972; Boddy and Crotty, 1975:12; Glyn and Harrison, 1980). But this raises the question, why did governments confronted with this sort of wage-push not simply use the macroeconomic instruments at their disposal to increase unemployment and as a result weaken the bargaining power of labor? Marxist writings provide two answers to this.

First, Boddy and Crotty (1974, 1975) argued that recessions can serve to cow the working class only temporarily. Prolonged unemployment would not successfully control the labour force since "the result . . . would be to effectively segment the labour force into those working, and those not only unemployed but, as time went on, increasingly unemployable because of deteriorating work skills and habits. The capitalists would once again be faced *de facto* with a militant, unfrightened workforce and tight labour markets even though measured unemployment remained high" (1975:9). This does not prevent governments from engineering short recessions to teach workers a lesson, but it does rule out the kind of really sustained recession that would put a stop to the steady wage-push inflation that Boddy and Crotty claim to have been present since the second world war.

Second, and more widespread, is an argument in terms of the "legitimation" needs of contemporary capitalism. This explanation has been most clearly applied to the postwar inflation in the work of O'Connor (1973) and Gough (1975, 1979). Assume, for the sake of argument, that capitalism produces a set of social and economic outcomes that would be considered unjust, at least by members of the working class. Its operations produce degraded working conditions, agglomerations of the population into urban areas in a way that is a menace to public health, disruption of the family (producing single-parent families and abandoned elderly), and, at best, periodic unemployment (Gough, 1979:32–36, 85–94). It also produces flagrant inequalities. In O'Connor's early work this process is, of course, tied into the emergence of undercon sumption and the creation of a secondary sector as a result of pricing behavior in the monopoly sector. If the needs for minimal regulation of working conditions, some maintenance of sanitary standards in urban areas, and a social safety net to deal with the human wreckage produced by the disruption of the family and recurrent unemployment were unmet, it is assumed by those who make these arguments, the capitalist system would be at risk. Workers would somehow rebel against the unreasonable conditions within which they have to work and live.[8] To avoid this, and to protect capitalism, the "state" (which serves the long-run interests of capital) is compelled to intervene to attenuate the worst damage caused by its operation. The result of this is what we have come to know as the welfare state, which is used to (modestly) redistribute income, provide minimal living standards for those who are casualties of the operation of a market economy, and through housing and health policy provide minimal general standards of public health. In doing this the state presents itself "as the representative of the common interests of 'a people' " (Gough, 1979:43) and, to some extent, quells the propensity of people to mobilize in response to the injustices produced by the operation of capitalism. The welfare state, in other words, legitimates capitalism. In doing so, furthermore, it ensures standards of housing, health, and education sufficient to ensure that employers have an adequate supply of labor power.

What does this all have to do with inflation? Well, all of these expenditures by the government needed to legitimate the capitalist system, added to the expenditures needed to provide a suitably trained labor force and to deal with the profit problems caused by underconsumption, strain the budgetary capacities of modern governments. In the postwar period, moreover, they have done so to a greater extent because, first, as argued by class conflict theorists, the working class has become more powerful so that it is necessary to spend more to secure its quiescence and, second, because "the unplanned relentless drive of capitalist development continually generates new needs. . . . Numerous 'social problems' from the middle-aged redundant to the victims of urban redevelopment to the thalidomide children, can be interpreted as the social costs associated with rapid economic and technological progress" (Gough, 1979:92). In other words, capitalism costs more and more to legitimate as its contradictions and irrationalities multiply.

The budgetary problems caused by the expenditures to deal with these multiplying needs (of legitimation and for subsidies to industries) tempt government to resort to inflationary finance. Governments cannot fund these expenditures out of taxes because to do so would further antagonize workers or compound the profit problems of corporations (Gough, 1975:86; 1979:125–126). So they have used deficit financing, and that is inflationary (O'Connor, 1973:43).

Now, as I observed at the beginning of this chapter, I have separated out a set of Marxist theories of crisis while, typically, two or more of them are combined in the relevant writings. Before going on to critically scrutinize these accounts and to avoid any notion that in separating out the component elements of these analyses I have somehow misrepresented them (on the very Marxist assumption that the whole is considerably more than its parts), let us examine one quite general explanation of the postwar inflation in its entirety.

Castells on the Inflationary Crisis of the 1970s

There are two elements to this (1980) analysis. There is a tendency toward economic crisis rooted *principally* in a falling rate of profit. Then there is a set of countertendencies designed to deal with the putative economic crisis caused by the falling rate of profit. Castell's falling rate of profit originates, first, in the rising power of workers (which is unexplained), which increases the attractiveness of capital equipment relative to labor (pp. 18, 48–49, 54, 61) and, second, in a rising organic composition of capital.

This tendency toward economic crisis is, moreover, exacerbated by aggregate demand problems caused by the development of a "dual economy." Like O'Connor he claims that the segmentation of the economy into a well-paid monopoly sector that accounts for a diminishing proportion of the labor force and a poorly paid competitive sector with an ever expanding labor force leads to aggregate demand problems: a crisis of underconsumption, in other words (p. 50).

What can be done about this crisis? Castell provides what is, in effect, a rag-bag of responses—almost all of which he presents as inflationary. Corporations with monopoly power respond to profit difficulties by increasing prices. This is inflationary (pp. 61–64). The corporate response to wage pressure is technical innovation that leads corporations into debt. Corporations deal with underconsumption problems by expanding their sales effort and liberalizing credit. Corporate indebtedness and personal indebtedness are both, according to Castells, inflationary (pp. 64–67). The internationalization of capital (with the growth of multinational corporations) liberates the private sector from national controls on credit and encourages speculation to boot (pp. 74–75). This too is inflationary. Finally, the government (or rather "state" in the portentous prose of fiscal crisis writers) spends money to support the profit rate (pp. 69 ff.). It takes on necessary but unprofitable activities (e.g., rail transportation or scientific research). It subsidizes private business. It bears the cost of "reproduction of social relations and . . . the organization of the social division of labor" (p. 71), which means that it pays a lot for "education, health, mass media, housing and transportation" or it forces private corporations to spend more on these activities. But because the state is limited in the extent to which it can tax private corporations it runs budget deficits and these are inflationary. Here, then, is the source of inflation. Corporations and governments respond to the declining rate of profit and deficient aggregate demand with, respectively, expanded credit and deficits that are financed through inflation rather than taxation.

Marxist Accounts: An Appraisal

I have divided my treatment of Marxist accounts of the postwar inflation into two parts: first, there are the theories of crisis that are the

centerpiece of each account; second there are a set of specific applications of why one of the *forms* taken by the crisis in the period after the
second world war has been a propensity to rising prices, particularly as
compared to the marked deflation of the 1930s. The answers to this latter
question are, as we have seen, as follows: for both falling rate of profit
theorists and underconsumptionists the postwar inflation originates in
the attempt of governments to spend their way out of the otherwise
inevitable stagnationary tendencies of capitalist economies, in the context of the policy options provided by the Keynesian revolution, and the
balance of payments deficits run up by the United States in the 1960s
and early 1970s together with the breakdown of the international financial discipline provided by the Bretton Woods agreement that it produced; for class conflict theorists there is a wage-push originating in a
working class made more powerful by the full employment and growing
social safety net of the postwar period, compounded by the need of the
government to spend large amounts of money to "legitimate" a capitalist system the inefficiency and injustice of which become ever more
obvious.

Consider first falling rate of profit and underconsumption accounts. If
you cast your mind back to some of the treatments of the postwar
inflation that I have reviewed in the previous chapters it should be
apparent that, purged of rhetoric, there is not a great deal of difference
between these explanations of the postwar inflation and one or another
of the non-Marxist accounts. For orthodox economists of either Keynesian or neoclassical disposition the postwar inflation originated, first, in a
set of policies designed to stimulate aggregate demand to produce higher rates of economic growth and lower rates of unemployment and,
second, in the transmission of inflation from the United States to the rest
of the world as a result of that country's Asian military adventure in the
1960s and early 1970s, in the context of the Bretton Woods fixed exchange rate regime. *In specific details,* falling rate of profit and underconsumptionist accounts of the postwar inflation are indistinguishable from
their bourgeois counterparts. They differ only in their assertion of one or
another underlying propensity to crisis. *They add absolutely nothing to our
understanding of postwar macroeconomics unless the particular crisis mechanism cited is correct.*

Here we run into an underlying difficulty. Marxists themselves cannot
agree on the plausibility of the various crisis theories. Underconsumptionist writers of the *Monthly Review* sort formally reject the falling rate of
profit argument as, in general, do neo-Ricardians. And it is quite clear
that for falling rate of profit theorists the *Monthly Review* underconsumptionists and the neo-Ricardians are nothing short of heretics (see, in
particular, Fine and Harris, 1976). Effective and perceptive criticism of

each of the crisis theories comes, as we shall see, from within the broad corpus of Marxist writings. But whether from within or without Marxist writings, there are some cogent criticisms of each of these theories of crisis.

Take first of all the falling rate of profit theory. It involves two central assertions: first that the organic composition of capital tends to rise and second that this inevitably produces a fall in the rate of profit. These assertions seem, at first sight, straightforward enough. But a close examination of the falling-rate-of-profit writings muddies this picture considerably. Marx recognized "counteracting tendencies that operate to prop up the rate of profit" (Sweezy, 1942:99 ff.); so do modern writers in this genre. "The actual capital accumulation process can be slowed down and is, in fact, constantly slowed down by non productive, i.e. nonprofitable capital expenditures, by the outright destruction of capital (as in time of war), and by interventions in the economy" (Mattick, 1969:99). There may be a "sudden fall in the average organic composition of capital, for example as a result of the massive penetration of capital into spheres (or countries) with a very low organic composition" (Mandel, 1975:115). Productivity improvements, moreover, might and often do mean that greater amounts of either consumption or investment goods can be produced with the same amount of capital and labor (Mandel, 1975:179). Where this occurs, its effect is to increase the average amount of surplus value being extracted from workers relative to wage costs (an increase in the "rate of exploitation") and, since capital costs remain constant, the rate of profit. At this point it is appropriate to ask, when does an "immanent" or "fundamental" tendency become transformed into an entirely contingent one?

As a matter of fact, it can be shown that there is no defensible "law of the falling rate of profit." Van Parijs (1980) has shown precisely this. The organic composition of capital need only rise if technical change is predominantly labor rather than capital saving. There is no reason why it should be so. Indeed, as van Parijs points out, why would a capitalist seeking to maximize profits substitute capital for labor unless doing so produced an increase in the rate of profit? The law of the falling rate of profit assumes that capitalists are irrational. And even if, for some reason, the organic composition tends to rise, that need not produce a fall in the rate of profit if productivity improvements allow capitalists to extract more surplus value from each worker—that is, to increase the rate of exploitation. In Wolff's words (1979:332; see also Steedman, 1979), "Marx's law of the falling rate of profit cannot be supported on theoretical grounds."

There have been some attempts to rebut van Parijs. Clawson (1983) argues that van Parijs is mistaken to construct a theory that assumes perfect competition. Marx, he argues, foresaw the centralization of capital the implication of which is, first, that when a crisis occurs it is much more disruptive and, second, that the competitive behavior of capitalists is transformed into a struggle over market shares that prevents them from, say, cutting production to deal with rising production costs. O'Connor (1987:85–86) argues that the increasing organization of the working class provides a very strong incentive to replace labor with capital. Each of these accounts deals with van Parijs' criticisms by asserting a different context of investment decisions—oligopolistic competition in the case of Clawson and an organized working class in the case of O'Connor. These changes in context may well be important. But neither objection explains why capitalists would choose to buy more capital equipment when doing so would produce lower profits (see also van Parijs, 1983).[9]

Castells (1980) has tried to respond to these difficulties. First, like O'Connor, he argues that the increasing organization of the working class increases the relative attractiveness of a more capital-intensive form of production organization (pp. 18, 48–49, 54, 61)—involving, of course, a higher organic composition of capital. Second, he makes a rather convoluted argument the gist of which is that competition forces capitalists to continually allocate funds to the purchase of capital equipment but that technical progress means that they are never able to realize the profits anticipated from their investment (pp. 48–58).[10]

There are difficulties with this line of argument too. It assumes such a frenetic pace of innovation that firms do not in practice realize the profits that might reasonably have been anticipated when the investment was undertaken. In my view, this assumes a rather romantic vision of the manufacturing industries of a number of countries. It is hard, for instance, to discover this frenetic pace of innovation in many of the U.S. industries described in the essays collected by Adams (1971). Canadian technical innovation is substantially dependent on that of the United States and, if anything, lags (Green, 1980:132–138). Nobody would accuse a substantial part of British industry of being particularly technically dynamic for most of the postwar period. Perhaps what Castell describes applies to Japan and Germany. But those are countries that were rather less damaged by the economic crisis of the 1970s and early 1980s.[11] In other words, the countries to which Castell's description of technical innovation best applies are precisely the ones whose economies have performed the best. The falling rate of profit mechanism propounded by Castells is no more convincing than the others.

Now consider the underconsumptionist theory of crisis—in its various versions. There is first of all the *Monthly Review* version, premised on a shift of major parts of capitalist economies from competitive to monopoly (or oligopoly) pricing, based in the growth of large firms and barriers to the entry of new competition into an industry, like high costs of entry and product differentiation (Bain, 1956). Or there is O'Connor's rather more complicated version of this argument.

One sort of evidence that this has taken place is the observation that many industrial prices are unresponsive to decreases in demand (Blair, 1972; Means, 1962). On the whole, however, subsequent research tends not to support these claims about pricing behavior. First, Stigler and Kindahl (1970) went to some lengths to show that price rigidity was much more a phenomenon of *list* than of *actual* prices; that, in practice, firms discount substantially from list prices so that the prices they actually charge do fall in response to recession. Using actual rather than list prices, there is much less evidence of the price asymmetry that the underconsumptionist argument (in the form presented by Baran and Sweezy) assumes. There is still, however, some evidence of price rigidity and it seems to have increased from the prewar to the postwar period (Cagan, 1979:73) in the way that the underconsumptionist argument would lead one to expect. Yet the increase in price rigidity *is not clearly associated with the concentration of an industry*. Price rigidity in the United States (which has been the focus of most of the research within this genre) increased in industries with intermediate levels of concentration by as much as it did in industries with high levels of concentration and by only a little bit more than it did in industries with very low levels of concentration (Cagan, 1979:82–90). In fact, as we saw earlier, Cagan's conclusion is that the downward inflexibility of prices in the postwar period is principally a consequence of ingrained inflationary expectations rather than of a change in the structure of industry (p. 94).

Semmler (1982:45–49) has reviewed another body of evidence bearing on this matter. There has been research on concentration ratios and entry barriers on the one hand and profits on the other.[12] He concludes that what evidence exists linking profit rates to concentration ratios can be explained by the relative efficiency of firms in concentrated industries, that tend to be large, rather than by market power. He also concludes that although entry barriers probably do support somewhat higher rates of profit, those barriers can also be *exit barriers*. Firms in industries that are costly to enter because they require high fixed capital investments are also difficult to leave when demand declines because of the high investment in capital equipment and its low scrap value. Such firms make high profits when demand is buoyant because it is difficult and costly for competitors to enter the industry but are also forced to tolerate low profits when demand is weak because it is not easy to move investment into other lines of activity. The North American steel industry in the 1970s provides a good example of this. So the relationship between profit rates and barriers to entry (and, usually, exit too) is not nearly as close *in the long run* as it seems in some cross-sectional studies. Semmler's general conclusion is that the pricing behavior of the modern corporation is not obviously inconsistent with the competitive assumptions of classical Marxism. Glick (1985) has provided further evidence that this is so. He shows that from 1958 to 1979 interindustry profit rates in the United States tended to converge, certainly to a degree that is not easily reconcilable with an argument based heavily on the assumption of monopoly pricing. The evidence on pricing behavior simply does not support the version of underconsumptionism that one finds either in writers of the *Monthly Review* style or in the writings of O'Connor.[13]

Besides, there are profound problems with its logic. Suppose that the underconsumptionists are right in their analysis of claims that monopoly pricing really does make a difference. In practice there are (of course!) a whole set of countervailing forces. Rising population, technological advance, and new foreign markets can all make investment more attractive (Baran and Sweezy, 1966:89 ff.). Government can intervene to buttress demand (Baran and Sweezy, 1966:109–110). The surplus can be mopped up with wasteful expenditures (on, for example, advertising) and militarism, imperialism, and wars (Baran and Sweezy, 1966:178 ff.). As in the case of the falling rate of profit we have a "tendency" here that can be scarcely said to "tend."

Now, it may well be that, in contradiction to the neoclassicists, there is no obvious mechanism tending to generate an equilibrium of prices, employment, and investment in this system. Wars may not come along at the right time; foreign markets may disappear; the government may bungle its demand management efforts and in looking for ways to "waste" the embarrassing surplus they are accumulating, the imagination of capitalists may fail them. Consequently, since nothing guarantees an equilibrium level of investment, the real world may, most of the time, involve both underinvestment and underconsumption. But this argument tends, as Wright acknowledges (1979:147), to collapse into a rather straightforward Keynesian or post-Keynesian view of the world that stresses "the subjective anticipations of profit on the part of capitalists as the key determinant of the rate of accumulation".

Furthermore, need a pattern of oligopolistic pricing in one sector of the economy and competitive pricing in another lead to a shift of income from workers to capitalists? Not necessarily. For the purchasers of the products of industries with concentrated market structures are very often other capitalists who function in fairly competitive markets (e.g., construction, machine tools—see Averitt 1968). In some industries (such as trucking) capitalists in an exceedingly competitive industry buy from producers in one or more concentrated industries (truck assembly and oil in the case of truckers) and negotiate with a labor force organized into a single union—where one would expect monopoly pricing on the part of labor. All this leads one to argue that the net result of market concentration may (in some countries, for some times) be less the shifting of income from workers to capitalists than the shifting of income from capitalists (in competitive markets) to other capitalists (in concentrated markets). This is a criticism of underconsumptionist arguments that has in fact been made (Wright, 1979:145).

What about the competitive version of this argument? Might one reasonably expect capitalists to cause a crisis by undercutting their own market through an aggressive approach to labor costs while at the same time continuing to invest in plant and equipment to eliminate intractable labor, preserve the growth that will maintain the loyalty of white-collar workers, and avoid losing market share?

There is an obvious difficulty in attempting to apply this to the postwar period. The analysis assumes that capitalists are confronting a weakened labor force. But during the period when rates of inflation in rich, capitalist countries were accelerating, rates of unemployment were generally low, union membership (outside of the United States) had been growing (Bain and Price, 1980), and the more common concern of political leaders was wage costs that were seen to be getting out of line— as reflected at the time by quite widespread experiments with incomes policy (Ulman and Flanagan, 1971). Certainly, to use this line of analysis to explain the postwar inflation one would have to start out dismissing out of hand the pretensions of the class conflict theorists. But that seems unreasonable because their assumptions about labor market and political conditions seem altogether more plausible.

Neither are the conditions identified by Devine (1983) requiring excessive investment particularly plausible. First, the importance of the intractability of labor is a bit overdone. Even in Britain, not known for its tractable labor force, it is possible to find evidence of quite large enterprises successfully using authoritarian techniques to direct their workers (e.g., Edwards and Scullion, 1982). Besides, a recession of the sort that underconsumption ought to produce does wonders to increase the tractability of labor, as the results of time series analyses of the relationship between unemployment and strikes tend to show (e.g., Paldam and Pedersen, 1984). Second, there is no evidence that I know of (or that Devine cites) that declining white-collar loyalty poses sufficient problems for managers of organizations that are not expanding to induce them to invest in production capacity for which they have no market. Third, although it is true that capitalists have to take into account the long-run implications for their market share of a decision to invest or not invest, they also have to take into account the implications of borrowing money for their future rate of profit. The one thing with respect to which the monopoly capital underconsumption writers are clearly correct is the degree to which, in North America at least, managerial careers are tied to profit performance. The competitive version of underconsumption theory is not terribly persuasive either.

Finally there is the class conflict theory of crises, and its application to the postwar inflation. It serves to explain the postwar inflation in two ways: as a result of wage-push, and as a source of pressures that require deficit financed expenses on "legitimation" to avoid a serious threat to the stability and continuity of capitalist societies. The underlying crisis-generating mechanism is quite straightforward. It is the assertion that social classes play a central role in social change and that the direction of historical change in capitalist societies has tended to strengthen the relative power of the working class.

Now, it should be clear that many of the specifics of this account of the postwar inflation are indistinguishable from those of the non Marxist wage-push theories described in Chapter 5. These latter also write about the effects of sustained full employment and the exhaustion of labor reserves. Perhaps more surprisingly, a number of the elements of the accounts of Marxist class conflict theorists are indistinguishable from those of many generally rather conservative neoclassical economists. Consider, in particular, Gough's account. As we saw above, he attributes some of the postwar economic difficulties in capitalist nations to the effect on work incentives of the development of the welfare state social safety net and of sustained full employment, compounded by the militancy of public sector unions and the fiscal difficulties caused by the need to develop an ever more elaborate welfare state to both maintain social peace and to deal with the increasing needs created as capitalism, with all its irrationalities, evolves. These, of course, are all staples of conservative accounts of postwar economic difficulties too.[14] What, then, makes Gough's account Marxist rather than conservative?

Obviously the moral judgments that are attached to each account and the rhetoric in terms of which the account is rendered are one element. But, more fundamentally, there are two assumptions that distinguish Gough's Marxist account from the accounts of conservative economists. The economists assume that these sources of economic difficulties originate in policy errors; that it has been harder to manage capitalist economies since World War II than it should have been because unemployment insurance benefits (among other welfare provisions)[15] were too high; because (as we saw) Keynesian economists incorrectly believed that there was a long-run, significantly nonvertical, Phillips curve and that, as a result, they contributed to the creation of overfull employment; that governments did not take a sufficiently strong line with public sector unions; and that governments gave away more in welfare benefits than the economy could support, and inefficiently administered the provision of those benefits, to boot. Gough assumes that governments had no alternative but to provide relatively generous unemployment insurance, maintain full employment, concede to public sector unions, and create a welfare state because they were forced to do so by an ever more powerful working class.

Which assumptions are more plausible? At the end of the 1970s a number of extremely conservative leaders were elected to office in western capitalist societies, in particular, Margaret Thatcher, Ronald Reagan, and Helmut Kohl. Each presided over a substantial increase in her or his nation's unemployment rate. Each has weakened the welfare system over which she or he presided. Yet none of them has been seriously troubled by threats to social peace and each of them has been reelected; in the case of Margaret Thatcher, twice. We have had about as direct a test of Gough's (and, to a greater or lesser extent, the other class conflict writers) assumptions as one could imagine: and they do not come out of the test in very good shape. The conservative economists come out of the test looking rather better, in the following very specific sense: the absence of disorder accompanying the substantial modifications to the institutions that were produced by the "postwar consensus" suggests that their architects had considerably more choice over whether or not to construct them in the way they did and to the degree they did (see also Zimmerman, 1984:322). Whether or not the conservative economists are right in their judgments about the wisdom (or, rather, lack of wisdom) of those architects is another matter altogether. But comments like that, of course, spring from a reformist mentality wholly alien to the sterner historical logic of Marxists.

Conclusion

If we set aside the quite savage disagreements between the various Marxist sects, a common element in analyses of the postwar inflation within this genre remains: each asserts a crisis-causing mechanism and explains the inflation *principally* as a product of the efforts of government to respond to that crisis. For falling-rate-of-profit and underconsumption theorists inflation was caused by desperate government attempts to offset the inherent tendencies within capitalism toward either periodic or secular stagnation. For class conflict theorists it was, as well as being in part a result of straightforward wage-push, a product of deficit financed government expenditures to shore up the increasingly rickety popular foundations of the capitalist economy.

Now, there is no question but that the period starting in the early
1970s was one of genuine crisis for a number of capitalist economies and
of some difficulties for all of them.[16] There is some evidence of falling
rates of profit in some countries for some periods (Bruno and Sachs,
1985:10, 54, 55). Unemployment rose throughout the capitalist world
and did so to very high levels in some countries. The rate of increase in
productivity and the rate of economic growth fell substantially. And, of
course, the rate of inflation rose. Is all of this not evidence that a Marxist
theory of some sort—that is, a theory at the center of which is the
inherent tendencies of capitalism towards crisis—is probably correct? It
should be clear that the answer to this is a resounding no.

For the observed difficulties of the capitalist economy can be just as
well explained by *almost* any one of the several alternative non-Marxist
theories that have been reviewed in previous chapters.[17] Indeed, those
theories—whether Keynesian, or mark I monetarist, or public choice, or
wage-push—include exactly the same kinds of factors that are incorporated *in the specific applications* of Marxist theory to the postwar period.
The export of inflation from the United States during the Vietnam war,
the breakdown of Bretton Woods that it produced, the rise in government expenditures on welfare, the growth of public sector unions, and
the sustained full employment of the early postwar period appear in
each kind of theory and can be subsumed within each. The plausibility
of each Marxist theory stands or falls on the distinctive crisis-generating
mechanism it postulates.

But there are fairly compelling grounds for rejecting each of them.
There are no good theoretic grounds for asserting that the rate of profit
has to fall; indeed, that is largely conceded in the relevant Marxist discussions of "countertendencies." There are rather better grounds for arguing that capitalist economies have a tendency to settle at lower than
desirable levels of economic activity, not least because there are some
quite persuasive arguments to that effect within the corpus of Keynesian
writing. But the evidence tends to suggest that that is not on account of
the monopoly pricing that is at the core of the monopoly capital version
of the underconsumptionist account. Besides, as we saw earlier, underconsumptionist arguments of any kind strain credulity where the relative bargaining power of workers is high (as compared, say, to the
1930s), as it clearly was during most of the postwar period.

Finally, as we saw in the last chapter, although there is some evidence
of an inflation-generating wage-push for some countries for some periods it is fairly clear that wage-push was only one factor among several
producing the postwar record of inflation and that, in addition, where it
occurred it was largely a response to wage compressions of the
mid-1960s—a fact that does not fit terribly well with the presumptions of

the class conflict account. There is absolutely no evidence, however, that the construction of the welfare state was a result of a threat of disorder. In applications of the "legitimation" component of this theory to the United States, for example, much is made of the "great society" programs under Lyndon Johnson; it is argued that they were a *response* to ghetto disorders (Piven and Cloward, 1971; O'Connor, 1973:167; Castells, 1980:154). But this is factually wrong. Harrington (1976:304) has pointed out that the bulk of the great society reforms were passed *before* the riots broke out. And there is certainly no evidence that the retreat from full employment in Britain, the United States, West Germany, and a number of other capitalist countries has produced any sort of threat to the continuity of capitalism. Quite the contrary, in fact.[18]

It may be true that, as Schott (1984a:77 ff.) has argued, recent Marxist *political* writings (e.g., those collected in Holloway and Picciotto, 1978) have the distinctive virtue of at least paying some attention to the distribution of power as an explanatory factor, in a way that orthodox economic theories (and, as we saw, in particular Keynesian ones) do not. But that has not helped Marxists to produce convincing accounts of the postwar stagnation. Those accounts depend on a set of entirely empirically and theoretically dubious crisis-generating mechanisms. Writing (sympathetically) of the underconsumptionist account Franklin (1977:168) observed that "the tendency toward stagnation is not always apparent" and that "Discovering the evidence of this process thus requires historical imagination." On the whole, I believe that Marxist theories of crisis *in general* require altogether too much "historical imagination." The available alternative accounts of what has happened in capitalist economies since the war require less heroic leaps of faith. Marxist theories have nothing useful to add to them.

Notes

1. Although, of course, part of the Marxist reaction to the economic success in the earlier period had been to produce theories either conceding the growth potential of capitalism but denouncing moral impoverishment that accompanied it (e.g., Marcuse, 1964) or, alternatively, explaining how the "state" had developed to diffuse the effects of capitalism's inevitable contradictions (e.g., Poulantzas, 1973).

2. This is even true of the falling rate of profit theory and the monopoly capital version of underconsumption theory that I outline below and that are flatly contradictory. Wright (1978:163–180), for example, has argued that both theories are correct, but apply to different periods of time.

3. But, like pretty much all social and economic theory, it has very venerable antecedents. Bleaney (1976) provides the best review of the theoretical tradition.

In his history of underconsumption theory he radically distinguishes *underconsumption* from *overinvestment* theory, with Baran and Sweezy an example of the former and Steindl an example of the latter (p. 11). The distinction rests in the fact that underconsumptionists argue that secular tendencies to stagnation within capitalism originate in deficient consumption, whereas writers in the second tradition locate the tendency toward stagnation within investment behavior. For present purposes I do not regard this radical distinction as terribly useful, particularly since Bleaney himself writes of the bulk of underconsumption theories as follows: "The difficulty . . . is that all underconsumption theories . . . consistently underestimate the role of investment expenditure, and although this is what lends them their specifically underconsumption quality, it is also a fundamental mistake" (p. 209).

4. Like most analyses of crisis the details of O'Connor's analysis are specific to a single country—in this case the United States. But he does claim a certain generality for his argument (1973:6).

5. Note, however, that in his later work O'Connor argues that a monopolistic market structure tends to reduce the rate of innovation by slowing down the diffusion of new technology (1984:80).

6. See also O'Connor (1984:59) for an interpretation of the great depression along these lines.

7. The editors of the *Monthly Review* started their October 1974 edition by noting the prescience of Paul Baran's analysis of the conditions leading to inflation. This is a striking example of either self-deception or hypocrisy. The relevant discussion of the conditions that might lead to inflation by Baran (1957:124–125) is, in actual fact, presented as an extraordinarily improbable outcome since inflation of any magnitude so contradicts the interests of capitalists. In the major book by Baran and Sweezy together (1966), inflation is not even considered as a possibility!

8. It is not made clear precisely what form this rebellion would take—whether in the streets or through the ballot box.

9. Hunt (1982, 1983) has attempted to rebut both van Parijs and Steedman. In my view his defense of the notion that a rising organic composition of capital must produce a falling rate of profit is largely tautological; that is, if you define the rising organic composition of capital in such a way that a rising rate of exploitation is excluded, you must end up with a falling rate of profit. This seems to me to not be terribly helpful.

10. It is worth noting in passing that this stress on the tendency of innovation to constantly undercut the rate of return on investment is a central element in Veblen's theory of business crises (Veblen, 1904:110–111).

11. Neither is what Castells describes consistent with the findings of a particularly interesting micro study of the decision to innovate. See Lewis (1988).

12. Semmler also discusses studies of the affects on profits of collusive behavior, capital output ratios, and unit wage costs, and of the association between firm size and variability of profit and growth rates. These seem to me less central to his argument than the studies and findings I discuss in the text.

13. There is further discussion of the evidence in Sherman (1983) and Semmler (1983).

14. For examples of conservative treatments of these issues see Grubel and Walker (1978) on the effects of unemployment insurance; Cagan (1979:206–216) on the notion that, if price stability was an objective, the postwar period has

been one of overfull employment; and Christensen (1980) on the disruptive effects of public sector unions.

15.   In the British case, a much cited source of labor cost increasing inhibitions on the mobility of labor is the widespread provision of public housing, access to which requires "queuing" within a particular local housing authority and which, as a result, provides a strong disincentive to move. For a review of the evidence on this see Green (1984:36–39).

16.   It has also, of course, been a period of even more severe economic crisis for most of the rest of the world and, in particular, for the noncapitalist part of it. In my view the relatively even less impressive performance of socialist countries on a wide range of indicators poses a serious problem for Marxist theory, one which is not dealt with by designating all of the countries in question as something other than socialist ("state capitalist," for example). But that raises a whole set of other issues for which there is not space here. For a relevant discussion see van den Berg and Smith (1981) or, better still, van den Berg (1988).

17.   The one exception, it seems to me, is the "rational expectations" approach of monetarism mark II, for which any economic difficulties that are not pretty much epiphenomenal are hard to explain.

18.   There *were* riots in inner cities in Britain between 1979 and 1985. These certainly originated, in part, in genuine deprivation. But tensions between the largely nonwhite rioters and police played a major role in precipitating the riots. And, besides, they certainly did not invoke much support among the bulk of the population outside the riot areas. On the riots see Jacobs (1986).

9

CONCLUSION

In the social sciences, judging the relative adequacy of theories is never an easy business. Without controlled experiments we have to make tentative decisions about relative plausibility on the cumulative basis of bits and pieces of, typically, rather unsatisfactory evidence. Still, the material examined in this book suggests quite strongly that the account of the postwar inflation most usually favored by sociologists and political scientists is generally incorrect and adds little to what we already know from orthodox economic accounts. In the first half of this chapter I review the evidence from the previous chapters that leads to this conclusion. In the second half I discuss some of the implications of this conclusion for attempts to construct an "economic sociology."

What *Did* Cause the Postwar Inflation?

The core of the sociological account is the claim that the postwar inflation was produced by distributional conflict, particularly class-based distributional conflict, and that variations across nations reflect differences in the extent to which institutions that can regulate class conflict are present. The argument assumes that inflation was caused by larger demands from workers and an increase in their power so that they were better able to translate those demands into a wage-push inflation and to narrow the range of political options available to governments, ruling out aggressively deflationary policies—in the long run, at least (see Goldthrope, 1987a:376–382).

Now, I do not doubt that organized labor has created some problems for macroeconomic policy, in some years, in some countries. In Britain, for example, I would think it fairly clear that trade unions sought, and sometimes succeeded, in opposing changes in work arrangements likely to increase productivity, and that the struggles over wage relativities in some industries produced patterns of industrial disputes that seriously disrupted production and reduced competitiveness. In Italy, the trade

241

union movement put together a sufficiently intimidating display of discontent in the "hot autumn" of 1969 to induce the government to introduce a set of laws that made labor even more difficult to control. In
Germany, wage growth burst out of the normal pattern in 1969 and 1970
in response to the attempt to contain it under "concerted action"
(Schultze, 1987:272). In Sweden, the context of macroeconomic policy is
changing, and it is likely that macroeconomic policy will change too,
because the wage leadership of the exposed sector that has been at the
heart of the normal operation of the "Scandinavian model" is threatened
by the growing power of public sector unions. In both Europe and
North America, deflation produces some unemployment because nominal wages are rigid.[1] So the capacity of organized labor to gum up the
macroeconomic works, so to speak, is not at issue here.

What is at issue is the extent to which this capacity can be used to
explain the postwar inflation. In this book I have tried to show that this
is rather unlikely. As we saw in Chapter 4, with the exception of Scandinavia, it is very hard to find much evidence that the postwar inflation
has had, to any great extent, a wage-push character. The time series
evidence on militancy, wages, and prices is anything but robust. Where
it occurred, the widely remarked surge in wages at the beginning of the
1970s seems to have been produced by some success in squeezing wages
in the mid-1960s (there was no such surge in Austria, where wages had
not been squeezed in the 1960s)—which makes it an odd indication of
rising worker power. Productivity growth seems to have turned down
in some countries before the 1973 oil shock but disproportionately did so
in countries with low rates of industrial conflict (usually taken to be an
indicator of low worker militancy), suggesting that the source of the
turn-down was factors other than worker militancy (e.g., excessively
high rates of capacity utilization at the end of the 1960s).

In any case, the claims about a decline in normative restraint and
increases in worker power are in some instances poorly documented
and in others overstated. There is simply no serious evidence on normative changes from the pre- to the postwar period. Although there *is*
evidence of increasing worker power it has involved, I would argue, a
much less ineluctable process than has been assumed in recent writing.
The first and most important source of increased worker power in the
early postwar period was the sustained full employment through to the
early 1970s, and the fact that minimizing unemployment was a central
policy concern of all (even Canadian and U.S.) governments through
part of that period. Second, with the exception of the United States, the
percentage of the labor force unionized has been generally higher since
the second world war than it was before it. Third, again with the excep-

tion of the United States, the legal basis for union action was stronger after the second world war than it was before it.

What is important to note here is that in a number of countries there has been a retreat from the situation in the early 1970s, with most governments willing to allow unemployment to rise, a number willing to allow or encourage union membership to fall, and several narrowing the legislative privileges of the union movement. This suggests that much of whatever rise in working class power occurred had a quite fragile character and that, insofar as it fed into higher inflation rates (in some way that is not contradicted by the weakness of the evidence for a direct wage-push), it depended on the tolerance of elected governments.

In Chapter 7 I reviewed a third kind of evidence tending to contradict the standard sociological account. If, as the sociological account assumes, rising power in the context of normative collapse worsens economic performance and increases inflation, then the inflation might be offset by centralized bargaining institutions that reintegrate trade unions into the collaborative pursuit of stable growth. This is the claim that the presence of neocorporatist institutions produces a general improvement in macroeconomic performance, including relative price stability.

There has been a substantial number of tests of this claim, but their methodological quality varies from the dubious to the downright appalling. There is a significant degree of dissensus on which countries should be considered neocorporatist and, in several instances, a dogged determination to push countries that clearly do not have centralized bargaining into the neocorporatist category, if they have an economic performance that is in any way impressive. This has particularly been the case for Japan, Switzerland, and, I would argue, Germany.[2] The data in these studies are aggregated into time periods that include widely varying economic and political situations. In analyses of economic growth, there is usually no adjustment for differences in the initial productivity level. And factors that might be important (e.g., central bank independence, trade dependence) are not controlled. Even countries that clearly *are* neocorporatist, such as Austria and Sweden, seem not to work the way the neocorporatist model (outlined in Chapter 6) says they should. In particular, in both cases wage growth seems to have been no better connected to productivity growth than anywhere else. Indeed, when Germany briefly (and, it is true, half-heartedly) experimented with corporatism during the "concerted action" period, wage growth and productivity were at their most disconnected.

None of this is to deny the importance of distributional conflict that has been, I take it, omnipresent in capitalist societies since the second world war. Nor is it to deny that the distributional implications of macroeconomic decisions greatly complicate government policy making. The point is, rather, that as far as I can tell, distributional conflict is present in pretty much all societies all of the time and, therefore, does not provide much of an explanation for the shift from the deflationary 1930s to the persistently inflationary postwar period. It may be true, as Horsman (1988:266–267) argues, that shocks, such as a rise in commodity prices or an unusual degree of governmental irresponsibility, can precipitate inflation and a distributional struggle that precipitates still more inflation. Something like this seems to have gone on in the 1970s in some of the countries of interest in this study. But all of the same countries were able to bring their inflations down below the peaks of the 1970s and none slipped into hyperinflation. These outcomes are consistent, I would suggest, with a view of distributional conflict as complicating factor in the process of controlling inflation rather than as ineluctable force based in a secular process of intensification of the class struggle.

But if it is not the normative estrangement and rising power of the working class, what does explain the postwar inflation, and variations across countries in its incidence? Remember that the critical elements of the orthodox economic account are "ignorance and error" and electoral opportunism that can often be characterized as political irresponsibility. What evidence do we have that bears on these interpretations?

With respect to ignorance and error the general issue is whether or not stabilization policies produced significantly more inflation than was intended, or produced about the intended additional inflation but without improved growth or employment performance. There are a number of bits and pieces of evidence that are relevant here, some discussed earlier and some not.

First, it is worth repeating that a useful stabilization policy (certainly, one that goes beyond "automatic stabilizers") requires some capacity to forecast how the economy would perform with or without some set of policies. But such forecasts seem not to be very accurate, particularly when economic conditions are changing in ways that might warrant intervention (e.g., after the oil shock). This provides a generalized context of ignorance. It follows from this that when governments have tried to stabilize, much of the time they are likely to have erred.[3] Second, across Keynesian (Blinder, 1979) and monetarist commentators (Cagan, 1979), there is some consensus that macroeconomic policy in the 1970s in the United States tended to make things worse rather than better, including periods when it exacerbated inflationary tendencies. Third, it is quite clear that British policy-makers during the 1960s were led to believe, probably incorrectly, that they could exploit a long-run, negatively sloped, Phillips curve and this led them to adopt aggressive, demand increasing, policies (Smith, 1982:310–313). Fourth, a similar view was cultivated in the United States in the 1960s by the Council of Economic Advisors and provided a backdrop for the deficit financing of the Vietnam war and Great Society programs, with the implications that that had for worldwide inflation (Tobin, 1974:34–39). Fifth, when the French socialist government of François Mitterand took office in 1981 it assumed that it could spend its way out of the worldwide recession, but quickly changed its mind in the face of rising inflation and a depreciating franc, and retrenched (e.g., Duhamel, 1984:1). Alesina's data (1989) suggest that this is a recurrent pattern for left wing governments, who come into office believing that they have macroeconomic policy options that turn out not to exist.[4] Sixth, it has been frequently assumed by policy-makers that demand could be maintained at a higher level if there were some statutory mechanism for regulating incomes and, sometimes, prices. It *is* possible to find some examples of *very* modest success of such policies (e.g., McCallum, 1986). But, by and large, beneficial effects appear to have been temporary; and, there is evidence that they have sometimes made things worse in the long run—the best example of which is the explosion of militancy at the end of the 1960s in response to (usually) government-initiated wage compression in the mid-1960s (Soskice, 1978). Seventh, Helliwell (1990:129–134) examined the relationship between indicators of demand-increasing stabilization policy and economic performance. For the same 18 countries appearing in Figure 7.3, he finds the following: there is a negative relationship between inflation and productivity growth, between inflation and real GNP growth, and, more weakly, between government spending on the one hand, and growth in productivity and real GNP on the other.[5] In other words, contrary to what one would expect if stabilization policy had worked, countries with an accumulation of the sort of outcomes likely to be produced by stabilization policy—higher rates of inflation and rising government expenditure, have relatively poorer performance.

I think the evidence for the role of ignorance and error in the generation of the postwar inflation is substantial. There is a certain irony here. For in order to set aside ignorance and error as an account, as Goldthorpe has done explicitly (1978:188–190) and most other sociologists and political scientists have done by simply ignoring them, it is necessary to give a great deal more credit to economics than it really deserves! This is not to dispute the capacity of economics to create more or less plausible interpretations of phenomena (as well as some wildly implausible ones!); it is, rather, to emphasize the incapacity of economics to go beyond explanation to the provision of the sort of policy advice that would allow a stabilization policy that did more good than harm, in most circumstances. (To claim that successful stabilization policies are impossible would be to go too far.) There is, as we saw in Chapter 2, a body of economists who claim that stabilization policy is both necessary and feasible. And since high unemployment and low economic growth are usually (and usually properly) thought of as problems, it follows that failed stabilization policy will tend to cluster on the stimulative side.

So ignorance and error plays some role in the *generality* of the postwar inflation. In an interdependent world during periods when exchange rates are more or less fixed, inflationary stimulus in one country is spread to other countries. In particular, if Tobin is correct, the inflationary finance of the Vietnam war and the Great Society program in the United States was facilitated because it was legitimated by Keynesian economic advisors. And that inflation, of course, spread to the rest of the capitalist world. Ignorance and error also explain some *intercountry variation*. For example, into the 1970s, the conviction that stimulative economic policies were necessary and desirable was distinctively well rooted in the United Kingdom and the result was an appalling record of inflation. Moreover, given its dependence on the British economy, this would also partially account for Ireland's poor inflation record.

Now consider "political irresponsibility" as an explanation. In this respect, note first that inflation was markedly higher after the collapse of the Bretton Woods agreement than it was before it. Fixed exchange rates imposed an external discipline on countries that prevented most from pursuing distinctly inflationary policies for any length of time. In this period, inflationary episodes took the form of short divergencies from the average for capitalist industrial countries followed by a prompt return to average, or below average rates of increase.[6] It is true, of course, that the growing inflation of the late 1960s was one of the reasons that Bretton Woods collapsed; but that does not change the fact that, during the period the treaty was in effect, countries with rates of inflation that diverged from the average returned to it reasonably promptly, and that this was even true for subsequently high inflation countries such as Italy and the United Kingdom. It is clear that the removal of the external discipline provided by Bretton Woods widened the policy options available to governments. But it did so to a much lesser extent for those small countries dependent on trade with a larger partner (Austria, the Netherlands, Ireland, Canada) and the inflation rates of those countries was largely dictated by the inflation rate of their trading partners. It is also clear that the development of the European Monetary System is an attempt to narrow policy options for a wider range of countries, including larger ones such as Italy, France, and the United Kingdom.

Second, the Bretton Woods system broke down because United States governments exploited the reserve currency status of the dollar to finance the Vietnam war and the Great Society program. This increased inflation throughout the world and constitutes, one can reasonably argue, political irresponsibility writ large. Here was a case where U.S. governments could spend without weakening their political base by dispersing the cost to people in other countries who could not vote in U.S. elections.

Third, Germany has exemplary price stability. It also has an independent central bank that we know to have repulsed inflationary policies that originated with a social democrat-led coalition government in the 1970s. Alesina (1989) claims that Japan had an independent central bank and, after the 1973 shock, it inaugurated and has since maintained a policy of monetary austerity so that, in the 1980s, Japan had the lowest average rate of inflation among the countries for which I present data. The Federal Reserve in the United States seems to have substantial (but certainly not complete) autonomy and, except for the Vietnam war years, the United States has been a relatively low inflation country. One would not, I take it, regard the Vietnam war inflation as contradicting the general claim that the Federal Reserve is to some extent a bulwark against inflation; it is widely accepted that principles of government finance are different in war time than during peace time. The country with the lowest average inflation rate from 1954 to 1972 was Canada. This was, in part, because of a very low rate of inflation up to 1961. Note that during this time the Bank of Canada was acting in a sufficiently independent way to induce the Diefenbaker government to force out its governor and modify the relevant legislation.[7] Since, Canada has usually maintained a higher rate of inflation than the United States, except during years when United States prices were growing at an unusually high rate (Smith, 1987:381–384).

Here, then, are cases where low rates of inflation can be explained by central bank independence. Moreover, the price stability produced by the central banks of Germany and the United States spreads to neighboring countries. For good economic *and* electoral reasons, Canadian governments do not usually allow the value of the Canadian dollar to vary greatly with respect to the U.S. dollar. A widely fluctuating exchange rate would disrupt trade and a depreciating dollar, in particular, would upset the electorate, a fact of which politicians are well aware (e.g., Stursberg, 1975:251–264). The consequence of all this is that the (usually relatively low, even post-Coyne) Canadian rate of inflation is substantially explained by the American rate. Similarly, German central bank autonomy produces low inflation in Austria (especially) and in the Netherlands and Belgium, to some extent.[8] I submit that, combined, this is strong evidence that international variations in the rate of inflation can *to a substantial extent* be explained by central bank autonomy, particularly after taking into account the effects of trade dependence on the policy options available to small countries.

There is also the case of Switzerland. Switzerland has exemplary price stability and an independent central bank. It also depends heavily on trade with Germany. If the argument above is correct, these factors on their own would account for the low rate of inflation in Switzerland. However, in the Swiss case, the constitutional limits on spending are sufficiently stringent that it is hard to imagine a government ever trying to spend its way out of a recession (see Aubert, 1979). This brings us to the fourth piece of evidence bearing on political irresponsibility.

Alesina (1989) has presented data tending to show that political instability is associated with poorer macroeconomic performance, including higher inflation. Most countries do not have autonomous central banks so, if there is to be a bulwark against political demands that exceed the capacity of the economy to deliver, it has to be found within governments themselves. But governments the legitimacy of which is in question, or that involve fragile coalitions, are likely to be more disposed to curry favor for short-run political advantage than to act as a bulwark against anything. Italy is the paradigmatic case here. Since 1973 it has been at or near the top of the inflation league table of rich capitalist countries. It has a history of rather short-lived minority governments and relatively vigorous parties of the extreme right and left doing their best to challenge government legitimacy (see also Salvati, 1985:554–555).[9] Also bear in mind that the high average rate of inflation in France prior to the oil shock was entirely produced during the period of constitutional instability of the 1950s and early 1960s.

Fifth, as discussed in Chapter 4, we know that parties have often competed in elections by promising to deliver more services or, sometimes, to cut taxes. This does not produce a predictable political business cycle. But it has produced a secular increase in government transfers— social security, unemployment insurance, education subsidies—because the costs of the programs promised, once installed, tend to grow with the eligible population *and* because as the programs mature, eligibility tends to be extended. Now, whether or not these programs address real and pressing needs is not at issue here. What is relevant is that these are programs that can be introduced or extended at an election but for which the burden of financing accrues to subsequent governments, often many years later. I am inclined to think that the balance of temptations here is obvious. Note further that, once it is introduced, it is very hard to eliminate a program or significantly restrict access to it.

We have already seen that the result of government weakness in Italy has been the accumulation of a range of social programs that have created a very serious, and inflationary, debt problem. In Canada, too, there has been an accumulation of costly transfer programs and a substantial government deficit. It has proven very difficult to cut back benefits or access to the programs (e.g., Myles, 1988:78–79). The result has been consistently higher rates of inflation than the United States and, to contain the inflation, an unusually high interest rate differential.[10] Consecutive weak Irish governments with, at best, marginal majorities, multiplied and expanded transfer programs and in doing so created an even higher ratio of debt to GDP than Italy (rising from 0.648 in 1971 to 1.413 in 1988) *and* very high taxes (see Dornbusch, 1989) *and*, not surprisingly, a rate of inflation that after closely tracking the U.K. rate for most of the postwar period was persistently and substantially higher from 1980 to 1985.

I would argue that any reasonably plausible explanation of the postwar inflation—in broad outline and in detailed country performance—will include substantial components of ignorance and error (produced by ever so fallible economic advice) and government irresponsibility—which means the tendency of politicians in government, *some of the time and under some circumstances*, to worry about next year's election and to let someone else worry about the next decade or so. Note that, in explaining the postwar inflation, such processes in large countries have been spread to their smaller trading partners.

In this account of the postwar inflation, a fundamental part is played by popular preferences within democratic political systems. People rarely turn down goods when they appear to be free; they are likely to vote for parties that promise goods disproportionately paid for by someone else—either the population at large or people who are richer than them. Furthermore, there is considerable evidence that after the second world war, and against the appalling background of the 1930s, there was a widespread popular preference for lower unemployment. Goldthorpe (1987a:366) includes this popular preference within what he has called "the Keynesian compromise." But for Goldthorpe, "the Keynesian compromise" is an expression of working class power.

This, I think, is where he goes wrong. In a paper some years ago I reviewed the survey data on concerns with unemployment, by class, in Britain (Smith, 1982:306–307). The data show that there was cross-class concern to minimize unemployment. In 1972 only 20% of the population thought that unemployment could be "justified" and, in Alt's (1979:191) data, even when respondents were *forced* to regard increasing unemployment as an alternative to putting up with high inflation, more than half of *all* income groups opted for reduced unemployment rather than reduced inflation. Nor was there any clear relationship between attitude to inflation and income.[11] The point is that, up to the early 1970s, hardly anyone found significant rates of unemployment appealing (one doubts that even the 20% who thought that it could be "justified" were enthused by it!).

Quite apart from the fact that it is just possible that *even* parts of the bourgeoisie have hearts, there is also the fact that, even if blue-collar workers are most negatively affected, *almost* everyone—white-collar workers, high-income groups, entrepreneurs—do worse during a recession.[12] I have seen no evidence suggesting that Britain is exceptional in this respect. So, where unrestrained in their policy choices by the glowering presence of an independent central bank or trade dependence on a low inflation country, governments of either right or left would have been likely to err on the side of demand stimulation because to do so would be politically popular across classes. This helps to explain an inflationary bias in the capitalist world up to the early 1970s. Then, however, things changed. When inflation accelerated after the oil shock it shifted (as we saw in Chapter 3) from minor irritant to major concern within the electorate. Governments, which still had to get reelected, shifted their priorities accordingly or, if they failed to do so, they lost office to parties that did make inflation a more central concern. The rise and fall of inflation in the postwar period, then, to some extent rest on the changing preferences of the electorate.

I cannot claim, of course, that this is an exhaustive account of the postwar inflation. But I can claim that there is much more evidence for the ignorance and error/political irresponsibility argument than there is for the class conflict alternative favored by most sociologists interested in the subject.

Did Secular Processes Produce the Postwar Inflation?

The possibilities of Marxist theory will no doubt continue to exercise some attraction for sociologists and political scientists, many of whom have, after all, invested a good part of a career as exegetes of, or apologists for, Marxism. But, as we saw in Chapter 8, even if there were any reason to have confidence in the (contradictory) crisis-producing mechanisms Marxists emphasize, the secular tendency of capitalism toward crisis proves on only moderately close inspection to be largely contingent, once a very large number of "countertendencies" is taken into account. Beyond the (contradictory) crisis-producing mechanisms the only difference between Marxist accounts and one or another orthodox economic account is their rhetoric. We can set them aside.

I argued in Chapter 4 that, although more original, there are serious problems with Hirsch's (1976) analysis of moral decay and with the hegemonic decline interpretation of Gilpin (1981, 1987). Although these analyses have been picked up and integrated into sociological accounts of the postwar inflation there are a number of problems with the details of each argument and neither explains what governments have to gain by dealing with the long-run problems of moral decay or hegemonic decline with the inevitably short-run benefits of an inflationary policy.[13] It is, in fact, hard to see how they could help us to explain the postwar inflation *unless* supplemented with some sort of public choice theory that accounted for the tendency of politicians to stress shorter over longer run consequences.

The other theory of secular decline that I considered was Olson's (1982) analysis of "institutional sclerosis," which has been less favorably treated in sociological writings on macroeconomic outcomes. Should it have been? As we saw in Chapter 4, in terms of the postwar inflation Olson makes two central assertions: first, that distributional coalitions reduce economic growth, even (but to a lesser extent) where coalitions are incorporated into "encompassing organizations"; second, countries with relatively low growth rates are likely to cast around for ways to improve them and, since institutional sclerosis not only obstructs price decreases but also slows the process of price increases, it makes possible (temporarily, and only once or twice) successful Keynesian demand stimulus.

I observed in Chapter 4 that there is at least *some* evidence tending to support the theory. In contrast, there is very little evidence in support of Hirsch's theory of moral decay or of the more general neocorporatist theory into which it has been incorporated.[14] Still, I am skeptical of quantitative research testing the theory of institutional sclerosis for the same sorts of reasons that I am skeptical of the quantitative research on neocorporatism. However, there is other evidence that, it seems to me, lends *some* credence to Olson's theory.

First, in recent sociological writings it is the role of "encompassing organizations" that is critical. Olson allows that, if interest groups become encompassing, they can no longer free ride; in their actions they are compelled to consider more general issues of economic growth. In this his analysis converges on a part of the neocorporatist theory discussed in Chapter 5. But, contrary to neocorporatist theory, Olson regards encompassing organizations as a second best solution because, he says, they *slow decision making*. What does the evidence show? Schwerin (1984) has assembled a body of data and claims that, all in all, there is no evidence that the group of countries that comes closest to having encompassing organizations, the Nordic democracies—Denmark, Finland, Norway, and Sweden, do any worse than any other countries on a variety of economic performance measures. However, his analysis stops in 1980 and his treatment of economic growth is superficial.[15] If we look at the labor productivity growth figures for the period 1960 to 1985 drawn from Helliwell, it turns out that all four Nordic democracies are underperformers—that is, they have lower rates of productivity growth than would be predicted from their 1960 level of labor productivity.[16] I take it this would be the sort of result one would expect where the crowded agendas of encompassing organizations delayed the process of reallocating labor from less to more productive jobs (see also Jonung, 1990).

Second, consider the case of the United Kingdom, a well-known poor performer for most of the postwar period. What were the distinctive characteristics of the organization of the U.K. economy (until the political change in 1979)? The mobility of labor was *considerably* restricted by a system of government-provided housing that rewarded queuing within a particular housing district and discouraged movement out of that district (Green, 1984). The allocation of capital was influenced by a fairly elaborate system of regional subsidies and some spectacular cases of subsidies or nationalizations to prevent unprofitable firms from going under. In a number of industries there were strong labor unions, particularly at the shop floor level and these greatly complicated the process of wage setting and of the renewal and efficient exploitation of capital equipment (Maitland, 1983). Financial institutions seem to have been particularly well organized and effective at protecting their interests and to have induced governments to pursue policies that kept interest rates and the exchange rate high and, in so doing, deterred manufacturing investment (Hall, 1990:130). From the National Economic Development Council system onward (Shonfield, 1965:151–155) there were repeated attempts to construct corporatist structures, culminating in the "social contract" of the Callaghan government in the 1970s, involving both centralized bargaining with labor and a set of laws strengthening the positions of organized labor and of workers (Clegg, 1979:312–313).[17]

Notwithstanding the free trade and immigration emphasized by De Vries (1983), this pattern is, I would have thought, the sort of thing that would be suggested by Olson's theory. Interest groups have sought and received protections that have imposed substantial inhibitions on the mobility of labor and capital and, in the case of financial institutions, policies that have deterred investment. In the context of these inhibitions and the widespread problems of labor relations on the shop floor both Labour and pre-1979 Conservative governments have sought to establish arrangements that would harness interest groups, but particularly organized labor, in the pursuit of shared goals. In the meantime, U.K. governments have confronted a chronic growth problem and, in the Keynesian climate provided by the British Treasury (Brittan, 1971; Keegan and Pennant-Rea, 1979), floundered into a series of inflationary policies that brought temporary but, across inflations, consecutively diminished, accelerations of growth.

If the Nordic democracies, then, are closest to having encompassing organizations, that has *not* secured them a record of superior growth in labor productivity. The United Kingdom clearly did develop a set of growth-reducing distributional coalitions within a Keynesian economic climate, and has a history of attempts to inflate into growth. This certainly does not mean that economic performance is some mechanical function of time since the last socially cataclysmic event (war, invasion, rebellion, etc.). The formation of distributional coalitions, after all, depends on laws and political arrangements that influence and regulate their organization and activity. This seems to be particularly relevant to labor unions. In generally high-performing Germany, the activities of labor unions are complicated by a relatively repressive body of labor law. In also high-performing Japan, the labor movement seems, for whatever reasons, to be chronically weak. And in the United States, which is also a high performer, when initial level of productivity or GNP is taken into account, the variability in federal labor law has made it possible for antiunion states to undercut the labor movement as a whole (Juris and Roomkin, 1980:198–199). But Olson's analysis assumes (and the British case suggests that he is correct in this) that workers are likely to seek to protect their interests in growth-damaging ways. So, where institutions and laws prevent them from doing so, irrespective of time since cataclysm, one would expect superior economic performance. And that is what one observes.

Power, Norms, and Economic Sociology

As a competing explanatory framework, economic sociology replaces the individual maximizing exchanges that underlie economic theory with norms and power. There is, I would have thought, overwhelming evidence of the importance of both norms and power in influencing economic outcomes. For example, people exploit the sense of obligation of their friends and relatives to find jobs (Granovetter, 1974), simplify commodity exchanges by principally confining them to coreligionists (Coleman, 1988), discriminate against racial minorities (Henry and Ginsberg, 1985), and, within multidivisional firms, managers manipulate information and exchanges to make the performance of their own divisions look better (Eccles and White, 1988). All this is evidence of the role of norms and power at the *micro* level. It is also evidence of processes that pose some problems for standard economics.[18]

Conclusion

There are other areas where the application of sociological theory to economic processes has been much less successful. For example, much sociological effort has been deployed to show that the distribution of earnings is influenced by the exercise of power by trade unions and professional associations, and by the extent to which concentrated market structures allow managers more discretion over the prices they set (e.g., Kalleberg, Wallace, and Althauser, 1981). But on close inspection it turns out that there is little or nothing to distinguish such analyses from those produced by economists: that restricting the supply of labor forces up its price and that governments can pay more to their employees because they can fund themselves from taxes can hardly be considered a sociological discovery (see Smith, 1990). The bulk of sociological interpretations of earnings is simply relabeled economics (see also the comments by Sørensen in Swedberg, 1990:311–312).

There is something similar to this in the material reviewed in this book. As we saw in Chapter 8, net of rhetoric and postulated "fundamental" crisis tendency, Marxist analyses of inflation have been little other than relabeled economics (of some sort). This, along with the sociological writing on earnings, illustrates one of the false directions likely to be taken by sociologists attempting to explain economic outcomes—the tendency to relabel commonplace economics, making liberal use of terms such as "power," "inequality," "class," and, sometimes, "exploitation."

The main current of sociological work on inflation reviewed in this book illustrates a second hazard—a tendency to greatly exaggerate the importance of social classes, both as bases for the politically relevant distribution of power and as sources of norms.

One of the principal theoretic legacies of social theory is a concern with social class. It is true that there has been a current of sociological theory, reaching its apogee in the work of Talcott Parsons, from which classes largely disappeared. Still, Parsons has very little influence on contemporary economic sociology, which is usually inspired by the concerns with inequality and its political effects found in the writings of Marx and Weber. For the sake of argument, ignore the conceptual confusion around precisely what "social class" means (and whether its operationalization has rendered it increasingly indistinguishable from the concept of "status group"). Let us simply proceed on the assumption that the existence of social classes implies a distributional struggle in which, in the final analysis, workers are on one side and capitalists on the other.

Now, when the performance of the Western economies turned down in the 1970s, inflation accelerated, and it looked as if there were some points to be scored off economics, most sociologists naturally chose a familiar explanatory path: it was all a result of another stage of the class struggle, caused by the fact that the working class was more powerful. By extension, countries varied in their performance because some handled class conflict better. That is, more successful countries did not try to suppress the newly powerful working class, which, in any case, would be a vain effort (see Goldthorpe, 1987a:366–382). Instead, in successful countries labor's power had been recognized and harnessed within neocorporatist institutions into a collective national effort in quest of growth and justice. As we have seen, in this account it was the combination of rising working class *power* conjoined with changes in *norms* produced within capitalist democracies (the collapse of normative restraint, the development of the norm of a right to a job) that explained the generality of inflation; and it was variations in the success of *normative reintegration* (in centralized bargaining institutions) that explained intercountry performance differentials).

Now, I have not in this book disputed the idea that workers in capitalist societies were, on the whole, in a better bargaining position after the second world war than they had been before it. A commitment to full employment and greater unionization within a more favorable legal framework no doubt encouraged many workers to demand and secure higher wages than they would otherwise have done and probably made nominal wage cuts even less likely. The policy changes that produced these outcomes were no doubt rooted in power and norms (what else is there?). But whose power and norms?

Take first of all norms. I take it that it would not be disputed that the memories of the 1930s produced a popular distaste for unemployment that shaped postwar macroeconomic policy. As I have pointed out before, although it may be possible to find evidence of class differences in the incidence of unemployment, there are quite good reasons for thinking that *nobody*, capitalist or proletarian, wanted a repeat of the 1930s. There is, to start with, the survey evidence from Britain that I cited earlier that shows that, in the early 1970s, a majority in all income groups were more concerned with unemployment than with inflation. Why this popular consensus? A class power account might argue that there was a fear that a repeat of the 1930s would bring revolution (e.g., Cuneo, 1979b). But the dominant feature of the history of the "working class" is, surely, its failure to meet its appointed destiny with revolution. Indeed, the unreliability of the revolutionary inspiration of workers is the leitmotif of a good chunk of Marxist theory (see van den Berg, 1988:473–474).

So where did the postwar antiunemployment consensus come from? Oddly enough, there seems to be little research on this. But we do know that some political leaders and those who advised them were appalled at the suffering produced by the Great Depression.[19] This suffering was an important theme in popular literature too.[20] Add to this principled objection to unemployment (even of someone else) the fact that industrial capitalists, bankers, farmers, and white-collar workers are also economically damaged by recessions.[21] These, I submit, provide a good part of the explanation for the postwar "Keynesian consensus"—which involved a cross-class antipathy toward unemployment.

In the 1970s, circumstances changed. Inflation accelerated. In some countries the view spread that many of the unemployed were not genuinely "deserving." As unions exercised their new power, they inconvenienced the public, including other union members, and that reduced popular support for them (Smith, 1978; Edwards and Bain, 1988). The result of this was a shift in the norms with which the electorate judged policy alternatives. Whereas the relative proportions no doubt varied by (one or another definition of) social class, the shift took place across classes so that Barry, in his 1985 paper, felt obliged to come up with a set of reasons for discounting the popular judgment that inflation *mattered*. As the relative popular concern with unemployment and inflation changed, so did policy.

However, I am not suggesting that policy is nothing more than a mechanical reflection of popular norms. Those norms are shaped by the options provided by political leaders. The suffering of the 1930s had also marked the policy preferences of political leaders and their advisors. Many of them were therefore, no doubt, disposed to respond sympathetically to arguments that stabilization policies could be used to avoid a repeat of the 1930s. But in the 1970s the views of political leaders also changed. There were two sources of this change. One was the changes in popular concerns about inflation referred to above. The second was that they were being offered an alternative interpretation of economic events—and one that probably seemed more consistent with what they were actually observing. Contrary to what was popularly expected, unemployment and inflation were rising together. As unemployment rose, vacancies remained quite high in many countries. The composition of unemployment had changed, with women and young people constituting a larger proportion. Where attempted, a record of relative failures had accumulated in previous stabilization efforts. Together, these aspects of the macroeconomic record would have increased the receptiveness of those in government—both politicians and senior civil servants—to arguments that the rate of unemployment was no longer the key indicator of welfare that it had once been, and that demand stimulus was not a reliable path to eliminating it and securing higher growth. The general point that I want to make here is that in the

determination of macroeconomic policy the norms of people in governments, and those from whom they take their advice, matter a great deal.
Why is this so? The starting point must be that the effects of monetary
and fiscal policy are difficult to gauge. The uncertainties with respect to
what will and will not work are so huge that the influence of ideas, often
of academic origin, are of considerable importance. Such ideas can
create norms. For example, whether an increase in the unemployment
rate of, say three percentage points, is thought by policy-makers to be
unacceptable depends on whether those policy-makers have been persuaded that a significant proportion of that unemployment is made up
of young people who tend to frequently switch jobs; or whether they
have been persuaded that doing something about the unemployment
(say, through a demand stimulus) will produce even worse effects—like
more inflation (which in turn depends on whether or not they are con-
vinced that inflation has real, negative, effects); and so on. Consequently, there is a lot of latitude for *intellectual conversion*.[22] Then, con-
verting a relatively small number of people can make a large difference
to policy.

Johnson (1970) observed that Keynesian policy became much more
entrenched in Britain than in the United States. He argued that the
intellectual influence of Kenyesianism in Britain rested in the fact that it
carried the day at Oxford and Cambridge; other British universities were
so much less prestigious that it was impossible for those employed at
them to mount an effective attack on Keynesianism. In the United
States, in contrast, the size and diversity of the university system meant
that, even if Harvard became predominantly Keynesian, Chicago and
other universities remained to provide effective intellectual competition.
This account may or may not be right. Clearly, however, it provides an
example of the *kind* of analysis of changes in norms and their effects that
I have in mind here.

So I would argue that the norms that are most relevant in the explanation of shifts in postwar macroeconomic policy are not the class-based
ones identified in sociological theories of the postwar inflation. The
relevant norms are, first, popular (substantially class-transcending)
norms formed largely by personal and family experience and, second,
the norms of politicians and their advisors (which also have some impact
on the distribution of popular norms).

In the explanation of the postwar inflation, where does *power* come in?
It appears in various forms in earlier chapters: the international power of
the United States as a reserve currency nation and its capacity to use that
power to export inflation to the rest of the world; the presence or absence of international constraints on government policy choices—inter-

national capital markets and trade dependency; the relative power of the central bank *vis à vis* the elected government; and the political vulnerability of governments with unstable majorities. There is also the fact that when parties of the left get elected into office they usually (the Lange government in New Zealand was an exception) exercise power to reduce unemployment, although in the medium term they are frequently forced to retreat by the other sources of constraint listed above.

I suggest that these are the forms of power that are relevant in the explanation of the postwar inflation—in its generality and in intercountry differences. Only in the final example can social class be regarded as a principal organizing basis. A disproportionate share of the vote for social democratic parties comes from the "working class" (however defined). If left wing parties put a higher priority on keeping unemployment low than in controlling inflation *and* if they use demand-stimulating policies to do so (as opposed to, say, public employment and higher taxes as in the case of Austria), then the result is likely to be somewhat higher inflation. So I cannot argue that class power is irrelevant in the explanation of the postwar inflation.

But the observation that parties of the left committed to stimulative policies produce higher inflation is not, I would have thought, very exciting or profound. It is certainly much less exciting than an interpretation that says that governments were compelled to keep unemployment low and to inflate by a less normatively restrained, more powerful working class. The ultimate evidence that it was not a historical transformation in the character of the working class that produced inflation lies in the relative ease with which most governments of capitalist societies after the mid-1970s accepted sustained high unemployment, often combined with a legislated weakening of trade unions who found that they had quite a lot less power than they thought they had.

Consistent with the sociological approach to economic behavior, norms and power certainly played a role in the postwar inflation; but the evidence tends to suggest that social classes did not provide the principal organizing basis for them. Social class played a role in the election of social democratic governments that, under some circumstances and for some periods, adopted more inflationary policies. But the power and norms that really mattered in the postwar inflation were popular distaste for high unemployment in many countries that was a legacy of the 1930s, the presence or absence of international constraint on policy options, the extent to which political institutions allowed or encouraged politicians to prize the short over the long run, and, within those broad limits, the policy norms of politicians and their advisors, in which academic advice played a significant (probably largely pernicious!) part.

All of this is to say, then, that in searching for sociological explanations for economic phenomena it makes sense to be a little less determined to discover that it is the conflict of social classes that is the master force in economic change but a little more interested in the legal, institutional, and international limits on policy discretion, and in the social processes *within academe and government* that underlie the rise and decline of alternative economic interpretations. This may produce explanations that are rather less congenial to the social democratic tastes of most sociologists and political scientists who write on economic subjects. But my guess is that they will be explanations that, on the whole, make better sense of the available evidence.

Notes

1. Implicit contract theory would suggest that the downward rigidity of wages is not limited to the unionized work force. I take it, however, that unionization spreads the phenomenon.

2. For a brief, relevant discussion of the Swiss case see Smith (1987:369). For a study that documents the weakness of organized labor vis-à-vis capital, its internal divisions, and the legislated prohibition on representational monopoly but *still* insists on putting Switzerland into the neocorporatist category, see Parri (1987:75–76, 82).

3. Hardiman's (1988:119) description of Irish macroeconomic policy is interesting in this respect: "Government strategies tended not to be informed by a high degree of intellectual rigour, nor did governments experience any need to justify their 'policy mix' in terms of an ideologically coherent set of priorities."

4. Of course, to the extent that members of a left wing government are aware that the policies will not work but introduce them to please their constituency they are acting in a politically irresponsible fashion, and this factor should be reallocated to that category.

5. In each case, initial level (of productivity or GNP) is controlled for, along with growth in "openness" of the economy—which means the sum of the value of imports and exports, divided by GNP.

6. Examples of temporary surges of this sort are Sweden in 1960 and 1966, the Netherlands in 1957, 1960, and 1969, Australia in 1964 and 1969, New Zealand in 1959 and 1967, Denmark in 1955, 1962, and 1969, France in 1953 to 1954 (followed by devaluation), and Italy in 1962 to 1965.

7. Governor Coyne was forced out in 1960 but Canada still had an inflation rate that was more than half a point lower than the United States' in 1961. I take it that it is reasonable to regard this as a lagged effect of Governor Coyne's monetary stringency.

8. Note that Denmark, that is also a small country contiguous to Germany, has had a generally poor record of inflation. But its principal source of imports is Sweden, with its mediocre inflation record and, until 1976, its largest single export destination was the high inflation United Kingdom. In the last decade and a half its dependence on trade with Germany has tended to increase and, along with that, it has improved from being a very high inflation country prior to the oil shocks to an intermediate inflation country. See Smith (1987:379–380).

9. It is worth reiterating here that Giavazzi and Spaventa (1989) have made an interesting case to the effect that Italy's high inflation rate in the 1970s provided a sensible economic policy in the context of a pervasive downward rigidity of real wages in Italy. First note, however, that they regard the inflationary policy as a "second best solution" (p. 138) made necessary by a set of institutional bases of wage rigidity that, arguably, had been conceded by weak governments in the past. Second, since Italy's high inflation rates of the 1970s had persisted into the 1980s its room for demand stimulation is now presumed considerably narrowed since a further acceleration would push it up toward the hyperinflation level, that nobody regards as desirable. Third, Giavazzi and Spaventa leave open the possibility that Italy's very substantial public debt, presumably in part accumulated as a result of government weakness, may cause serious problems in the future.

10. There are some relevant figures in Roubini and Sachs (1989:107, 110).

11. The closest thing to a relationship between attitudes toward unemployment and class is provided by Hibbs (1975:31-37), using the same data set as Alt. His analysis of occupational data shows that a narrow majority of the higher managerial and professional category did opt for steady prices rather than full employment. But the differences between the responses of this category and the blue-collar category are, in fact, very small indeed and Hibbs finds no clear relationship between attitudes toward a trade-off and class. Jonung and Wadensjö's study of Swedish attitudes, cited earlier, is also relevant here.

12. I made this point in my 1982 paper. Goldthorpe (1987a:380) seems to concede it (without acknowledgment) but simply fails to grasp the fact that this, to some degree, poses a problem for a class struggle account.

13. Goldthorpe (1987a:372-373) makes Hirsch's argument a central part of his most recent analysis of macroeconomic performance, but fails to consider— or even acknowledge—the critical treatments to which it has been subjected in Heath and Kumar (1983).

14. With respect to quantitative tests of Olson's theory it is worth underlining that the institutional sclerosis emphasized by Olson is unlikely to be the only source of economic difficulties. For example, if Alesina is correct, many of the institutions and expenditures encumbering the Italian economy are produced by the particular party system that Italy has inherited, with its unstable coalitions and rather strong extremes. These presumably do not have their principal origins in an Olsonian accretion of voluntary associations since Italy was invaded and defeated during the second world war. Controlling for this and other variables (central bank independence?) would presumably modify Olson's results.

15. See Schwerin (1984:235). He reports a simple bivariate correlation between growth in GDP and Cameron's (1985) index of "organized power of labour." It is not clear whether it is real or nominal GDP that is involved and he does not control for initial level of either labor productivity or GDP. Also, the GDP figures for Norway are, of course, substantially affected by oil discoveries and their effects.

16. It is true that they all do rather better in GNP growth (Helliwell, 1990:125). Sweden and Denmark grew by about what would be predicted from their 1960 level and Finland and Norway by more. But Norway's GNP growth is inflated by oil and Finland seems not to work according to the Nordic model since it has had a high level of industrial conflict (see Adams, 1982:471).

17. For further examples see Jones (1985:106). Note, however, that this study

presents a strong plea for the development of centralized bargaining institutions in Britain.

18. But it is not clear that this is behavior that it is *impossible* for economists to deal with, once standard economic analysis is extended to include imperfections in information. A clear example of this would be the idea of "statistical discrimination." On this see Phelps (1972a).

19. For the effects of this experience on a Conservative British politician see Macmillan (1938). For the effect on a U.S. politician of rather direct and personal deprivation see Humphrey (1976:30–36). On evidence of Keynesian attitudes in the Canadian civil service see Bryce (1986:65, 116, 119–122).

20. Some indication of the literature involved can be found in Reid (1979) and Peeler (1987).

21. For some relevant evidence, see Hamilton (1975:Ch. 2).

22. As Odell (1982) has shown for international monetary policy.

REFERENCES

Aaron, Benjamin 1972. "Methods of industrial action: Courts, administrative agencies and legislatures." Pp. 69–126 in Benjamin Aaron and K. W. Wedderburn (eds.), *Industrial Conflict: A Comparative Legal Survey.* London: Longman.

Abegglen, James C., and George Stalk, Jr. 1985. *Kaisha: The Japanese Corporation.* New York: Basic Books.

Abramovitz, Moses. 1983. "Notes on international differences in productivity growth rates." Pp. 79–89 in Dennis C. Mueller (ed.), *The Political Economy of Growth.* New Haven: Yale University Press.

Adams, Roy J. 1982. "Industrial-relations systems in Europe and North America." Pp. 457–480 in John Anderson and Morley Gunderson (eds.), *Union-Management Relations in Canada.* Don Mills, Ontario: Addison-Wesley.

Adams, Walter (ed.) 1971. *The Structure of American Industry* (4th ed.). New York: Macmillan.

Adler, P. S. 1985. "Rethinking the skill requirements of new technologies." Pp. 85–112 in D. Whittington (ed.), *High Hopes for High Tech: Microelectronics Policy in North Carolina.* Chapel Hill: University of North Carolina Press.

Ahlén, Kristina. 1988a. "Recent trends in Swedish collective bargaining: Collapse of the Swedish model." *Current Sweden* No. 358.

Ahlén, Kristina. 1988b. "Recent trends in Swedish collective bargaining: Heading toward negotiated incomes policy?" *Current Sweden* No. 359.

Ahlén, Kristina. 1989. "Swedish collective bargaining under pressure: Interunion rivalry and incomes policies." *British Journal of Industrial Relations* 27:330–346.

Albåge, Lars-Gunnar. 1986. "Recent trends in collective bargaining in Sweden: An employer's view." *International Labour Review* 125:107–122.

Alesina, Alberto. 1989. "Politics and business cycles in industrial democracies." *Economic Policy* 4:55–98.

Alexander, David. 1984. "Immediate antiques as good as gold are a Thai speciality." *Smithsonian* 15:100–109.

Allen, Bruce T. 1976. "Average concentration in manufacturing, 1947–1972." *Journal of Economic Issues* 10:664–673.

Allen, Christopher S. 1989. "The underdevelopment of Keynesianism in the Federal Republic of Germany." Pp. 263–290 in Peter A. Hall (ed.), *The Politi-*

cal Power of Economic Ideas: Keynesianism Across Nations. Princeton, NJ: Princeton University Press.

Alt, James E. 1979. *The Politics of Economic Decline: Economic Management and Political Behaviour in Britain since 1964.* Cambridge: Cambridge University Press.

Alt, James E. 1985a. "Political parties, world demand, and unemployment: Domestic and international sources of economic activity." *American Political Science Review* 79:1016–1040.

Alt, James E. 1985b. "Party strategies, world demand, and unemployment in Britain and the United States, 1947–1983." Pp. 32–61 in Heinz Eulau and Michael S. Lewis-Beck (eds.), *Economic Conditions and Electoral Outcomes: The United States and Western Europe.* New York: Agathon Press.

Alt, James E. 1988. "Crude politics: Oil and the political economy of unemployment in Britain and Norway, 1970–85." *British Journal of Political Science* 17:149–199.

Alt, James E., and Alec Chrystal. 1981. "Politico-economic models of British fiscal policy." Pp. 185–208 in Douglas A. Hibbs and Heino Fassbender (eds.), *Contemporary Political Economy: Studies on the Interdependence of Politics and Economics.* Amsterdam: North-Holland Publishing Company.

Alt, James E., and K. Alec Chrystal. 1983. *Political Economics.* Brighton: Wheatsheaf Books.

Altvater, Elmer. 1973. "Notes on some problems of state interventionism (II)." *Kapitalistate* No. 2:76–83.

Alvarez, R. Michael, Geoffrey Garrett, and Peter Lange. 1991. "Government partisanship, labor organization, and macroeconomic performance." *American Political Science Review* 85:539–556.

Andriulaitis, R. J. 1986. *Deregulation and Airline Employment: Myth Versus Fact.* Vancouver: Centre for Transportation Studies, U.B.C.

Archibald, G. C. 1969. "The Phillips curve and the distribution of unemployment." *American Economic Review* (Papers and Proceedings 59:124–134.

Artus, Jacques. 1982. "Commentary." Pp. 35–41 in Sven W. Arndt (ed.), *The Political Economy of Austria.* Washington, D.C.: American Enterprise Institute for Public Policy Research.

Ashenfelter, Orley, and George E. Johnson. 1969. "Bargaining theory, trade unions and industrial strike activity." *American Economic Review* 59:35–49.

Ashenfelter, O. C., G. E. Johnson, and J. H. Pencavel. 1972. "Trade unions and the rate of change of money wage rates in United States manufacturing industry." *Review of Economic Studies* 39:27–54.

Asselain, J.-C., and C. Morrisson. 1983. "Economic growth and interest groups: The French experience." Pp. 157–175 in Dennis C. Mueller (ed.), *The Political Economy of Growth.* New Haven, CT: Yale University Press.

Atkinson, A. B. 1983. *Social Justice and Public Policy.* Cambridge, Massachusetts: MIT Press.

Aubert, Jean Francois. 1979. *Petite Histoire Constitutionelle de la Suisse.* Berne: Francke Editions.

Aukrust, Odd. 1977. "Inflation in the open economy: A Norwegian model." Pp.

107–153 in L. B. Krause and W. S. Salant (eds.), *Worldwide Inflation*. Washington, DC: The Brookings Institution.

Averitt, Robert T. 1968. *The Dual Economy: The Dynamics of American Industrial Structure*. New York: W. W. Norton.

Bachrach, Peter, and Morton S. Baratz. 1970. *Power and Poverty: Theory and Practice*. New York: Oxford University Press.

Bain, George Sayers. 1970. *The Growth of White Collar Unionism*. London: Oxford University Press.

Bain, George Sayers, and Faroukh Elsheikh. 1976. *Union Growth and the Business Cycle: An Econometric Analysis*. Oxford: Basil Blackwell.

Bain, George Sayers, and Robert Price. 1980. *Profiles of Union Growth: A Comparative Statistical Portrait of Eight Countries*. Oxford: Blackwell.

Bain, Joe S. 1956. *Barriers to New Competition*. Cambridge, MA: Harvard University Press.

Balassa, Bela. 1964. "The purchasing-power parity doctrine: A reappraisal." *Journal of Political Economy* 72:584–596.

Banaian, King, Leroy A. Laney, and Thomas D. Willett. 1983. "Central bank independence: An international comparison." *Economic Review of the Federal Reserve Bank of Dallas* March:1–14.

Baran, Paul A. 1957. *The Political Economy of Growth*. New York: Monthly Review Press.

Baran, Paul A., and Paul M. Sweezy. 1966. *Monopoly Capital: An Essay on the American Economic and Social Order*. New York: Monthly Review Press.

Barber, Clarence L., and John C. P. McCallum. 1982. *Controlling Inflation: Learning from Experience in Canada, Europe and Japan*. Toronto: Lorimer.

Barkin, Solomon (ed.). 1975. *Worker Militancy and its Consequences, 1965–75*. New York: Praeger.

Baron, James N., and Andrew E. Newman. 1990. "For what it's worth: Organizations, occupations, and the value of work done by women and non-whites." *American Sociological Review* 55:155–175.

Barry, Brian. 1985. "Does democracy cause inflation? Political ideas of some economists." Pp. 280–317 in Leon N. Lindberg and Charles S. Maier (eds.), *The Politics of Inflation and Economic Stagnation*. Washington, DC: Brookings Institution.

Barry, Brian. 1983. "Some questions about explanation." *International Studies Quarterly* 27:17–27.

Batstone, Eric. 1984. *Working Order: Workplace Industrial Relations over Two Decades*. Oxford: Basil Blackwell.

Baumol, William J. 1979. "On some microeconomic issues in inflation theory." Pp. 55–78 in James H. Gapinski and Charles E. Rockwood (eds.), *Essays in Post-Keynesian Inflation*. Cambridge, MA: Ballinger Publishing Company.

Beck, Nathaniel. 1982a. "Does there exist a political business cycle?" *Public Choice* 38:208–217.

Beck, Nathaniel. 1982b. "Presidential influence on the Federal Reserve in the 1970's." *American Journal of Political Science* 26:415–445.

Beck, Nathaniel. 1982c. "Parties, administrations, and American macroeconomic outcomes." *American Political Science Review* 76:83–93.

Beck, Nathaniel. 1984. "Domestic political sources of American monetary policy: 1955–82." *Journal of Politics* 46:786–817.

Beck, Nathaniel. 1987. "Domestic politics and monetary policy: A comparative perspective." *American Journal of Political Science* 31:194–216.

Beck, Nathaniel. 1990. "Political monetary cycles." Pp. 115–130 in Thomas Mayer (ed.), *The Political Economy of American Monetary Policy*. Cambridge: Cambridge University Press.

Becker, Gary. 1981. *A Treatise on the Family*. Cambridge, MA: Harvard University Press.

Bellon, Bertrand, and Jorge Niosi. 1988. *The Decline of the American Economy*. Montreal: Black Rose Books.

Bendix, Reinhard. 1964. *Nation Building and Citizenship: Studies of our Changing Social Order*. New York: Wiley.

Benson, Leslie. 1978. *Proletarians and Parties: Five Essays in Social Class*. Wellington, New Zealand: Methuen.

Bergmann, Joachim, and Walter Muller-Jentsch. 1975. "The Federal Republic of Germany: Cooperative unionism and dual bargaining system challenged." Pp. 235–276 in Solomon Barkin (ed.), *Worker Militancy and Its Consequences, 1965–75: New Directions in Western Industrial Relations*. New York: Praeger.

Bergsten, C. Fred. 1975. *The Dilemmas of the Dollar: The Economics and Politics of United States International Monetary Policy*. New York: New York University Press.

Berry, Brian J. L. 1991. *Long-Wave Rhythms in Economic Development and Political Behaviour*. Baltimore, MD: The Johns Hopkins University Press.

Blair, John. 1972. *Economic Concentration: Structure, Behaviour and Public Policy*. New York: Harcourt, Brace, Jovanovich.

Blais, André, and John McCallum. 1986. "Government, special interest groups and economic growth." Pp. 153–201 in David Laidler (ed.), *Responses to Economic Change*. Toronto: University of Toronto Press in cooperation with the Royal Commission on the Economic Union and Development Prospects for Canada.

Blanchard, Olivier Jean. 1987. "Aggregate and individual price adjustment." *Brookings Papers on Economic Activity*:57–109.

Blaug, Mark. 1976. "The empirical status of human capital theory: A slightly jaundiced view." *Journal of Economic Literature* 14:827–855.

Bleaney, Michael. 1976. *Under-Consumption Theories: A History and Critical Analysis*. New York: International Publishers.

Blinder, Alan S. 1979. *Economic Policy and the Great Stagflation*. New York: Academic Press.

Blinder, Alan S. 1987. *Hard Heads, Soft Hearts: Tough Minded Economics for a Just Society*. Reading, MA: Addison-Wesley.

Block, Fred L. 1977. *The Origins of International Economic Disorder: A Study of United States International Monetary Policy from World War II to the Present*. Berkeley, CA: University of California Press.

Block, Fred. 1990. *Postindustrial Possibilities: A Critique of Economic Discourse.* Berkeley, CA: University of California Press.

Bluestone, Barry, and Bennett Harrison. 1982. *The Deindustrialization of America: Plant Closings, Community Abandonment and the Dismantling of Basic Industry.* New York: Basic Books.

Blumberg, Paul. 1980. *Inequality in an Age of Decline.* New York: Oxford University Press.

Blyth, Conrad A. 1977. *Inflation in New Zealand.* Hornsby, N.S.W.: George Allen and Unwin Australia.

Boddy, Raford, and James Crotty. 1974. "Class conflict, Keynesian policies and the business cycle." *Monthly Review* 26:1–17.

Boddy, Raford, and James Crotty. 1975. "Class conflict and macro-policy: The political business cycle." *Review of Radical Political Economics* 7:1–19.

Bond, D. E., and R. A. Shearer. 1972. *The Economics of the Canadian Financial System: Theory, Policy and Institutions.* Scarborough, Ontario: Prentice-Hall.

Bond, Marian E. 1983. "Exchange rates, inflation and vicious circles." *IMF Staff Papers* 27:9–23.

Bosworth, Barry P., and Robert Z. Lawrence. 1987. "Adjusting to slower economic growth: The domestic economy." Pp. 22–54 in Barry P. Bosworth and Alice M. Rivlin (eds.), *The Swedish Economy.* Washington, DC: The Brookings Institution.

Bourdon, Clint. 1979. "Pattern bargaining, wage determination, and inflation: Some preliminary observations on the 1976–78 wage round." Pp. 115–133 in Michael J. Piore (ed.), *Unemployment and Inflation: Institutionalist and Structuralist Views.* Armonk, NY: M. E. Sharpe Inc.

Bradley, Keith, and Alan Gelb. 1980. "The radical potential of cash nexus breaks." *British Journal of Sociology* 31:188–203.

Brandini, Pietro Merli. 1975. "Italy: Creating a new industrial relations system from the bottom." Pp. 82–117 in Solomon Barkin (ed.), *Worker Militancy and Its Consequences, 1965–75: New Directions in Western Industrial Relations.* New York: Praeger.

Brandt, Gerhard. 1984. "Industrial relations in the Federal Republic of Germany under conditions of economic crisis." Pp. 5–20 in Tokunaga Shigeyoshi and Joachim Bergmann (eds.), *Industrial Relations in Transition: The Cases of Japan and the Federal Republic of Germany.* Tokyo: University of Tokyo Press.

Braverman, Harry. 1974. *Labor and Monopoly Capital.* New York: Monthly Review Press.

Brecher, Jeremy. 1972. *Strike!* Greenwich, CT: Straight Arrow Books.

Brenner, Reuven. 1985. *Betting on Ideas: Wars, Inventions, Inflation.* Chicago: University of Chicago Press.

Brittan, Samuel. 1971. *Steering the Economy: The British Experiment.* New York: Library Press.

Brittan, Samuel. 1978. "Inflation and democracy." Pp. 161–185 in Fred Hirsch and John H. Goldthorpe (eds.), *The Political Economy of Inflation.* Cambridge, MA: Harvard University Press.

Brittan, Samuel, and P. Lilley. 1977. *The Delusion of Incomes Policy.* London: Temple Smith.

Bronfenbrenner, Martin, and Yasukichi Yasuba. 1987. "Economic welfare." Pp. 93–136 in Kozo Yamamura and Yasukichi Yasuba (eds.), *The Political Economy of Japan,* Vol. 1. Stanford, CA: Stanford University Press.

Brown, A. J. 1985. *World Inflation since 1950: An International Comparative Study.* London: Cambridge University Press.

Brown, William. 1990. "Class and industrial relations: Sociological bricks without straw." Pp. 213–221 in Jon Clark, Celia Modgil, and Sohan Modgil (eds.), *John H. Goldthorpe: Consensus and Controversy.* London: The Falmer Press.

Browning, Edgar K., & William R. Johnson. 1984. "The trade-off between equality and efficiency." *Journal of Political Economy.* 92:175–203.

Brunner, Karl. 1975. "Comment." *Journal of Law and Economics* 18:837–857.

Bruno, Michael, and Jeffrey Sachs. 1985. *Economics of Worldwide Stagflation.* Cambridge, MA: Harvard University Press.

Bryce, Robert B. 1986. *Maturing in Hard Times: Canada's Department of Finance through the Great Depression.* Kingston and Montreal: McGill-Queen's University Press.

Buchanan, James M. 1987. *Economics: Between Predictive Science and Moral Philosophy.* College Station, TX: Texas A&M University Press.

Buchanan, James M., and Gordon Tullock. 1962. *The Calculus of Consent.* Ann Arbor: University of Michigan Press.

Buchanan, James, M., and Richard E. Wagner. 1977. *Democracy in Deficit: The Political Legacy of Lord Keynes.* New York: Academic Press.

Buiter, Willem H. 1980. "The macroeconomics of Dr. Pangloss: A critical survey of the new classical macroeconomics." *Economic Journal* 90:34–50.

Burtt, Everett Johnson. 1979. *Labor in the American Economy.* New York: St. Martin's Press.

Bush, W., and A. Denzau. 1977. "The voting behaviour of bureaucrats and public sector growth." Pp. 90–99 in Thomas E. Borcheding (ed.), *Budgets and Bureaucrats: The Sources of Government Growth.* Durham, NC: Duke University Press.

Butschek, Felix. 1982. "Full employment during recession." Pp. 101–129 in Sven W. Arndt (ed.), *The Political Economy of Austria.* Washington, DC: American Enterprise Institute for Public Policy Research.

Cagan, Phillip. 1979. *Persistent Inflation: Historical and Policy Essays.* New York: Columbia University Press.

Cairncross, Alec. 1966. *Introduction to Economics* (4th ed.). London: Butterworth.

Calder, Kent E. 1988. *Crisis and Compensation: Public Policy and Political Stability in Japan, 1949–1986.* Princeton, NJ: Princeton University Press.

Calleo, David P. 1982. *The Imperious Economy.* Cambridge, MA: Harvard University Press.

Calleo, David P. 1987. *Beyond American Hegemony: The Future of the Western Alliance.* New York: Basic Books.

Calmfors, Lars. 1977. "Inflation in Sweden." Pp. 493–537 in L. B. Krause and

W. S. Salant (eds.), *Worldwide Inflation*. Washington, DC: The Brookings Institution.

Calmfors, Lars. 1987. "Comments." Pp. 174–181 in Barry P. Bosworth and Alice M. Rivlin (eds.), *The Swedish Economy*. Washington, DC: Brookings Institution.

Calmfors, Lars, and John Driffill. 1988. "Bargaining structure, corporatism and macroeconomic performance." *Economic Policy* 2:14–47.

Cameron, David R. 1978. "The expansion of the public economy: A comparative analysis." *American Political Science Review* 72:1243–1261.

Cameron, David, R. 1982. "On the limits of the public economy: A comparative analysis." *The Annals of the American Academy of Political and Social Science* 72:1243–1261.

Cameron, David R. 1984. "Social democracy, corporatism, labour quiescence, and the representation of economic interest in advanced capitalist society." Pp. 143–179 in John H. Goldthorpe (ed.), *Order and Conflict in Contemporary Capitalism: Studies in the Political Economy of Western European Nations*. Oxford: Clarendon Press.

Cameron, David R. 1985. "Does government cause inflation? Taxes, spending, and deficits." Pp. 224–279 in Leon N. Lindberg and Charles S. Maier (ed.), *The Politics of Inflation and Economic Stagnation*. Washington, DC: Brookings Institution.

Carter, Donald D. 1982. "Collective bargaining legislation in Canada." Pp. 29–94 in John Anderson and Morley Gunderson (eds.), *Union-Management Relations in Canada*. Don Mills, Ontario: Addison-Wesley.

Castells, Manuel. 1980. *The Economic Crisis and American Society*. Princeton, NJ: Princeton University Press.

Castles, Francis G. 1982. "The impact of parties on public expenditure." In Francis G. Castles (ed.), *The Impact of Parties: Politics and Policies in Democratic Capitalist States*. London: Sage Publications.

Castles, Francis G. 1986. "Social expenditures and the political right: A methodological note." *European Journal of Political Research* 14:669–676.

Castles, Francis G. 1987. "Neocorporatism and the 'happiness index', or what the trade unions get for their cooperation." *European Journal of Political Research* 15:381–393.

Cecchetti, Stephen G. 1986. "The frequency of price adjustments: A study of the newsstand prices of magazines." *Journal of Econometrics* 31:255–274.

Cerny, K. (ed.). 1977. *Scandinavia at the Polls*. Washington, DC: American Enterprise Institute.

Chaison, Gary N. 1982. "Unions: Growth, structure and dynamics." Pp. 147–172 in John Anderson and Morley Gunderson (eds.), *Union-Management Relations in Canada*. Don Mills, Ontario: Addison-Wesley.

Chalmers, Norma J. 1989. *Industrial Relations in Japan: The Peripheral Workforce*. London: Routledge.

Chamberlin, Edwin H. 1933. *The Theory of Monopolistic Competition*. Cambridge, MA: Harvard University Press.

Chirot, Daniel. 1977. *Social Change in the Twentieth Century*. New York: Harcourt, Brace Jovanovich.

Choi, Kwang. 1983a. *Theories of Comparative Economic Growth.* Ames, IA: Iowa State University Press.

Choi, Kwang. 1983b. "A statistical test of Olson's model." Pp. 57–78 in Dennis C. Mueller (ed.), *The Political Economy of Growth.* New Haven, CT: Yale University Press.

Christensen, Sandra. 1980. *Unions and the Public Interest.* Vancouver: The Fraser Institute.

Chrystal, K. A., and J. E. Alt. 1981. "Some problems in formulating and testing a politico-economic model of the U.K." *Economic Journal* 91:730–736.

Cipolla, Carlo M. (ed.). 1970. *The Economic Decline of Empires.* London: Methuen.

Clarke, Harold D., William Mishler, and Paul Whitely. 1990. "Recapturing the Falklands: Models of Conservative Popularity, 1979–83." *British Journal of Political Science* 20:63–81.

Clawson, Dan. 1980. *Bureaucracy and the Labor Process: The Transformation of U.S. Industry, 1860–1920.* New York: Monthly Review Press.

Clawson, Patrick. 1983. "A comment on van Parij's obituary." *Review of Radical Political Economics* 15:107–110.

Clegg, Hugh. 1971. *How to Run an Incomes Policy and Why We Made Such a Mess of the Last One.* London: Heinemann.

Clegg, Hugh Armstrong. 1979. *The Changing System of Industrial Relations in Britain.* Oxford: Basil Blackwell.

Clemens, John. 1983. *Polls, Politics and Populism.* Aldershot, Hants.: Gower.

Cohen, Benjamin J. 1982. "Balance of payments financing: Evolution of a regime." *International Organization* 36:457–478.

Colbjørnsen, Tom. 1986. *Dividers in the Labour Market.* Oslo: Norwegian University Press.

Coleman, James S. 1988. "Social capital in the creation of human capital." *American Journal of Sociology* 94 (supplement):S95–S120.

Coombs, Rod, Paolo Saviotti, and Vivien Walsh. 1987. *Economics of Technological Change.* Totowa, NJ: Rowman and Littlefield.

Coughlin, Richard M. 1980. *Attitudes Towards Taxing and Spending in Industrialized Societies.* Berkeley, California: Institute of International Studies Research Series, No. 42.

Courant, Paul N. 1987. "Fiscal policy and European economic growth." Pp. 423–507 in Robert Z. Lawrence and Charles L. Schultze (eds.), *Barriers to European Growth: A Transatlantic View.* Washington, DC: Brookings Institution.

Cripps, Francis. 1977. "The money supply, wages and inflation." *Cambridge Journal of Economics* 1:101–112.

Crispo, John H. G., and H. W. Arthurs. 1968. "Industrial unrest in Canada: A diagnosis of recent experience." *Relations Industrielles/Industrial Relations* 23:237–262.

Crompton, Rosemary, and Stuart Reid. 1982. "The deskilling of clerical work." Pp. 163–178 in Stephen Wood (ed.), *The Degradation of Work? Skill, Deskilling and the Labour Process.* London: Hutchinson.

Crossman, Richard. 1976. *Diaries of a Cabinet Minister,* Volume 2. London: Hamish Hamilton and Jonathan Cape.

Crouch, Colin. 1978. "Inflation and the political organization of economic interests." Pp. 217–239 in Fred Hirsch and John H. Goldthorpe (eds.), *The Political Economy of Inflation*. Cambridge, MA: Harvard University Press.

Crouch, Colin. 1979. *The Politics of Industrial Relations*. Glasgow: Fontana.

Crouch, Colin. 1985a. "Conditions for trade union wage restraint." Pp. 105–139 in Leon N. Lindberg and Charles S. Maier (eds.), *The Politics of Inflation and Economic Stagnation*. Washington, DC: Brookings Institution.

Crouch, Colin. 1985b. "Corporatism in industrial relations: A formal model." Pp. 62–88 in Wyn Grant (ed.), *The Political Economy of Corporatism*. London: Macmillan.

Crouch, Colin, and Alessandro Pizzorno (eds.). 1978. *The Resurgence of Class Conflict in Western Europe since 1968*. London: Macmillan.

Crouigneau, Françoise. 1986. "En République d'Irlande: La monnaie est dévaluée en douceur pour compenser la baisse du sterling et du dollar." *Le Devoir* August 7:11.

Cuneo, Carl J. 1979a. "Class contradictions in Canada's international setting." *Canadian Review of Sociology and Anthropology* 16:1–20.

Cuneo, Carl J. 1979b. "State, class, and reserve labour: The case of the 1941 Canadian unemployment insurance act." *Canadian Review of Sociology and Anthropology* 16:147–170.

Daniel, W. W. 1976. *Wage Determination in Industry*. London: PEP Report No. 563.

Darby, Michael R., and James R. Lothian. 1983. *The International Transmission of Inflation*. Chicago: University of Chicago Press.

Daub, Mervin. 1984. "Some reflections on the importance of forecasting to policy-making." *Canadian Public Policy* 10:377–383.

Davies, Robert J. 1983. "Incomes and anti-inflation policy." Pp. 419–456 in George Bain (ed.), *Industrial Relations in Britain*. Oxford: Blackwell.

Davis, Lance E., and Robert A. Huttenback. 1982. "The cost of empire." Pp. 41–70 in Roger L. Ransom, Richard Sutch, and Gary M. Walton (eds.), *Explorations in the New Economic History: Essays in Honor of Douglass C. North*. New York: Academic Press.

deBrunhoff, Suzanne, and Jean Cartelier. 1974. "Une analyse marxiste de l'inflation." *Chronique Sociale de France* 4:47–60.

Dell'Aringa, Carlo, and Claudio Lucifora. 1990. "Wage determination and union behaviour in Italy: An efficiency wage interpretation." Pp. 391–413 in Renato Brunetta and Carlo Dell'Aringa (eds.), *Labour Relations and Economic Performance*. London: Macmillan.

de Vries, Jan. 1983. "The rise and decline of nations in historical perspective." *International Studies Quarterly* 27:11–16.

Dennison, E. F. 1973. "The shift to services and the rate of productivity change." *Survey of Current Business* No. 10:20–35.

Devine, James. 1983. "Underconsumption, over-investment and the origins of the great depression." *Review of Radical Political Economics* 15:1–27.

Dinkel, Reiner. 1981. "Political business cycles in Germany and the United States: Some theoretical and empirical considerations." Pp. 209–230 in Douglas A. Hibbs and Heino Fassbender (eds.), *Contemporary Political Economy: Studies on the Interdependence of Politics and Economics*. Amsterdam: North-Holland Publishing Company.

Dodge, William. 1977. *Skilled Labour Supply Imbalances: The Canadian Experience.* Montreal: British North America Committee.

Dornbusch, Rudiger. 1989. "Credibility, debt and unemployment: Ireland's failed stabilization." *Economic Policy* 4:174–209.

Dowrick, Steve, and Duc-Tho Nguyen. 1989. "OECD comparative economic growth 1950–85: Catch-up and convergence." *American Economic Review* 79:1010–1030.

Downs, Anthony. 1965. "Why the government bureaucracy is too small in a democracy." Pp. 76–95 in Edmund Phelps (ed.), *Private Wants and Public Needs* (rev. ed.). New York: Norton.

Duda, Helga, and Franz Tödtling. 1986. "Austrian trade unions in the economic crisis." Pp. 227–268 in Richard Edwards, Paolo Garonna, and Franz Tödtling (eds.), *Unions in Crisis and Beyond: Perspectives from Six Countries.* Dover, MA: Auburn House.

Duhamel, Alain. 1984. "Transhumance ideologique." *Le Monde* June 12th:1.

Dunlop, John T. 1957. "The task of contemporary wage theory." Pp. 117–139 in George W. Taylor and Frank C. Pierson (eds.), *New Concepts of Wage Determination.* New York: McGraw-Hill.

Dunn, Robert M. 1971. *Canada's Experience with Fixed and Flexible Exchange Rates in a North American Capital Market.* Washington DC: National Planning Association.

Dunn, Robert M. 1978. *The Canada-U.S. Capital Market: Intermediation, Integration and Policy Independence.* Montreal: C. D. Howe Institute.

Durkheim, Emile. 1933. *The Division of Labor in Society.* New York: Macmillan.

Dyson, Kenneth. 1982. "The politics of economic recession in Western Germany." Pp. 32–64 in Andrew Cox (ed.), *Politics, Policy and the European Recession.* New York: St. Martin's Press.

Eastwood, David B. 1985. *The Economics of Consumer Behavior.* Boston: Allyn & Bacon.

Eccles, Robert G., and Harrison C. White. 1988. "Price and authority in inter-profit center transactions." *American Journal of Sociology* 94 (Supplement):S17–S51.

Editors, The. 1981. "Reagan and the nemesis of inflation." *Monthly Review* 32:1–10.

Edwards, P. K., and Hugh Scullion. 1982. *The Social Organization of Industrial Conflict: Control and Resistance in the Workplace.* Oxford: Basil Blackwell.

Edwards, P. K., and George Sayers Bain. 1988. "Why are trade unions becoming more popular? Unions and public opinion in Britain." *British Journal of Industrial Relations* 26:311–326.

Ellis, Adrian, and Anthony Heath. 1983. "Positional competition, or an offer you can't refuse?" Pp. 1–22 in Adrian Heath and Krishan Kumar (eds.), *Dilemmas of Liberal Democracies: Studies in Fred Hirsch's 'Social Limits to Growth'.* London: Tavistock.

Ellis, Adrian, and Krishan Kumar. 1983. *Dilemmas of Liberal Democracies: Studies in Fred Hirsch's 'Social Limits to Growth'.* London: Tavistock.

Elster, Jon. 1989. *The Cement of Society: A Study of Social Order.* Cambridge: Cambridge University Press.

Esping-Andersen, Gösta. 1990. *The Three Worlds of Welfare Capitalism*. Princeton, NJ: Princeton University Press.

Esping-Andersen, Gösta, and Walter Korpi. 1984. "Social policy as class politics in post-war capitalism: Scandinavia, Austria, and Germany." Pp. 179–208 in John H. Goldthorpe (ed.), *Order and Conflict in Contemporary Capitalism: Studies in the Political Economy of Western European Nations*. Oxford: Clarendon Press.

Etzioni, Amitai. 1988. *The Moral Dimension: Toward a New Economics*. New York: Free Press.

Evans, Peter. 1979. *Dependent Development: The Alliance of Multinationals, State, and Local Capital in Brazil*. Princeton, NJ: Princeton University Press.

Fair, Don. 1979. "The independence of central banks." *The Banker* 129:31–41.

Feldstein, Martin. 1982. "Inflation and the American economy." *The Public Interest* No. 67:63–70.

Fender, John. 1990. *Inflation: Welfare Costs, Positive Theory, and Policy Options*. Ann Arbor: University of Michigan Press.

Fine, Ben, and Laurence Harris. 1976. "State expenditure in advanced capitalism: A reply." *New Left Review* 98:97–112.

Fiorito, Jack, and Robert C. Dauffenbach. 1982. "Market and non market influences on curriculum choice by college students." *Industrial and Labor Relations Review* 36:88–101.

Fischer, Stanley. 1977. "Long term contracts, rational expectations, and the optimal money supply rule." *Journal of Political Economy* 85:191–205.

Fitoussi, Jean-Paul, and Edmund S. Pehlps. 1988. *The Slump in Europe: Reconstructing Open Economy Theory*. Oxford: Basil Blackwell.

Flanagan, Robert J., David W. Soskice, and Lloyd Ulman. 1983. *Unionism, Economic Stabilization, and Incomes Policies: European Experience*. Washington, DC: Brookings Institution.

Fleming, J. S. 1978. "The economic explanation of inflation." Pp. 13–36 in Fred Hirsch and John H. Goldthorpe (eds.), *The Political Economy of Inflation*. Cambridge, MA: Harvard University Press.

Franke, Walter, and Irwin Sobel. 1970. *The Shortage of Skilled and Technical Workers*. Lexington, Massachusetts: Heath Lexington.

Franklin, Raymond S. 1977. *American Capitalism: Two Visions*. New York: Random House.

Frey, Bruno, S., and W. W. Pommerehne. 1982. "How powerful are public bureaucrats as voters?" *Public Choice* 38:253–262.

Frey, Bruno, S., and Friedrich Schneider. 1978a. "An empirical study of politico-economic interaction in the U.S." *Review of Economics and Statistics* 60:174–183.

Frey, Bruno, S., and Friedrich Schneider. 1978b. "A politico-economic model of the United Kingdom." *Economic Journal* 88:243–253.

Frey, Bruno S., and Friedrich Schneider. 1979. "An econometric model with endogenous government sector." *Public Choice* 23:29–43.

Frey, Bruno S., and Friedrich Schneider. 1981. "Recent research on empirical politico-economic models." Pp. 11–30 in Douglas A. Hibbs and Heino Fassbender (eds.), *Contemporary Political Economy: Studies on the Interdependence of Politics and Economics*. Amsterdam: North Holland Publishing Company.

Friedland, Roger, and Jimy Sanders. 1985. "The public economy and growth in Western market economies." *American Sociological Review* 50:421–437.

Friedman, Milton. 1962. *Capitalism and Freedom*. Chicago: University of Chicago Press.

Friedman, Milton. 1968a. "The role of monetary policy." *American Economic Review* 58:1–17.

Friedman, Milton. 1968b. *Dollars and Deficits*. Englewood Cliffs, NJ: Prentice Hall.

Friedman, Milton. 1975. *Unemployment Versus Inflation? An Evaluation of the Phillips Curve*. London: Institute for Economic Affairs.

Friedman, Milton, and Anna Schwartz. 1963. *A Monetary History of the United States, 1867–1960*. Princeton, NJ: Princeton University Press.

Frisch, Helmut. 1982. "Macroeconomic adjustment in small open economies." Pp. 42–60 in Sven W. Arndt (ed.), *The Political Economy of Austria*. Washington, DC: American Enterprise Institute for Public Policy Research.

Frisch, Helmut. 1986. "The role of incomes policy in Austria." Pp. 199–204 in John Sargent (ed.), *Foreign Macroeconomic Experience: A Symposium*. Toronto: University of Toronto Press in cooperation with the Royal Commission on the Economic Union and Development Prospects for Canada.

Galbraith, John Kenneth. 1979. *The Affluent Society* (3rd ed.). Harmondsworth, Middlesex: Penguin.

Gale, Dennis E. 1984. *Neighbourhood Revitalization and the Postindustrial City: A Multinational Perspective*. Lexington, MA: Lexington Books.

Galenson, Walter, and Konosuke Odaka. 1976. "The Japanese labour market." Pp. 587–671 in Hugh Patrick and Henry Rosovsky (eds.), *Asia's New Giant— How the Japanese Economy Works*. Washington, DC: Brookings Institution.

Gamble, Andrew, and Paul Walton. 1976. *Capitalism in Crisis: Inflation and the State*. London: Macmillan.

Gardner, Richard. 1980. *Sterling-Dollar Diplomacy in Current Perspective*. New York: Columbia University Press.

Garrett, Geoffrey, and Peter Lange. 1986. "Performance in a hostile world: Economic growth in capitalist democracies, 1974–1982." *World Politics* 38:517–545.

Gennard, John. 1977. *Financing Strikers*. London: Macmillan.

Gennard, John, and Roger Lasko. 1975. "The individual and the strike." *British Journal of Industrial Relations* 13:346–370.

Gerlich, Peter, Edgar Grande, and Wolfgang C. Müller. 1988. "Corporatism in crisis: Stability and change of social partnership in Austria." *Political Studies* 36:209–223.

Gershuny, Jonathon. 1983. "Technical change and 'social limits'." Pp. 23–44 in Adrian Heath and Krishan Kumar (eds.), *Dilemmas of Liberal Democracies: Studies in Fred Hirsch's 'Social Limits to Growth'*. London: Tavistock.

Giavazzi, Francesco, and Luigi Spaventa. 1989. "Italy: The real effects of inflation and disinflation." *Economic Policy* 4:133–172.

Gilbert, Michael. 1981. "A sociological model of inflation." *Sociology* 15:185–209.

Gilbert, Michael. 1986. *Inflation and Social Conflict: A Sociology of Economic Life in Advanced Societies.* Brighton, Sussex: Wheatsheaf Books.

Gill, Louis. 1989. *Les Limites du Partenariat: Les Expériences Social-Démocrates de Gestion Économique en Suède, en Allemagne, en Autriche et en Norvège.* Montreal: Boréal.

Gill, Stephen. 1990. *American Hegemony and the Trilateral Commission.* Cambridge: Cambridge University Press.

Gilpin, Robert. 1981. *War and Change in World Politics.* Cambridge: Cambridge University Press.

Gilpin, Robert. 1987. *The Political Economy of International Relations.* Princeton, New Jersey: Princeton University Press.

Giugni, Gino. 1972. "The peace obligation." Pp. 127–174 in Benjamin Aaron and K. W. Wedderburn (eds.), *Industrial Conflict: A Comparative Legal Survey.* London: Longman.

Glenn, Norval D., Patricia A. Taylor, and Charles N. Weaver. 1977. "Age and job satisfaction among males and females: A multivariate, multisurvey study." *Journal of Applied Psychology* 62:189–193.

Glick, Mark. 1985. "Monopoly or competition in the U.S. economy?" *Review of Radical Political Economics* 17:121–127.

Glyn, Andrew, and John Harrison. 1980. *The British Economic Disaster.* London: Pluto Press.

Glyn, Andrew, and Bob Sutcliffe. 1972. *Capitalism in Crisis.* New York: Random House.

Godfrey, L. 1971. "The Phillips curve: Incomes policy and trade union effects." Pp. 9–124 in H. G. Johnson and A. R. Nobay (eds.), *The Current Inflation.* London: Macmillan.

Golden, D., and J. Poterba. 1980. "The price of popularity: The political business cycle reexamined." *American Journal of Political Science* 24:696–714.

Goldthorpe, John H. 1974. "Industrial relations in Great Britain: A critique of reformism." *Politics and Society* 4:419–452.

Goldthorpe, John H. 1978. "The current inflation: Towards a sociological account." Pp. 186–213 in Fred Hirsch and John H. Goldthorpe (eds.), *The Political Economy of Inflation.* Cambridge, MA: Harvard University Press.

Goldthorpe, John H. 1984. "The end of convergence: corporatist and dualist tendencies in modern western societies." Pp. 315–43 in John H. Goldthorpe (ed.), *Order and Conflict in Contemporary Capitalism: Studies in the Political Economy of Western European Nations.* Oxford: Clarendon Press.

Goldthorpe, John H. 1987a. "Problems of political economy after the postwar period." Pp. 363–407 in Charles S. Maier (ed.), *Changing Boundaries of the Political: Essays on the Evolving Balance Between the State and Society, Public and Private in Europe.* Cambridge: Cambridge University Press.

Goldthorpe, John H. (with Catriona Llewellyn and Clive Payne). 1987b. *Social Mobility and Class Structure in Modern Britain.* Oxford: Clarendon Press.

Goldthorpe, John H. 1990. "A response." Pp. 399–438 in Jon Clark, Celia Modgil, and Sohan Modgil (eds.), *John H. Goldthorpe: Consensus and Controversy.* London: The Falmer Press.

Goldthorpe, John H., and Philippa Bevan. 1977. "The study of social stratification in Great Britain: 1946–1976." *Social Science Information* 16:279–334.

Goldthorpe, John H., David Lockwood, Frank Bechhofer, and Jennifer Platt. 1968. *The Affluent Worker: Industrial Attitudes and Behaviour.* Cambridge: Cambridge University Press.

Goldthorpe, John H., David Lockwood, Frank Bechhofer, and Jennifer Platt. 1969. *The Affluent Worker in the Class Structure.* Cambridge: Cambridge University Press.

Gonick, Cy. 1983. "Boom and bust: State policy and the economics of restructuring." *Studies in Political Economy* No. 11:27–48.

Goodhart, C. A. E., and R. J. Bhansali. 1970. "Political economy." *Political Studies* 18:43–106.

Gordon, Robert J. 1978. *Macroeconomics.* Boston: MA: Little Brown and Company.

Gordon, Robert J. 1982. "Why U.S. wage and employment behaviour differs from that in Britain and Japan." *Economic Journal* 92:13–44.

Gough, Ian. 1975. "State expenditure in advanced capitalism." *New Left Review.* No. 92:53–92.

Gough, Ian. 1979. *The Political Economy of the Welfare State.* London: Macmillan.

Gourevitch, Peter, Andrew Martin, George Ross, Christopher Allan, Stephen Bornstein, and Andrei Markovits. 1984. *Unions and Economic Crisis: Britain, West Germany and Sweden.* London: George Allen & Unwin.

Gowa, Joanne. 1983. *Closing the Gold Window: Domestic Politics and the End of Bretton Woods.* Ithaca, NY: Cornell University Press.

Gramlich, Edward M. 1987. "Rethinking the role of the public sector." Pp. 250–286 in Barry P. Bosworth and Alice M. Rivlin (eds.), *The Swedish Economy.* Washington, DC: Brookings Institution.

Gramlich, Edward M., and D. L. Rubinfield. 1982. "Voting on public spending: Differences between public employees, transfer recipients, and private workers." *Journal of Policy Analysis and Management* 1:516–533.

Granatstein, J. L. 1986. *Canada 1957–1967: The Years of Uncertainty and Innovation.* Toronto: McClelland and Stewart.

Granovetter, Mark. 1974. *Getting a Job: A Study of Contacts and Careers.* Cambridge, MA: Harvard University Press.

Grant, Wyn. 1985. "Introduction." Pp. 1–31 in Wyn Grant (ed.), *The Political Economy of Corporatism.* London: Macmillan.

Green, Christoper. 1980. *Canadian Industrial Organization and Policy.* Toronto: McGraw Hill-Ryerson.

Green, Christopher. 1984. *Industrial Policy: The Fixities Hypothesis.* Toronto: Ontario Economic Council.

Grier, Kevin B. 1987. "Presidential elections and Federal Reserve policy: An empirical test." *Southern Economic Journal* 54:475–486.

Grier, Kevin B. 1989. "On the existence of a political monetary cycle." *American Journal of Political Science* 33:376–389.

Grubel, H. G., and M. A. Walker (eds.). 1978. *Unemployment Insurance: Global Evidence of its Effects on Unemployment.* Vancouver: Fraser Institute.

Guttman, William, and Patricia Meehan. 1975. *The Great German Inflation: Germany 1919–23.* Westmead, Hants. Saxon House.

Haberler, Gottfried. 1982. "Austria's economic development after the two world wars: A mirror picture of the world economy." Pp. 61–75 in Sven W. Arndt (ed.), *The Political Economy of Austria.* Washington, DC: American Enterprise Institute for Public Policy Research.

Hadley, Eleanor M. 1989. "The diffusion of Keynesian ideas in Japan." Pp. 291–310 in Peter A. Hall (ed.), *The Political Power of Economic Ideas: Keynesianism Across Nations.* Princeton, NJ: Princeton University Press.

Halberstam, David. 1972. *The Best and the Brightest.* New York: Random House.

Hall, Peter (ed.). 1989. *The Political Power of Economic Ideas: Keynesianism Across Nations.* Princeton, NJ: Princeton University Press.

Hall, John A. 1990. "Will the United States decline as did Britain?" Pp. 114–145 in J. M. Mann (ed.), *The Rise and Decline of the Nation State.* Oxford: Blackwell.

Hamilton, Richard F. 1967. *Affluence and the French Worker in the Fourth Republic.* Princeton, NJ: Princeton University Press.

Hamilton, Richard. 1975. *Restraining Myths: Critical Studies of U.S. Social Structure and Politics.* New York: Wiley.

Hamilton, Richard F., and James D. Wright. 1986. *The State of the Masses.* New York: Aldine.

Hammermesh, Daniel S. 1975. "The effect of government ownership on union wages." Pp. 227–255 in Daniel S. Hamermesh (ed.), *Labor in the Public and Nonprofit Sectors.* Princeton, NJ: Princeton University Press.

Hanson, Charles G. 1978. "Collective bargaining: The balance of market advantage." Pp. 23–29 in *Trade Unions: Public Goods or Public 'Bads'?* London: Institute of Economic Affairs.

Hardiman, Niamh. 1988. *Pay, Politics, and Economic Performance in Ireland 1970–1987.* Oxford: Clarendon Press.

Harrington, Michael. 1976. *The Twilight of Capitalism.* New York: Simon and Schuster.

Harrod, Roy F. 1951. *The Life of John Maynard Keynes.* London: Macmillan.

Harvey, David. 1982. *The Limits to Capital.* Oxford: Basil Blackwell.

Hayek, Friedrich A. 1960. *The Constitution of Liberty.* Chicago: Henry Regnery.

Heath, Adrian, and Krishan Kumar (eds.). 1983. *Dilemmas of Liberal Democracies: Studies in Fred Hirsch's 'Social Limits to Growth'.* London: Tavistock.

Heclo, Hugh, and Henrik Madsen. 1987. *Policy and Politics in Sweden: Principled Pragmatism.* Philadelphia: Temple University Press.

Helliwell, John F. 1988. "Comparative macroeconomics of stagflation." *Journal of Economic Literature* 26:1–28.

Helliwell, John F. 1990. "Globalization and the national economy." Pp. 121–138 in K. Newton, T. Scweitzer, and J.-P. Voyer (eds.), *Perspective 2000: Proceedings of a Conference Sponsored by the Economic Council of Canada, December 1988.* Ottawa: Ministry of Supply and Services.

Hempel, Carl G. 1959. "The logic of functional analysis." Pp. 271–307 in Llewellyn Gross (ed.), *Symposium on Sociological Theory.* New York: Harper & Row.

Hennart, Jean-Francois. 1983. "The political economy of comparative growth rates: The case of France." Pp. 176–202 in Dennis C. Mueller (ed.), *The Political Economy of Growth*. New Haven, CT: Yale University Press.

Henrekson, Magnus, and Johan A. Lybeck. 1988. "Explaining the growth of government in Sweden: A disequilibrium approach." *Public Choice* 57:213–232.

Henry, Frances, and Effi Ginsberg. 1985. *Who Gets the Work? A Test of Racial Discrimination in Employment*. Toronto: Urban Alliance on Race Relations and the Social Planning Council of Metropolitan Toronto.

Henry, S. G. B., and P. Ormerod. 1978. "Incomes policy and wage inflation: Empirical evidence for the UK, 1961–77." *National Institute Economic Review* No. 85:31–39.

Henry, S. G. B., M. C. Sawyer, and P. Smith. 1976. "Models of inflation in the United Kingdom." *National Institute Economic Review* No. 77:60–71.

Hepple, Bob. 1983. "Individual labour law." Pp. 393–418 in George Bain (ed.), *Industrial Relations in Britain*. Oxford: Blackwell.

Hibbs, Douglas A. 1976. *Economic interest and the Politics of Macroeconomic Policy*. Centre for International Studies, MIT Monograph Series, C/75-14.

Hibbs, Douglas A. 1977. "Political Parties and Macroeconomic Policy." *American Political Science Review* 71:1467–1487.

Hibbs, Douglas. 1978. "On the political economy of strike activity." *British Journal of Political Science* 8:153–175.

Hibbs, Douglas A. 1979. Letter. *American Political Science Review* 73:185–190.

Hibbs, Douglas A. 1982. "Public concern about inflation and unemployment in the United States: Trends, correlates and political implications." Pp. 211–232 in Robert E. Hall (ed.), *Inflation: Causes and Effects*. Chicago: University of Chicago Press.

Hibbs, Douglas A. 1987. *The American Political Economy: Macroeconomics and Electoral Politics*. Cambridge, MA: Harvard University Press.

Hibbs, Douglas A. 1991. "Market forces, trade union ideology and trends in Swedish wage dispersion." *Acta Sociologica* 34:89–102.

Hibbs, Douglas A., and Nicholas Vasilatos. 1981. "Macroeconomic performance and mass political support in the United States and Great Britain." Pp. 31–48 in Douglas A. Hibbs and Heino Fassbender (eds.), *Contemporary Political Economy: Studies on the Interdependence of Politics and Economics*. Amsterdam: North-Holland Publishing Company.

Hicks, Alexander. 1988. "Social democratic corporatism and economic growth." *Journal of Politics* 50:677–704.

Hicks, Alexander, Duane H. Swank, and Martin Ambuhl. 1989. "Welfare expansion revisited: Policy routines and their mediation by party, class and crisis, 1957–1982." *European Journal of Political Research* 17:401–430.

Hicks, John R. 1974. *The Crisis in Keynesian Economics*. Oxford: Blackwell.

Hines, A. G. 1964. "Trade unions and wage inflation in the United Kingdom, 1893–1961." *Review of Economic Studies* 31:221–252.

Hines, A. G. 1971. "The determinants of the rate of change of money wage rates and the effectiveness of incomes policy." Pp. 143–178 in H. G. Johnson and A. R. Nobay (eds.), *The Current Inflation*. London: Macmillan.

Hinton, James. 1973. *The First Shop Stewards Movement*. London: George Allen & Unwin.

Hirsch, Fred. 1976. *Social Limits to Growth*. Cambridge, MA: Harvard University Press.

Hirsch, Fred. 1978. "The Ideological Underlay of Inflation." Pp. 263–284 in Fred Hirsch and John H. Goldthorpe (eds.), *The Political Economy of Inflation*. Cambridge: MA: Harvard University Press.

Hirsch, Fred, and John H. Goldthorpe (eds.). 1978. *The Political Economy of Inflation*. Cambridge, MA: Harvard University Press.

Holloway, John, and Sol Picciotto (eds.). 1978. *State and Capital, A Marxist Debate*. London: Edward Arnold.

Holt, Charles C. 1970. "Job search, Phillips' wage relation, and union influence: Theory and evidence." Pp. 53–123 in Edmund S. Phelps (ed.). *Microeconomic Foundations of Employment and Inflation theory*. London: Macmillan.

Hondrich, Karl Otto. 1989. "Value changes in Western societies—The last thirty years." Pp. 131–158 in Burkhard Strümpel (ed.), *Industrial Societies after the Stagnation of the 1970s—Taking Stock from an Interdisciplinary Perspective*. Berlin: Walter de Gruyter.

Hoover, Kevin D. 1984. "Two types of monetarism." *Journal of Economic Literature* 22:58–76.

Horsman, George. 1988. *Inflation in the Twentieth Century: Evidence from Europe and North America*. Hemel Hempstead, Hertfordshire: Wheatsheaf.

Humphrey, Hubert H. 1976. *The Education of a Public Man: My Life and Politics*. Garden City, New Jersey: Doubleday.

Hunt, Ian. 1982. "The labors of Steedman on Marx." *Review of Radical Political Economics* 14:52-68.

Hunt, Ian. 1983. "An obituary or a new life for the tendency of the rate of profit to fall?" *Review of Radical Political Economics* 15:131–148.

Hyman, Richard, and Ian Brough. 1975. *Social Values and Industrial Relations: A Study of Fairness and Equality*. Oxford: Basil Blackwell.

Ingham, Geoffrey K. 1974. *Strikes and Industrial Conflict. Britain and Scandinavia*. London: Macmillan.

Ingham, Geoffrey. 1984. *Capitalism Divided? The City and Industry in British Social Development*. London: MacMillan.

Jackson, Dudley, H. A. Turner, and Frank Wilkinson. 1975. *Do Trade Unions Cause Inflation: Two Studies with a theoretical Introduction and Policy Conclusion* (2nd ed.). Cambridge: Cambridge University Press.

Jacobs, Brian D. 1986. *Black Politics and Urban Crisis*. Cambridge: Cambridge University Press.

Janis, Irving L. 1972. *Victims of Groupthink: A Psychological Study of Foreign Policy Decisions and Fiascoes*. Boston, MA: Houghton Mifflin.

Jessop, Bob, Otto Jacobi, and Hans Kastendieck. 1986. "Corporatist and liberal responses to the crisis of postwar capitalism." Pp. 1–13 in Otto Jaccob, Bob Jessop, Hans Kastendieck, and Marino Regini (eds.), *Economic Crisis, Trade Unions and the State*. London: Croom Helm.

Johnson, Harry G. 1970. "Monetary theory and monetary policy." *Euromoney*

2:16–20. Reprinted in Harry G. Johnson, *Further Essays in Monetary Economics*. Cambridge, MA: Harvard University Press.

Johnson, Harry G., and P. Mieszkowski. 1970. "The effects of unionization on the distribution of income: A general equilibrium approach." *Quarterly Journal of Economics* 84:539–561.

Johnston, J. 1972. "A model of wage determination under bilateral monopoly." *Economic Journal* 82:837–852.

Johnston, J., and M. C. Timbrell. 1973. "Empirical tests of a bargaining model of wage rate determination." *Manchester School* 41:141–167.

Jones, Aubrey. 1985. *Britain's Economy: The Roots of Stagnation*. Cambridge: Cambridge University Press.

Jonung, Lars. 1990. *The Political Economy of Price Controls: The Swedish Experience 1970–1987*. Aldershot: Avebury.

Jonung, Lars, and Eskil Wadensjö. 1987. "Rational, adaptive and learning behaviour of voters: Evidence from disaggregated popularity functions for Sweden." *Public Choice* 54:197–210.

Juris, Hervey A., and Myron Roomkin. 1980. "The shrinking perimeter: Unions and collective bargaining." Pp. 197–211 in Hervey A. Juris and Myron Roomkin (eds.), *The Shrinking Perimeter: Unions and Labour Relations in the Manufacturing Sector*. Lexington, MA: Lexington Books.

Kalleberg, Arne L., Michael Wallace, and Robert P. Althauser. 1981. "Economic segmentation, worker power, and income inequality." *American Journal of Sociology* 87:651–683.

Katzenstein, Peter J. 1984. *Corporatism and Change: Austria, Switzerland, and the Politics of Industry*. Ithaca: Cornell University Press.

Katzenstein, Peter J. 1985. "Small nations in an open international economy: The converging balance of state and society in Switzerland and Austria." Pp. 227–251 in Peter B. Evans, Dietrich Rueschemeyer, and Theda Skocpol (eds.), *Bringing the State Back In*. Cambridge, MA: Harvard University Press.

Katzenstein, Peter J. 1987. *Policy and Politics in West Germany: The Growth of a Semisovereign State*. Philadelphia: Temple University Press.

Kavanaugh, Dennis. 1990. "Ideology, sociology and the strategy of the British Labour Party." Pp. 171–183 in Jon Clark, Celia Modgil, and Sohan Modgil (eds.), *John H. Goldthorpe: Consensus and Controversy*. London: The Falmer Press.

Keegan, W., and R. Pennant-Rea. 1979. *Who Runs the Economy? Control and Influence in British Economic Policy*. London: Maurice Temple Smith.

Kellman, Mitchell, and Oded Izraeli. 1985. "The political business cycle: An international perspective." Pp. 71–83 in Paul M. Johnson and William R. Thompson (eds.), *Rhythms in Politics and Economics*. New York: Praeger.

Kelman, Steven. 1987. "'Public choice' and public spirit." *The Public Interest* No. 87:80–94.

Kendix, Michael, and Mancur Olson. 1990. "Changing unemployment rates in Europe and the USA: Institutional structure and regional variation." Pp. 40–67 in Renato Brunetta and Carlo Dell'Aringa (eds.), *Labour Relations and Economic Performance*. London: Macmillan.

Kenen, Peter B., and Raymond Lubitz. 1971. *International Economics* (3rd. ed.). Englewood Cliffs, New Jersey: Prentice-Hall.

Kennedy, Paul. 1988. *The Rise and Fall of the Great Powers: Economic Change and Military Conflict from 1500 to 2000*. London: Unwin Hyman.

Keohane, Robert O. 1980. "The theory of hegemonic stability and changes in international economic regimes, 1967–1977." Pp. 131–162 in Ole Holsti et al., *Change in the International System*. Boulder: Westview Press.

Keohane, Robert O. 1984a. "The world political economy and the crisis of embedded liberalism." Pp. 15–38 in John H. Goldthorpe (ed.), *Order and Conflict in Contemporary Capitalism: Studies in the Political Economy of Western European Nations*. Oxford: Clarendon Press.

Keohane, Robert O. 1984b. *After Hegemony: Cooperation and Discord in the World Political Economy*. Princeton, NJ: Princeton University Press.

Keohane, Robert O. 1985. "The international politics of inflation." Pp. 78–104 in Leon Lindberg and Charles Maier (eds.), *The Politics of Inflation and Economic Stagnation: Theoretical Approaches and Case Studies*. Washington, DC: Brookings Institution.

Kiewit, D. Roderick. 1983. *Macroeconomics and Micropolitics: The Electoral Effects of Economic Issues*. Chicago: University of Chicago Press.

Kinder, Donald R., and D. Roderick Kiewit. 1979. "Economic discontent and political behaviour: The role of personal grievances and collective economic judgements in congressional voting." *American Journal of Political Science* 23:475–517.

Kindleberger, Charles P. 1973. *The World in Depression, 1929–1939*. Berkeley: University of California Press.

Kindleberger, Charles P. 1978. *Manias, Panics and Crashes*. Cambridge: Harvard University Press.

Kindleberger, Charles P. 1983. "On the rise and decline of nations." *International Studies Quarterly* 27:5–10.

Klein, Rudolf. 1985. "Public expenditure in an inflationary world." Pp. 196–223 in Leon N. Lindberg and Charles S. Maier (eds.), *The Politics of Inflation and Economic Stagnation: Theoretical Approaches and International Case Studies*. Washington, DC: Brookings Institution.

Kloten, Norbert, Karl-Heinz Ketterer, and Rainer Vollmer. 1985. "West Germany's stabilization performance." Pp. 353–402 in Leon N. Lindberg and Charles S. Maier (eds.), *The Politics of Inflation and Economic Stagnation: Theoretical Approaches and International Case Studies*. Washington, DC: Brookings Institution.

Knott, Jack H. 1981. *Managing the German Economy: Budgetary Politics in a Federal State*. Lexington, MA: D. C. Heath.

Koike, Kazuo. 1987. "Human resource development and labor-management relations." Pp. 289–330 in Kozo Yamamura and Yasukichi Yasuba (eds.), *The Political Economy of Japan*, Vol. 1. Stanford, CA: Stanford University Press.

Korpi, Walter. 1978. *The Working Class in Welfare Capitalism: Work, Unions and Politics in Sweden*. London: Routledge & Kegan Paul.

Korpi, Walter. 1983. *The Democratic Class Struggle*. London: Routledge & Kegan Paul.

Korpi, Walter. 1990. "Political and economic explanations for unemployment: A cross-national and long-term analysis." *British Journal of Political Science* 21:315–348.

Kosters, Marvin H. 1982. "Commentary." Pp. 124–129 in Sven W. Arndt (ed.), *The Political Economy of Austria*. Washington, DC: American Enterprise Institute for Public Policy Research.

Kramer, G. 1971. "Short run fluctuations in U.S. voting behaviour, 1896–1964." *American Political Science Review* 65:131–143.

Kudrle, Robert T., and Davis B. Bobrow. 1990. "The G-7 after hegemony: Compatibility, cooperation, and conflict." Pp. 147–168 in David P. Rapkin (ed.), *World Leadership and Hegemony*. Boulder, CO: Lynne Reinner Publishers.

Lacroix, Robert. 1987. *Les Grèves au Canada: Causes et Conséquences*. Montreal: Les Presses de l'Université de Montréal.

Lafay, Jean-Dominique. 1985. "Political change and stability of the popularity function: The French general election of 1981." Pp. 78–97 in Heinz Eulau and Michael S. Lewis-Beck (eds.), *Economic Conditions and Electoral Outcomes: The United States and Western Europe*. New York: Agathon Press.

Laidler, David. 1981a. "Monetarism: An interpretation and an assessment." *Economic Journal* 91:1–28.

Laidler, David. 1981b. "Inflation and unemployment in an open economy: A monetarist view." *Canadian Public Policy* 7 (supplement):179–188.

Laidler, David, and Michael Parkin. 1975. "Inflation: A survey." *Economic Journal* 85:741–809.

Landes, David S. 1972. *The Unbound Prometheus: Technological Change and Industrial Development in Western Europe from 1750 to the Present*. Cambridge: Cambridge University Press.

Lane, Jan-Erik, and Svante Ersson. 1986. "Political institutions, public policy and economic growth." *Scandinavian Journal of Political Studies* 9:19–34.

Laney, L., and T. Willett. 1983. "Presidential politics, budget deficits and monetary policy in the United States: 1960–1976." *Public Choice* 40:53–69.

Lange, Peter. 1984. "Unions, workers, and wage regulation: The rational bases of consent." Pp. 98–123 in John H. Goldthorpe (ed.), *Order and Conflict in Contemporary Capitalism: Studies in the Political Economy of Western European Nations*. Oxford: Clarendon Press.

Lange, Peter, and Geoffrey Garrett. 1985. "The politics of growth: Strategic interaction and economic performance in the advanced industrial democracies, 1974–1980." *Journal of Politics* 47:792–827.

Lash, Scott, and John Urry. 1987. *The End of Organized Capitalism*. Madison: University of Wisconsin Press.

Lauman, Edward O., and James S. House. 1973. "Living-room styles and social attributes: The patterning of material artifacts in a modern urban community." Pp. 430–440 in H. H. Kassarjian and T. S. Robertson (eds.), *Perspectives in Consumer Behavior*. Glenview, IL: Scott, Foresman.

Lawrence, Robert Z., and Barry P. Bosworth. 1987. "Adjusting to slower economic growth: The External Sector." Pp. 55–88 in Barry P. Bosworth and Alice M. Rivlin (eds.), *The Swedish Economy*. Washington, DC: Brookings Institution.

Lawrence, Robert Z., and Charles L. Schultze. 1987. *Barriers to Growth: A Transatlantic View*. Washington, DC: Brookings Institution.

Lebaube, Alain. 1986. "Le nombre de chômeurs japonais n'est pas aussi faible que l'indiquent les chiffres officiels." *Le Devoir* 26 August:9–10.

Lebowitz, Michael A. 1982. "The general and the specific in Marx's theory of crisis." *Studies in Political Economy* No. 7:5–26.

Lehmbruch, Gerhard. 1979. "Consociational democracy, class conflict and the new corporatism." Pp. 53–62 in Philippe C. Schmitter and Gerhard Lehmbruch (eds.), *Trends Towards Corporatist Intermediation*. Beverly Hills, CA: Sage Publications.

Lehmbruch, Gerhard. 1982. "Introduction: Neocorporatism in comparative perspective." Pp. 1–28 in Gerhard Lehmbruch and Manfred Schmitter (eds.), *Patterns of Corporatist Policy-Making*. Beverly Hills, CA: Sage.

Lehmbruch, Gerhard. 1983. "Neokorporatismus im Westeuropa: Hauptprobleme in internationalen vergleich." In Klaus Armingeon et al. (eds.), *Neokorporatistische Politik in Westeuropa*. Universität Konstanz, Diskussionsbeiträge nv1.

Lehmbruch, Gerhard. 1984. "Concertation and the structure of corporatist networks." Pp. 60–80 in John H. Goldthorpe (ed.), *Order and Conflict in Contemporary Capitalism: Studies in the Political Economy of Western European Nations*. Oxford: Clarendon Press.

Leijonhufvud, Axel. 1973. "Life among the econ." *Western Economic Journal* 11:327–337.

Lewis, Alan. 1988. "Technology and management: A study of the diffusion of numerical control machinery in central Canada." Unpublished Ph.D. thesis. Montreal: McGill University.

Lewis, Roy. 1983. "Collective labour law." Pp. 361–392 in George Bain (ed.), *Industrial Relations in Britain*. Oxford: Blackwell.

Lindbeck, Assar. 1974. *Swedish Economic Policy*. Berkeley, CA: University of California Press.

Lindberg, Leon. 1982. "Inflation, recession, and the political process: Challenges to Theory and Practice." Pp. 1–43 in Richard Medley (ed.), *The Politics of Inflation: A Comparative Analysis*. New York: Pergamon Press.

Lindberg, Leon N. 1985. "Models of the inflation-disinflation process." Pp. 25–50 in Leon N. Lindberg and Charles S. Maier (eds.), *The Politics of Inflation and Economic Stagnation: Theoretical Approaches and International Case Studies*. Washington, DC: Brookings Institution.

Lipietz, Alain. 1985. *The Enchanted World: Inflation, Credit and the World Crisis*. London: Verso.

Lipsey, Richard D. 1960. "The relation between unemployment and the rate of change of money wage rates in the United Kingdom, 1862–1957: A further analysis." *Economica* 27:1–31.

Lipsey, Richard. 1976. "Wage-price controls: How to do a lot of harm by trying to do a little good." *Canadian Public Policy* 3:1–13.

Lipsey, Richard, and J. M. Parkin. 1970. "Incomes policy: A reappraisal." *Economica* (N.S.) 37:115–138.

Littler, Craig R. 1982. *The Development of the Labour Process in Capitalist Societies: A Comparative Study of Transformation of Work Organization in Britain, Japan and the USA*. London: Heinemann.

Llewellyn, David T. 1982. "Introduction." Pp. 1–36 in David T. Llewellyn et al. (eds.), *The Framework of UK Monetary Policy*. London: Heinemann Educational Books.

Long, John B., and Charles I. Plosser. 1983. "Real business cycles." *Journal of Political Economy* 91:39–69.

Lucas, Robert E. 1980. "Rules, discretion, and the role of the economic advisor." Pp. 199–210 in Stanley Fisher (ed.), *Rational Expectations and Economic Policy.* Chicago: University of Chicago Press.

Lucas, Robert E. 1981. "Tobin and monetarism: A review article." *Journal of Economic Literature* 19:558–567.

Lundberg, Erik. 1985. "The rise and fall of the Swedish model." *Journal of Economic Literature* 23:1–36.

Macmillan, Harold. 1938. *The Middle Way: A Study of the Problem of Economic and Social Progress in a Free Society.* London: Macmillan.

Maddison, Angus. 1982. *Phases of Capitalist Development.* Oxford: Oxford University Press.

Maddock, Rodney, and Michael Carter. 1982. "A child's guide to rational expectations." *Journal of Economic Literature* 20:39–51.

Maier, Charles S. 1975. *Recasting Bourgeois Europe: Stabilization in France, Germany, and Italy in the Decade after World War I.* Princeton, NJ: Princeton University Press.

Maier, Charles S. 1978. "The politics of inflation in the twentieth century." Pp. 37–72 in Fred Hirsch and John F. Goldthorpe (eds.), *The Political Economy of Inflation.* Cambridge, MA: Harvard University Press.

Maier, Charles S. 1984. "Preconditions for corporatism." Pp. 39–59 in John H. Goldthorpe (ed.), *Order and Conflict in Contemporary Capitalism: Studies in the Political Economy of Western European Nations.* Oxford: Clarendon Press.

Maier, Charles. 1985. "Inflation and stagnation as politics and history." Pp. 3–24 in Leon N. Lindberg and Charles S. Maier (eds.), *The Politics of Inflation and Economic Stagnation: theoretical Approaches and International Case Studies.* Washington, DC: Brookings Institution.

Maier, Charles S. 1987. *In Search of Stability: Explorations in Historical Political Economy.* New York: Cambridge University Press.

Maier, Charles S., and Leon N. Lindberg. 1985. "Alternatives and future crises." Pp. 567–588 in Leon N. Lindberg and Charles S. Maier (eds.), *The Politics of Inflation and Economic Stagnation: Theoretical Approaches and International Case Studies.* Washington, DC: Brookings Institution.

Maitland, Ian. 1983. *The Causes of Industrial Disorder: A Comparison of a British and a German Factory.* London: Routledge & Kegan Paul.

Mandel, Ernest. 1975. *Late Capitalism.* London: New Left Books.

Mandel, Ernest. 1978. *The Second Slump: A Marxist Analysis of Recession in the Seventies.* London: New Left Books.

Mankiw, N. Gregory. 1989. "Real business cycles: A new Keynesian perspective." *Journal of Economic Perspectives* 3:79–90.

Mankiw, N. Gregory. 1990. "A quick refresher course in macroeconomics." *Journal of Economic Literature* 28:1645–1660.

Marcuse, Herbert. 1964. *One Dimensional Man: Studies in the Ideology of Advanced Industrial Society.* Boston: Beacon Press.

Marin, Bend. 1985. "Austria—The paradigmatic case of liberal corporatism." Pp.

89–125 in Wyn Grant (ed.), *The Political Economy of Corporatism*. New York: St. Martin's Press.

Markovits, Andrei S., and Christopher S. Allen. 1984. "Trade unions and the economic crisis: The West German case." Pp. 91–188 in Peter Gourevitch et al. (eds.), *Unions and Economic Crisis: Britain, West Germany and Sweden*. London: George Allen & Unwin.

Marks, Gary. 1986. "Neocorporatism and incomes policy in Western Europe and North America." *Comparative Politics* 18:253–277.

Marmor, Theodore R., and Jerry L. Mashaw (eds.). 1988. *Social Security: Beyond the Rhetoric of Crisis*. Princeton, NJ: Princeton University Press.

Marshall, Gordon, Carolyn Vogler, David Rose, and Howard Newby. 1987. "Distributional struggle and moral order in a market society." *Sociology* 21:55–73.

Marshall, Gordon, Howard Newby, David Rose, and Carolyn Vogler. 1988. *Social Class in Modern Britain*. London: Hutchinson.

Martin, Andrew. 1984. "Trade unions in Sweden: Strategic responses to change and crisis." Pp. 191–359 in Peter Gourevitch, Andrew Martin, George Ross, Christopher Allen, Stephan Bornstein, and Andrei Markovits (eds.), *Unions and Economic Crisis: Britain, West Germany and Sweden*. London: George Allen & Unwin.

Martin, Andrew. 1985. "Wages, profits, and investment in Sweden." Pp. 403–466 in Leon N. Lindberg and Charles S. Maier (eds.), *The Politics of Inflation and Economic Stagnation: Theoretical Approaches and International Case Studies*. Washington, DC: Brookings Institution.

Martin, Jack K., and Constance Shehan. 1989. "Education and job satisfaction: The influence of gender, wage-earning status, and job values." *Work and Occupations* 16:184–199.

Masters, Marick F., and John D. Robertson. 1988. "Class compromises in industrial democracies." *American Political Science Review* 82:1183–1201.

Mattick, Paul. 1969. *Marx and Keynes: The Limits of the Mixed Economy*. Boston, MA: Porter Sargent.

Mattick, Paul. 1978. *Economics, Politics and the Age of Inflation*. Armonk, NY: M. E. Sharpe.

Maynard, Geoffrey, and W. van Ryckeghem. 1976. *A World of Inflation*. London: B. T. Batsford.

McCallum, Bennet. 1978. "The political business cycle: An empirical test." *Southern Economic Journal* 45:504–515.

McCallum, John. 1983. "Inflation and social consensus in the seventies." *Economic Journal* 93:784–805.

McCallum, John. 1986. "Two cheers for the AIB." *Canadian Public Policy* 12:133–147.

McCallum, John. 1990. "Incomes policies in a North American setting." Pp. 215–228 in Renato Brunetta and Carlo Dell'Aringa (eds.), *Labour Relations and Economic Performance*. London: Macmillan.

McKean, Margaret A. 1989. "Equality." Pp. 201–224 in Takeshidi Ishida and Ellis S. Krauss (eds.), *Democracy in Japan*. Pittsburgh, PA: University of Pittsburgh Press.

McKendrick, Neil, John Brewer, and J. H. Plumb. 1982. *The Birth of a Consumer*

Society: The Commercialization of Eighteenth-Century England. London: Europa Publications.

Meade, James E. 1982. *Stagflation. Volume 1, Wage-Fixing*. London: George Allen & Unwin.

Means, Gardener. 1962. *Pricing Power and the Public Interest: A Study Based on Steel*. New York: Harper.

Meltz, Noah M. 1982. *Economic Analysis of Labour Shortages: The Case of Tool and Die Makers in Ontario*. Toronto: Ontario Economic Council.

Merton, Robert K. 1949. *Social Theory and Social Structure: Toward the Codification of Social Research*. Illinois: The Free Press of Glencoe.

Metcalf David. 1990. "Trade unions and economic performance: The British evidence." Pp. 283–303 in Renato Brunetta and Carlo Dell'Aringa (eds.), *Labour Relations and Economic Performance*. London: Macmillan.

Michels, Robert. 1962. *Political Parties: A Sociological Study of Oligarchical Tendencies of Modern Democracy*. New York: Free Press.

Miliband, Ralph. 1969. *The State in Capitalist Society: The Analysis of the Western System of Power*. London: Weidenfeld and Nicholson.

Miller, Arthur H., and Ola Listhaug. 1985. "Economic effects on the vote in Norway." Pp. 125–143 in Heinz Eulau and Michael S. Lewis-Beck (eds.), *Economic Conditions and Electoral Outcomes: The United States and Western Europe*. New York: Agathon Press.

Milner, Henry. 1989. *Sweden: Social Democracy in Practice*. Oxford: Oxford University Press.

Minford, Patrick. 1983. *Unemployment: Cause and Cure*. Oxford: Martin Robertson.

Minkin, Lewis. 1986. "Against the tide: Trade unions, political communication and the 1983 general election." Pp. 190–206 in Ivor Crewe and Martin Harrop (eds.), *Political Communications: The General Election of 1983*. Cambridge: Cambridge University Press.

Mintz, Beth, and Michael Schwartz. 1985. *The Power Structure of American Business*. Chicago: University of Chicago Press.

Mintz, Beth, and Michael Schwartz. 1990. "Capital flows and the process of financial hegemony." Pp. 203–226 in Sharon Zukin and Paul DiMaggio (eds.), *The Structure of Capital: The Social Organization of the Economy*. Cambridge: Cambridge University Press.

Mishan, E. J. 1982. *Cost-Benefit Analysis: An Informal Introduction* (3rd ed.). London: George Allen & Unwin.

Mitton, Roger, Peter Willmott, and Phyllis Willmott. 1983. *Unemployment, Poverty and Social Policy in Europe: A Comparative Study in Britain, France and Germany*. London: Bedford Square Press.

Monroe, K. 1979. "Econometric analyses of electoral behaviour: A critical review." *Political Behaviour* 1:137–173.

Moore, Barrington. 1978. *Injustice: The Social Origins of Obedience and Revolt*. White Plains, New York: M. E. Sharpe.

Moore, Basil J. 1979. "The endogenous money stock." *Journal of Post Keynesian Economics* 2:49–70.

Morley, Samuel A. 1979. *Inflation and Unemployment* (2nd ed.). Hinsdale, IL: The Dryden Press.

Morris, Jacob. 1973. "The crisis of inflation." *Monthly Review* 25:1–22.

Mueckenberger, Ulrich. 1986. "Labour law and industrial relations." Pp. 236–257 in Otto Jacobi, Bob Jessop, Hans Kastendiek, and Marino Regini (eds.), *Economic Crisis, Trade Unions and the State*. London: Croom Helm.

Mueller, Dennis C. 1986. "Rational egoism versus adaptive egoism as fundamental postulate for a descriptive theory of human behaviour." *Public Choice* 51:3–23.

Muir, J. Douglas. 1975. "Highlights in the development of the legal system." Pp. 97–108 in S. M. A. Hameed (ed.), *Canadian Industrial Relations*. Toronto: Butterworth.

Murray, Charles A. 1984. *Losing Ground: American Social Policy, 1950–1980*. New York: Basic Books.

Murrell, Peter. 1983. "The comparative structure of the growth of the West German and British manufacturing industries." Pp. 109–131 in Denis C. Mueller (ed.), *The Political Economy of Growth*. New Haven, CT: Yale University Press.

Muszynski, L., and D. A. Wolfe. 1989. "New technology and training: Lessons from abroad." *Canadian Public Policy* 15:245–264.

Myles, John. 1988. "Decline or impasse? The current state of the welfare state." *Studies in Political Economy* 26:73–108.

Nakamura, Takafusa. 1981. *The Postwar Japanese Economy: Its Development and Structure*. Tokyo: University of Tokyo Press.

Newton, Scott, and Dilwyn Porter. 1988. *Modernization Frustrated: The Politics of Industrial Decline in Great Britain since 1900*. London: Unwin Hyman.

Niskanen, William A. 1971. *Bureaucracy and Representative Government*. Chicago: Aldine.

Noguchi, Yukio. 1987. "Public finance." Pp. 186–222 in Kozo Yamamura and Yasukichi Yasuba (eds.), *The Political Economy of Japan* (Vol. 1). Stanford, CA: Stanford University Press.

Nordhaus, William D. 1975. "The political business cycle." *Review of Economic Studies* 42:169–190.

Nordhaus, William D. 1989. "Alternative approaches to the political business cycle." *Brookings Papers on Economic Activity* No. 2:1–65.

Norman, Frank. 1977. *The Fake's Progress: Being the Cautionary History of the Master Painter and Simulator Mr. Tom Keating*. London: Hutchinson.

Norpoth, Helmut. 1985. "Economics, politics, and the cycle of presidential popularity." Pp. 167–186 in Heinz Eulau and Michael S. Lewis-Beck (eds.), *Economic Conditions and Electoral Outcomes: The United States and Western Europe*. New York: Agathon Press.

Norpoth, Helmut. 1987. "Guns and butter and government popularity in Britain." *American Political Science Review* 81:949–959.

North, Douglass C. 1981. *Structure and Change in Economic History*. New York: Norton.

O'Connor, James. 1973. *The Fiscal Crisis of the State*. New York: St. Martin's Press.

288   References

O'Connor, James. 1984. *Accumulation Crisis*. Oxford: Blackwell.
O'Connor, James. 1987. *The Meaning of Crisis: A Theoretical Introduction*. London: Basil Blackwell.
Oberschall, Anthony, and Eric M. Leifer. 1986. "Efficiency and social institutions: Uses and misuses of economic reasoning in sociology." *Annual Review of Sociology* 12:233–253.
Odell, John S. 1982. *U.S. International Monetary Policy: Markets, Power, and Ideas as Sources of Change*. Princeton, NJ: Princeton University Press.
Okun, Arthur M. 1983. *Economics for Policymaking: Selected Essays of Arthur Okun* (edited by Joseph A. Pechman). Cambridge, MA: MIT Press.
Olson, Mancur. 1965. *The Logic of Collective Goods: Public Goods and the Theory of Groups*. New York: Schocken.
Olson, Mancur. 1979. "An evolutionary approach to inflation." Pp. 137–161 in James H. Gapinski and Charles E. Rockwood (eds.), *Essays in Post-Keynesian Inflation*. Cambridge, MA: Ballinger Publishing Company.
Olson, Mancur. 1982. *The Rise and Decline of Nations: Economic Growth, Stagflation and Social Rigidities*. New Haven, CT: Yale University Press.
Olson, Mancur. 1983a. "The political economy of comparative growth rates." Pp. 7–52 in Dennis C. Mueller (ed.), *The Political Economy of Growth*. New Haven, CT: Yale University Press.
Olson, Mancur. 1983b. "Towards a mature social science." *International Studies Quarterly* 27:29–37.
Olson, Mancur. 1984. "Beyond Keynesianism and Monetarism." *Economic Inquiry* 22:297–322.
Olson, Mancur, and Richard Zeckhauser. 1966. "An economic theory of alliances." *Review of Economics and Statistics* 48:266–279.
Ouchi, William. 1984. *The M-Form Society: How American Teamwork Can Recapture the Competitive Edge*. Reading, MA: Addison-Wesley.
Pal, Leslie A. 1988. *State, Class and Bureaucracy: Canadian Unemployment Insurance and Public Policy*. Kingston and Montreal: McGill-Queen's University Press.
Paldam, M. 1979. "Is there an election cycle? A comparative study of national accounts." *Scandinavian Journal of Economics* 81:323–342.
Paldam, M. 1981. "A preliminary survey of the European theories and findings on vote and popularity functions." *Journal of Political Research* 9:181–200.
Paldam, Martin, and Peder J. Pedersen. 1984. "The large pattern of industrial conflict—A comparative study of 18 countries, 1919–1979." *International Journal of Social Economics* 11:3–29.
Panitch, Leo. 1976. *Social Democracy and Industrial Militancy: The Labour Party, the Trade Unions and Incomes Policy, 1946–1974*. Cambridge: Cambridge University Press.
Panitch, Leo. 1977a. "The development of corporatism in liberal democracies." *Comparative Political Studies* 10:61–90.
Panitch, Leo. 1977b. "Profits and politics: Labour and the crisis of British corporatism." *Politics and Society* 7:477–508.
Panitch, Leo. 1980. "Recent theorizations of corporatism: Reflections on a growth industry." *British Journal of Sociology* 31:159–187.

Panitch, Leo. 1988. "Corporatism: A growth industry reaches the monopoly stage." *Canadian Journal of Political Science* 21:813–822.

Panitch, Leo, and Donald Swartz. 1988. *The Assault on Trade Union Freedoms.* Toronto: Garamond.

Parkin, Frank. 1979. *Marxism and Class Theory: A Bourgeois Critique.* New York: Columbia University Press.

Parkin, J. M., M. T. Sumner, and R. A. Jones. 1972. "A survey of the econometric evidence on effects of incomes policy on the rate of inflation." Pp. 1–29 in J. M. Parkin and M. T. Sumner (eds.), *Incomes Policy and Inflation.* Manchester: Manchester University Press.

Parkin, Michael. 1975. "The politics of inflation." *Government and Opposition* 10:189–202.

Parri, Leonardo. 1987. "Neo-corporatist arrangements, 'Konkordanz' and direct democracy: The Swiss experience." Pp. 70–94 in Ilja Scholten (ed.), *Political Stability and Neo-Corporatism: Corporatist Integration and Societal Cleavages in Western Europe.* London: Sage Publications.

Parsons, Talcott, and Neil J. Smelser. 1956. *Economy and Society: A Study in the Integration of Economic and Social Theory.* New York: Free Press.

Payne, James L. 1979. "Inflation, unemployment, and left-wing political parties: A reanalysis." *American Political Science Review* 73:181–185.

Payne, James L. 1991. "Elections and government spending." *Public Choice* 70:71–82.

Peeler, David P. 1987. *Hope Among Us Yet: Social Criticism and Social Solace in Depression America.* Athens, GA: University of Georgia Press.

Pekkarinen, Jukka. 1989. "Keynesianism and the Scandinavian models of economic policy." Pp. 311–346 in Peter A. Hall (ed.), *The Political Power of Economic Ideas: Keynesianism Across Nations.* Princeton, NJ: Princeton University Press.

Pempel, T. J., and K. Tsunekawa. 1979. "Corporatism without labor? The Japanese anomaly." Pp. 231–270 in P. C. Schmitter and D. Lehmbruch (eds.), *Trends Towards Corporatist Intermediation.* Beverly Hills, CA: Sage.

Pencavel, John H. 1970. "An investigation into industrial strike activity in Britain." *Economica* 37:239–256.

Penn, Roger. 1982. "Skilled manual workers in the labour process, 1856–1964." Pp. 90–108 in Stephen Wood (ed.), *The Degradation of Work? Skill, Deskilling and the Labour Process.* London: Hutchinson.

Perrucci, Carolyn, Robert Perrucci, Dena B. Targ, and Harry R. Targ. 1988. *Plant Closings: International Context and Social Class.* New York: Aldine De Gruyter.

Phelps, Edmund S. 1972a. "The statistical theory of racism and sexism." *American Economic Review* 64:59–61.

Phelps, Edmund S. 1972b. *Inflation Policy and Unemployment Theory.* New York: Norton.

Phelps, Edmund S., and John B. Taylor. 1977. "Stabilizing powers of monetary policy under rational expectations." *Journal of Political Economy* 85:163–190.

Phelps Brown, H. 1975. "A non monetarist view of the pay explosion." *Three Banks Review* 105:3–24.

Phelps Brown, Henry. 1977. *The Inequality of Pay.* Berkeley, CA: University of California Press.

Phelps Brown, Henry. 1983. *The Origins of Trade Union Power.* Oxford: Clarendon Press.

Phelps Brown, Henry, and Sheila V. Hopkins. 1981. *A Perspective of Wages and Prices.* London: Methuen.

Piven, Francis Fox, and Richard A. Cloward. 1971. *Regulating the Poor.* New York: Vintage Books.

Plosser, Charles I. 1989. "Understanding real business cycles." *Journal of Economic Perspectives* 3:51–77.

Polanyi, Karl. 1957. *The Great Transformation: The Political and Economic Origins of our Time.* Boston: Beacon Press.

Posner, Richard A. 1973. "Economic justice and the economist." *The Public Interest* 33:109–19.

Pothier, John T. 1982. "The political causes and effects of Argentine inflation." Pp. 186–224 in Richard Medley (ed.), *The Politics of Inflation: A Comparative Analysis.* New York: Pergamon Press.

Poulantzas, Nicos. 1975. *Political Power and Social Classes.* London: New Left Books.

Prescott, Edward C. 1986. "Theory ahead of business-cycle measurement." Pp. 11–44 in Karl Brunner and Allan H. Meltzer (eds.), *Real Business Cycles, Real Exchange Rates and Actual Policies.* Amsterdam: North-Holland.

Pryor, Frederick L. 1983. "A quasi-test of Olson's hypotheses." Pp. 90–108 in Dennis C. Mueller (ed.), *The Political Economy of Growth.* New Haven, CT: Yale University Press.

Pryor, Frederick L. 1988. "Corporatism as an economic system: A review essay." *Journal of Comparative Economics* 12:317–344.

Przeworski, Adam, and Michael Wallerstein. 1988. "Structural dependence of the state on capital." *American Political Science Review* 82:11–29.

Purdy, D. L., and G. Zis. 1973. "Trade unions and wage inflation in the U.K.: A reappraisal." Pp. 294–327 in J. M. Parkin (ed.), *Essays in Modern Economics.* London: Longmans.

Purvis, Douglas. 1979. "Wage responsiveness and the insulation properties of a flexible exchange rate." Pp. 225–248 in Assar Lindbeck (ed.), *Inflation and Unemployment in Open Economies.* Amsterdam: North Holland Publishing Company.

Purvis, Douglas. 1980. "Monetarism: A review." *Canadian Journal of Economics* 13:96–122.

Quinn, Robert P., Graham L. Staines, and Margaret R. McCullough. 1974. *Job Satisfaction: Is there a Trend?* U.S. Department of Labor Manpower Research Monograph No. 30, Washington, DC: U.S. Government Printing Office.

Rae, John B. 1971. *The Road and Car in American Life.* Cambridge, MA: MIT Press.

Reder, Melvin W. 1948. "The theoretical problems of a national wage-price policy." *Canadian Journal of Economics and Political Science* 14;46–61.

Reder, Melvin. 1982. "Chicago economics: Permanence and change." *Journal of Economic Literature* 20:1–38.

Reid, Ian. 1979. *Fiction and the Great Depression: Australia and New Zealand, 1930–1950*. Melbourne: E. Arnold.

Renshaw, Geoffrey. 1986. *Adjustment and Economic Performance in Industrialized Countries: A Synthesis*. Geneva: International Labour Office.

Rinehart, James W. 1978. "Contradictions of work-related attitudes and behaviour: An interpretation." *Canadian Review of Sociology and Anthropology* 13:1–15.

Rinehart, James W. 1987. *The Tyranny of Work* (2nd ed.). Toronto: Longmans Canada.

Ringen, Stein. 1987. *The Possibility of Politics: A Study in the Political Economy of the Welfare State*. Oxford Clarendon.

Robinson, Joan. 1933. *The Economics of Imperfect Competition*. London: Macmillan.

Roche, William. 1990. "Social Class, social integration and industrial relations." Pp. 191–212 in Jon Clark, Celia Modgil, and Sohan Modgil (eds.), *John H. Goldthorpe: Consensus and Controversy*. London: The Falmer Press.

Rosenbluth, Frances McCall. 1989. *Financial Politics in Contemporary Japan*. Ithaca, NY: Cornell University Press.

Ross, Arthur M. 1948. *Trade Union Wage Policy*. Berkeley, CA: University of California Press.

Roubini, Nouriel, and Jeffrey Sachs. 1989. "Government spending and budget deficits in the industrial countries." *Economic Policy* 4:100–132.

Rowthorn, R. E. 1977. "Conflict, inflation and money." *Cambridge Journal of Economics* 1:215–239.

Ruggie, John Gerard. 1982. "International regimes, transactions, and change: Embedded liberalism in the postwar economic order." *International Organization* 36:397–415.

Runciman, W. G. 1966. *Relative Deprivation and Social Justice: A Study of Attitudes to Social Equality in Twentieth Century England*. London: Routledge.

Sachs, Jeffrey D. 1979. "Wages, profits and macroeconomic adjustment: A comparative study." *Brookings Papers on Economic Activity* No. 1:269–319.

Sachs, Jeffrey D. 1980. "The changing cyclical behaviour of wages and prices 1890–1976." *American Economic Review* 70:78–90.

Salvati, Michele, and Giorgio Brosio. 1979. "The rise of market politics: Industrial relations in the seventies." *Daedalus* 108:43–71.

Salvati, Michele. 1985. "The Italian inflation." Pp. 509–563 in Leon N. Lindberg and Charles S. Maier (eds.), *The Politics of Inflation and Economic Stagnation: Theoretical Approaches and International Case Studies*. Washington, DC: Brookings Institution.

Sanders, David, Hugh Ward, and David Marsh. 1987. "Government popularity and the Falklands war: A reassessment." *British Journal of Political Science* 17:281–313.

Sanders, David, David Marsh, and Hugh Ward. 1990. "A reply to Clarke, Mishler and Whitely." *British Journal of Political Science* 20:83–90.

Sargent, Thomas J. 1986. *Rational Expectations and Inflation*. New York: Harper & Row.

Sato, Kazuo. 1987. "Saving and investment." Pp. 137–185 in Kozo Yamamura and Yasukichi Yasuba (eds.), *The Political Economy of Japan*. Stanford, CA: Stanford University Press.

Saunders, Christopher, and David Marsden. 1981. *Pay Inequalities in the European Community*. London: Butterworths.

Sawyer, Malcolm. 1976. *Income Distribution in OECD Countries*. OECD Economic Outlook Occasional Papers.

Scase, Richard. 1977. *Social Democracy in Capitalist Society: Working-Class Politics in Britain and Sweden*. London: Croom Helm.

Scharpf, Fritz W. 1984. "Economic and institutional constraints of full-employment strategies: Sweden, Austria, and West Germany, 1973–1982." Pp. 257–290 in John Goldthorpe (ed.), *Order and Conflict in Contemporary Capitalism: Studies in the Political Economy of Western Nations*. Oxford: Clarendon.

Scharpf, Fritz W. 1989. "Antagonism and cooperation in four countries: Economic policies and performance." Pp. 79–100 in Burkhard Strümpel (ed.), *Industrial Societies after the Stagnation of the 1970s—Taking Stock from an Interdisciplinary Perspective*. Berlin: Walter de Gruyter.

Schmidt, Folke. 1972. "Industrial action: The role of trade unions and employers' associations." Pp. 1–68 in Benjamin Aaron and K. W. Wedderburn (eds.), *Industrial Conflict: A Comparative Legal Survey*. London: Longman.

Schmidt, Manfred G. 1982. "Does corporatism matter? Economic crisis, politics, and the rate of unemployment in capitalist democracies in the 1970s." Pp. 237–258 in Gerhard Lehmbruch and Manfred Schmitter (eds.), *Patterns of Corporatist Policy-Making*. Beverly Hills, CA: Sage.

Schmidt, Manfred G. 1989. "The political management of mixed economies: Political aspects of macroeconomic performance in OECD nations (1960–1984)." Pp. 101–127 in Burkhard Strümpel (ed.), *Industrial Societies after the Stagnation of the 1970s—Taking Stock from an Interdisciplinary Perspective*. Berlin: Walter de Gruyter.

Schmitter, Philippe C. 1979. "Modes of interest intermediation and models of societal change in Western Europe." Pp. 63–94 in Philippe C. Schmitter and Gerhard Lehmbruch (eds.), *Trends Towards Corporatist Intermediation*. Beverly Hills, CA: Sage Publications.

Schmitter, Philippe C. 1985. "Neo-corporatism and the state." Pp. 32–62 in Wyn Grant (ed.), *The Political Economy of Corporatism*. London: Macmillan.

Schneider, Friedrich, Werner W. Pommerehne, and Bruno S. Frey. 1981. "Politico-economic interdependence in a direct democracy: The case of Switzerland." Pp. 231–248 in Douglas A. Hibbs and Heino Fassbender (eds.), *Contemporary Political Economy: Studies on the Interdependence of Politics and Economics*. Amsterdam: North-Holland Publishing Company.

Schott, Kerry. 1984a. *Policy, Power and Order: The Persistence of Economic Problems in Capitalist States*. New Haven, CT: Yale University Press.

Schott, Kerry. 1984b. "Investment, order, and conflict in a simple dynamic model of capitalism." Pp. 81–97 in John H. Goldthorpe (ed.), *Order and Conflict in Contemporary Capitalism: Studies in the Political Economy of Western European Nations*. Oxford: Clarendon Press.

Schrank, R., and S. Stein. 1971. "Yearning, learning, and status." Pp. 318–341 in

S. Levitan (ed.), *Blue Collar Workers: A Symposium on Middle America.* New York: McGraw-Hill.

Schultze, Charles L. 1987. "Real wages, real wage aspirations, and unemployment in Europe." Pp. 230–291 in Robert Z. Lawrence and Charles L. Schultze (eds.), *Barriers to European Growth: A Transatlantic View.* Washington, DC: Brookings Institution.

Schwerin, Don S. 1984. "Historic compromise and pluralist decline? Profits and capital in the Nordic Countries." Pp. 231–256 in John H. Goldthorpe (ed.), *Order and Conflict in Contemporary Capitalism: Studies in the Political Economy of Western European Nations.* Oxford: Clarendon Press.

Seidel, Hans. 1982. "The Austrian economy: An overview." Pp. 7–25 in Sven W. Arndt (ed.), *The Political Economy of Austria.* Washington, DC: American Enterprise Institute for Public Policy Research.

Semmler, Willi. 1982. "Competition, monopoly, and differentials of profit rates: Theoretical considerations and empirical evidence." *Review of Radical Political Economics* 13:39–52.

Semmler, Willi. 1983. "Competition, monopoly, and differentials of profit rates: A reply." *Review of Radical Political Economics* 15:92–99.

Shalev, M. 1990. "Class conflict, corporatism and comparison: A Japanese enigma." Pp. 60–93 in S. N. Eisenstadt and Eyal Ben-Ari (eds.), *Japanese Models of Conflict Resolution.* London: Kegan Paul.

Shannon, Russell, and Myles S. Wallace. 1985. "Wages and inflation: An investigation into causality." *Journal of Post Keynesian Economics* 8:182–191.

Shepherd, William G. 1979. *The Economics of Industrial Organization.* Englewood Cliffs, NJ: Prentice-Hall.

Shepherd, William G. 1982. "Causes of increased competition in the U.S. economy, 1939–1980." *Review of Economics and Statistics* 14:613–626.

Sheriff, T. D. 1980. "The lessons of wage equations." Pp. 213–227 in F. T. Blackaby (ed.), *The Future of Pay Bargaining.* London: Heinemann.

Sherman, Howard. 1976. *Stagflation: A Political Theory of Unemployment and Inflation.* New York: Harper & Row.

Sherman, Howard. 1983. "Monopoly power and profit rates." *Review of Radical Political Economics* 15:125–133.

Shigeyoshi, Tokunaga. 1984. "The structure of the Japanese labour market." Pp. 25–55 in Tokunaga Shigeyoshi and Joachim Bergmann (eds.), *Industrial Relations in Transition: The Cases of Japan and the Federal Republic of Germany.* Tokyo: University of Tokyo Press.

Shinkai, Yoichi. 1982. "Oil crises and stagflation in Japan." Pp. 173–193 in Kozo Yamamura (ed.), *Policy and Trade Issues of the Japanese Economy: American and Japanese Perspectives.* Seattle, WA: University of Washington Press.

Shonfield, Andrew. 1958. *British Economic Policy Since the War.* Harmondsworth, Middlesex: Penguin.

Shonfield, Andrew. 1965. *Modern Capitalism: The Changing Balance of Public and Private Power.* London: Oxford University Press.

Shonfield, Andrew. 1984. *In Defence of the Mixed Economy.* Oxford: Oxford University Press.

Shorter, Edward, and Charles Tilly. 1974. *Strikes in France, 1830–1968.* London: Cambridge University Press.

Shostak, Arthur B., and David Skocik. 1986. *The Air Traffic Controllers' Controversy: Lessons from the PATCO Strike.* New York: Human Sciences Press.

Simon, Herbert A. 1979. "Rational decision making in organizations." *American Economic Review* 69:493–453.

Simons, Henry C. 1948. *Economic Policy for a Free Society.* Chicago: University of Chicago Press.

Skidelsky, Robert. 1979. "The decline of Keynesian politics." Pp. 55–87 in Colin Crouch (ed.), *The State and Economy in Contemporary Capitalism.* New York: St. Martins Press.

Smelser, Neil. 1976. *The Sociology of Economic Life* (2nd ed.). Englewood Cliffs, NJ: Prentice-Hall.

Smith, Adam. 1937. *The Wealth of Nations.* New York: Modern Library.

Smith, Michael R. 1978. "The effects of strikes on workers: A Critical analysis." *Canadian Journal of Sociology* 3:457–472.

Smith, Michael R. 1979a. "Characterizations of Canadian strikes: Some critical comments." *Relations Industrielles/Industrial Relations* 34:592–605.

Smith, Michael R. 1979b. "Institutional setting and industrial conflict in Quebec." *American Journal of Sociology* 85:109–134.

Smith, Michael R. 1981. "Industrial conflict in postwar Ontario: Or, one cheer for the Woods Report." *Canadian Review of Sociology and Anthropology* 18:370–392.

Smith, Michael R. 1982. "Accounting for inflation in Britain." *British Journal of Sociology* 33:301–329.

Smith, Michael R. 1987. "The political bases of inflation in postwar Canada." *Canadian Journal of Sociology* 12:363–392.

Smith, Michael R. 1988. "Wages and inflation in Quebec." *Canadian Review of Sociology and Anthropology* 25:577–602.

Smith, Michael R. 1990. "What is new in 'new structuralist' analyses of earnings?" *American Sociological Review* 55:827–841.

Solow, Robert M. 1975. "The intelligent citizen's guide to inflation." *The Public Interest* 38:30–60.

Solow, Robert M. 1979. "Alternative approaches to macroeconomic theory: A partial view." *Canadian Journal of Economics* 12:339–354.

Solow, Robert M. 1980. "On theories of unemployment." *American Economic Review* 70:1–11.

Sorensen, Aage. 1990. "Throwing the sociologists out? A reply to Smith." *American Sociological Review* 55:842–845.

Soskice, David. 1978. "Strike waves and wage explosions, 1968–1970: An economic interpretation." Pp. 221–246 in Colin Crouch and Alessandro Pizzorno (eds.), *The Resurgence of Class Conflict In Western Europe since 1968* (Vol. 2). London: Macmillan.

Spenner, Kenneth I. 1979. "Temporal changes in work content." *American Sociological Review* 44:968–975.

Spenner, Kenneth I. 1983. "Deciphering Prometheus: Temporal change in the skill level of work." *American Sociological Review* 48:824–837.

Stearns, Linda Brewster. 1990. "Capital market effects on the external control of corporations." Pp. 175–202 in Sharon Zukin and Paul DiMaggio (eds.), *The Structure of Capital: The Social Organization of the Economy.* Cambridge: Cambridge University Press.

Steedman, Ian. 1977. *Marx After Sraffa.* London: New Left Books.

Steindl, Josef. 1976. *Maturity and Stagnation in American Capitalism.* New York: Monthly Review Press.

Stephens, John D. 1979. *The Transition from Capitalism to Socialism.* London: Macmillan.

Stewart, Michael. 1972. *Keynes and After* (2nd ed.). Harmondsworth, Middlesex: Penguin.

Stigler, George J. 1973. "General economic conditions and national elections." *American Economic Review* 63:160–167.

Stigler, George. 1975. *The Citizen and the State: Essays on Regulation.* Chicago: University of Chicago Press.

Stigler, George, and James Kindahl. 1970. *The Behavior of Industrial Prices.* New York: National Bureau of Economic Research.

Stiglitz, Joseph. 1986. "Theories of wage rigidity." Pp. 153–206 in James L. Butkiewicz, Kenneth J. Koford, and Jeffrey B. Miller (eds.), *Keynes' Economic Legacy: Contemporary Economic Theories.* New York: Praeger.

Stinchcombe, Arthur. 1968. *Constructing Social Theories.* New York: Harcourt, Brace and Wold.

Streeck, Wolfgang. 1984. *Industrial Relations in West Germany.* London: Heinemann.

Stursberg, Peter. 1975. *Diefenbaker: Leadership Gained 1956–62.* Toronto: University of Toronto Press.

Suzuki, Midoshi. 1991. "The rationality of economic voting and the macroeconomic regime." *American Journal of Political Science* 35:624–642.

Suzuki, Yoshio. 1986. *Money, Finance, and Macroeconomic Performance in Japan.* New Haven: Yale University Press.

Swedberg, Richard. 1987. "Economic sociology: Past and present." *Current Sociology* 35:1–221.

Swedberg, Richard. 1990. *Economics and Sociology: Redefining their Boundaries: Conversations with Economists and Sociologists.* Princeton, NJ: Princeton University Press.

Sweezy, Paul. 1942. *The Theory of Capitalist Development.* New York: Monthly Review Press.

Sylos-Labini, Paolo. 1974. *Trade Unions, Inflation and Productivity.* Lexington, MA: D. C. Heath.

Tanzi, Vito. 1985. "The deficit experience in industrial countries." Pp. 81–120 in Phillip Cagan (ed.), *Essays in Contemporary Economic Problems, 1985: The Economy in Deficit.* Washington, DC: American Enterprise Institute.

Tarantelli, Ezio. 1986. "The regulation of inflation and unemployment." *Industrial Relations* 25:1–15.

Taveggia, Thomas C., and Bruce Ross. 1978. "Generational differences in work orientations: Fact or fiction?" *Pacific Sociological Review* 22:331–349.

Taylor-Gooby, Peter. 1983. "The distributional compulsion and the moral order of the welfare state." Pp. 98–121 in Adrian Ellis and Krishan Kumar (eds.),

Dilemmas of Liberal Democracies: Studies in Fred Hirsch's 'Social Limits to Growth'. London: Tavistock.

Templeman, Donald C. 1981. *The Italian Economy*. New York: Praeger.

Thaler, Richard H. 1989. "Anomalies: Interindustry wage differentials." *Journal of Economic Perspectives* 3:181–184.

Thomas, Barry, and David Deaton. 1977. *Labour Shortages and Economic Analysis: A Study of Occupational Labour Markets*. Oxford: Blackwell.

Thompson, W., and G. Zuk. 1983. "American elections and the international electoral-economic cycle: A test of the Tufte hypothesis." *American Journal of Political Science* 27:464–484.

Thorns, David C. 1972. *Suburbia*. London: MacGibbon and Kee.

Tichy, Gunther. 1984. "Strategy and implementation of employment policy in Austria." *Kyklos* 37:363–386.

Tobin, James. 1972. "Inflation and unemployment." *American Economic Review* 62:1–18.

Tobin, James. 1974. *The New Economics One Decade Older*. Princeton, NJ: Princeton University Press.

Tobin, James. 1977. "How dead is Keynes?" *Economic Inquiry* 15:459–468.

Tobin, James. 1980. *Asset Accumulation and Economic Activity: Reflections on Contemporary Macroeconomic Theory*. Chicago: University of Chicago Press.

Tobin, James. 1981. "The monetarist counter-revolution today—An appraisal." *Economic Journal* 91:29–42.

Trevithick, James Anthony, and Charles Mulvey. 1975. *The Economics of Inflation*. New York: Wiley.

Tuchman, Barbara W. 1984. *The March of Folly: From Troy to Vietnam*. London: Michael Joseph.

Tufte, Edward R. 1978. *Political Control of the Economy*. Princeton, NJ: Princeton University Press.

Tullock, Gordon. 1980. "The welfare costs of tariffs, monopolies and theft." Pp. 39–50 in James M. Buchanan, Robert D. Tollison, and Gordon Tullock (eds.), *Towards a Theory of the Rent-Seeking Society*. College Station, TX: Texas A&M Press.

Tylecote, Andrew. 1981. *The Causes of the Present Inflation: An Interdisciplinary Explanation of Inflation in Britain, Germany and the United States*. London: Macmillan.

Uchino, Tatsurō. 1983. *Japan's Postwar Economy: An Insider's View of its History and Future*. Tokyo: Kodansha International.

Ullman, Lloyd, and Robert J. Flanagan. 1971. *Wage Restraint: A Study of Incomes Policies in Western Europe*. Berkeley, CA: University of California Press.

van den Berg, Axel. 1988. *The Immanent Utopia: From Marxism on the State to the State of Marxism*. Princeton, NJ: Princeton University Press.

van den Berg, Axel, and Michael R. Smith. 1981. "Review essay: The Marxist theory of the state in practice." *Canadian Journal of Sociology* 6:505–519.

van den Berg, Axel, and Joseph Smucker. 1992. "Labor markets and government interventions: A comparison of Canadian and Swedish labor market policies." *International Journal of Contemporary Sociology*, in press.

van Parijs, Philippe. 1980. "The falling-rate-of-profit theory of crisis: A rational reconstruction by way of obituary." *Review of Radical Political Economics* 12:1–16.

van Parijs, Philippe. 1983. "Why Marxist economics needs microfoundations: Postscript to an obituary." *Review of Radical Political Economics* 15:11–24.

Veblen, Thorstein. 1904. *The Theory of Business Enterprise.* New York: Scribners.

Vogel, Ezra. 1979. *Japan as Number One: Lessons for America.* New York: Harper & Row.

Warburton, P. 1980. "Comment on Chapter 10." Pp. 228–233 in F. T. Blackaby (ed.), *The Future of Pay Bargaining.* London: Heinemann.

Ward, R., and G. Zis. 1974. "Trade union militancy as an explanation of inflation: An International Comparison." *Manchester School* 42:45–65.

Webb, P. 1987. "Union, party and class in Britain: The changing electoral relationship, 1964–1983." *Politics* 7:15–21.

Webber, Douglas, and Gabriele Nass. 1984. "Employment policy in West Germany." Pp. 167–192 in Jeremy Richardson and Roger Henning (eds.), *Unemployment: Policy Responses of Western Democracies.* Beverly Hills, CA: Sage.

Weede, Erich. 1986a. "Catch-up, distributional coalitions and government as determinants of economic growth or decline in industrialized democracies." *British Journal of Sociology* 37:194–220.

Weede, Erich. 1986b. "Sectoral reallocation, distributional coalitions and the welfare state as determinants of economic growth rates in industrialized democracies." *European Journal of Political Research* 14:501–519.

Weeks, John. 1981. *Capital and Exploitation.* Princeton, NJ: Princeton University Press.

Weintraub, Sidney. 1978. *Capitalism's Inflation and Unemployment Crisis: Beyond Monetarism and Keynesianism.* Reading, MA: Addison-Wesley.

Westley, William, and Margaret Westley. 1971. *The Emerging Worker: Equality and Conflict in the Mass Consumption Society.* Montreal: McGill-Queen's University Press.

Westphal, Uwe. 1986. "The German experience." Pp. 185–188 in John Sargent (ed.), *Foreign Macroeconomic Experience: A Symposium.* Toronto: University of Toronto Press in cooperation with the Royal Commission on the Economic Union and Development Prospects for Canada.

Wijkman, Per Magnus. 1987. "Comments." Pp. 92–96 in Barry P. Bosworth and Alice M. Rivlin (eds.), *The Swedish Economy.* Washington, DC: Brookings Institution.

Wilensky, Harold L. 1975. *The Welfare State and Equality: Structural and Ideological Roots of the Public Expenditures.* Berkeley, CA: University of California Press.

Wilensky, Harold L., et al. 1985. *Comparative Social Policy: Theories, Methods, Findings.* Berkeley, CA: Institute of International Studies, University of California.

Wilensky, Harold L., and Lowell Turner. 1987. *Democratic Corporatism and Policy Linkages: The Interdependence of Industrial, Labor-Market Incomes, and Social Policies in Eight Countries.* Berkeley, CA: Institute of International Studies, University of California.

Wiles, Peter. 1973. "Cost inflation and the state of economic theory." *Economic Journal* 83:377–398.

Williamson, Oliver E. 1985. *The Economic Institutions of Capitalism: Firms, Markets, Relational Contracting.* New York: Free Press.

Williamson, Peter J. 1985. *Varieties of Corporatism: A Conceptual Discussion.* Cambridge: Cambridge University Press.

Wilton, David W. 1984. "An evaluation of wage and price controls in Canada." *Canadian Public Policy* 10:167–176.

Wolff, Edward N. 1979. "The rate of surplus value, the organic composition and the general rate of profit in the U.S. economy 1946–67." *American Economic Review* 69:329–341.

Wonnacott, Paul. 1965. *The Canadian Dollar, 1948–62.* Toronto: University of Toronto Press.

Wood, Adrian. 1978. *A Theory of Pay.* Cambridge: Cambridge University Press.

Woolley, John T. 1978. "Monetary policy instrumentation and the relationship of central banks and governments." *Annals of the American Academy of Political and Social Science* 434:151–173.

Woolley, John T. 1984. *Monetary Politics: The Federal Reserve and the Politics of Monetary Policy.* Cambridge: Cambridge University Press.

Woolley, John T. 1985. "Central banks and inflation." Pp. 318–348 in Leon N. Lindberg and Charles S. Maier (eds.), *The Politics of Inflation and Economic Stagnation: Theoretical Approaches and International Case Studies.* Washington, DC: Brookings Institution.

Wright, Erik Olin. 1978. *Class, Crisis and the State.* London: Verso.

Wright, Erik Olin. 1985. *Classes.* London: Verso.

Wright, James D., and Richard F. Hamilton. 1978. "Work satisfaction and age: Some evidence for the 'job change' hypothesis." *Social Forces* 56:1140–1158.

Wright, James D., and Richard F. Hamilton. 1979. "Education and job attitudes among blue collar workers." *Sociology of Work and Occupations* 6:59–83.

Yaffe, David S. 1973. "The crisis of profitability: A critique of the Glyn-Sutcliffe thesis." *New Left Review* 80:45–62.

Yellen, Janet L. 1984. "Efficiency wage models of unemployment." *American Economic Review* 74:200–205.

Yuchtman-Yaar, Ephraim. 1989. "Economic culture in post-industrial society: Orientations toward growth, technology, and work." Pp. 159–184 in Burkhard Strümpel (ed.), *Industrial Societies after the Stagnation of the 1970s— Taking Stock from an Interdisciplinary Perspective.* Berlin: Walter de Gruyter.

Zeigler, Harmon. 1988. *Pluralism, Corporatism, and Confucianism: Political Association and Conflict Regulation in the United States, Europe, and Taiwan.* Philadelphia: Temple University Press.

Zimmermann, Ekkart. 1984. "The study of crises in liberal democracies: Pitfalls and promises." *International Political Science Review* 5:319–343.

Zysman, John. 1985. "Inflation and the politics of supply." Pp. 140–172 in Leon N. Lindberg and Charles S. Maier (eds.), *The Politics of Inflation and Economic Stagnation: theoretical Approaches and International Case Studies.* Washington, DC: Brookings Institution.

INDEX

Active labor market policies in Sweden, 199, 202-203
Affluent workers, 134n17
Age of program and government spending, 55, 63
Aggregate demand, 8, 15, 17, 35, 56, 78, 71-72, 195, 198, 221, 224, 227, 231; effect of wages on, 98, 133n5; stimulus to, 15-16, 18-20, 30-33, 40, 51, 79, 118-122, 139, 228, 232, 244-245, 256-257; reduction in, 16, 116-117, 129, 220
Aggregate supply, 8, 17, 72 (*see also* "Oil shocks," "Commodity price shocks")
Alienation, 101, 111-12, 134n21, 204
Aspirations of workers, 100-102, 131; of young workers, 111, 134n19, 134n20
Australia, 7-9, 60, 145, 165-168, 171-172, 177-178, 259n6
Austria, 1, 7-9, 10, 11, 106, 129-130, 145, 161n18, 165-169, 171-172, 176, 177-178, 181, 191-198, 203, 211, 213n10, 214n26, 242, 243, 246, 247, 258
Automatic stabilizers, 27

Bank of Canada, 61-62, 247
Bank of Japan, 209
Barriers to entry and exit, 231-232
Belgium, 7-9, 126, 129, 136n36, 165-168, 171-172, 176, 177-178, 247
Bivariate analysis, 58-59; as a methodological problem, 178-180
Bolshevik inflation, 1, 11n1
Brazil, 50, 73
Bretton Woods, 30, 36, 38n15, 50, 83, 85, 87, 196, 224, 228, 236, 246

Budget balance, at high employment, 43
Bundesbank, 61

Canada, 7-9, 27, 30, 31, 32, 38n11, 38n13, 67n18, 106, 107, 115, 120, 134n15, 136n36, 145, 165-168, 171-172, 175, 177-178, 180, 208, 213n18, 214n35, 230, 242, 246, 248, 259n7, 261n19; Diefenbaker government, 247; Progressive Conservative Party, 61-62
Capacity utilization, 32, 121-122, 130, 195, 220, 242
Capital, capitalists, 3, 4, 10, 18, 22, 79, 97, 99, 103-104, 116, 117, 124, 138, 143, 144, 146, 147, 152, 156-159, 169, 196, 208, 217-218, 220-221, 222, 223, 224, 225, 229, 230, 252, 254, 256; failure of imagination, 232; internationalization of, 32, 108, 180, 227
Capitalism, amorality of, 4, 70, 75, 237n1, 250-251; moral basis of, 9, 71
Capital markets, 2
"Catch-up," and economic growth, 81, 84, 85-86, 92n8, 176-178, 192, 207, 253, 259n5
Central bank, 50; autonomy of, 11, 44, 50-51, 60-62, 63, 180, 183, 190-191, 243, 247, 248, 250, 257; reaction function, 123
Centralized bargaining, 10, 125, 182, 185-186, 188-189, 202, 211; absence in Japan, 209; and coercion, 142, 151-152, 157, 160n6, 203-204, 214n32; and economic adjustment, 143-144, and norms, 160n8, 255;

cle"); relative concern with inflation and unemployment, 50, 64–66, 255–256
Empires, decline of, 69–70, 91n1 (*see also* "Hegemony, declining")
Employment, effects of inflation on, 19 (*see also* "Phillips curve")
Encompassing organizations, 77–78, 251
Entitlement programs, 53
Europe, 120–122; European Monetary System, 175, 246
Exchange rates, 24, 56, 59, 196; and interests of United States, 88–89
Exchange rates, fixed, 30–31, 50, 87, 228, 246, 252; interwar level in United Kingdom, 89–90; and similar rates of inflation, 32, 83, 85, 247
Exchange rates, flexible, 31–32, 51, 175, 246; and dispersed rates of inflation, 32, 85; and effectiveness of monetary and fiscal policy, 51
Expectations, adaptive, 20, 72–73; rational, 22, 25, 27–28, 239n17
Explanation of inflation, prerequisites, 7–8, 71–72, 99
Export delivery dates, and worker power, 108, 131–132

Fairness, unfairness, 2, 3, 4, 5, 144, 154, 187; worker perceptions of, 112–113
Falklands war, 67
Falling rate of profit, 3, 219–220, 223–224, 226, 228–230, 235, 236, 237n2; and productivity improvements, 229; and shares of capital and labor, 229
Fascism and corporatism, 137
Finland, 7–9, 60, 114, 165–168, 171–172, 178, 251, 260n16
Fiscal policy, 13, 207; and elections, 46–47; limits on, 51
Flexibility of prices and wages, 33–34
Foreign labor, 197 (*see also* "Immigration")

France, 7–9, 82, 93n9, 106, 110, 125, 126, 127, 129, 134n15, 135n29, 135n35, 136n36, 165–168, 171–172, 178, 246, 248, 259n6; Mitterand government, 245
Free riders, 76, 77, 84
Full employment, 17, 43, 114, 118, 123, 126, 132, 192, 194, 234–235, 236, 237, 242; definition, 43; as neocorporatist goal, 138, 143, 199–200, 202; overfull employment, 234; and stickiness of wages, 121–122; and worker bargaining power, 101–103, 105–106, 113–118, 139, 222, 228, 254
Functional alternatives, 169–170
Functional distribution of income (shares of labor and capital), 3, 4, 99–100, 116, 117, 124, 126, 155–160, 224
Functional representation, 138, 192

GATT (General Agreement on Tariffs and Trade), 83, 108
Germany, interwar inflation, 11n1, 129
Germany, Federal Republic of, 7–9, 10, 11, 44, 45, 46, 47, 50, 54, 57, 60, 62, 75, 77, 81, 82, 106, 108–109, 110, 114, 126, 129–130, 134n15, 136n36, 165–169, 170–175, 176, 177–178, 181, 183–191, 196, 211, 212–213n8, 213n10, 213n15, 213n18, 214n21, 214n28, 230, 237, 242, 243, 247, 253, 259n8; Christian Democratic Party, 185; Free Democratic Party, 185; Helmut Kohl, 235
Government employment, 196–197, 212; and worker power, 107–108
Government, growth of, 40
Government ownership of industry, 193
Government policy; as source of economic instability, 14, 23, 24, 249 (*see also* "Ignorance and error"); and strength of the labor movement, 132, 228; where inflation is

For Product Safety Concerns and Information please contact our
EU representative GPSR@taylorandfrancis.com Taylor & Francis
Verlag GmbH, Kaufingerstraße 24, 80331 München, Germany